ONCE UPON
A CHILDHOOD

ONCE UPON A CHILDHOOD

STORIES AND MEMOIRS
OF AMERICAN YOUTH

EDITED BY BARBARA H. SOLOMON
AND EILEEN PANETTA

NEW AMERICAN LIBRARY

New American Library
Published by New American Library, a division of
Penguin Group (USA) Inc., 375 Hudson Street,
New York, New York 10014, USA
Penguin Group (Canada), 10 Alcorn Avenue, Toronto,
Ontario M4V 3B2, Canada (a division of Pearson Penguin Canada Inc.)
Penguin Books Ltd., 80 Strand, London WC2R 0RL, England
Penguin Ireland, 25 St. Stephen's Green, Dublin 2,
Ireland (a division of Penguin Books Ltd.)
Penguin Group (Australia), 250 Camberwell Road, Camberwell, Victoria 3124,
Australia (a division of Pearson Australia Group Pty. Ltd.)
Penguin Books India Pvt. Ltd., 11 Community Centre, Panchsheel Park,
New Delhi - 110 017, India
Penguin Group (NZ), Cnr Airborne and Rosedale Roads, Albany,
Auckland 1310, New Zealand (a division of Pearson New Zealand Ltd.)
Penguin Books (South Africa) (Pty.) Ltd., 24 Sturdee Avenue,
Rosebank, Johannesburg 2196, South Africa

Penguin Books Ltd., Registered Offices:
80 Strand, London WC2R 0RL, England

First published by New American Library,
a division of Penguin Group (USA) Inc.

First New American Library Printing, October 2004
10 9 8 7 6 5 4 3 2 1

Copyright © Barbara H. Solomon and Eileen Panetta, 2004
All rights reserved

(Author copyrights and permissions can be found on pages 307–8.)

REGISTERED TRADEMARK—MARCA REGISTRADA

LIBRARY OF CONGRESS CATALOGING-IN-PUBLICATION DATA:

Once upon a childhood : stories and memoirs of American youth / edited by Barbara H. Soloman and Eileen
   Panetta.
      p. cm.
   ISBN 0-451-21296-7 (trade pbk.)
   1. Youth—Fiction. 2. Children—Fiction. 3. Children—United States—Biography. 4. Youth—United
States—Biography. 5. American prose literature. I. Soloman, Barbara H. II. Panetta, Eileen.
   PS648.Y68O53 2004
   810.8'0354—dc22   2004055243

Set in American Typewriter and Galliard
Designed by Ginger Legato

Printed in the United States of America

This book is for
STANLEY, NANCY, AND JEN
ROGER, JANE, AND CLAIRE

ACKNOWLEDGMENTS

We would like to express our appreciation to Karla Sundstrom and Dina Lally, Department of English student secretaries, and to Susan Robinson, Ryan Library Reference and Document Delivery Librarian, for their help in securing and assembling materials. To Iona College, Eileen Panetta is indebted for a recent Faculty Fellowship and Barbara H. Solomon is indebted for a current Faculty Fellowship.

CONTENTS

NONFICTION

INTRODUCTION

A mong the most compelling topics in literature are those dealing with experiences of childhood and adolescence. In British novels, ranging from Dickens's *Great Expectations* to D. H. Lawrence's *Sons and Lovers* and Joyce's *A Portrait of the Artist as a Young Man,* and in American novels, ranging from Alcott's *Little Women,* Twain's *Huck Finn,* and Salinger's *The Catcher in the Rye* to Knowles's *A Separate Peace* and Morrison's *The Bluest Eye,* writers of fiction have dramatized their visions of the relationships between children and adults or with other children.

In nonfiction as well, memoirists have recalled in vivid detail their early surroundings, relationships with parents, siblings, or other relatives, their friendships and schooling. Sometimes the stories and memoirs depict a traumatic or sad event. Sometimes they celebrate a childhood pleasure or recall a child's developing sense of selfhood or the discovery of some deeply embedded character trait or talent or of one's special place within the family and the community.

Often a subtheme of the authors' stories and recollections in this collection is that of the disparity between the idea of childhood as an innocent and carefree time filled with learning, play, and affection in the heart of a loving family and the reality of their own experiences of traumatic loss through death, divorce, or illness, their sense of isolation, unjust or harsh punishment, a frustrating lack of autonomy, or the painful sense of being insufficiently loved and valued by parents.

Although few children have the analytical ability to adequately express their basic needs, adults writing about childhood have described through both positive and negative scenes the kind of world that makes for a nurturing and comfortable time of exploration, learning, attachment, and growth. Clearly, children want obvious and unconditional love from family members—love that is often reflected in affection and approval. They crave stability, the kind provided by parents who have a loving or at least harmonious relationship, parents who are contented with their circumstances, not bitter or resentful. Children long to know that they were wanted and not merely accidents.

Children want to live with parents who are reasonable and, even, predictable, not whimsical in their reactions; they need parents who create routines and structures, but who are not excessively controlling or possessive. They want their parents to have ample time for them, for eating together regularly and for other opportunities during which they can talk about their achievements or their problems. Children need parents who are proactive in protecting them, whether from some teenager's bullying or some adult's sexual advances.

When children misbehave, they want their parents to be reasonable about appropriate punishments, and they fear unrestrained anger and violent reactions; they fear the pain and physical harm that an adult authority is capable of inflicting and that they are helpless to avoid. Children, particularly adolescents, want to be cut some slack when they are disobedient and rebellious, when they get into mischief or serious trouble.

They want to explore the boundaries of acceptable behavior, but also enjoy having some experiences with behavior that their parents would deem bad or unacceptable. In the Tillie Olsen story "I Stand Here Ironing," a mother reflects on the extraordinarily docile behavior of her daughter, Emily, who did not want to be sent off each day to the unpleasant nursery school. Now, many years later, the mother recalls that Emily never directly rebelled or protested and she remembers the other reluctant children with their "explosions, the tempers, the denunciations, the demands," realizing that Emily's behavior was not that of a healthy and secure child. With a sinking heart, she questions: "What in me demanded that goodness in her? And what was the cost, the cost to her of such goodness?" Emily's mother now wisely understands that children have their own inner agendas, strong desires and frustrations and that something is seriously amiss when they are unable to express their feelings.

Children often believe that they are competing with a sibling or with a divorced parent's boyfriend or girlfriend for attention and affection. They may be uncomfortable with how much they dislike the traits and behavior of brothers and sisters and may be bewildered by the fact that it seems possible to experience hatred and deep caring for relatives almost simultaneously.

Children want to have friends and particularly want to have a best friend with whom to share their feelings and thoughts. They want to spend time with another child who has similar interests in playing and exploring their surroundings. Early in Sandra Cisneros's *The House on Mango Street,* Esperanza describes some of the comforts of having a best friend: "One I can tell my secrets to. One who will understand my jokes without my having to explain them." In a subsequent passage, she expresses her sympathy for an older girl, Sally, who has fought with her best friend. Esperanza understands that since that time "you don't have a best friend to lean against the school yard fence with, to laugh behind your hands at what the boys say. There is no one to lend you her hairbrush." Although a child with friends may be quite contented without being a member of the "in crowd" at school, most children are quite perceptive about where they would be categorized on a scale of popularity. Being at the bottom of the social hierarchy may invite teasing or bullying or lead to the humiliation of eating lunch alone.

Children need stimulation. They need books, games, toys, and puzzles to stretch their imagination, to learn, to practice social skills, and to be entertained. They want to be rescued from boredom. Often, they request lessons for activities, such as playing an instrument, dancing, or swimming. They need to engage in sports activities, sometimes as a member of a team and sometimes individually. They want to go to the movies or ball games or parties. Generally, they like to visit interesting places, to go on vacations or make trips to beaches or amusement parks.

While children may not think abstractly about the advantages of great wealth, they are made very uneasy when parents worry about money or make the lack of funds a central topic of daily life. They are self-conscious about being on an equal footing with other children. Thus, they desire to be as well dressed as their peers in school and in the neighborhood, to have similar toys and games as others, and to live in housing that is not dramatically inferior to the homes of friends or relatives they visit. At an early age, impoverished children who associate with those who are much better off financially often develop a sense of pride and try to disguise or minimize their own deprivations.

Many of the stories and memoirs in this volume depict the difficult external circumstances that fill childhood with painful problems and are clearly beyond any individual child's ability to control. Among these, poverty, racism, and sexism often exact a high toll. Other pieces dramatize internal problems caused by the insensitivity, cruelty, selfishness, or irresponsibility of family members. But surprisingly, the very point of much of the literature of childhood is to dramatize the resilient, energetic, and creative ways in which children contrive to survive and overcome the hostile elements of their environments. The desire to lead normal, fulfilling, and successful lives seems to drive many children to intuit the steps they must take to be healed and enjoy the happiness that life can offer.

In excerpts from their memoirs, Veronica Chambers's *Mama's Girl* and Rebecca Walker's *Black, White and Jewish,* the daughters of divorcing parents describe the momentous impacts of this break in their lives. Chambers records the horrifying violence that occurs just prior to the separation as her father swings a hammer at the head of her mother, hitting her with one powerful stroke and gouging a hole in her head: "I think I am dead. I must be dead and I must be in hell. Where else would I see something like this?"

Paralyzed with fear, Veronica fails to summon aid for her profusely bleeding mother and is endlessly haunted by her inability to help: "It is a moment I will play over and over in my mind. I know now that faced with calamity, I am ineffective."

Rebecca Walker, whose parents seem to have kept the widening gap between them out of sight of their eight-year-old, experiences a totally unexpected shock to her being:

> I stop making sense in third grade. Right after my parents sit me down
> and tell me they are not getting along, that me and Mama are going to
> move to another neighborhood and Daddy will come to pick me up on
> weekends. They might as well have told me we were moving to live with
> penguins on the North Pole, but I nod my head and help Mama pack
> books and generally move as if nothing is wrong, as if there isn't this big
> crack in the middle of the painting that is supposed to be my life.

Rebecca's new life of spending time with each parent separately catapults her into two strikingly different familial environments. Her mother, Alice Walker, is an African-American writer who had not yet achieved the literary success she now enjoys and, thus, had little money compared to Rebecca's father, a Jewish middle-class civil rights lawyer. When she is with her white stepmother, father, or grandmother, Rebecca longs to be identified as one of them. When she visits her black relatives, Rebecca is enthralled by their way of life, the television programs they watch, the huge pots of seafood simmering on the stove, the lessons they give her on how to use a gun, and the motorcycle rides she takes clinging to the back of her favorite cousin. But her uncle Bobby uses the word "cracker" to refer to Rebecca, and when she realizes that the word refers to a certain kind of hostile and unpleasant white person, she is forced to think of herself as both an insider and an outsider in her mother's family.

Two stories, "Deadman's Float" by Katherine L. Hester and "Danny in Transit" by David Leavitt, dramatize the plight of children when parents divorce and abandon responsibility for their children while they pursue new lives that don't include the families they created. As might well be expected, children can be shaken to the core when they realize how fragile the bonds of family relations can be. They sometimes discover that not only have their parents ceased to love one another, but that their mothers and fathers have become enraged antagonists who cannot agree on anything.

Often, children must now live with single parents who feel burdened by familial responsibilities and stressed by new economic realities. They must adjust to dramatic changes about where and with whom they live, face the rancor of bitter adults, and as new marriages occur, they must adjust to relationships with stepfamilies who may or may not prove to be congenial relatives.

In David Leavitt's "Danny in Transit," Danny has been living for two months in the household of his affluent aunt, uncle, and maternal grandmother. He is the only child of Elaine and Allen, whose separation has irrevocably destroyed Danny's safe childhood world. Everyone in the family, including Danny, is aware that his parents believe that they can no longer give their son a home—Elaine because of her debilitating mental illness and hospitalization and Allen because of his new union with a gay lover. Danny has become a difficult and annoying child to live with, sometimes sullen, sometimes "bursting into tears, into screams, into hysterical fits at the slightest inclination." He shares no interests or bonds with his two male cousins—athletic boys who are the obvious pride and joy of their father, Danny's uncle.

A perceptive and imaginative child, he realizes that in order to fit into this household, to be the "good" boy they would not resent, he would have to reinvent himself, that he would have to destroy his own identity. In a moment of profound insight, "his face full of a pain too strong for a child to mimic," he tells his father, "'I can't change. I can't change.'"

Narrated from the center of consciousness of Leah, a seventh grader, "Deadman's Float" by Katherine L. Hester depicts the effects of the departure of her father, now separated or divorced from her mother. Leah's brother, a high school student, has become a truant and juvenile delinquent; he has finally moved out of the household.

Although Leah is at summer camp, the disintegration of family life permeates her camp experience. She is painfully aware of her mother's lack of money as she wears a wrinkled Girl Scout sash that was purchased at a secondhand store. The house where she grew up has been sold and she and her mother now live in an apartment. The effects of dislocation, stress, and rejection become palpable as she becomes a sleepwalker.

In a number of stories and memoirs, race, religion, or ethnic background is the catalyst for dramatic events or tense and stressful environments. Alliances with others and acceptance by peer groups often depend on how tolerant children are of those who come from a different background or have a different physical appearance from themselves. Another important element is the attitude toward outsiders that is expressed within the family. When prejudice and racism are freely and frequently asserted by parents or siblings, it becomes difficult for any child to associate with or befriend the outsider who would be scorned by relatives. They come to consider racist behavior the right thing to do.

In Piri Thomas's "Alien Turf," Piri becomes the object of a gang's venom for one reason only: he is a dark-skinned Puerto Rican who has moved into their Italian neighborhood in New York City. Almost immediately, a gang of Italian youths on his block begins to taunt him about his ethnic and racial heritage. They throw debris at him, call him a "spic," and joke about the way they will violate any sisters he has. After one encounter, Piri describes the effect that the fear he must keep hidden is having on him: "I wanted to do something tough, like spitting in their direction. But you gotta have spit in your mouth in order to spit, and my mouth was hurt dry. I just stood there with my back to them." For a month, he bravely endures their threatening behavior. When he encounters them on his way home, they grin at him "like a bunch of hungry alley cats that could get to their mouse anytime they wanted." Piri knows that a physical confrontation with them is inevitable, and when it comes, he will be a lone child facing a gang of opponents.

For minority children, there is often the terrible tension between clinging to one's culture, patterns of speech, and other group members and the desire to become assimilated, to change certain elements of one's behavior, mannerisms, or speech to gain acceptance by the majority culture or the idealized "American" culture of the media.

For example, in *Living up the Street*, Gary Soto, a Mexican-American, recalls the influence television shows such as *Father Knows Best* and *Leave It to Beaver* had on him. After watching the way that the affluent members of those TV families dress for meals, he tries to begin to imitate them by asking his brother, Rick, and his sister, Deb, to wear shoes to dinner. They respond by ridiculing him, and that night Rick arrives at the supper table dressed only in swim trunks. But Soto's discontent is not deeply felt, as is evident when he describes his family's typical, informal meals at which they consume their beans in a congenial and supportive atmosphere "laughing and chewing loudly." During a conversation with Deb and Rick later, he explains his interest in clothes:

> I tried to convince them that if we improved the way we looked we might get along better in life. White people would like us more. They might invite us to places, like their homes or front yard. They might not hate us so much.

His sister's response is a simple statement: "They'll never like us."

In *The Rice Room*, Ben Fong-Torres recalls his pleasure at the age of twelve of being accepted "as just another new kid in town" when he begins to attend Horace Mann Junior High School in Amarillo, Texas. Far from his family's home in Oakland's Chinatown, he remembers being the only Chinese-American student among that school's population of 433 and believes that music was the key to acceptance:

> Inside the jukebox, there were no racial borders, no segregation. The coolest sounds were being made by Elvis and Jerry Lee and Buddy Holly, but also by Little Richard and Chuck Berry. . . . Rock and roll was an equalizer. And for me, it was more than a way to have fun or to feel like part of the crowd. It was a way to feel Americanized.

Ben also notes, however, his determination "to try and sound, as well as be, more 'American'" by choosing English electives of speech and drama so that he might improve the way he pronounced certain sounds and learn to bridge words more smoothly. He is humiliated to find that it is not a school bully or bigot, but his own physical education teacher who insults him by clapping his hands together and calling "Let's go, Chop Chop." Fong-Torres comments:

> For a kid who was longing to belong, it was a devastating blow. Trying only to fit in, I had been singled out; I was that round little yellow-skinned guy in the comic book. I was the Ching-Chong Chinaman. I had to be; after all, it was a teacher who was saying so.

According to James McBride in *The Color of Water*, from early childhood he was disturbed by the difference in appearance between his white mother and himself and his eleven brothers and sisters. When he was nine years old, in 1966, and living in St. Albans, Queens, he realized that the spreading concept of black power had "permeated every element of [the] neighborhood." But this political movement that was being wholeheartedly embraced by many around him was fraught with danger for James. Ever mindful that his mother was a white woman living in an African-American environment, any hostility expressed toward whites made him fear for her safety.

James's mother and her children are subjected to the prejudice and hatred of both white and black bigots. He remembers the behavior of some white people "when we rode the subway, sometimes laughing at us, pointing, muttering things like, 'Look at her with those little niggers.'" He also recalls a time "when a white man shoved her angrily as she led a group of us onto an escalator . . . as well as two black women pointing at us, saying, 'Look at that white bitch,' and a white man screaming at Mommy somewhere in Manhattan, calling her a 'nigger lover.'" His mother's policy, generally, was to ignore all of these racial attacks "unless the insults threatened her children, at which time she would turn and fight back like an alley cat, hissing, angry, and fearless." McBride describes the highly successful strategies his mother contrived for keeping her children safely off the dark streets, for getting the best possible education for them in New York City's public school system, and for instilling in them the Christian principles of her faith.

In a considerable number of memoirs by women, including those by Kate Simon and Beverly Donofrio, it is apparent that their being female was a dominant fact that determined the attitudes and expectations with which they were raised. In families with both male and female children there was frequently a significant disparity between the activities approved for the boys as opposed to those approved for their sisters.

In Kate Simon's *Bronx Primitive,* young Kate is often criticized by her discontented father. He is selfish and cheap in ways that affect both his son and daughter, but the accusations he hurls at Kate are often sexist and based on his contempt for females. He objects to the amount of reading that she does. Moreover, he accuses her of not properly caring for her younger brother. Most of all, she is guilty of associating with the neighborhood boys, engaging in the same activities that they do:

> I climbed with boys, I ran with boys, I skated with them on far streets. . . .
> And how would this life, this playing with boys, end? I would surely become a street girl, a prostitute, and wind up being shipped to a filthy, diseased brothel crawling with hairy tropical bugs, in Buenos Aires.

Kate's mother, a woman of farsighted and humane values, gives her daughter advice that is very different from that which other women in their building give to their daughters. While they emphasize quickly finding a husband "who makes a nice living," Kate's mother proclaims:

> Study. Learn. Go to college. Be a schoolteacher . . . and don't get married until you have a profession. With a profession you can have men friends and even children, if you want. You're free. But don't get married, at least not until you can support yourself and make a careful choice. Or don't get married at all, better still.

Her father's behavior often inspires hatred in Kate, but in her mother, she has a supportive and inspiring role model.

In the first chapter of *Riding in Cars with Boys,* Beverly Donofrio introduces the antagonistic relationship she had with her policeman father during puberty: "The guy stopped looking at me at the first appearance of my breasts, way back in the fifth grade." The oldest of three girls, she recalls the seating arrangements at dinner with her father and brother at the ends of the table while her mother "sat on the sidelines with us girls."

As high school sophomores, Beverly and her friends decided that they

> were sick to death of boys having all the fun, so we started acting like them: We got drunk in the parking lot before school dances and rode real

low in cars, elbows stuck out windows, tossing beer cans, flicking butts, and occasionally pulling down our pants and shaking our fannies at passing vehicles.

At the same time, Beverly discovers that there is a price to be paid for behaving as she pleases. She comes to realize that the sort of boys she likes, "collegiate, popular, seniors," would not even consider dating her or any of her friends. She and her friends were no longer "nice" girls.

Several works that touch on the topic of the intense rivalry that occurs as adolescents engage in dating or fall in love are Art Buchwald's chapter "Flossie and the Marines" from his memoir *Leaving Home*, F. Scott Fitzgerald's story "Bernice Bobs Her Hair," and Bharati Mukherjee's story "Danny's Girls." The process for adolescents of establishing an identity and becoming romantically attractive to others is often a painful one of learning, of overcoming real or imagined inadequacies, of dealing with external barriers, and of having inevitable failures. Although teenagers tend to emphasize their intense romantic feelings and passion, they frequently encounter unexpected significant barriers posed by their race or religion, social status, and financial and educational limitations.

Art Buchwald narrates the events surrounding his enlisting at the age of seventeen in the marine corps at the beginning of World War II. He travels to Greensboro, North Carolina, to say good-bye to a Southern belle with whom he had fallen in love when both of them had had summer jobs at a resort hotel. Penniless and dressed shabbily, he appears at Flossie's dorm room and is disillusioned to learn that she has a date for her college's special dance that weekend and she has no intention of breaking it. Instead, Flossie arranges for Art to attend the dance in an ill-fitting, borrowed tuxedo as her roommate's date. Her own date is a cadet from the Virginia Military Institute who arrives in his convertible. Buchwald recalls:

> The night of the dance, Flossie breezed into the ballroom as gorgeous as I had ever seen her, with the VMI cadet in dress uniform at her side. I, on the other hand, was fighting to keep Pete's tux on. It was too big for me and I kept getting lost in it. There were a few close moments when I thought I would lose my pants. . . . No one has ever accused me of being Fred Astaire, so I couldn't even put the VMI guy to shame with my jitterbugging.

One small victory over his rival occurs when Art leaves carrying the pint of liquor with which the cadet, no doubt, intended to entertain Flossie later that evening.

In F. Scott Fitzgerald's "Bernice Bobs Her Hair," money is not a problem for either Bernice or her popular cousin, Marjorie, with whom she is staying. But Bernice is a social burden for Marjorie, because she bores the eligible young men of her cousin's elite social circle. Marjorie undertakes to teach Bernice how to be poised and charming, how to improve her appearance and her personality. She explains the necessity of being nice to unattractive men—the "sad birds"—in order to practice her dancing and conversation with these clumsy and shy boys:

> If you go to a dance and really amuse, say, three sad birds that dance with you; if you talk so well to them that they forget they're stuck with you, you've done something. They'll come back next time, and gradually so many sad birds will dance with you that the attractive boys will see there's no danger of being stuck—then they'll dance with you.

Of course, Marjorie, who is a selfish and imperious beauty, never imagines that her dull cousin will be able to use her advice to transform herself into such an exciting and desirable date that Marjorie herself will have to compete with her.

In "Danny's Girls," by Bharati Mukherjee, the unnamed fifteen-year-old narrator lives with his mother and aunt among many immigrants in Flushing, Queens. His family is originally from India, and in America, his mother must work seven days a week selling newspapers at a subway stall. A street-smart kid, the boy runs errands for a neighborhood pimp and con man who is involved in illegal immigration scams that use desperate young women. He feels that he is living a lie when his mother tells everyone that he is planning to enroll in Columbia University's School of Engineering. He is painfully aware of his lower-class status when he attends his weekly Gujarati class. There he regularly sees:

> a girl from Syosset who called herself "Pammy Patel," a genuine Hindu-American Princess of the sort I had never seen before, whose skin and voice and eyes were as soft as the clouds. She wore expensive dresses and you could tell she'd spend hours making herself up just for the Gujarati classes in the Hindu Temple. Her father was a major surgeon, and he and Pammy's brothers would stand outside the class to protect her from any contact with boys like me.

To complicate matters, he becomes infatuated with one of the girls Danny has arranged to bring to America, a sensual Nepalese beauty. She is another girl he fears will be beyond his reach—not because of superior social status, but because Danny has become a possessive and powerful rival.

Clearly, misbehaving and getting into trouble are among the normal activities of childhood. Invariably, children are tempted to do what they feel like doing, even though there are prohibitions on certain behavior. Sometimes, they crave excitement. Other times their friends encourage them to join in group behavior that they would never participate in on their own. For teenagers there is generally a wide range of forbidden actions with which to signal their independence or rebellion: cursing, drinking, ignoring parental rules, smoking, lying, stealing, inflicting pain on weaker children or animals, vandalizing property, playing malicious jokes, taking drugs, cutting school, bullying, fighting, engaging in promiscuous sexuality, and displaying hostility to family members.

In two works, Tobias Wolff's memoir *This Boy's Life* and T. Coraghessan Boyle's "Rara Avis," the troubling actions of two boys seem connected to their uncomfortable sexual awakenings. Their aggressive acts seem to be an outlet for sexual anxiety, for insecurity about sexual attractiveness, or guilt about sexual cravings or activity, and they reflect their sense of being shut out of the adult world of sexual gratification.

Wolff depicts his relationship with two other eleven-year-olds, who spend all their after-school time together. Their anxiety about their physical appearance, growing sexual longing, and sense of being marginalized has rendered the boys discontented and envious, and their activities are calculated to show their contempt for the world that surrounds them.

During part of each afternoon, the boys watch *The Mickey Mouse Club*. They greet Annette's appearance on the screen with a show of masculine lust: "Taylor would start moaning and Silver would lick the screen with his tongue. 'Come here baby,' he'd say, 'I've got six inches of piping hot flesh just for you.'" At the end of the program, which they find completely absorbing with its many innocent and childlike activities, they would rouse themselves "and talk dirty about Annette."

The reason that the Thunderbird convertible, with its red leather upholstery, is an irresistible target for the boys' vandalism is obvious. The young man driving it is well dressed, "handsome and fresh." He is, no doubt, on his way to pick up a beautiful young woman, the sort that these boys can only dream about.

To the twelve-year-old narrator in T. Coraghessan Boyle's "Rara Avis," the world appears to be a cauldron bubbling with sexual activity. In the crowd that had gathered to watch a huge primordial bird that has landed on a store roof, he suspiciously notices his father whispering to a woman with wet lips. He wonders where his mother is. Next, he sees a girl wearing a sweater "leaning against the fender of a convertible while her boyfriend pressed himself against her as if he wanted to dance." The narrator recalls a similar crowd gathering a few weeks earlier when an abandoned house burned to the ground. At that house, he had "studied scraps of pornographic magazines with a fever beating through my body." Soon after, the boy recalls lying to a priest in a confessional about whether he has masturbated.

Into his world permeated with sexual temptation and prohibitions comes the bird. To him, it seems to embody an almost obscene femininity with its "wings folded like a shawl, long legs naked and exposed beneath a skirt of jagged feathers," and a "secret, raw, red, and wet" wound that flashes "just above the juncture of the legs." Tension and aggression merge in the boy's final action.

Whereas their own developing sexuality threatens Wolff's and Boyle's narrators from within, in two stories about adolescent girls, Julia Alvarez's "Trespass" and Sandra Cisneros's "The First Job," the humiliation of the girls, with their developing sexuality, and the threats of violation come from without. The threatening males are both boys and adult men.

In "Trespass," twelve-year-old Carla and her family have been in the United States for only one year. In order to reach the bus that will take her to her new school, where she is in seventh grade, she must walk for a mile along an empty Long Island farm lot and a deserted service road. Her encounter with a pervert who is seated in his car on her route horrifies her, but her experiences in the school playground prove to have even longer-lasting significance.

At recess a group of four or five boys regularly taunt her, pelting her with stones that they aim "at her feet so there would be no bruises." One pulls up her blouse and scornfully announces "no titties" while another pulls her socks down and pronounces her legs, which have begun to be covered with hair, to be "monkey legs." Dismayed by and ashamed of the changes occurring daily in her body, Carla feels that her persecutors are revealing the shameful creature she is becoming.

In "The First Job," Esperanza looks forward to working so that she can help to pay her tuition for the Catholic high school she attends. She follows instructions to lie about her age in order to get a job at a photo-finishing company. Afraid of eating in the lunchroom with adults who are strangers, she eats her food quickly while standing in one of the stalls in the washroom. Later, on a break, she retreats to the company coatroom. Alone and self-conscious, she is particularly vulnerable when an older employee seems to be understanding and welcoming. His betrayal of her trust is clearly damaging since Esperanza had liked his "nice eyes" and naively thought of him as a friend who was helping her to get over being a nervous outsider.

In Frank Conroy's *Stop-Time,* and the stories "Flight" by Alice Hoffman, "Bobby" by Michael Cunningham, and "Paul's Case" by Willa Cather, very different children in very different circumstances are engaged in destructive behavior of very different magnitudes. The adults about them seem baffled by the children's actions and are totally inadequate in dealing with them. Sometimes the cause of the behavior is apparent even to the adolescents themselves, while in other instances, the adolescents' motivation and problems seem inexplicable. Often they pay dearly for their bad judgment and "crimes."

From Conroy's description of the experimental boarding school at which he lived from the ages of nine to eleven, it is clear that a certain amount of wild behavior was inevitable. With a weak and alcoholic headmaster, as well as a school philosophy of extraordinary freedom, the boys felt encouraged to test the limits of authority or to ignore it.

On a rainy day, as many as forty unsupervised boys in the dorm join to torment Ligget, a classmate. Overweight and friendless, he is so demoralized or so depressed that he makes no attempt to defend himself at the extended mock trial that the boys conduct or to protect himself from the blows of the other boys after it. Not a single boy in the group is willing to question the actions of the group as a whole. Frank readily participates with his own goal, that of throwing "a clean, powerful punch completely unhindered and with none of the sloppiness of an actual fight." None of the boys identifies in the least with the outsider they have chosen to use as a human "punching bag." If Conroy learns anything from the experience, it is "that brutality happens easily."

In "Flight," one of the interconnected stories of Alice Hoffman's *Local Girls,* Gretel

Samuelson, her brother, Jason, and their mother, Frances, are living in the suburban Long Island house that Gretel's father has left on his way to a new life and a new wife. Gretel, who is highly articulate and a gifted writer, has gone into the lucrative "business" of writing term papers for many other high school students with her brother's best friend, a senior named Eugene Kessler. According to Gretel, he seems to be the only person who understands her feelings:

> On truly hot nights, when the air was so humid and thick it was a triumph
> to draw a deep breath, I would sometimes see Eugene out in his yard.
> Somehow, I knew how alone he felt, and it gave me the shivers to think
> that alienation could be a shared experience.

The indifference with which Gretel and Eugene flout the high school's rules against cheating is just one index of their contempt for and withdrawal from their community and the people who surround them.

In "Bobby," by Michael Cunningham, the first-person narrator recalls the events of a time when he was nine years old and his brother, Carlton, was sixteen. Carlton considers himself his brother's mentor and protector. He reassures Bobby on a morning when they have both taken acid at breakfast: "There's not a thing in this pretty world to be afraid of. I'm here."

Although Carlton is a habitual user of drugs and alcohol, and happily shares both with his fourth-grader brother, their parents seem generally unaware of their sons' troubled behavior. Bobby's mother suspects "something's going on," but she has been thwarted so often that she has given up trying to understand or control her eldest son:

> Carlton comes home whistling. Our mother treats him like a guest who's
> overstayed. He doesn't care. . . . He treats her as if she were harmless, and
> so she is. . . . She never hits Carlton. She suffers him the way farm girls
> suffer a thieving crow, with a grudge so old and endless it borders on rev-
> erence.

With all that is seriously amiss in her family, Bobby's mother confronts Carlton over tracking mud into the house.

From the opening scene of "Paul's Case" by Willa Cather, it is apparent that Paul, a Pittsburgh high school student who has been suspended for his "misdemeanors," is an enigma to his teachers. They see a defiant boy who barely bothers to hide the disgust with which he views them and their way of life. While they are insulted by his insolent smile, they also despair of helping him because they can't understand his hostile behavior. His drawing teacher remarks:

> I don't really believe that smile of his comes altogether from insolence;
> there's something sort of haunted about it. The boy is not strong for one
> thing. There is something wrong about the fellow.

A motherless boy who lives in a middle-class neighborhood with his father and sisters, Paul is revolted by the ordinary circumstances of his life. He continually lies to escape from his hated surroundings, his bedroom with "its horrible yellow wallpaper, the creaking bureau with the greasy collar-box" and the pictures of George Washington and John Calvin that hang over his bed. Paul feels alive only in the presence of beauty, of art, such as music, theater, and paintings, and of luxury. He temporarily escapes the existence he despises through his job as an usher at Pittsburgh's Carnegie Hall, where he can visit the picture gallery and take a seat behind the wealthy and well-dressed patrons to listen to the symphony. After an evening at such a concert, there is no comfort for him in returning to his own home:

> He approached it tonight with the nerveless sense of defeat, the hopeless feeling of sinking back forever into ugliness and commonness that he had always had when he came home. The moment he turned into Cordelia Street he felt the waters close above his head.

Paul's theft of his employer's bank deposit is the result of his depression, the isolation and hopelessness after his father has separated him from the only experiences that gave him any pleasure. He is a deeply disturbed youngster whose cravings for beauty reflect bewildering and intractable psychological problems.

In four works, the selections from Russell Baker's *Growing Up,* Laura Shaine Cunningham's *A Place in the Country,* Warren Kliewer's "The Best Christmas Present Ever," and Toni Cade Bambara's story "Raymond's Run," children have highly positive family experiences. They are comfortable members of a household with well-understood roles in their families, and as a result, they have a strong sense of belonging and of their own identity and are contented with it. When they test their abilities in the world, they don't experience a destructive fear of failure. In some way that they don't need to analyze, they are loved for themselves and this certainly enables them to function with security in a variety of situations.

In the second chapter of *Growing Up,* Russell Baker recounts his experiences over a period of three years of selling weekly issues of the *Saturday Evening Post* at five cents each. His mother, who has been a widow for two years, is very concerned that her son have a better way of life than that of her husband. A schoolteacher, she is determined that Russell will "not grow up like him and his people, with calluses on their hands, overalls on their backs, and fourth-grade educations in their heads." She had known all too well the world of her husband in which "men left with their lunch pails at sunup, worked with their hands until the grime ate into the pores, and died with a few sticks of mail-order furniture as their legacy."

Mrs. Baker has identified a flaw in her son's character, a lack of "gumption." With the example of his energetic and aggressive younger sister, Doris, before him, Russell pretty well agrees with his mother's evaluation. Her solution, however, does not please him. With the best of intentions, she sets her son to selling magazines to keep him busy and to help him learn to influence prospective customers as a kind of trial run for a career in business. When, as a realistic woman, she accepts the inevitable conclusion that her son will never succeed in a competitive business environment, she simply moves on and identifies a skill that her son does possess. With what might seem her casual suggestion, she has gladdened Russell's heart and inspired him with a goal that is, indeed, an appropriate and pleasing one for him.

At eight years old, after the death of her mother, Laura Shaine Cunningham finds herself at the center of a new family created by her bachelor uncles, Gabe and Len. This newly formed family of three begins housekeeping together, decorating the new, larger apartment in the building into which they have moved. The uncles make most decisions about their daily routine with the goal of pleasing the orphaned child with whom they consult about her preferences. Uncle Gabe and Uncle Len are clearly eccentric individualists who have very little information about raising an eight-year-old. They do, however, have respect for Laura's wishes and a good deal of wisdom about relationships and making one another feel valued.

When Laura, who is at a summer camp, insists on her right to bunk with a ten-year-old friend from home rather than with girls her own age, the camp managers refuse to break their rules. Her uncles come to her defense, with her uncle Len traveling by taxi from the Bronx to the Catskills to join the battle. Refusing to bed down with the eight-year-old Bluebells, Laura instead lies down on the basketball court, wondering about her rebellion:

> But how long, realistically, could I last out here in this alien dark and cold?
> Already, there were rustlings in the woods, the distant howl of a coyote.
> The mountain air chilled fast; soon the radiant heat left the asphalt court.
> I started to shiver. . . . Uncle Len took off his trench coat and covered me.
> Then, in a surprise move, he lay down on the court, too. "They are a tough
> bunch," he told me, but we would prevail.

Her unconventional "family," living life on their own terms and doggedly loyal to Laura, creates an environment in which a motherless child is able to act bravely to fulfill her own needs.

The settings of Kliewer's and Bambara's works are very different: a young boy celebrates Christmas with his Mennonite family in rural Minnesota and a young black girl celebrates May Day by participating, as she always does, in her elementary school's annual track meet.

Early in his memoir, Kliewer describes the house of his uncle Pete and aunt Anna, at which his large clan of relatives always gathers for a Christmas feast followed by the distribution of a gift for each child. He, along with numerous cousins, is impatient for the gift-giving ceremony that follows the festive meal:

> The red-and-green wrapped packages were stacked and waiting under the
> Christmas tree, but the grown-ups were delaying. We children would drift
> like a small flock of lost sparrows into the kitchen where we'd watch the

women putting food away, washing dishes, drying them, and laughing
and talking as if this were a plain, old, ordinary day, not Christmas. We
wanted to ask, "Aren't you almost done?" but no one dared.

Well-understood family tradition is the organizing force behind the day's activities.
Thus, the children eat their meal separately, after the adults are finished, and each child
will be given a gift purchased by the relative who picked that child's name out of a hat
that was circulated at the family's Thanksgiving reunion. Over the years, experience
taught Warren not to expect a very interesting gift: "My mind dwelt on things I didn't
want but someone probably thought I needed—dark brown, useful woolen scarves
and ugly red caps with earflaps." Fortunately, the gift that he receives not only pleases
him greatly, but helps him to discover an inner resource of his own that will become
an important part of his identity.

In "Raymond's Run," Hazel Elizabeth Deborah Parker is a young black girl who has
a strong sense of identity. She is the protector of her retarded brother, Raymond, and
she is a runner who wins. Comfortable with her role in the family, with the way that
everyone contributes to one another's well being, Squeaky—as she is nicknamed—takes
pride in the way that she deals with other children who want to tease and humiliate her
brother, and in her athletic ability. Having such a healthy sense of self, she dismisses the
May Pole dancing at the Harlem park, with the fancy white dress and baby-doll shoes
that the dancers must wear. She knows herself: "I do not dance on my toes. I run. That
is what I am all about." With her self-confidence and willingness to work hard, Squeaky
believes she can succeed at anything she decides to do.

Three poignant works—Mary McCarthy's "A Tin Butterfly," the excerpt from Mary
Crow Dog's *Lakota Woman,* and Jack London's "The Apostate"—depict incidents of
the brutalization or abuse of children. Some of the incidents were the result of mistaken good intentions or might not have been labeled child abuse at the time they
occurred. For example, Mary McCarthy's great-aunt Margaret's devout belief in the
benefits of fresh air for her four young charges leads her to keep them outdoors in the
Minnesota cold for a total of six hours every Saturday and Sunday. McCarthy recalls
that with the temperature

at fifteen, twenty, or twenty-four below zero we could not play, even if we
had had something to play with, and used simply to stand in the snow,
crying, and beating sometimes on the window with our frozen mittens,
till my aunt's angry face would appear there and drive us away.

Another example of child abuse that was widely countenanced during the nineteenth
century was the employment in factories, particularly fabric mills, of children as young
as eight and nine years old. And the use of child labor on family farms, which was generally viewed as helping with chores, became the use of children in the workforce
among immigrants and migrant workers in the harvesting of crops throughout the
twentieth century.

The most pervasive example of child abuse, however, remains the use of corporal punishment. In almost every memoir of childhood in this volume, the narrators—no matter what their ethnic, religious, and racial backgrounds—can recall an unjust or brutal punishment during which an angry adult inflicted considerable pain on them, or even a routine of such punishments. Often added to the pain was the shame of being forced to undress and being struck on a private part of the body.

With warnings passed on by generations of relatives and religious authorities against "sparing the rod," in a majority of American households, misbehavior was met with varying degrees of socially sanctioned corporal punishment. From a slap of a hand, to a spanking with a hairbrush, to a whipping with a strap or switch, adults seemed to believe that physical pain was an effective deterrent and a suitable outlet for the outrage of an adult whose rules had been ignored. Peaceful people who would never have dreamed of slapping, punching, or whipping another adult believed that it was their right—or even their duty—to do so to their own children.

In Mary McCarthy's chapter "A Tin Butterfly" in *Memories of a Catholic Girlhood,* she records that as a result of the deaths of her parents during the 1918 flu epidemic, she and her three brothers were sent to live with her middle-aged great-aunt Margaret and her husband, Myers Shriver. Myers, in effect, became the hired father surrogate for four children, all under seven years of age and to whom he was related by marriage, not by blood. A man who had no friends or relatives and no paying job, Myers clearly had no fondness or compassion for three of the four orphans.

When Mary, at age ten, wins a $25 prize in a children's essay contest, she knows that her great-aunt Margaret is "proud and happy." But when she arrives home after the award ceremony, her "uncle silently rose from his chair, led me into the dark downstairs lavatory . . . and furiously beat me with the razor strop—to teach me a lesson, he said, lest I become stuck-up." At the center of the chapter is the severe beating by both her aunt and uncle in order to make her confess to the theft of a butterfly pin. But the experience, far from breaking her spirit, a goal of her aunt and uncle, provides an inner victory that strengthens her spirit.

In *Lakota Woman,* Mary Crow Dog titles her chapter on life at the St. Francis mission school "Civilize Them with a Stick." Three generations of Sioux women in her family had been sent away from home to the school, and her grandmother, a devout Catholic, believed that for Mary an education there was the key to achieving the white man's comfortable lifestyle. Mary observes:

> Examples abounded all around her that it was the wrong key to the wrong
> door, that it would not change the shape of my cheekbones, or the slant
> of my eyes, the color of my hair, or the feelings inside me. She had only to
> open her eyes to see, but could not or would not.

The school's daily routine included a considerable amount of child labor, with classes sandwiched between scrubbing floors and tables as well as kitchen chores. Children caught resting when they were supposed to be working would often be slapped across the face with a dish towel. The dorm room was "icy cold" in the winter and the cheap, unpleasant food frequently contained insects or rocks.

Beatings with a strap were commonplace. Mary recalls:

> I did not escape my share of the strap. Once, when I was thirteen years old, I refused to go to Mass. I did not want to go to church because I did not feel well. A nun grabbed me by the hair, dragged me upstairs, made me stoop over, pulled my dress up . . . pulled my panties down, and gave me what they called "swats"—twenty-five swats with a board around which Scotch tape had been wound. She hurt me badly.

But as she grew older, she confronted the nuns. With two other strong-willed girls, in what she termed "a Sioux uprising," she wrote and distributed an issue of a newspaper that described the inhumane treatment of the children at the school. And when a nun was about to swat a shy little girl who was ashamed to remove her underpants for the evening shower, Mary defended the child: "I went up to the sister, pushed her veil off, and knocked her down. I told her that if she wanted to hit a little girl she should pick on me, pick one her own size. She got herself transferred out of the dorm a week later."

In Jack London's 1911 story "The Apostate," the brutalization of a child is not a matter of punishment, but of a way of life in an impoverished, fatherless household. The story chronicles the work history of Johnny, who began to toil in a mill before he was seven years old. Each morning he is "torn bodily by his mother from the grip of sleep" and given a meager breakfast that does not satisfy his hunger; then he must trudge a considerable distance to the mill where he works a ten-hour day. His child's wages, which help to support his mother and younger siblings, only make the difference between "acute starvation and chronic underfeeding."

By the age of twelve he is worn out, and the endless hours of serving machines with repetitive machinelike precision have rendered him incapable of thinking or even dreaming. He is a stunted creature who is "a travesty of the human." In portraying Johnny as the victim of poverty and the exploitation of factory owners and overseers, London has dramatized not some far-fetched fictional experience, but the typical world experienced by hundreds of thousands of child laborers before the passage of child-labor laws. Moreover, in contemporary America the children of seasonal workers remain unprotected by legislation. Children as young as six years of age pack lettuce and cabbage, harvest tomatoes on Virginia's eastern shore, and pick berries or grapes in the fields of Oregon and California. They are paid slave wages and suffer a much larger proportion of farm injuries than do adult workers.

In two very different stories, "Indian Camp" by Ernest Hemingway and "Gospel Song" by Dorothy Allison, a parent fails to protect a vulnerable child from a hurtful situation. In Hemingway's story, a well-meaning father fails to anticipate his young son's reaction to an emergency operation. In Allison's story, a mother willfully fails to protect her albino daughter, whom the world views as ugly, from two kinds of harm.

In "Indian Camp," Nick Adams's father inappropriately takes his young son to an Indian shanty where a pregnant woman has been in labor for two days. He jokingly refers to Nick, who has been holding a basin as his father performs a caesarean, as an "interne." Dr. Adams even suggests that Nick might want to watch as he sews up the incision he has made. Nick does not. With typical Hemingway understatement, we are told that Nick's "curiosity had been gone for a long time."

The doctor, who has been rather cavalier about the woman's suffering and who has told Nick that "her screams are not important," only begins to realize how wrong he was to bring Nick when the experience comes to involve an unexpected death as well as a new life. Perfectly willing to teach Nick how babies come into the world, Dr. Adams is now faced with a child's questions about death.

Nick's reaction to the dawning day and to the security of being in a boat rowed by his father is to embrace life. He asserts the child's view of invulnerability.

In "Gospel Song," the nine-year-old narrator befriends Shannon Pearl when the albino girl boards the school bus for the first time and is shunned by all of the students. They refuse to allow her to take a seat next to any of them because of "her skull showing blue-white through the thin, colorless hair and those watery pink eyes flicking back and forth, drifting in and out of focus." The narrator welcomes Shannon by pulling her by the arm into her own row; she has no fear of being teased as a result of her association. She is secure because

> everyone at Greenville Elementary knew me and my family—particularly
> my matched sets of cousins, big unruly boys who would just as soon toss
> a boy as a penny against the school walls if they heard of an insult against
> any of us.

The nine-year-old begins to travel with Shannon and her parents to country churches in search of gospel choirs or gospel soloists to book for revival meetings. Increasingly, the narrator becomes aware of the drinking and sexual behavior that occur backstage at large gospel performances. Shannon and the narrator have to learn "to walk carefully backstage, with all those hands reaching out to stroke our thighs and pinch the nipples we barely had yet." Shannon's mother laughingly pronounces the harassers "playful boys" and seems unable to smell the liquor fumes on the costumes of the singers. In contrast to the spirited defense of Shannon that the nine-year-old friend exhibits when a male singing star cruelly insults her, Mrs. Pearl flirts with the entertainer.

As the authors of the stories and memoirs of this collection vividly demonstrate, there is a compelling attraction to the recollection, depiction, and analysis of childhood experience. Long after more recent events have been forgotten, it seems as though adults can recall with surprising clarity and emotion pleasurable or painful childhood occurrences and the relationships that were reflected by them. One poignant element that emerges as adults recollect their childhood is the vulnerability that all children share. Lacking knowledge and experience of the world or power within it, they depend on family members and other adults to protect and defend them. Lacking autonomy in much of their lives, children can only hope that their desires will count in the decisions that adults make about them. Most grown-ups believe strongly that what happened to them as children was very significant. The gratifications, disappointments, and hurt of childhood often remain as lifelong, joyful, and inspiring memories or as bitter regrets about what should have been.

Finally, a word about the selections in this collection. We have grouped them according to their sources as short stories or excerpts from autobiographies or memoirs. They are the work of established—often very well-known—writers. In some cases, the distinction between an autobiographical story and a memoir is a blurry one at best. Some of the memoir excerpts, such as Mary McCarthy's "A Tin Butterfly" and Kate Simon's "Coney and Gypsies" read like short stories. The incidents recounted have the shape and dynamism of a contrived formal narrative and resonate with complex images. So too, some of the short stories have the tone of candor and intimacy, the immediacy of detail, the quirkiness of remembered experiences, which, in refashioned form, they undoubtedly are. To return to the world of childhood, whether in search of the hidden sources of the adult self or as an exercise in nostalgia or bitter reminiscence or as a rich mine for one's art, is to enter the world of longing and desire as much as the world of fact. Whether in memoir or short story, the exploration of the sometimes remote, sometimes inescapably near worlds of childhood and adolescence is the calling forth of an elusive but never-to-be-exorcised ghost. What results is simultaneously a work of self-validation and self-creation, a marriage of memory and art.

—Barbara H. Solomon
and Eileen Panetta

NOTE: Block ornaments in the text indicate an elision of that selection.

FICTION

DOROTHY ALLISON

(1949–)

Dorothy Allison considers her birth in Greenville, South Carolina, to an impoverished, unwed mother who had just turned fifteen years old to be the "central fact" of her life. From the ages of five to eleven years old, she was the victim of her abusive stepfather, who often beat and raped her. As an adolescent, she worked after school at a job created through Lyndon Johnson's War on Poverty program, received charity glasses from the Lions Club, and stole books that she was too poor to buy. A National Merit scholarship enabled her to attend Florida Presbyterian College. In the early 1970s, Allison recalls, she worked for the Social Security Administration, where she was rebuked for wearing pantsuits to work. Allison was a member of a feminist collective household and very much a part of the radical women's movement of the 1970s. She credits feminism with saving her life. In her introduction to a revised and expanded edition of her story collection *Trash* (2002), she observes that forgiving her family "took place in large part through the writing of these stories, in a process of making peace with the violence of my childhood, in owning up to it and finding a way to talk about it that did not make me more ashamed of myself or those I loved." She has published a book of poetry, *The Women Who Hate Me* (1983); an autobiographical novel, *Bastard Out of Carolina* (1992), which was a finalist for the National Book Award; *Two or Three Things I Know for Sure* (1994); *Skin: Talking About Sex, Class & Literature* (1994); and the novel *Cavedweller* (1998).

Gospel Song

At nine, I knew exactly who and what I wanted to be. Early every Sunday morning I got up to watch *The Sunrise Gospel Hour* and practice my secret ambition. More than anything in the world I wanted to be a gospel singer—a little girl in a white fringe vest with silver and gold crosses embroidered on the back. I wanted gray-headed ladies to cry when they saw my pink cheeks. I wanted people to moan when they heard the throb in my voice when I sang of the miracle in my life. I wanted a miracle in my life. I wanted to be a gospel singer and be loved by the whole wide world.

All that summer, while Mama was off at work, I haunted the White Horse Cafe over on the highway. They had three Teresa Brewer songs on the jukebox, and the truckers loved Teresa as much as I did. I'd sit out under the jalousie windows and hum along with her, imagining myself crooning with a raw and desperate voice. Half asleep in the sun, reassured by the familiar smell of frying fat, I'd make promises to God. If only He'd let it happen! I knew I'd probably turn to whiskey and rock 'n' roll like they all did, but not for years, I promised. Not for years, Lord. Not till I had glorified His Name and bought my mama a yellow Cadillac and a house on Old Henderson Road.

Jesus, make me a gospel singer, I prayed, while Teresa sang of what might have been God, and then again might have been some black-eyed man. Make me, oh make me! But Jesus must have been busy with Teresa 'cause my voice went high and shrill every time I got excited, and cracked and went hoarse if I tried to croon. The preacher at Bushy Creek Baptist wouldn't even let me stand near the choir to turn the pages of a hymnal. Without a voice like Teresa's or June Carter's, I couldn't sing gospel. I could just listen to it and watch the gray-headed ladies cry. It was an injustice I could not understand or forgive. It left me with a wild aching hunger in my heart and a deep resentment I hid from everyone but God.

My friend Shannon Pearl had the same glint of hunger in her watery pink eyes. An albino, perennially six inches shorter than me, Shannon had white skin, white hair, pale eyes, and fine blue blood vessels showing against the ivory of her scalp. Blue threads under the linen, her mama was always saying. Sometimes, Shannon seemed strangely beautiful to me, as she surely was to her mother. Sometimes, but not often. Not often at all. But every chance she could get, Mrs. Pearl would sit her daughter between her knees and purr over that gossamer hair and puffy pale skin.

"My little angel," Mrs. Pearl would croon, and my stomach would push up against my heart.

It was a lesson in the power of love. Looking back at me from between her mother's legs, Shannon was wholly monstrous, a lurching hunched creature shining with sweat and smug satisfaction. There had to be something wrong with me I was sure, the way I went from awe to disgust where Shannon was concerned. When Shannon sat between her mama's legs or chewed licorice strings her daddy held out for her, I purely hated her. But when other people would look at her hatefully or the boys up at Lee Highway would call her "Lard Eyes," I felt a fierce and protective love for her as if she were more my sister than Reese. I felt as if I belonged to her in a funny kind of way, as if her "affliction" put me deeply in her debt. It was a mystery, I guessed, a sign of grace like my Catholic Aunt Maybelle was always talking about.

I met Shannon Pearl on the first Monday of school the year I entered the third grade. She got on the bus two stops after Reese and me, walking stolidly past a dozen hooting boys and another dozen flushed and whispering girls. As she made her way up the aisle, I watched each boy slide to the end of his seat to block her sitting with him and every girl flinch away as if whatever Shannon had might be catching. In the seat ahead of us Danny Powell leaned far over into the aisle and began to make retching noises.

"Cootie Train! Cootie Train!" somebody yelled as the bus lurched into motion and Shannon still hadn't found a seat.

I watched her face—impassive, contemptuous, and stubborn. Sweat was showing on her dress but nothing showed in her face except for the eyes. There was fire in those pink eyes, a deep fire I recognized, banked and raging. Before I knew it I was on my feet and leaning forward to catch her arm. I pulled her into our row without a word. Reese stared at me like I was crazy, but Shannon settled herself and started cleaning her bottle-glass lenses as if nothing at all was happening.

I glared at Danny Powell's open mouth until he turned away from us. Reese pulled a strand of her lank blond hair into her mouth and pretended she was sitting alone. Slowly, the boys sitting near us turned their heads and began to mutter to each other. There was one soft "Cootie Bitch" hissed in my direction, but no yelling. Nobody knew exactly why I had taken a shine to Shannon, but everyone at Greenville Elementary knew me and my family—particularly my matched sets of cousins, big unruly boys who would just as soon toss a boy as a penny against the school walls if they heard of an insult against any of us.

Shannon Pearl spent a good five minutes cleaning her glasses and then sat silent for the rest of the ride to school. I understood intuitively that she would not say anything, would in fact generously pretend to have fallen into our seat. I sat there beside her watching the pinched faces of my classmates as they kept looking back toward us. Just the way they stared made me want to start a conversation with Shannon. I imagined us discussing all the enemies we had in common while half the bus craned their necks to try to hear. But I couldn't bring myself to actually do that, couldn't even imagine what to say to her. Not till the bus crossed the railroad tracks at the south corner of Greenville Elementary did I manage to force my mouth open enough to say my name and then Reese's.

She nodded impartially and whispered "Shannon Pearl" before taking off her glasses to begin cleaning them all over again. With her glasses off she half shut her eyes and hunched her shoulders. Much later, I would realize that she cleaned her glasses whenever she needed a quiet moment to regain her composure, or more often, just to put everything around her at a distance. Without glasses, the world became a soft blur, but she also behaved as if the glasses were all that made it possible for her to hear. Commotion or insults made while she was cleaning her glasses never seemed to register at all. It was a valuable trick when you were the object of as much ridicule as Shannon Pearl.

Christian charity, I knew, would have had me smile at Shannon but avoid her like everyone else. It wasn't Christian charity that made me give her my seat on the bus, trade my third-grade picture for hers, sit at her kitchen table while her mama tried another trick on her wispy hair—"Egg and cornmeal, that'll do the trick. We gonna put curls in this hair, darling, or my name an't Roseanne Pearl"—or follow her to the Bushy Creek Highway Store and share the blue Popsicle she bought us. Not Christian charity, my fascination with her felt more like the restlessness that made me worry the scabs on my ankles. As disgusting as it all seemed, I couldn't put away the need to scratch my ankles, or hang around what Granny called "that strange and ugly child."

Other people had no such problem. Other than her mother and I, no one could stand Shannon. No amount of Jesus's grace would make her even marginally acceptable, and people had been known to suddenly lose their lunch from the sight of the clammy sheen of her skin, her skull showing blue-white through the thin, colorless hair and those watery pink eyes flicking back and forth, drifting in and out of focus.

"Lord! But that child is ugly."

"It's a trial, Jesus knows, a trial for her poor parents."

"They should keep her home."

"Now, honey. That's not like you. Remember, the Lord loves a charitable heart."

"I don't care. The Lord didn't intend me to get nauseous in the middle of Sunday services. That child is a shock to the digestion."

Driving from Greenville to Greer on Highway 85 past the Sears, Roebuck warehouse, the airbase, the rolling green-and-red mud hills—a trip we made almost every other day—my stepfather never failed to get us all to sing like some traveling gospel family. *WHILE I WAS SLEEPING SOMEBODY TOUCHED ME, WHILE I WAS SLEEPING, OH! SOMEBODY TOUCHED ME . . . MUST'HA BEEN THE HAND OF THE LORD . . .*

Full-voice, all-out, late-evening gospel music filled the car and shocked the passing traffic. My stepfather never drove fast, and not a one of us could sing worth a damn. My sisters howled and screeched, my mama's voice broke like she, too, dreamed of Teresa Brewer, and my stepfather made sounds that would have scared cows. None of them cared, and I tried not to let it bother me. I'd put my head out the window and howl for all I was worth. The wind filled my mouth and the roar obscured the fact that I sang as badly as any of them. Sometimes at the house I'd even go sing into the electric fan. It made my voice buzz and waver like a slide guitar, an effect I particularly liked, though Mama complained it gave her a headache and would give me an earache if I didn't cut it out.

I took the fan out on the back porch and sang to myself. Maybe I wouldn't get to be the star on the stage, maybe I'd wind up singing background in a "family"—all of us dressed alike in electric blue fringed blouses with silver embroidery. All I needed was a chance to turn my soulful brown eyes on a tent full of believers, sing out the little break in my mournful voice. I knew I could make them love me. There was a secret to it, but I would find it out. If Shannon Pearl could do it to me, I would find a way to do it to the world.

I had the idea that because she was so ugly on the outside, it was only reasonable that Shannon would turn out to be saintlike when you got to know her. That was the way it would have been in any storybook the local ladies' society would have let me borrow. I thought of *Little Women, The Bobbsey Twins,* and all those novels about poor British families at Christmas. Tiny Tim, for Christ's sake! Shannon, I was sure, would be like that. A patient and gentle soul had to be hidden behind those pale and sweaty features. She would be generous, insightful, understanding, and wise beyond her years. She would be the friend I had always needed.

That she was none of these was something I could never quite accept. Once she relaxed with me, Shannon invariably told horrible stories, most of which were about the gruesome deaths of innocent children. ". . . And then the tractor backed up over him, cutting his body in three pieces, but nobody seen it or heard it, you see, 'cause of the noise the thresher made. So then his mama come out with iced tea for everybody. And she put her foot down right in his little torn-open stomach. And oh Lord! Don't you know . . ."

I couldn't help myself. I'd sit and listen, open-mouthed and fascinated, while this shining creature went on and on about decapitations. She loved best little children who had fallen in the way of large machines. It was something none of the grown-ups knew a thing about, though once in a while I'd hear a much shorter, much tamer version of one of Shannon's stories from her mama. At those moments, Shannon would give me a grin of smug pride. Can't I tell it better? she seemed to be saying. Gradually I admitted to myself what hid behind Shannon's impassive pink-and-white features. Shannon Pearl simply and completely hated everyone who had ever hurt her, and spent most of her time brooding on punishments either she or God would visit on them. The fire that burned in her eyes was the fire of outrage. Had she been stronger or smarter, Shannon Pearl would have been dangerous. But half-blind, sickly, and ostracized, she was not much of a threat to anyone.

"I like your family," Shannon sometimes said, though we both knew that was a polite lie. "Your mama's a fine woman," Roseanne Pearl would agree, while she eyed my too-tight raggedy dresses. She reminded me of my stepfather's sisters looking at us out of smug, superior faces, laughing at my mama's loose teeth and my sister's curls done up in paper scraps. Whenever the Pearls talked about my people, I'd take off and not go back for weeks. I didn't want the two parts of my life to come together.

We were living out past Henderson Road, on the other side of White Horse Highway. Up near the highway a revival tent had been erected. Some evenings I would walk up there on my own to sit outside and listen. The preacher was a shouter, something I had never liked. He'd rave and threaten, and it didn't seem as if he was ever gonna get to the invocation. I sat in the dark, trying not to think about anything, especially not about the whipping I was going to get if I stayed too long. I kept seeing my Uncle Jack in the men who stood near the highway sharing a bottle in a paper sack, black-headed men with blasted rough-hewn faces. Was it hatred or sorrow that made them look like that, their necks so stiff and their eyes so cold?

Did I look like that?

Would I look like that when I grew up? I remembered Aunt Grace putting her big hands over my ears and turning my face to catch the light, saying, "Just as well you smart; you an't never gonna be a beauty."

At least I wasn't as ugly as Shannon Pearl, I told myself, and was immediately ashamed. Shannon hadn't made herself ugly, but if I kept thinking that way I just might. Mama always said people could see your soul in your face, could see your hatefulness and lack of charity. With all the hatefulness I was trying to hide, it was a wonder I wasn't uglier than a toad in mud season.

The singing started. I sat back on my heels and hugged my knees, humming. Revivals are funny. People get pretty enthusiastic, but they sometimes forget just which hymn it is they're singing. I grinned to myself and watched the men near the road punch each other lightly and curse in a friendly fashion.

You bastard.

You son of a bitch.

The preacher said something I didn't understand. There was a moment of silence, and then a pure tenor voice rose up into the night sky. The spit soured in my mouth. They had a real singer in there, a real gospel choir.

SWING LOW, SWEET CHARIOT . . . COMING FOR TO CARRY ME HOME . . . AS I WALKED OUT IN THE STREETS OF LAREDO . . . SWEET JESUS . . . LIFT ME UP, LIFT ME UP IN THE AIR. . . .

The night seemed to wrap all around me like a blanket. My insides felt as if they had melted, and I could just feel the wind in my mouth. The sweet gospel music poured through me and made all my nastiness, all my jealousy and hatred, swell in my heart. I knew. I knew I was the most disgusting person in the world. I didn't deserve to live another day. I started hiccupping and crying.

"I'm sorry. Jesus, I'm sorry."

How could I live with myself? How could God stand me? Was this why Jesus wouldn't speak to my heart? The music washed over me . . . *SOFTLY AND TENDERLY.* The music was a river trying to wash me clean. I sobbed and dug my heels into the dirt, drunk on grief and that pure, pure voice. It didn't matter then if it was whiskey backstage or tongue kissing in the dressing room. Whatever it took to make that juice was necessary, was fine. I wiped my eyes and swore out loud. Get those boys another bottle, I said. Find that girl a hard-headed husband. But goddamn, get them to make that music. Make that music! Lord, make me drunk on that music.

The next Sunday I went off with Shannon and the Pearls for another gospel drive.

Driving backcountry with the Pearls meant stopping in at little country churches listening to gospel choirs. Mostly all those choirs had was a little echo of the real stuff. "Pitiful, an't it?" Shannon sounded like her father's daughter. "Organ music just can't stand against a slide guitar." I nodded, but I wasn't sure she was right.

Sometimes one pure voice would stand out, one little girl; one set of brothers whose eyes would lift when they sang. Those were the ones who could make you want to scream low against all the darkness in the world. "That one," Shannon would whisper smugly, but I didn't need her to tell me. I could always tell which one Mr. Pearl would take aside and invite over to Gaston for revival week.

"Child!" he'd say. "You got a gift from God."

Uh huh, yeah.

Sometimes I couldn't stand it. I couldn't go in one more church, hear one more choir. Never mind loving the music, why couldn't God give me a voice? I hadn't asked for thick eyelashes. I had asked for, begged for, gospel. Didn't God give a good goddamn what I wanted? If He'd take bastards into heaven, how come He couldn't put me in front of those hot lights and all that dispensation? Gospel singers always had money in their pockets, another bottle under their seats. Gospel singers had love and safety and the whole wide world to fall back on—women and church and red clay solid under their feet. All I wanted, I whispered, all I wanted was a piece, a piece, a little piece of it.

Shannon looked at me sympathetically.

She knows, I thought, she knows what it is to want what you are never going to have.

There was a circuit that ran from North Carolina to South Carolina, Tennessee, Georgia, Alabama. The gospel singers moved back and forth on it, a tide of gilt and fringe jackets that intersected and paralleled the country-western circuit. Sometimes you couldn't tell the difference, and as times got harder certainly Mr. Pearl stopped making distinctions, booking any act that would get him a little cash up front. More and more, I got to go off with the Pearls in their old yellow DeSoto, the trunk stuffed with boxes of religious supplies and Mrs. Pearl's sewing machine, the backseat crowded with Shannon and me and piles of sewing. Pulling into small towns in the afternoon so Mr. Pearl could do the setup and Mrs. Pearl could repair tears and frayed edges of embroidery, Shannon and I would go off to picnic alone on cold chicken and chow-chow. Mrs. Pearl always brought tea in a mason jar, but Shannon would rub her eyes and complain of a headache until her mama gave in and bought us RC Colas.

Most of the singers arrived late.

It was a wonder to me that the truth never seemed to register with Mr. and Mrs. Pearl. No matter who fell over the boxes backstage, they never caught on that the whole Tuckerton family had to be pointed in the direction of the stage, nor that Little Pammie Gleason—Lord, just thirteen!—had to wear her frilly blouse long-sleeved 'cause she had bruises all up and down her arms from that redheaded boy her daddy wouldn't let her marry. They never seemed to see all the "boys" passing bourbon in paper cups backstage or their angel daughter, Shannon, begging for "just a sip." Maybe Jesus shielded their eyes the way he kept old Shadrach, Meshach, and Abednego safe in the fiery furnace. Certainly sin didn't touch them the way it did Shannon and me. Both of us had learned to walk carefully backstage, with all those hands reaching out to stroke our thighs and pinch the nipples we barely had yet.

"Playful boys," Mrs. Pearl would laugh, stitching the sleeves back on their jackets, the rips in their pants. It was a wonder to me that she couldn't smell the whiskey breath set deep in her fine embroidery. But she didn't, and I wasn't gonna commit the sin of telling her what God surely didn't intend her to know.

"Sometimes you'd think Mama's simple," Shannon told me. It was one of those times I was keeping my head down, not wanting to say anything. It was her mama. I wouldn't talk about my mama that way even if she was crazy. I wished Shannon would shut up and the music would start. I was still hungry. Mrs. Pearl had packed less food than usual, and Mama had told me I was always to leave something on my plate when I ate with Shannon. I wasn't supposed to make them think they had to feed me. Not that that particular tactic worked. I'd left half a biscuit, and damned if Shannon hadn't popped it in her mouth.

"Maybe it's all that tugging at her throttle." Shannon started giggling funny, and I knew somebody had finally given her a pull at a paper cup. Now, I thought, now her mama will have to see. But when Shannon fell over her sewing machine, Mrs. Pearl just laid her down with a wet rag on her forehead.

"It's the weather," she whispered to me, over Shannon's sodden head. It was so hot; the heat was wilting the pictures off the paper fans provided by the local funeral home. But if there had been snow up to the hubcaps, Mrs. Pearl would have said it was the chill in the air. An hour later, one of the Tuckerton cousins spilled a paper cup on Mrs. Pearl's sleeve, and I saw her take a deep, painful breath. Catching my eye, she just said, "Can't expect that frail soul to cope without a little help."

I didn't tell her that it seemed to me that all those "boys" and "girls" were getting a hell of a lot of "help." I just muttered an almost inaudible "yeah" and cut my sinful eyes at them all.

"We could go sit under the stage," Shannon suggested. "It's real nice under there."

It was nice, close and dark and full of the sound of people stomping on the stage. I put my head back and let the dust drift down on my face enjoying the feeling of being safe and hidden, away from all the people. The music seemed to be vibrating in my bones. *TAKING YOUR MEASURE, TAKING YOUR MEASURE, JESUS AND THE HOLY GHOST ARE TAKING YOUR MEASURE . . .*

I didn't like the new music they were singing. It was a little too gimmicky. *TWO CUPS, THREE CUPS, A TEASPOON OF RIGHTEOUS. HOW WILL YOU MEASURE WHEN THEY CALL OUT YOUR NAME?* Shannon started laughing. She put her hands around me and rocked her head back and forth. The music was too loud and I could smell whiskey all around us. My head hurt terribly; the smell of Shannon's hair was making me sick.

"Uh huh uh." I started to gag. Desperately I pushed Shannon away and crawled for the side of the stage as fast as I could. Air, I had to have air.

"Uh huh uh." I rolled out from under the stage and hit the side of the tent. Retching now, I jerked up the side of the tarp and wiggled through. Out in the damp evening air, I just let my head hang down and vomited between my widespread hands. Behind me Shannon was gasping and giggling.

"You're sick, you poor baby." I felt her hand on the small of my back pushing down comfortingly.

"Lord God!"

I looked up. A very tall man in a purple shirt was standing in front of me. I dropped my head and puked again. He had silver boots with cracked heels. I watched him step back out of range.

"Lord God!"

"It's all right." Shannon got to her feet beside me, keeping her hand on my back.

"She's just a little sick." She paused. "If you got her a Co-Cola, it might settle her stomach."

I wiped my mouth, and then wiped my hand on the grass. I looked up. Shannon was standing still, sweat running down into her eyes and making her blink. I could see she was hoping for two Cokes. The man was still standing there with his mouth hanging open, a look of horror and shock on his face.

"Lord God," he said again, and I knew before he spoke what he was gonna say. It wasn't me who'd surprised him.

"Child, you are the ugliest thing I have ever seen."

Shannon froze. Her mouth fell open, and as I watched, her whole face seemed to cave in. Her eyes shrank to little dots and her mouth became a cup of sorrow. I pushed myself up.

"You bastard!" I staggered forward and he backed up, rocking on his little silver heels. "You goddamned gutless son of a bitch!" His eyes kept moving from my face to Shannon's wilting figure. "You think you so pretty? You ugly sack of shit! You shit-faced turd-eating . . ."

"SHANNON PEARL!"

Mrs. Pearl was coming round the tent.

"You girls . . ." She gathered Shannon up in her arms. "Where have you been?" The man backed further away. I breathed through my mouth, though I no longer felt so sick. I felt angry and helpless and I was trying hard not to start crying. Mrs. Pearl clucked between her teeth and stroked Shannon's limp hair. "What have you been doing?"

Shannon moaned and buried her face in her mama's dress. Mrs. Pearl turned to me. "What were you saying?" Her eyes glittered in the arc lights from the front of the tent. I wiped my mouth again and said nothing. Mrs. Pearl looked to the man in the purple shirt. The confusion on her face seemed to melt and quickly became a blur of excitement and interest.

"I hope they weren't bothering you," she told him. "Don't you go on next?"

"Uh, yeah." He looked like he wasn't sure. He couldn't take his eyes off Shannon. He shook himself. "You Mrs. Pearl?"

"Why, that's right." Mrs. Pearl's face was glowing.

"I'd heard about you. I just never met your daughter before."

Mrs. Pearl seemed to shiver all over but then catch herself. Pressed to her mama's stomach, Shannon began to wail.

"Shannon, what are you going on for?" She pushed her daughter away from her side and pulled out a blue embroidered handkerchief to wipe her face.

"I think we all kind of surprised each other." The man stepped forward and gave Mrs. Pearl a slow smile, but his eyes kept wandering back to Shannon. I wiped my mouth again and stopped myself from spitting. Mrs. Pearl went on wiping her daughter's face but looking up into the man's eyes.

"I love it when you sing," she said and half giggled. Shannon pulled away from her and stared up at them both. The hate in her face was terrible. For a moment I loved her with all my heart.

"Well," the man said. He rocked from one boot to the other. "Well . . ."

I reached for Shannon's hand. She slapped mine away. Her face was blazing. I felt as if a great fire was burning close to me, using up all the oxygen, making me pant to catch my breath. I laced the fingers of my hands together and tilted my head back to look up at the stars. If there was a God, then there would be justice. If there was justice, then Shannon and I would someday make them all burn. We walked away from the tent toward Mr. Pearl's battered DeSoto.

"Someday," Shannon whispered.

"Yeah," I whispered back. We knew exactly what we meant.

JULIA ALVAREZ
(1950–)

Although she was born in New York City, Julia Alvarez was taken to the Dominican Republic when she was three months old and did not return to the United States until she was ten, when her parents fled the Trujillo regime. Asked what made her a writer, she points to the watershed experience of coming to the United States: "Not understanding the language, I had to pay close attention to each word—great training for a writer. I also discovered the welcoming world of the imagination and books." Alvarez graduated summa cum laude from Middlebury College, was elected to Phi Beta Kappa, and returned to Middlebury almost twenty years later as a faculty member in the English department. In 1998 she became writer-in-residence there and still serves as adviser to Latino students. The year of her tenure at Middlebury, she published her first novel, *How the García Girls Lost Their Accents* (1991). Since then she has published *In the Time of the Butterflies* (1994); a book of essays entitled *Something to Declare* (1998); *In the Name of Salome* (2000); a children's book called *How Tía Lola Came to Stay* (2001); *A Cafecito Story* (2002), which received the Nebraska Book Award for Fiction; and *Before We Were Free* (2002). She has been the recipient of numerous awards for fiction and poetry. In 1999, her novel *How the García Girls Lost Their Accents* was picked by New York librarians as one of twenty-one classics for the twenty-first century. It was also selected as one of four texts for the national reading project "A Latino National Conversation," sponsored by the Great Books Foundation, 2001–2.

---

from *How the García Girls Lost Their Accents*

Trespass

CARLA

The day the Garcías were one American year old, they had a celebration at dinner. Mami had baked a nice flan and stuck a candle in the center. "Guess what day it is today?" She looked around the table at her daughters' baffled faces. "One year ago today," Papi began orating, "we came to the shores of this great country." When he was done misquoting the poem on the Statue of Liberty, the youngest, Fifi, asked if she could blow out the candle, and Mami said only after everyone had made a wish.

What do you wish for on the first celebration of the day you lost everything? Carla wondered. Everyone else around the table had their eyes closed as if they had no trouble deciding. Carla closed her eyes too. She should make an effort and not wish for

33

what she always wished for in her homesickness. But just this last time, she would let herself. "Dear God," she began. She could not get used to this American wish-making without bringing God into it. "Let us please go back home, please," she half prayed and half wished. It seemed a less and less likely prospect. In fact, her parents were sinking roots here. Only a month ago, they had moved out of the city to a neighborhood on Long Island so that the girls could have a yard to play in, so Mami said. The little green squares around each look-alike house seemed more like carpeting that had to be kept clean than yards to play in. The trees were no taller than little Fifi. Carla thought yearningly of the lush grasses and thick-limbed, vine-ladened trees around the compound back home. Under the *amapola* tree her best-friend cousin, Lucinda, and she had told each other what each knew about how babies were made. What is Lucinda doing right this moment? Carla wondered.

Down the block the neighborhood dead-ended in abandoned farmland that Mami read in the local paper the developers were negotiating to buy. Grasses and real trees and real bushes still grew beyond the barbed-wire fence posted with a big sign: PRIVATE, NO TRESPASSING. The sign had surprised Carla since "forgive us our trespasses" was the only other context in which she had heard the word. She pointed the sign out to Mami on one of their first walks to the bus stop. "Isn't that funny, Mami? A sign that you have to be good." Her mother did not understand at first until Carla explained about the Lord's Prayer. Mami laughed. Words sometimes meant two things in English too. This trespass meant that no one must go inside the property because it was not public like a park, but private. Carla nodded, disappointed. She would never get the hang of this new country.

Mami walked her to the bus stop for her first month at her new school over in the next parish. The first week, Mami even rode the buses with her, transferring, going and coming, twice a day, until Carla learned the way. Her sisters had all been enrolled at the neighborhood Catholic school only one block away from the house the Garcías had rented at the end of the summer. But by then, Carla's seventh grade was full. The nun who was the principal had suggested that Carla stay back a year in sixth grade, where they still had two spaces left. At twelve, though, Carla was at least a year older than most sixth graders, and she felt mortified at the thought of having to repeat yet another year. All four girls had been put back a year when they arrived in the country. Sure, Carla could use the practice with her English, but that also meant she would be in the same grade as her younger sister Sandi. That she could not bear. "Please," she pleaded with her mother, "let me go to the other school!" The public school was a mere two blocks beyond the Catholic school, but Laura García would not hear of it. Public schools, she had learned from other Catholic parents, were where juvenile delinquents went and where teachers taught those new crazy ideas about how we all came from monkeys. No child of hers was going to forget her family name and think she was nothing but a kissing cousin to an orangutan.

Carla soon knew her school route *by heart,* an expression she used for weeks after she learned it. First, she walked down the block by heart, noting the infinitesimal differences between the look-alike houses: different color drapes, an azalea bush on the left side of the door instead of on the right, a mailbox or door with a doodad of some kind. Then by heart, she walked the long mile by the deserted farmland lot with the funny sign. Finally, a sharp right down the service road into the main thoroughfare, where by heart she boarded the bus. "A young lady señorita," her mother pronounced the first morning Carla set out by herself, her heart drumming in her chest. It was a long and scary trek, but she was too grateful to have escaped the embarrassment of being put back a year to complain.

And as the months went by, she neglected to complain about an even scarier development. Every day on the playground and in the halls of her new school, a gang of boys chased after her, calling her names, some of which she had heard before from the old lady neighbor in the apartment they had rented in the city. Out of sight of the nuns, the boys pelted Carla with stones, aiming them at her feet so there would be no bruises. "Go back to where you came from, you dirty spic!" One of them, standing behind her in line, pulled her blouse out of her skirt where it was tucked in and lifted it high. "No titties," he snickered. Another yanked down her socks, displaying her legs, which had begun growing soft, dark hairs. "Monkey legs!" he yelled to his pals.

"Stop!" Carla cried. "Please stop."

"Eh-stop!" they mimicked her. "Plees eh-stop."

They were disclosing her secret shame: her body was changing. The girl she had been back home in Spanish was being shed. In her place—almost as if the boys' ugly words and taunts had the power of spells—was a hairy, breast-budding grown-up no one would ever love.

Every day, Carla set out on her long journey to school with a host of confused feelings. First of all, there was this body whose daily changes she noted behind the closed bathroom door until one of her sisters knocked that Carla's turn was over. How she wished she could wrap her body up the way she'd heard Chinese girls had their feet bound so they wouldn't grow big. She would stay herself, a quick, skinny girl with brown eyes and a braid down her back, a girl she had just begun to feel could get things in this world.

But then, too, Carla felt relieved to be setting out towards her very own school in her proper grade away from the crowding that was her family of four girls too close in age. She could come home with stories of what had happened that day and not have a chorus of three naysayers to correct her. But she also felt dread. There, in the playground, they would be waiting for her—the gang of four or five boys, blond, snotty-nosed, freckled-faced. They looked bland and unknowable, the way all Americans did. Their faces betrayed no sign of human warmth. Their eyes were too clear for cleaving, intimate looks. Their pale bodies did not seem real but were like costumes they were wearing as they played the part of her persecutors.

She watched them. In the classroom, they bent over workbooks or wore scared faces when Sister Beatrice, their beefy, no-nonsense teacher, scolded them for missing their homework. Sometimes Carla spied them in the playground, looking through the chain link fence and talking about the cars parked on the sidewalk. To Carla's bafflement, those cars had names beyond the names of their color or size. All she knew of their family car, for instance, was that it was a big black car where all four sisters could ride in the back, though Fifi always made a fuss and was allowed up front. Carla could also identify Volkswagens because that had been the car (in black) of the secret police back home; every time Mami saw one she made the sign of the cross and said a prayer for Tío Mundo, who had not been allowed to leave the Island. Beyond Volkswagens and medium blue cars or big black cars, Carla could not tell one car from the other.

But the boys at the fence talked excitedly about Fords and Falcons and Corvairs and Plymouth Valiants. They argued over how fast each car could go and what models were better than others. Carla sometimes imagined herself being driven to school in a flashy red car the boys would admire. Except there was no one *to* drive her. Her immigrant father with his thick mustache and accent and three-piece suit would only bring her more ridicule. Her mother did not yet know how to drive. Even though Carla could imagine owning a very expensive car, she could not imagine her parents as different from what they were. They were, like this new body she was growing into, givens.

One day when she had been attending Sacred Heart about a month, she was followed by a car on her mile walk home from the bus stop. It was a lime green car, sort of medium sized, and with a kind of long snout, so had it been a person, Carla would have described it as having a long nose. A long-nosed, lime green car. It drove slowly, trailing her. Carla figured the driver was looking for an address, just as Papi drove slowly and got honked at when he was reading the signs of shops before stopping at a particular one.

A blat from the horn made Carla jump and turn to the car, now fully stopped just a little ahead of her. She could see the driver clearly, from the shoulders up, a man in a red shirt about the age of her parents—though it was hard for Carla to tell with Americans how old they were. They were like cars to her, identifiable by the color of their clothes and a general age group—a little kid younger than herself, a kid her same age, a teenager in high school, and then the vast indistinguishable group of American grown-ups.

This grown-up American man about her parents' age beckoned for her to come up to the window. Carla dreaded being asked directions since she had just moved into this area right before school started, and all she knew for sure was the route home from the bus stop. Besides, her English was still just classroom English, a foreign language. She knew the neutral bland things: how to ask for a glass of water, how to say good morning and good afternoon and good night. How to thank someone and say they were welcomed. But if a grown-up American of indeterminable age asked her for directions, invariably speaking too quickly, she merely shrugged and smiled an inane smile. "I don't speak very much English," she would say in a small voice by way of apology. She hated having to admit this since such an admission proved, no doubt, the boy gang's point that she didn't belong here.

As Carla drew closer, the driver leaned over and rolled down the passenger door window. Carla bent down as if she were about to speak to a little kid and peeked in. The man smiled a friendly smile, but there was something wrong with it that Carla couldn't put her finger on: this smile had a bruised, sorry quality as if the man were someone who'd been picked on all his life, and so his smiles were appeasing, not friendly. He was wearing his red shirt unbuttoned, which seemed normal given the warm Indian-summer day. In fact, if Carla's legs hadn't begun to grow hairs, she would have taken off her school green knee socks and walked home bare-legged.

The man spoke up. "Whereyagoin?" he asked, running all his words together the way the Americans always did. Carla was, as usual, not quite sure if she had heard right.

"Excuse me?" she asked politely, leaning into the car to hear the man's whispery voice better. Something caught her eye. She looked down and stared, aghast.

The man had tied his two shirtends just above his waist and was naked from there on down. String encircled his waist, the loose ends knotted in front and then looped around his penis. As Carla watched, his big blunt-headed thing grew so that it filled and strained at the lasso it was caught in.

"Where ya' going?" His voice had slowed down when he spoke this time, so that Carla definitely understood him. Her eyes snapped back up to his eyes.

"Excuse me?" she said again dumbly.

He leaned towards the passenger door and clicked it open. "C'moninere." He nodded towards the seat beside him. "C'm'on," he moaned. He cupped his hand over his thing as if it were a flame that might blow out.

Carla clutched her bookbag tighter in her hand. Her mouth hung open. Not one word, English or Spanish, occurred to her. She backed away from the big green car, all the while keeping her eyes on the man. A pained, urgent expression was deepening on his face like a plea that Carla did not know how to answer. His arm pumped at something Carla could not see, and then after much agitation, he was still. The face relaxed into something like peacefulness. The man bowed his head as if in prayer. Carla turned and fled down the street, her bookbag banging against her leg like a whip she was using to make herself go faster, faster.

Her mother called the police after piecing together the breathless, frantic story Carla told. The enormity of what she had seen was now topped by the further enormity of involving the police. Carla and her sisters feared the American police almost as much as the SIM back home. Their father, too, seemed uneasy around policemen; whenever a cop car was behind them in traffic, he kept looking at the rearview mirror and insisting on silence in the car so he could think. If officers stood on the sidewalk as he walked by, he bowed ingratiatingly at them. Back home, he had been tailed by the secret police for months and the family had only narrowly escaped capture their last day on the Island. Of course, Carla knew American policemen were "nice guys," but still she felt uneasy around them.

The doorbell rang only minutes after Carla's mother had called the station. This was a law-abiding family neighborhood, and no one wanted a creep like this on the loose among so many children, least of all the police. As her mother answered the door, Carla stayed behind in the kitchen, listening with a racing heart to her mother's explanation. Mami's voice was high and hesitant and slightly apologetic—a small, accented woman's voice among the booming, impersonal American male voices that interrogated her.

"My daughter, she was walking home—"

"Where exactly!" a male voice demanded.

"That street, you know?" Carla's mother must have pointed. "The one that comes up the avenue, I don't know the name of it."

"Must be the service road," a nicer male voice offered.

"Yes, yes, the service road." Her mother's jubilant voice seemed to conclude whatever had been the problem.

"Please go on, ma'am."

"Well, my daughter, she said this, this crazy man in this car—" Her voice lowered. Carla heard snatches: something, something "to come in the car—"

"Where's your daughter, ma'am?" the male voice with authority asked.

Carla cringed behind the kitchen door. Her mother had promised that she would not involve Carla with the police but would do all the talking herself.

"She is just a young girl," her mother excused Carla.

"Well, ma'am, if you want to file charges, we have to talk to her."

"File charges? What does that mean, file charges?"

There was a sigh of exasperation. A too-patient voice with dividers between each word explained the legal procedures as if repeating a history lesson Carla's mother should have learned long before she had troubled the police or moved into this neighborhood.

"I don't want any trouble," her mother protested. "I just think this is a crazy man who should not be allowed on the streets."

"You're absolutely right, ma'am, but our hands are tied unless you, as a responsible citizen, help us out."

Oh no, Carla groaned, now she was in for it. The magic words had been uttered. The Garcías were only legal residents, not citizens, but for the police to mistake Mami for a citizen was a compliment too great to spare a child discomfort. "Carla!" her mother called from the door.

"What's the girl's name?" the officer with the voice in charge asked.

Her mother repeated Carla's full name and spelled it for the officer, then called out again in her voice of authority, "Carla Antonia!"

Slowly, sullenly, Carla wrapped herself around the kitchen door, only her head poking out and into the hallway. "*¿Sí, Mami?*" she answered in a polite, law-abiding voice to impress the cops.

"Come here," her mother said, motioning. "These very nice officers need for you to explain what you saw." There was an apologetic look on her face. "Come on, Cuca, don't be afraid."

"There's nothing to be afraid of," the policeman said in his gruff, scary voice.

Carla kept her head down as she approached the front door, glancing up briefly when the two officers introduced themselves. One was an embarrassingly young man with a face no older than the boys' faces at school on top of a large, muscular man's body. The other man, also big and fair-skinned, looked older because of his meaner, sharp-featured face like an animal's in a beast fable a child knows by looking at the picture not to trust. Belts were slung around both their hips, guns poking out of the holsters. Their very masculinity offended and threatened. They were so big, so strong, so male, so American.

After a few facts about her had been established, the mean-faced cop with the big voice and the pad asked her if she would answer a few questions. Not knowing she could refuse, Carla nodded meekly, on the verge of tears.

"Could you describe the vehicle the suspect was driving?"

She wasn't sure what a vehicle was or a suspect, for that matter. Her mother translated into simpler English, "What car was the man driving, Carla?"

"A big green car," Carla mumbled.

As if she hadn't answered in English, her mother repeated for the officers, "A big green car."

"What make?" the officer wanted to know.

"Make?" Carla asked.

"You know, Ford, Chrysler, Plymouth." The man ended his catalogue with a sigh. Carla and her mother were wasting his time.

"*¿Qué clase de carro?*" her mother asked in Spanish, but of course she knew Carla wouldn't know the make of a car. Carla shook her head, and her mother explained to the officer, helping her save face, "She doesn't remember."

"Can't she talk?" the gruff cop snapped. The boyish-looking one now asked Carla a question. "Carla," he began, pronouncing her name so that Carla felt herself coated all over with something warm and too sweet. "Carla," he coaxed, "can you please describe the man you saw?"

All memory of the man's face fled. She remembered only the bruised smile and a few strands of dirty blond hair laid carefully over a bald pate. But she could not remember the word for bald and so she said, "He had almost nothing on his head."

"You mean no hat?" the gentle cop suggested.

"Almost no hair," Carla explained, looking up as if she had taken a guess and wanted to know if she was wrong or right.

"Bald?" The gruff cop pointed first to a hairy stretch of wrist beyond his uniform's cuff, then to his pink, hairless palm.

"Bald, yes." Carla nodded. The sight of the man's few dark hairs had disgusted her. She thought of her own legs sprouting dark hairs, of the changes going on in secret in her body, turning her into one of these grown-up persons. No wonder the high-voiced boys with smooth, hairless cheeks hated her. They could see that her body was already betraying her.

The interrogation proceeded through a description of the man's appearance, and then the dreaded question came.

"What did you see?" the boy-faced cop asked.

Carla looked down at the cops' feet. The black tips of their shoes poked out from under their cuffs like the snouts of wily animals. "The man was naked all down here." She gestured with her hand. "And he had a string around his waist."

"A string?" The man's voice was like a hand trying to lift her chin to make her look up, which is precisely what her mother did when the man repeated, "A string?"

Carla was forced to confront the cop's face. It was indeed an adult version of the sickly white faces of the boys in the playground. This is what they would look like once they grew up. There was no meanness in this face, no kindness either. No recognition of the difficulty she was having in trying to describe what she had seen with her tiny English vocabulary. It was the face of someone in a movie Carla was watching asking her, "What was he doing with the string?"

She shrugged, tears peeping at the corners of her eyes.

Her mother intervened. "The string was holding up this man's—"

"Please, ma'am," the cop who was writing said. "Let your daughter describe what she saw."

Carla thought hard for what could be the name of a man's genitals. They had come to this country before she had reached puberty in Spanish, so a lot of the key words she would have been picking up in the last year, she had missed. Now, she was learning English in a Catholic classroom, where no nun had ever mentioned the words she was needing. "He had a string around his waist," Carla explained. By the ease with which the man was writing, she could tell she was now making perfect sense.

"And it came up to the front"—she showed on herself—"and here it was tied in a—" She held up her fingers and made the sign for zero.

"A noose?" the gentle cop offered.

"A noose, and his thing—" Carla pointed to the policeman's crotch. The cop writing scowled. "His thing was inside that noose and it got bigger and bigger," she blurted, her voice wobbling.

The friendly cop lifted his eyebrows and pushed his cap back on his head. His big hand wiped the small beads of sweat that had accumulated on his brow.

Carla prayed without prayer that this interview would stop now. What she had begun fearing was that her picture—but who was there to take a picture?—would appear in the paper the next day and the gang of mean boys would torment her with what she had seen. She wondered if she could report them now to these young officers. "By the way," she could say, and the gruff one would begin to take notes. She would have the words to describe them: their mean, snickering faces she knew by heart. Their pale look-alike sickly bodies. Their high voices squealing with delight when Carla mispronounced some word they coaxed her to repeat.

But soon after her description of the incident, the interview ended. The cop snapped his pad closed, and each officer gave Carla and her mother a salute of farewell. They drove off in their squad car, and all down the block, drapes fell back to rest, half-opened shades closed like eyes that saw no evil.

For the next two months before Carla's mother moved her to the public school close to home for the second half of her seventh grade, she took Carla on the bus to school and was there at the end of the day to pick her up. The tauntings and chasings stopped. The boys must have thought Carla had complained, and so her mother was along to defend her. Even during class times, when her mother was not around, they now ignored her, their sharp, clear eyes roaming the classroom for another victim, someone too fat, too ugly, too poor, too different. Carla had faded into the walls.

But their faces did not fade as fast from Carla's life. They trespassed in her dreams and in her waking moments. Sometimes when she woke in the dark, they were perched at the foot of her bed, a grim chorus of urchin faces, boys without bodies, chanting without words, "Go back! Go back!"

So as not to see them, Carla would close her eyes and wish them gone. In that dark she created by keeping her eyes shut, she would pray, beginning with the names of her own sisters, for all those she wanted God to especially care for, here and back home. The seemingly endless list of familiar names would coax her back to sleep with a feeling of safety, of a world still peopled by those who loved her.

TONI CADE BAMBARA

(1939–95)

Raised in New York's Harlem and Bedford-Stuyvesant neighborhoods, Toni Cade added "Bambara," a maternal family name, as a tribute to the elders of the Bambara people of the Sudan after she had begun to publish her fiction. She received a B.A. from Queens College in 1959 and an M.A. from City College of the City University of New York in 1963. A social worker for the New York State Department of Welfare, she described herself as "a community organizer, educator, parent, writer, and apprentice filmmaker." She taught at Rutgers University, City College, Duke University, and Atlanta University, as well as becoming a writer-in-residence at Spelman College in Atlanta, Georgia. Her stories often reflected her disgust with the unrealistic and stereotypical portraits of black women in fiction. Her dedication for the anthology *The Black Woman* (1970) expresses her belief in the need for change: "To the uptown mammas who nudged me to just set it down in print so it gets to be a habit to write letters to each other, so maybe that way we don't keep treadmilling the same ole ground." In addition to editing another anthology, *Tales and Stories for Black Folks* (1971), and writing numerous critical articles, Bambara published three collections of short stories: *Gorilla, My Love* (1972), *The Seabirds Are Still Alive* (1977), and *Collected Stories* (1977). In 1980, she published the novel *The Salt Eaters*.

Raymond's Run

I don't have much work to do around the house like some girls. My mother does that. And I don't have to earn my pocket money by hustling; George runs errands for the big boys and sells Christmas cards. And anything else that's got to get done, my father does. All I have to do in life is mind my brother Raymond, which is enough.

Sometimes I slip and say my little brother Raymond. But as any fool can see he's much bigger and he's older too. But a lot of people call him my little brother cause he needs looking after cause he's not quite right. And a lot of smart mouths got lots to say about that too, especially when George was minding him. But now, if anybody has anything to say to Raymond, anything to say about his big head, they have to come by me. And I don't play the dozens or believe in standing around with somebody in my face doing a lot of talking. I much rather just knock you down and take my chances even if I am a little girl with skinny arms and a squeaky voice, which is how I got the name Squeaky. And if things get too rough, I run. And as anybody can tell you, I'm the fastest thing on two feet.

There is no track meet that I don't win the first place medal. I used to win the twenty-yard dash when I was a little kid in kindergarten. Nowadays, it's the fifty-yard dash. And tomorrow I'm subject to run the quarter-meter relay all by myself and come in first, second, and third. The big kids call me Mercury cause I'm the swiftest thing in the neighborhood. Everybody knows that—except two people who know better, my father and me. He can beat me to Amsterdam Avenue with me having a two fire-hydrant headstart and him running with his hands in his pockets and whistling. But that's private information. Cause you can imagine some thirty-five-year-old man stuffing himself into PAL shorts to race little kids? So as far as everyone's concerned, I'm the fastest and that goes for Gretchen, too, who has put out the tale that she is going to win the first-place medal this year. Ridiculous. In the second place, she's got short legs. In the third place, she's got freckles. In the first place, no one can beat me and that's all there is to it.

I'm standing on the corner admiring the weather and about to take a stroll down Broadway so I can practice my breathing exercises, and I've got Raymond walking on the inside close to the buildings, cause he's subject to fits of fantasy and starts thinking he's a circus performer and that the curb is a tightrope strung high in the air. And sometimes after a rain he likes to step down off his tightrope right into the gutter and slosh around getting his shoes and cuffs wet. Then I get hit when I get home. Or sometimes if you don't watch him he'll dash across traffic to the island in the middle of Broadway and give the pigeons a fit. Then I have to go behind him apologizing to all the old people sitting around trying to get some sun and getting all upset with the pigeons fluttering around them, scattering their newspapers and upsetting the waxpaper lunches in their laps. So I keep Raymond on the inside of me, and he plays like he's driving a stage coach which is O.K. by me so long as he doesn't run me over or interrupt my breathing exercises, which I have to do on account of I'm serious about my running, and I don't care who knows it.

Now some people like to act like things come easy to them, won't let on that they practice. Not me. I'll high-prance down 34th Street like a rodeo pony to keep my knees strong even if it does get my mother uptight so that she walks ahead like she's not with me, don't know me, is all by herself on a shopping trip, and I am somebody else's crazy child. Now you take Cynthia Procter for instance. She's just the opposite. If there's a test tomorrow, she'll say something like, "Oh, I guess I'll play handball this afternoon and watch television tonight," just to let you know she ain't thinking about the test. Or like last week when she won the spelling bee for the millionth time, "A good thing you got 'receive,' Squeaky, cause I would have got it wrong. I completely forgot about the spelling bee." And she'll clutch the lace on her blouse like it was a narrow escape. Oh, brother. But of course when I pass her house on my early morning trots around the block, she is practicing the scales on the piano over and over and over and over. Then in music class she always lets herself get bumped around so she falls accidentally on purpose onto the piano stool and is so surprised to find herself sitting there that she decides just for fun to try out the ole keys. And what do you know— Chopin's waltzes just spring out of her fingertips and she's the most surprised thing in the world. A regular prodigy. I could kill people like that. I stay up all night studying the words for the spelling bee. And you can see me any time of day practicing running.

I never walk if I can trot, and shame on Raymond if he can't keep up. But of course he does, cause if he hangs back someone's liable to walk up to him and get smart, or take his allowance from him, or ask him where he got that great big pumpkin head. People are so stupid sometimes.

So I'm strolling down Broadway breathing out and breathing in on counts of seven, which is my lucky number, and here comes Gretchen and her sidekicks: Mary Louise, who used to be a friend of mine when she first moved to Harlem from Baltimore and got beat up by everybody till I took up for her on account of her mother and my mother used to sing in the same choir when they were young girls, but people ain't grateful, so now she hangs out with the new girl Gretchen and talks about me like a dog; and Rosie, who is as fat as I am skinny and has a big mouth where Raymond is concerned and is too stupid to know that there is not a big deal of difference between herself and Raymond and that she can't afford to throw stones. So they are steady coming up Broadway and I see right away that it's going to be one of those Dodge City scenes cause the street ain't that big and they're close to the buildings just as we are. First I think I'll step into the candy store and look over the new comics and let them pass. But that's chicken and I've got a reputation to consider. So then I think I'll just walk straight on through them or even over them if necessary. But as they get to me, they slow down. I'm ready to fight, cause like I said I don't feature a whole lot of chit-chat, I much prefer to just knock you down right from the jump and save everybody a lotta precious time.

"You signing up for the May Day races?" smiles Mary Louise, only it's not a smile at all. A dumb question like that doesn't deserve an answer. Besides, there's just me and Gretchen standing there really, so no use wasting my breath talking to shadows.

"I don't think you're going to win this time," says Rosie, trying to signify with her hands on her hips all salty, completely forgetting that I have whupped her behind many times for less salt than that.

"I always win cause I'm the best," I say straight at Gretchen who is, as far as I'm concerned, the only one talking in this ventriloquist-dummy routine. Gretchen smiles, but it's not a smile, and I'm thinking that girls never really smile at each other because they don't know how and don't want to know how and there's probably no one to teach us how, cause grown-up girls don't know either. Then they all look at Raymond who has just brought his mule team to a standstill. And they're about to see what trouble they can get into through him.

"What grade you in now, Raymond?"

"You got anything to say to my brother, you say it to me, Mary Louise Williams of Raggedy Town, Baltimore."

"What are you, his mother?" sasses Rosie.

"That's right, Fatso. And the next word out of anybody and I'll be *their* mother too." So they just stand there and Gretchen shifts from one leg to the other and so do they. Then Gretchen puts her hands on her hips and is about to say something with her freckle-face self but doesn't. Then she walks around me looking me up and down but keeps walking up Broadway, and her sidekicks follow her. So me and Raymond smile at each other and he says, "Gidyap" to his team and I continue with my breathing exercises, strolling down Broadway toward the ice man on 145th with not a care in the world cause I am Miss Quicksilver herself.

I take my time getting to the park on May Day because the track meet is the last thing on the program. The biggest thing on the program is the May Pole dancing, which I can do without, thank you, even if my mother thinks it's a shame I don't take part and act like a girl for a change. You'd think my mother'd be grateful not to have to make me a white organdy dress with a big satin sash and buy me new white baby-doll shoes that can't be taken out of the box till the big day. You'd think she'd be glad her daughter ain't out there prancing around a May Pole getting the new clothes all dirty and sweaty and trying to act like a fairy or a flower or whatever you're supposed to be when you should be trying to be yourself, whatever that is, which is, as far as I am concerned, a poor Black girl who really can't afford to buy shoes and a new dress you only wear once a lifetime cause it won't fit next year.

I was once a strawberry in a Hansel and Gretel pageant when I was in nursery school and didn't have no better sense than to dance on tiptoe with my arms in a circle over my head doing umbrella steps and being a perfect fool just so my mother and father could come dressed up and clap. You'd think they'd know better than to encourage that kind of nonsense. I am not a strawberry. I do not dance on my toes. I run. That is what I am all about. So I always come late to the May Day program, just in time to get my number pinned on and lay in the grass till they announce the fifty-yard dash.

I put Raymond in the little swings, which is a tight squeeze this year and will be impossible next year. Then I look around for Mr. Pearson, who pins the numbers on. I'm really looking for Gretchen if you want to know the truth, but she's not around. The park is jam-packed. Parents in hats and corsages and breast-pocket handkerchiefs peeking up. Kids in white dresses and light blue suits. The parkees unfolding chairs and chasing the rowdy kids from Lenox as if they had no right to be there. The big guys with their caps on backwards, leaning against the fence swirling the basketballs on the tips of their fingers, waiting for all these crazy people to clear out the park so they can play. Most of the kids in my class are carrying bass drums and glockenspiels and flutes. You'd think they'd put in a few bongos or something for real like that.

Then here comes Mr. Pearson with his clipboard and his cards and pencils and whistles and safety pins and fifty million other things he's always dropping all over the place with his clumsy self. He sticks out in a crowd because he's on stilts. We used to call him Jack and the Beanstalk to get him mad. But I'm the only one that can outrun him and get away, and I'm too grown for that silliness now.

"Well, Squeaky," he says, checking my name off the list and handing me number seven and two pins. And I'm thinking he's got no right to call me Squeaky, if I can't call him Beanstalk.

"Hazel Elizabeth Deborah Parker," I correct him and tell him to write it down on his board.

"Well, Hazel Elizabeth Deborah Parker, going to give someone else a break this year?" I squint at him real hard to see if he is seriously thinking I should lose the race on purpose just to give someone else a break. "Only six girls running this time," he continues, shaking his head sadly like it's my fault all of New York didn't turn out in sneakers. "That new girl should give you a run for your money." He looks around the park for Gretchen like a periscope in a submarine movie. "Wouldn't it be a nice gesture if you were . . . to ahhh . . ."

I give him such a look he couldn't finish putting that idea into words. Grown-ups got a lot of nerve sometimes. I pin number seven to myself and stomp away, I'm so burnt. And I go straight for the track and stretch out on the grass while the band winds up with "Oh, the Monkey Wrapped His Tail Around the Flag Pole," which my teacher calls by some other name. The man on the loudspeaker is calling everyone over to the track and I'm on my back looking at the sky, trying to pretend I'm in the country, but I can't, because even grass in the city feels hard as sidewalk, and there's just no pretending you are anywhere but in a "concrete jungle" as my grandfather says.

The twenty-yard dash takes all of two minutes cause most of the little kids don't know no better than to run off the track or run the wrong way or run smack into the fence and fall down and cry. One little kid, though, has got the good sense to run straight for the white ribbon up ahead so he wins. Then the second-graders line up for the thirty-yard dash and I don't even bother to turn my head to watch cause Raphael Perez always wins. He wins before he even begins by psyching the runners, telling them they're going to trip on their shoelaces and fall on their faces or lose their shorts or something, which he doesn't really have to do since he is very fast, almost as fast as I am. After that is the forty-yard dash which I used to run when I was in first grade. Raymond is hollering from the swings cause he knows I'm about to do my thing cause the man on the loudspeaker has just announced the fifty-yard dash, although he might just as well be giving a recipe for angel food cake cause you can hardly make out what he's sayin for the static. I get up and slip off my sweat pants and then I see Gretchen standing at the starting line, kicking her legs out like a pro. Then as I get into place I see that ole Raymond is on line on the other side of the fence, bending down with his fingers on the ground just like he knew what he was doing. I was going to yell at him but then I didn't. It burns up your energy to holler.

Every time, just before I take off in a race, I always feel like I'm in a dream, the kind of dream you have when you're sick with fever and feel all hot and weightless. I dream I'm flying over a sandy beach in the early morning sun, kissing the leaves of the trees as I fly by. And there's always the smell of apples, just like in the country when I was little and used to think I was a choo-choo train, running through the fields of corn and chugging up the hill to the orchard. And all the time I'm dreaming this, I get lighter and lighter until I'm flying over the beach again, getting blown through the sky like a feather that weighs nothing at all. But once I spread my fingers in the dirt and crouch over the Get on Your Mark, the dream goes and I am solid again and am telling myself, Squeaky you must win, you must win, you are the fastest thing in the world, you can even beat your father up Amsterdam if you really try. And then I feel my weight coming back just behind my knees then down to my feet then into the earth and the pistol shot explodes in my blood and I am off and weightless again, flying past the other runners, my arms pumping up and down and the whole world is quiet except for the crunch as I zoom over the gravel in the track. I glance to my left and there is no one. To the right, a blurred Gretchen, who's got her chin jutting out as if it would win the race all by itself. And on the other side of the fence is Raymond with his arms down to his side and the palms tucked up behind him, running in his very own style, and it's the first time I ever saw that and I almost stop to watch my brother Raymond on his first run. But the white ribbon is bouncing toward me and I tear past it, racing into the distance till my feet with a mind of their own start digging up footfuls of dirt and brake me short. Then all the kids standing on the side pile on me, banging me on the back and slapping my head with their May Day programs, for I have won again and everybody on 151st Street can walk tall for another year.

"In first place . . ." the man on the loudspeaker is clear as a bell now. But then he pauses and the loudspeaker starts to whine. Then static. And I lean down to catch my breath and here comes Gretchen walking back, for she's overshot the finish line too, huffing and puffing with her hands on her hips taking it slow, breathing in steady time like a real pro and I sort of like her a little for the first time. "In first place . . ." and then three or four voices get all mixed up on the loudspeaker and I dig my sneaker into the grass and stare at Gretchen who's staring back, we both wondering just who did win. I can hear old Beanstalk arguing with the man on the loudspeaker and then a few others running their mouths about what the stopwatches say. Then I hear Raymond yanking at the fence to call me and I wave to shush him, but he keeps rattling the fence like a gorilla in a cage like in them gorilla movies, but then like a dancer or something he starts climbing up nice and easy but very fast. And it occurs to me, watching how smoothly he climbs hand over hand and remembering how he looked running with his arms down to his side and with the wind pulling his mouth back and his teeth showing and all, it occurred to me that Raymond would make a very fine runner. Doesn't he always keep up with me on my trots? And he surely knows how to breathe in counts of seven cause he's always doing it at the dinner table, which drives my brother George up the wall. And I'm smiling to beat the band cause if I've lost this race, or if me and Gretchen tied, or even if I've won, I can always retire as a runner and begin a whole new career as a coach with Raymond as my champion. After all, with a little more study I can beat Cynthia and her phony self at the spelling bee. And if I bugged my mother, I could get piano lessons and become a star. And I have a big rep as the baddest thing around. And I've got a roomful of ribbons and medals and awards. But what has Raymond got to call his own?

So I stand there with my new plans, laughing out loud by this time as Raymond jumps down from the fence and runs over with his teeth showing and his arms down to the side, which no one before him has quite mastered as a running style. And by the time he comes over I'm jumping up and down so glad to see him—my brother Raymond, a great runner in the family tradition. But of course everyone thinks I'm jumping up and down because the men on the loudspeaker have finally gotten themselves together and compared notes and are announcing "In first place—Miss Hazel Elizabeth

Deborah Parker." (Dig that.) "In second place—Miss Gretchen P. Lewis." And I look over at Gretchen wondering what the "P" stands for. And I smile. Cause she's good, no doubt about it. Maybe she'd like to help me coach Raymond; she obviously is serious about running, as any fool can see. And she nods to congratulate me and then she smiles. And I smile. We stand there with this big smile of respect between us. It's about as real a smile as girls can do for each other, considering we don't practice real smiling every day, you know, cause maybe we too busy being flowers or fairies or strawberries instead of something honest and worthy of respect . . . you know . . . like being people.

T. CORAGHESSAN BOYLE
(1948-)

Born and raised in Peekskill, New York, Thomas Coraghessan Boyle earned a B.A. at the State University of New York at Potsdam, an M.F.A. at the University of Iowa Writers' Workshop, and a Ph.D. in nineteenth-century English literature at the University of Iowa. At the age of seventeen, he changed his name from Thomas John, replacing John with a maternal family name that is pronounced *Cor-RAG-ah-sen*. A professor of creative writing at the University of Southern California, he lives in a Frank Lloyd Wright house outside Santa Barbara. An enthusiastic performer of his own fiction, Boyle has given numerous readings throughout the country and has appeared on television programs such as *Today, Late Night with David Letterman,* and *The Charlie Rose Show.* He is the author of nine novels: *Water Music* (1982); *Budding Prospects* (1984); *World's End* (1987), which won the 1988 PEN/Faulkner Award for Best American Fiction; *East Is East* (1990); *The Road to Wellville* (1993), which was made into a film starring Anthony Hopkins and Bridget Fonda; *The Tortilla Curtain* (1995); *Riven Rock* (1998); *A Friend of the Earth* (2000); and *Drop City* (2003). His stories are collected in *Descent of Man* (1979), which received the 1980 St. Lawrence Award for short fiction; *Greasy Lake* (1985); *If the River Was Whiskey* (1989); *Without a Hero* (1994); and *T. C. Boyle Stories* (1998), a collection of sixty-eight tales that won the 1999 PEN/Malamud Award for Excellence in Short Fiction and was a *New York Times* Notable Book.

Rara Avis

It looked like a woman or a girl perched there on the roof of the furniture store, wings folded like a shawl, long legs naked and exposed beneath a skirt of jagged feathers the color of sepia. The sun was pale, poised at equinox. There was the slightest breeze. We stood there, thirty or forty of us, gaping up at the big motionless bird as if we expected it to talk, as if it weren't a bird at all but a plastic replica with a speaker concealed in its mouth. Sidor's Furniture, it would squawk, loveseats and three-piece sectionals.

I was twelve. I'd been banging a handball against the side of the store when a man in a Studebaker suddenly swerved into the parking lot, slammed on his brakes, and slid out of the driver's seat as if mesmerized. His head was tilted back, and he was shading his eyes, squinting to focus on something at the level of the roof. This was odd. Sidor's roof—a flat glaring expanse of crushed stone and tar relieved only by the neon characters that irradiated the proprietor's name—was no architectural wonder. What could be so captivating? I pocketed the handball and ambled round to the front of the store. Then I looked up.

There it was: stark and anomalous, a relic of a time before shopping centers, tract houses, gas stations, and landfill, a thing of swamps and tidal flats, of ooze, fetid water, and rich black festering muck. In the context of the minutely ordered universe of suburbia, it was startling, as unexpected as a downed meteor or the carcass of a woolly mammoth. I shouted out, whooped with surprise and sudden joy.

Already people were gathering. Mrs. Novak, all three hundred pounds of her, was lumbering across the lot from her house on the corner, a look of bewilderment creasing her heavy jowls. Robbie Matechik wheeled up on his bike, a pair of girls emerged from the rear of the store with jump ropes, an old man in baggy trousers struggled with a bag of groceries. Two more cars pulled in, and a third stopped out on the highway. Hopper, Moe, Jennings, Davidson, Sebesta: the news echoed through the neighborhood as if relayed by tribal drums, and people dropped rakes, edgers, pruning shears, and came running. Michael Donadio, sixteen years old and a heartthrob at the local high school, was pumping gas at the station up the block. He left the nozzle in the customer's tank, jumped the fence, and started across the blacktop, weaving under his pompadour. The customer followed him.

At its height, there must have been fifty people gathered there in front of Sidor's, shading their eyes and gazing up expectantly, as if the bird were the opening act of a musical comedy or an ingenious new type of vending machine. The mood was jocular, festive even. Sidor appeared at the door of his shop with two stockboys, gazed up at the bird for a minute, and then clapped his hands twice, as if he were shooing pigeons. The bird remained motionless, cast in wax. Sidor, a fleshless old man with a monk's tonsure and liver-spotted hands, shrugged his shoulders and mugged for the crowd. We all laughed. Then he ducked into the store and emerged with an end table, a lamp, a footstool, motioned to the stockboys, and had them haul out a sofa and an armchair. Finally he scrawled BIRD WATCHER'S SPECIAL on a strip of cardboard and taped it to the window. People laughed and shook their heads. "Hey, Sidor," Albert Moe's father shouted, "where'd you get that thing—the Bronx Zoo?"

I couldn't keep still. I danced round the fringe of the crowd, tugging at sleeves and skirts, shouting out that I'd seen the bird first—which wasn't strictly true, but I felt proprietary about this strange and wonderful creature, the cynosure of an otherwise pedestrian Saturday afternoon. Had I seen it in the air? people asked. Had it moved? I was tempted to lie, to tell them I'd spotted it over the school, the firehouse, the used-car lot, a hovering shadow, wings spread wider than the hood of a Cadillac, but I couldn't. "No," I said, quiet suddenly. I glanced up and saw my father in the back of the crowd, standing close to Mrs. Schlecta and whispering something in her ear. Her lips were wet. I didn't know where my mother was. At the far end of the lot a girl in a college sweater was leaning against the fender of a convertible while her boyfriend pressed himself against her as if he wanted to dance.

Six weeks earlier, at night, the community had come together as it came together now, but there had been no sense of magic or festivity about the occasion. The Novaks, Donadios, Schlectas, and the rest—they gathered to watch an abandoned house go up in flames. I didn't dance round the crowd that night. I stood beside my father, leaned against him, the acrid, unforgiving stink of the smoke almost drowned in the elemental odor of his sweat, the odor of armpit and crotch and secret hair, the sematic animal scent of him that had always repelled me—until that moment. Janine McCarty's mother was shrieking. Ragged and torn, her voice clawed at the starless night, the leaping flames. On the front lawn, just as they backed the ambulance in and the crowd parted, I caught a glimpse of Janine, lying there in the grass. Every face was shouting. The glare of the fire tore disordered lines across people's eyes and dug furrows in their cheeks.

There was a noise to that fire, a killing noise, steady and implacable. The flames were like the waves at Coney Island—ghost waves, insubstantial, yellow and red rather than green, but waves all the same. They rolled across the foundation, spat from the windows, beat at the roof. Wayne Sanders was white-faced. He was a tough guy, two years older than I but held back in school because of mental sloth and recalcitrance. Police and firemen and wild-eyed neighborhood men nosed round him, excited, like hounds. Even then, in the grip of confusion and clashing voices, safe at my father's side, I knew what they wanted to know. It was the same thing my father demanded of me whenever he caught me—in fact or by report—emerging from the deserted, vandalized, and crumbling house: What were you doing in there?

He couldn't know.

Spires, parapets, derelict staircases, closets that opened on closets, the place was magnetic, vestige of an age before the neat rows of ranches and Cape Cods that lined both sides of the block. Plaster pulled back from the ceilings to reveal slats like ribs, glass pebbled the floors, the walls were paisleyed with aerosol obscenities. There were bats in the basement, rats and mice in the hallways. The house breathed death and freedom. I went there whenever I could. I heaved my interdicted knife end-over-end at the lintels and peeling cupboards, I lit cigarettes and hung them from my lower lip, I studied scraps of pornographic magazines with a fever beating through my body. Two days before the fire I was there with Wayne Sanders and Janine. They were holding hands. He had a switchblade, stiff and cold as an icicle. He gave me Ex-Lax and told me it was chocolate. Janine giggled. He shuffled a deck of battered playing cards and showed me one at a time the murky photos imprinted on them. My throat went dry with guilt.

After the fire I went to church. In the confessional the priest asked me if I practiced self-pollution. The words were formal, unfamiliar, but I knew what he meant. So, I thought, kneeling there in the dark, crushed with shame, there's a name for it. I looked at the shadowy grill, looked toward the source of the soothing voice of absolution, the voice of forgiveness and hope, and I lied. "No," I whispered.

And then there was the bird.

It never moved, not once, through all the commotion at its feet, through all the noise and confusion, all the speculation regarding its needs, condition, origin, species: it never moved. It was a statue, eyes unblinking, only the wind-rustled feathers giving it away for flesh and blood, for living bird. "It's a crane," somebody said. "No, no, it's a herring—a blue herring." Someone else thought it was an eagle. My father later confided that he believed it was a stork.

"Is it sick, do you think?" Mrs. Novak said.

"Maybe it's broke its wing."

"It's a female," someone insisted. "She's getting ready to lay her eggs."

I looked around and was surprised to see that the crowd had thinned considerably. The girl in the college sweater was gone, Michael Donadio was back across the street pumping gas, the man in the Studebaker had driven off. I scanned the crowd for my father: he'd gone home, I guessed. Mrs. Schlecta had disappeared too, and I could see the great bulk of Mrs. Novak receding into her house on the corner like a sea lion vanishing into a swell. After a while Sidor took his lamp and end table back into the store.

One of the older guys had a rake. He heaved it straight up like a javelin, as high as the roof of the store, and then watched it slam down on the pavement. The bird never flinched. People lit cigarettes, shuffled their feet. They began to drift off, one by one. When I looked around again there were only eight of us left, six kids and two men I didn't recognize. The women and girls, more easily bored or perhaps less interested to begin with, had gone home to gas ranges and hopscotch squares: I could see a few of the girls in the distance, on the swings in front of the school, tiny, their skirts rippling like flags.

I waited. I wanted the bird to flap its wings, blink an eye, shift a foot; I wanted it desperately, wanted it more than anything I had ever wanted. Perched there at the lip of the roof, its feet clutching the drainpipe as if welded to it, the bird was a coil of possibility, a muscle relaxed against the moment of tension. Yes, it was magnificent, even in repose. And, yes, I could stare at it, examine its every line, from its knobbed knees to the cropped feathers at the back of its head, I could absorb it, become it, look out from its unblinking yellow eyes on the street grown quiet and the sun sinking behind the gas station. Yes, but that wasn't enough. I had to see it in flight, had to see the great impossible wings beating in the air, had to see it transposed into its native element.

Suddenly the wind came up—a gust that raked at our hair and scattered refuse across the parking lot—and the bird's feathers lifted like a petticoat. It was then that I understood. Secret, raw, red, and wet, the wound flashed just above the juncture of the legs before the wind died and the feathers fell back in place.

I turned and looked past the neighborhood kids—my playmates—at the two men, the strangers. They were lean and seedy, unshaven, slouching behind the brims of their hats. One of them was chewing a toothpick. I caught their eyes: they'd seen it too.

I threw the first stone.

WILLA CATHER
(1873–1947)

The oldest of seven children, Willa Cather was born near Winchester, Virginia, in a commodious brick farmhouse. Uprooted at the age of nine when her family moved to the prairies of Webster County, Nebraska, she spent her adolescence in the frontier village of Red Cloud. She attended a private high school in Lincoln and graduated with a degree in classics from the University of Nebraska in 1895. For a decade, she lived in Pittsburgh, where she worked first as an editor and journalist and, later, as a high school teacher of English and Latin. During that time, she published a poetry collection, *April Twilights* (1903), and a story collection, *The Troll Garden* (1905). She moved to New York City, where she became the managing editor of *McClure's Magazine.* In 1912, her first novel, *Alexander's Bridge,* was published in serial form by the magazine. Among her other novels are *O Pioneers!* (1913); *The Song of the Lark* (1915); *My Ántonia* (1918); *One of Ours* (1922), for which she was awarded the Pulitzer Prize; *A Lost Lady* (1923); *The Professor's House* (1925); *Death Comes for the Archbishop* (1927); and *Sapphira and the Slave Girl* (1940). When she received an honorary doctorate from Yale University in 1929, William Lyon Phelps introduced her by saying: "Her worst novel, *One of Ours,* received the Pulitzer Prize because in that year her worst novel was better than everybody else's masterpiece." Her stories have been collected in the posthumous volume *The Old Beauty and Others* (1948).

Paul's Case

It was Paul's afternoon to appear before the faculty of the Pittsburgh High School to account for his various misdemeanors. He had been suspended a week ago, and his father had called at the Principal's office and confessed his perplexity about his son. Paul entered the faculty room suave and smiling. His clothes were a trifle outgrown, and the tan velvet on the collar of his open overcoat was frayed and worn; but for all that there was something of a dandy about him, and he wore an opal pin in his neatly knotted black four-in-hand, and a red carnation in his buttonhole. This latter adornment the faculty somehow felt was not properly significant of the contrite spirit befitting a boy under the ban of suspension.

Paul was tall for his age and very thin, with high, cramped shoulders and a narrow chest. His eyes were remarkable for a certain hysterical brilliancy, and he continually used them in a conscious, theatrical sort of way, peculiarly offensive in a boy. The pupils were abnormally large, as though he were addicted to belladonna, but there was a glassy glitter about them which that drug does not produce.

When questioned by the Principal as to why he was there, Paul stated, politely

enough, that he wanted to come back to school. This was a lie, but Paul was quite accustomed to lying; found it, indeed, indispensable for overcoming friction. His teachers were asked to state their respective charges against him, which they did with such a
rancor and aggrievedness as evinced that this was not a usual case. Disorder and im-
pertinence were among the offences named, yet each of his instructors felt that it was
scarcely possible to put into words the real cause of the trouble, which lay in a sort of
hysterically defiant manner of the boy's; in the contempt which they all knew he felt
for them, and which he seemingly made not the least effort to conceal. Once, when he
had been making a synopsis of a paragraph at the blackboard, his English teacher had
stepped to his side and attempted to guide his hand. Paul had started back with
a shudder and thrust his hands violently behind him. The astonished woman could
scarcely have been more hurt and embarrassed had he struck at her. The insult was so
involuntary and definitely personal as to be unforgettable. In one way and another, he
had made all his teachers, men and women alike, conscious of the same feeling of
physical aversion. In one class he habitually sat with his hand shading his eyes; in another he always looked out of the window during the recitation; in another he made a
running commentary on the lecture, with humorous intent.

His teachers felt this afternoon that his whole attitude was symbolized by his shrug
and his flippantly red carnation flower, and they fell upon him without mercy, his English teacher leading the pack. He stood through it smiling, his pale lips parted over his
white teeth. (His lips were continually twitching, and he had a habit of raising his eyebrows that was contemptuous and irritating to the last degree.) Older boys than Paul
had broken down and shed tears under that ordeal, but his set smile did not once
desert him, and his only sign of discomfort was the nervous trembling of the fingers
that toyed with the buttons of his overcoat, and an occasional jerking of the other
hand which held his hat. Paul was always smiling, always glancing about him, seeming
to feel that people might be watching him and trying to detect something. This conscious expression, since it was as far as possible from boyish mirthfulness, was usually
attributed to insolence or "smartness."

As the inquisition proceeded, one of his instructors repeated an impertinent remark
of the boy's, and the Principal asked him whether he thought that a courteous speech
to make to a woman. Paul shrugged his shoulders slightly and his eyebrows twitched.

"I don't know," he replied. "I didn't mean to be polite or impolite, either. I guess
it's a sort of way I have, of saying things regardless."

The Principal asked him whether he didn't think that a way it would be well to get rid
of. Paul grinned and said he guessed so. When he was told that he could go, he bowed
gracefully and went out. His bow was like a repetition of the scandalous red carnation.

His teachers were in despair, and his drawing-master voiced the feeling of them all
when he declared there was something about the boy which none of them understood. He added: "I don't really believe that smile of his comes altogether from insolence; there's something sort of haunted about it. The boy is not strong for one thing.
There is something wrong about the fellow."

The drawing-master had come to realize that, in looking at Paul, one saw only his white teeth and the forced animation of his eyes. One warm afternoon the boy had gone to sleep at his drawing-board, and his master had noted with amazement what a white, blue-veined face it was; drawn and wrinkled like an old man's about the eyes, the lips twitching even in his sleep.

His teachers left the building dissatisfied and unhappy; humiliated to have felt so vindictive toward a mere boy, to have uttered this feeling in cutting terms, and to have set each other on, as it were, in the gruesome game of intemperate reproach. One of them remembered having seen a miserable street cat set at bay by a ring of tormentors.

As for Paul, he ran down the hill whistling the Soldiers' Chorus from *Faust,* looking behind him now and then to see whether some of his teachers were not there to witness his light-heartedness. As it was now late in the afternoon and Paul was on duty that evening as usher at Carnegie Hall, he decided that he would not go home to supper.

When he reached the concert hall, the doors were not yet open. It was chilly outside, and he decided to go up into the picture gallery—always deserted at this hour—where there were some of Raffelli's gay studies of Paris streets and an airy blue Venetian scene or two that always exhilarated him. He was delighted to find no one in the gallery but the old guard, who sat in the corner, a newspaper on his knee, a black patch over one eye and the other closed. Paul possessed himself of the place and walked confidently up and down, whistling under his breath. After a while he sat down before a blue Rico and lost himself. When he bethought him to look at his watch, it was after seven o'clock and he rose with a start and ran downstairs, making a face at Augustus Caesar, peering out from the cast-room, and an evil gesture at the Venus of Milo as he passed her on the stairway.

When Paul reached the ushers' dressing-room, half a dozen boys were there already, and he began excitedly to tumble into his uniform. It was one of the few that at all approached fitting, and Paul thought it very becoming—though he knew the tight, straight coat accentuated his narrow chest, about which he was exceedingly sensitive. He was always excited while he dressed, twanging all over to the tuning of the strings and the preliminary flourishes of the horns in the music-room; but tonight he seemed quite beside himself, and he teased and plagued the boys until, telling him that he was crazy, they put him down on the floor and sat on him.

Somewhat calmed by his suppression, Paul dashed out to the front of the house to seat the early comers. He was a model usher. Gracious and smiling he ran up and down the aisles. Nothing was too much trouble for him; he carried messages and brought programs as though it were his greatest pleasure in life, and all the people in his section thought him a charming boy, feeling that he remembered and admired them. As the house filled, he grew more and more vivacious and animated, and the color came to his cheeks and lips. It was very much as though this were a great reception and Paul were the host. Just as the musicians came out to take their places, his English teacher arrived with checks for the seats which a prominent manufacturer had taken for the season. She betrayed some embarrassment when she handed Paul the tickets, and a *hauteur* which subsequently made her feel very foolish. Paul was startled for a moment, and had the feeling of wanting to put her out; what business had she here among all these fine people and gay colors? He looked her over and decided that she was not appropriately dressed and must be a fool to sit downstairs in such togs. The tickets had probably been sent her out of kindness, he reflected, as he put down a seat for her, and she had about as much right to sit there as he had.

When the symphony began, Paul sank into one of the rear seats with a long sigh of relief, and lost himself as he had done before the Rico. It was not that symphonies, as such, meant anything in particular to Paul, but the first sight of the instruments seemed to free some hilarious spirit within him; something that struggled there like the Genius in the bottle found by the Arab fisherman. He felt a sudden zest of life; the lights danced before his eyes and the concert hall blazed into unimaginable splendor. When the soprano soloist came on, Paul forgot even the nastiness of his teacher's being there, and gave himself up to the peculiar intoxication such personages always had for him. The soloist chanced to be a German woman, by no means in her first youth, and the mother of many children; but she wore a satin gown and a tiara, and she had that indefinable air of achievement, that world-shine upon her, which always blinded Paul to any possible defects.

After a concert was over, Paul was often irritable and wretched until he got to sleep—and tonight he was even more than usually restless. He had the feeling of not being able to let down; of its being impossible to give up this delicious excitement which was the only thing that could be called living at all. During the last number he withdrew and, after hastily changing his clothes in the dressing-room, slipped out to the side door where the singer's carriage stood. Here he began pacing rapidly up and down the walk, waiting to see her come out.

Over yonder the Schenley, in its vacant stretch, loomed big and square through the fine rain, the windows of its twelve stories glowing like those of a lighted cardboard house under a Christmas tree. All the actors and singers of any importance stayed there when they were in Pittsburgh, and a number of the big manufacturers of the place lived there in the winter. Paul had often hung about the hotel, watching the people go in and out, longing to enter and leave schoolmasters and dull care behind him forever.

At last the singer came out, accompanied by the conductor, who helped her into her carriage and closed the door with a cordial *auf wiedersehen*—which set Paul to wondering whether she were not an old sweetheart of his. Paul followed the carriage over to the hotel, walking so rapidly as not to be far from the entrance when the singer alighted and disappeared behind the swinging glass doors which were opened by a Negro in a tall hat and a long coat. In the moment that the door was ajar, it seemed to Paul that he, too, entered. He seemed to feel himself go after her up the steps, into the warm, lighted building, into an exotic, a tropical world of shiny, glistening surfaces and basking ease. He reflected upon the mysterious dishes that were brought into the dining-room, the green bottles in buckets of ice, as he had seen them in the supper-party pictures of the Sunday supplement. A quick gust of wind brought the rain down with sudden vehemence, and Paul was startled to find that he was still outside in the slush of the gravel driveway; that his boots were letting in the water and his scanty overcoat was clinging wet about him; that the lights in front of the concert hall were out, and that the rain was driving in sheets between him and the orange glow of the windows above him. There it was, what he wanted—tangibly before him, like the fairy world of a Christmas pantomime; as the rain beat in his face, Paul wondered whether he were destined always to shiver in the black night outside, looking up at it.

He turned and walked reluctantly toward the car tracks. The end had to come sometime; his father in his night-clothes at the top of the stairs, explanations that did not explain, hastily improvised fictions that were forever tripping him up, his upstairs room and its horrible yellow wallpaper, the creaking bureau with the greasy plush collar-box, and over his painted wooden bed the pictures of George Washington and John Calvin, and the framed motto, "Feed my Lambs," which had been worked in red worsted by his mother, whom Paul could not remember.

Half an hour later, Paul alighted from the Negley Avenue car and went slowly down one of the side streets off the main thoroughfare. It was a highly respectable street, where all the houses were exactly alike, and where business men of moderate means begot and reared large families of children, all of whom went to Sabbath School and learned the shorter catechism, and were interested in arithmetic; all of whom were as exactly alike as their homes, and of a piece with the monotony in which they lived. Paul never went up Cordelia Street without a shudder of loathing. His home was next to the house of the Cumberland minister. He approached it tonight with the nerveless sense of defeat, the hopeless feeling of sinking back forever into ugliness and commonness that he had always had when he came home. The moment he turned into Cordelia Street he felt the waters close above his head. After each of these orgies of living, he experienced all the physical depression which follows a debauch; the loathing of respectable beds, of common food, of a house permeated by kitchen odors; a shuddering repulsion for the flavorless, colorless mass of everyday existence; a morbid desire for cool things and soft lights and fresh flowers.

The nearer he approached the house, the more absolutely unequal Paul felt to the sight of it all: his ugly sleeping chamber; the old bathroom with the grimy zinc tub, the cracked mirror, the dripping spigots; his father, at the top of the stairs, his hairy legs sticking out from his nightshirt, his feet thrust into carpet slippers. He was so much later than usual that there would certainly be inquiries and reproaches. Paul stopped short before the door. He felt that he could not be accosted by his father tonight; that he could not toss again on that miserable bed. He would not go in. He would tell his father that he had no carfare, and it was raining so hard he had gone home with one of the boys and stayed all night.

Meanwhile, he was wet and cold. He went around to the back of the house and tried one of the basement windows, found it open, and raised it cautiously, and scrambled down the cellar wall to the floor. There he stood, holding his breath, terrified by the noise he had made; but the floor above him was silent, and there was no creak on the stairs. He found a soap-box, and carried it over to the soft ring of light that streamed from the furnace door, and sat down. He was horribly afraid of rats, so he did not try to sleep, but sat looking distrustfully at the dark, still terrified lest he might have awakened his father. In such reactions, after one of the experiences which made days and nights out of the dreary blanks of the calendar, when his senses were deadened, Paul's head was always singularly clear. Suppose his father had heard him getting in at the window and had come down and shot him for a burglar? Then, again, suppose his father had come down, pistol in hand, and he had cried out in time to save himself, and his father had been horrified to think how nearly he had killed him? Then again, suppose a day should come when his father would remember that night, and wish there had been no warning cry to stay his hand? With this last supposition Paul entertained himself until daybreak.

The following Sunday was fine; the sodden November chill was broken by the last flash of autumnal summer. In the morning Paul had to go to church and Sabbath School, as always. On seasonable Sunday afternoons the burghers of Cordelia Street usually sat out on their front "stoops," and talked to their neighbors on the next stoop, or called to those across the street in neighborly fashion. The men sat placidly on gay cushions placed upon the steps that led down to the sidewalk, while the women, in their Sunday "waists," sat in rockers on the cramped porches, pretending to be greatly at their ease. The children played in the streets; there were so many of them that the place resembled the recreation grounds of a kindergarten. The men on the steps—all in their shirtsleeves, their vests unbuttoned, sat with their legs well apart, their stomachs comfortably protruding, and talked of the prices of things, or told anecdotes of the sagacity of their various chiefs and overlords. They occasionally looked over the multitude of squabbling children, listened affectionately to their high-pitched, nasal voices, smiling to see their own proclivities reproduced in their offspring, and interspersed their legends of the iron kings with remarks about their sons' progress at school, their grades in arithmetic, and the amounts they had saved in their toy banks.

On this last Sunday of November, Paul sat all afternoon on the lowest step of his "stoop," staring into the street, while his sisters, in their rockers, were talking to the minister's daughters next door about how many shirtwaists they had made in the last week, and how many waffles someone had eaten at the last church supper. When the weather was warm, and his father was in a particularly jovial frame of mind, the girls made lemonade, which was always brought out in a red-glass pitcher, ornamented with forget-me-nots in blue enamel. This the girls thought very fine, and the neighbors joked about the suspicious color of the pitcher.

Today Paul's father, on the top step, was talking to a young man who shifted a restless baby from knee to knee. He happened to be the young man who was daily held up to Paul as a model, and after whom it was his father's dearest hope that he would pattern. This young man was of a ruddy complexion, with a compressed, red mouth, and faded, near-sighted eyes, over which he wore thick spectacles, with gold bows that curved about his ears. He was clerk to one of the magnates of a great steel corporation, and was looked upon in Cordelia Street as a young man with a future. There was a story that, some five years ago—he was now barely twenty-six—he had been a trifle "dissipated," but in order to curb his appetites and save the loss of time and strength that a sowing of wild oats might have entailed, he had taken his chief's advice, oft reiterated to his employees, and at twenty-one had married the first woman whom he could persuade to share his fortunes. She happened to be an angular schoolmistress, much older than he, who also wore thick glasses, and who had now borne him four children, all near-sighted like herself.

The young man was relating how his chief, now cruising in the Mediterranean, kept in touch with all the details of the business, arranging his office hours on his yacht just as though he were at home, and "knocking off work enough to keep two stenographers busy." His father told, in turn, the plan his corporation was considering, of putting in an electric railway plant at Cairo. Paul snapped his teeth; he had an awful apprehension that they might spoil it all before he got there. Yet he rather liked to hear these legends of the iron kings, that were told and retold on Sundays and holidays; these stories of palaces in Venice, yachts on the Mediterranean, and high play at Monte Carlo appealed to his fancy, and he was interested in the triumphs of cash-boys who had become famous, though he had no mind for the cash-boy stage.

After supper was over, and he had helped to dry the dishes, Paul nervously asked his father whether he could go to George's to get some help in his geometry, and still more nervously asked for carfare. This latter request he had to repeat, as his father, on principle, did not like to hear requests for money, whether much or little. He asked Paul whether he could not go to some boy who lived nearer, and told him that he ought not to leave his school work until Sunday; but he gave him the dime. He was not a poor man, but he had a worthy ambition to come up in the world. His only reason for allowing Paul to usher was that he thought a boy ought to be earning a little.

Paul bounded upstairs, scrubbed the greasy odor of the dishwater from his hands with the ill-smelling soap he hated, and then shook over his fingers a few drops of violet water from the bottle he kept hidden in his drawer. He left the house with his geometry conspicuously under his arm, and the moment he got out of Cordelia Street and boarded a downtown car, he shook off the lethargy of two deadening days, and began to live again.

The leading juvenile of the permanent stock company which played at one of the downtown theaters was an acquaintance of Paul's, and the boy had been invited to drop in at the Sunday-night rehearsals whenever he could. For more than a year Paul had spent every available moment loitering about Charley Edwards's dressing-room. He had won a place among Edwards's following not only because the young actor, who could not afford to employ a dresser, often found him useful, but because he recognized in Paul something akin to what churchmen term "vocation."

It was at the theater and at Carnegie Hall that Paul really lived; the rest was but a sleep and a forgetting. This was Paul's fairy tale, and it had for him all the allurement of a secret love. The moment he inhaled the gassy, painty, dusty odor behind the scenes, he breathed like a prisoner set free, and felt within him the possibility of doing or saying splendid, brilliant things. The moment the cracked orchestra beat out the overture from *Martha*, or jerked at the serenade from *Rigoletto*, all stupid and ugly things slid from him, and his senses were deliciously, yet delicately fired.

Perhaps it was because, in Paul's world, the natural nearly always wore the guise of ugliness, that a certain element of artificiality seemed to him necessary in beauty.

Perhaps it was because his experience of life elsewhere was so full of Sabbath-School picnics, petty economies, wholesome advice as to how to succeed in life, and the unescapable odors of cooking, that he found this existence so alluring, these smartly clad men and women so attractive, that he was so moved by these starry apple orchards that bloomed perennially under the limelight.

It would be difficult to put it strongly enough how convincingly the stage entrance of the theater was for Paul the actual portal of Romance. Certainly none of the company ever suspected it, least of all Charley Edwards. It was very like the old stories that used to float about London of fabulously rich Jews, who had subterranean halls, with palms, and fountains, and soft lamps and richly appareled women who never saw the disenchanting light of London day. So, in the midst of that smoke-palled city, enamored of figures and grimy toil, Paul had his secret temple, his wishing-carpet, his bit of blue-and-white Mediterranean shore bathed in perpetual sunshine.

Several of Paul's teachers had a theory that his imagination had been perverted by garish fiction; but the truth was, he scarcely ever read at all. The books at home were not such as would either tempt or corrupt a youthful mind, and as for reading the novels that some of his friends urged upon him—well, he got what he wanted much more quickly from music; any sort of music, from an orchestra to a barrel-organ. He needed only the spark, the indescribable thrill that made his imagination master of his senses, and he could make plots and pictures enough of his own. It was equally true that he was not stage-struck—not, at any rate, in the usual acceptation of the expression. He had no desire to become an actor, any more than he had to become a musician. He felt no necessity to do any of these things; what he wanted was to see, to be in the atmosphere, float on the wave of it, to be carried out, blue league after league, away from everything.

After a night behind the scenes, Paul found the schoolroom more than ever repulsive; the bare floors and naked walls; the prosy men who never wore frock coats, or violets in their buttonholes; the women with their dull gowns, shrill voices, and pitiful seriousness about prepositions that govern the dative. He could not bear to have the other pupils think, for a moment, that he took these people seriously; he must convey to them that he considered it all trivial, and was there only by the way of a joke, anyway. He had autographed pictures of all the members of the stock company which he showed his classmates, telling them the most incredible stories of his familiarity with these people, of his acquaintance with the soloists who came to Carnegie Hall, his suppers with them and the flowers he sent them. When these stories lost their effect, and his audience grew listless, he would bid all the boys goodbye, announcing that he was going to travel for a while; going to Naples, to California, to Egypt. Then, next Monday, he would slip back, conscious and nervously smiling; his sister was ill, and he would have to defer his voyage until spring.

Matters went steadily worse with Paul at school. In the itch to let his instructors know how heartily he despised them, and how thoroughly he was appreciated elsewhere, he mentioned once or twice that he had no time to fool with theorems; adding—with a twitch of the eyebrows and a touch of that nervous bravado which so perplexed them—that he was helping the people down at the stock company; they were old friends of his.

The upshot of the matter was that the Principal went to Paul's father, and Paul was taken out of school and put to work. The manager at Carnegie Hall was told to get another usher in his stead; the doorkeeper at the theater was warned not to admit him to the house; and Charley Edwards remorsefully promised the boy's father not to see him again.

The members of the stock company were vastly amused when some of Paul's stories reached them—especially the women. They were hard-working women, most of them supporting indolent husbands or brothers, and they laughed rather bitterly at having stirred the boy to such fervid and florid inventions. They agreed with the faculty and with his father, that Paul's was a bad case.

The east-bound train was plowing through a January snowstorm; the dull dawn was beginning to show grey when the engine whistled a mile out of Newark. Paul started up from the seat where he had lain curled in uneasy slumber, rubbed the breath-misted window-glass with his hand, and peered out. The snow was whirling in curling eddies above the white bottom lands, and the drifts lay already deep in the fields and along the fences, while here and there the tall dead grass and dried weed stalks protruded black above it. Lights shone from the scattered houses, and a gang of laborers who stood beside the track waved their lanterns.

Paul had slept very little, and he felt grimy and uncomfortable. He had made the all-night journey in a day coach because he was afraid if he took a Pullman he might be seen by some Pittsburgh business man who had noticed him in Denny & Carson's office. When the whistle woke him, he clutched quickly at his breast pocket, glancing about him with an uncertain smile. But the little, clay-bespattered Italians were still sleeping, the slatternly women across the aisle were in open-mouthed oblivion, and even the crumby, crying babies were for the nonce stilled. Paul settled back to struggle with his impatience as best he could.

When he arrived at the Jersey City station, he hurried through his breakfast, manifestly ill at ease and keeping a sharp eye about him. After he reached the Twenty-third Street station, he consulted a cabman, and had himself driven to a men's furnishing establishment which was just opening for the day. He spent upward of two hours there, buying with endless reconsidering and great care. His new street suit he put on in the fitting-room; the frock coat and dress clothes he had bundled into the cab with his new shirts. Then he drove to a hatter's and a shoe house. His next errand was at Tiffany's, where he selected silver-mounted brushes and a scarf-pin. He would not wait to have his silver marked, he said. Lastly, he stopped at a trunk shop on Broadway, and had his purchases packed into various traveling-bags.

It was a little after one o'clock when he drove up to the Waldorf, and, after settling with the cabman, went into the office. He registered from Washington; said his mother and father had been abroad, and that he had come down to await the arrival of their steamer. He told his story plausibly and had no trouble, since he offered to pay for them in advance, in engaging his rooms; a sleeping-room, sitting-room, and bath.

Not once, but a hundred times Paul had planned this entry into New York. He had gone over every detail of it with Charley Edwards, and in his scrapbook at home there were pages of description about New York hotels, cut from the Sunday papers.

When he was shown to his sitting-room on the eighth floor, he saw at a glance that everything was as it should be; there was but one detail in his mental picture that the place did not realize, so he rang for the bell-boy and sent him down for flowers. He moved about nervously until the boy returned, putting away his new linen and fingering it delightedly as he did so. When the flowers came, he put them hastily into water, and then tumbled into a hot bath. Presently he came out of his white bathroom, resplendent in his new silk underwear, and playing with the tassels of his red robe. The snow was whirling so fiercely outside his windows that he could scarcely see across the street; but within, the air was deliciously soft and fragrant. He put the violets and jonquils on the taboret beside the couch, and threw himself down with a long sigh, covering himself with a Roman blanket. He was thoroughly tired; he had been in such haste, he had stood up to such a strain, covered so much ground in the last twenty-four hours, that he wanted to think how it had all come about. Lulled by the sound of the wind, the warm air, and the cool fragrance of the flowers, he sank into deep, drowsy retrospection.

It had been wonderfully simple; when they had shut him out of the theater and concert hall, when they had taken away his bone, the whole thing was virtually determined. The rest was a mere matter of opportunity. The only thing that at all surprised him was his own courage—for he realized well enough that he had always been tormented by fear, a sort of apprehensive dread which, of late years, as the meshes of the lies he had told closed about him, had been pulling the muscles of his body tighter and tighter. Until now, he could not remember a time when he had not been dreading something. Even when he was a little boy, it was always there—behind him, or before, or on either side. There had always been the shadowed corner, the dark place into which he dared not look, but from which something seemed always to be watching him—and Paul had done things that were not pretty to watch, he knew.

But now he had a curious sense of relief, as though he had at last thrown down the gauntlet to the thing in the corner.

Yet it was but a day since he had been sulking in the traces; but yesterday afternoon that he had been sent to the bank with Denny & Carson's deposit, as usual—but this time he was instructed to leave the book to be balanced. There was above two thousand dollars in checks, and nearly a thousand in the banknotes which he had taken from the book and quietly transferred to his pocket. At the bank he had made out a new deposit slip. His nerves had been steady enough to permit of his returning to the office, where he had finished his work and asked for a full day's holiday tomorrow, Saturday, giving a perfectly reasonable pretext. The bank book, he knew, would not be returned before Monday or Tuesday, and his father would be out of town for the next week. From the time he slipped the banknotes into his pocket until he boarded the night train for New York, he had not known a moment's hesitation.

How astonishingly easy it had all been; here he was, the thing done; and this time there would be no awakening, no figure at the top of the stairs. He watched the snowflakes whirling by his window until he fell asleep.

When he awoke, it was four o'clock in the afternoon. He bounded up with a start; one of his precious days gone already! He spent nearly an hour in dressing, watching every stage of his toilet carefully in the mirror. Everything was quite perfect; he was exactly the kind of boy he had always wanted to be.

When he went downstairs, Paul took a carriage and drove up Fifth Avenue toward the Park. The snow had somewhat abated; carriages and tradesmen's wagons were hurrying soundlessly to and fro in the winter twilight; boys in woolen mufflers were shoveling off the doorsteps; the Avenue stages made fine spots of color against the white street. Here and there on the corners whole flower gardens blooming behind glass windows, against which the snowflakes stuck and melted; violets, roses, carnations, lilies-of-the-valley—somehow vastly more lovely and alluring that they blossomed thus unnaturally in the snow. The Park itself was a wonderful stage winter-piece.

When he returned, the pause of the twilight had ceased, and the tune of the streets had changed. The snow was falling faster, lights streamed from the hotels that reared their many stories fearlessly up into the storm, defying the raging Atlantic winds. A long, black stream of carriages poured down the Avenue, intersected here and there by other streams, tending horizontally. There were a score of cabs about the entrance of his hotel, and his driver had to wait. Boys in livery were running in and out of the awning stretched across the sidewalk, up and down the red velvet carpet laid from the door to the street. Above, about, within it all, was the rumble and roar, the hurry and toss of thousands of human beings as hot for pleasure as himself, and on every side of him towered the glaring affirmation of the omnipotence of wealth.

The boy set his teeth and drew his shoulders together in a spasm of realization; the plot of all dramas, the text of all romances, the nerve-stuff of all sensations was whirling about him like the snowflakes. He burnt like a faggot in a tempest.

When Paul came down to dinner, the music of the orchestra floated up the elevator shaft to greet him. As he stepped into the thronged corridor, he sank back into one of the chairs against the wall to get his breath. The lights, the chatter, the perfumes, the bewildering medley of color—he had, for a moment, the feeling of not being able to stand it. But only for a moment; these were his own people, he told himself. He went slowly about the corridors, through the writing-rooms, smoking-rooms, reception-rooms, as though he were exploring the chambers of an enchanted palace, built and peopled for him alone.

When he reached the dining-room he sat down at a table near a window. The flowers, the white linen, the many-colored wine-glasses, the gay toilettes of the women, the low popping of corks, the undulating repetitions of the "Blue Danube" from the orchestra, all flooded Paul's dream with bewildering radiance. When the roseate tinge of his champagne was added—that cold, precious, bubbling stuff that creamed and foamed in his glass—Paul wondered that there were honest men in the world at all. This was what all the world was fighting for, he reflected; this was what all the struggle was about. He doubted the reality of his past. Had he ever known a place called Cordelia

Street, a place where fagged-looking business men boarded the early car? Mere rivets in a machine they seemed to Paul—sickening men, with combings of children's hair always hanging to their coats, and the smell of cooking in their clothes. Cordelia Street— Ah, that belonged to another time and country! Had he not always been thus, had he not sat here night after night, from as far back as he could remember, looking pensively over just such shimmering textures, and slowly twirling the stem of a glass like this one between his thumb and middle finger? He rather thought he had.

He was not in the least abashed or lonely. He had no especial desire to meet or to know any of these people; all he demanded was the right to look on and conjecture, to watch the pageant. The mere stage properties were all he contended for. Nor was he lonely later in the evening, in his loge at the Opera. He was entirely rid of his nervous misgivings, of his forced aggressiveness, of the imperative desire to show himself different from his surroundings. He felt now that his surroundings explained him. Nobody questioned the purple; he had only to wear it passively. He had only to glance down at his dress coat to reassure himself that here it would be impossible for anyone to humiliate him.

He found it hard to leave his beautiful sitting-room to go to bed that night, and sat long watching the raging storm from his turret window. When he went to sleep, it was with the lights turned on in his bedroom; partly because of his old timidity, and partly so that, if he should wake in the night, there would be no wretched moment of doubt, no horrible suspicion of yellow wallpaper, or of Washington and Calvin above his bed.

On Sunday morning the city was practically snowbound. Paul breakfasted late, and in the afternoon he fell in with a wild San Francisco boy, a freshman at Yale, who said he had run down for a "little flyer" over Sunday. The young man offered to show Paul the night side of the town, and the two boys went off together after dinner, not returning to the hotel until seven o'clock the next morning. They had started out in the confiding warmth of a champagne friendship, but their parting in the elevator was singularly cool. The freshman pulled himself together to make his train, and Paul went to bed. He awoke at two o'clock in the afternoon, very thirsty and dizzy, and rang for icewater, coffee, and the Pittsburgh papers.

On the part of the hotel management, Paul excited no suspicion. There was this to be said for him, that he wore his spoils with dignity and in no way made himself conspicuous. His chief greediness lay in his ears and eyes, and his excesses were not offensive ones. His dearest pleasures were the grey winter twilights in his sitting-room; his quiet enjoyment of his flowers, his clothes, his wide divan, his cigarette, and his sense of power. He could not remember a time when he had felt so at peace with himself. The mere release from the necessity of petty lying, lying every day and every day, restored his self-respect. He had never lied for pleasure, even at school; but to make himself noticed and admired, to assert his difference from other Cordelia Street boys; and he felt a good deal more manly, more honest, even, now that he had no need for boastful pretensions, now that he could, as his actor friends used to say, "dress the part." It was characteristic that remorse did not occur to him. His golden days went by without a shadow, and he made each as perfect as he could.

On the eighth day after his arrival in New York, he found the whole affair exploited in the Pittsburgh papers, exploited with a wealth of detail which indicated that local news of a sensational nature was at a low ebb. The firm of Denny & Carson announced that the boy's father had refunded the full amount of his theft, and that they had no intention of prosecuting. The Cumberland minister had been interviewed, and expressed his hope of yet reclaiming the motherless lad, and Paul's Sabbath-School teacher declared that she would spare no effort to that end. The rumor had reached Pittsburgh that the boy had been seen in a New York hotel, and his father had gone East to find him and bring him home.

Paul had just come in to dress for dinner; he sank into the chair, weak in the knees, and clasped his head in his hands. It was to be worse than jail, even; the tepid waters of Cordelia Street were to close over him finally and forever. The grey monotony stretched before him in hopeless, unrelieved years;—Sabbath School, Young People's Meeting, the yellow-papered room, the damp dish-towels; it all rushed back upon him with sickening vividness. He had the old feeling that the orchestra had suddenly stopped, the sinking sensation that the play was over. The sweat broke out on his face, and he sprang to his feet, looked about him with his white, conscious smile, and winked at himself in the mirror. With something of the childish belief in miracles with which he had so often gone to class, all his lessons unlearned, Paul dressed and dashed whistling down the corridor to the elevator.

He had no sooner entered the dining-room and caught the measure of the music than his remembrance was lightened by his old elastic power of claiming the moment, mounting with it, and finding it all-sufficient. The glare and glitter about him, the mere scenic accessories had again, and for the last time, their old potency. He would show himself that he was game, he would finish the thing splendidly. He doubted, more than ever, the existence of Cordelia Street, and for the first time he drank his wine recklessly. Was he not, after all, one of these fortunate beings? Was he not still himself, and in his own place? He drummed a nervous accompaniment to the music and looked about him, telling himself over and over that it had paid.

He reflected drowsily, to the swell of the violin and the chill sweetness of his wine, that he might have done it more wisely. He might have caught an outbound steamer and been well out of their clutches before now. But the other side of the world had seemed too far away and too uncertain then; he could not have waited for it; his need had been too sharp. If he had to choose over again, he would do the same thing to-morrow. He looked affectionately about the dining-room, now gilded with a soft mist. Ah, it had paid indeed!

Paul was awakened next morning by a painful throbbing in his head and feet. He had thrown himself across the bed without undressing, and had slept with his shoes on. His limbs and hands were lead-heavy, and his tongue and throat were parched. There came upon him one of those fateful attacks of clear-headedness that never occurred except when he was physically exhausted and his nerves hung loose. He lay still and closed his eyes and let the tide of realities wash over him.

His father was in New York; "stopping at some joint or other," he told himself. The memory of successive summers on the front stoop fell upon him like a weight of black water. He had not a hundred dollars left; and he knew now, more than ever, that money was everything, the wall that stood between all he loathed and all he wanted. The thing was winding itself up; he had thought of that on his first glorious day in New York, and had even provided a way to snap the thread. It lay on his dressing-table now; he had got it out last night when he came blindly up from dinner—but the shiny metal hurt his eyes, and he disliked the look of it, anyway.

He rose and moved about with a painful effort, succumbing now and again to attacks of nausea. It was the old depression exaggerated; all the world had become Cordelia Street. Yet somehow he was not afraid of anything, was absolutely calm; perhaps because he had looked into the dark corner at last, and knew. It was bad enough, what he saw there; but somehow not so bad as his long fear of it had been. He saw everything clearly now. He had a feeling that he had made the best of it, that he had lived the sort of life he was meant to live, and for half an hour he sat staring at the revolver. But he told himself that was not the way, so he went downstairs and took a cab to the ferry.

When Paul arrived at Newark, he got off the train and took another cab, directing the driver to follow the Pennsylvania tracks out of town. The snow lay heavy on the roadways and had drifted deep in the open fields. Only here and there the dead grass or dried weed stalks projected, singularly black, above it.

Once well into the country, Paul dismissed the carriage and walked, floundering along the tracks, his mind a medley of irrelevant things. He seemed to hold in his brain an actual picture of everything he had seen that morning. He remembered every feature of both his drivers, the toothless old woman from whom he had bought the red flowers in his coat, the agent from whom he had got his ticket, and all of his fellow-passengers on the ferry. His mind, unable to cope with vital matters near at hand, worked feverishly and deftly at sorting and grouping these images. They made for him a part of the ugliness of the world, of the ache in his head, and the bitter burning on his tongue. He stooped and put a handful of snow into his mouth as he walked, but that, too, seemed hot. When he reached a little hillside, where the tracks ran through a cut some twenty feet below him, he stopped and sat down.

The carnations in his coat were drooping with cold, he noticed; all their red glory over. It occurred to him that all the flowers he had seen in the show windows that first night must have gone the same way, long before this. It was only one splendid breath they had, in spite of their brave mockery at the winter outside the glass. It was a losing game in the end, it seemed, this revolt against the homilies by which the world is run. Paul took one of the blossoms carefully from his coat and scooped a little hole in the snow, where he covered it up. Then he dozed awhile, from his weak condition, seeming insensible to the cold.

The sound of an approaching train woke him and he started to his feet, remembering only his resolution, and afraid lest he should be too late. He stood watching the approaching locomotive, his teeth chattering, his lips drawn away from them in a frightened smile; once or twice he glanced nervously sidewise, as though he were being watched. When the right moment came, he jumped. As he fell, the folly of his haste occurred to him with merciless clearness, the vastness of what he had left undone. There flashed through his brain, clearer than ever before, the blue of Adriatic water, the yellow of Algerian sands.

He felt something strike his chest—his body being thrown swiftly through the air, on and on, immeasurably far and fast, while his limbs gently relaxed. Then, because the picture making mechanism was crushed, the disturbing visions flashed into black, and Paul dropped back into the immense design of things.

SANDRA CISNEROS
(1954–)

Born in Chicago to a Mexican father and a Mexican-American mother, Sandra Cisneros was the only daughter in a family with six sons. During her childhood, her family often lived in Mexico City as well as in Chicago. She received a B.A. from Loyola University and an M.F.A. from the University of Iowa Writers' Workshop. She has worked as a high school teacher for dropout students and a Loyola University recruiter and counselor for minority students, as well as having visiting professorships at California State University, Chico; University of California, Berkeley; University of California, Irvine; University of Michigan; and University of New Mexico. She has been awarded two National Endowment for the Arts Fellowships (1982; 1988), a Paisano Dobie Fellowship (1986), a Lannan Foundation Literary Award (1991), an honorary doctorate from the State University of New York at Purchase (1993), and a MacArthur Foundation Fellowship (1995). According to Cisneros, she discovered in a course at University of Iowa the unique narrative voice with which she writes—one influenced by the two different speech patterns of her parents. Sifting through her background and the experiences that her classmates could know nothing about, she recalls: "I chose to write about third-floor flats, and fear of rats, and drunk husbands sending rocks through windows. . . . And this is when I discovered the voice I'd been suppressing all along without realizing it." Her collections of poetry are *Bad Boys* (1980), *My Wicked, Wicked Ways* (1987), and *Loose Woman* (1994). She has also published *The House on Mango Street* (1984), a collection of connected vignettes written from the first-person point of view of a Latina girl; *Woman Hollering Creek and Other Stories* (1991); and the novel *Caramelo* (2002).

---

from *The House on Mango Street*

The House on Mango Street

We didn't always live on Mango Street. Before that we lived on Loomis on the third floor, and before that we lived on Keeler. Before Keeler it was Paulina, and before that I can't remember. But what I remember most is moving a lot. Each time it seemed there'd be one more of us. By the time we got to Mango Street we were six—Mama, Papa, Carlos, Kiki, my sister Nenny and me.

The house on Mango Street is ours, and we don't have to pay rent to anybody, or share the yard with the people downstairs, or be careful not to make too much noise, and there isn't a landlord banging on the ceiling with a broom. But even so, it's not the house we'd thought we'd get.

We had to leave the flat on Loomis quick. The water pipes broke and the landlord wouldn't fix them because the house was too old. We had to leave fast. We were using the washroom next door and carrying water over in empty milk gallons. That's why Mama and Papa looked for a house, and that's why we moved into the house on Mango Street, far away, on the other side of town.

They always told us that one day we would move into a house, a real house that would be ours for always so we wouldn't have to move each year. And our house would have running water and pipes that worked. And inside it would have real stairs, not hallway stairs, but stairs inside like the houses on TV. And we'd have a basement and at least three washrooms so when we took a bath we wouldn't have to tell everybody. Our house would be white with trees around it, a great big yard and grass growing without a fence. This was the house Papa talked about when he held a lottery ticket and this was the house Mama dreamed up in the stories she told us before we went to bed.

But the house on Mango Street is not the way they told it at all. It's small and red with tight steps in front and windows so small you'd think they were holding their breath. Bricks are crumbling in places, and the front door is so swollen you have to push hard to get in. There is no front yard, only four little elms the city planted by the curb. Out back is a small garage for the car we don't own yet and a small yard that looks smaller between the two buildings on either side. There are stairs in our house, but they're ordinary hallway stairs, and the house has only one washroom. Everybody has to share a bedroom—Mama and Papa, Carlos and Kiki, me and Nenny.

Once when we were living on Loomis, a nun from my school passed by and saw me playing out front. The laundromat downstairs had been boarded up because it had been robbed two days before and the owner had painted on the wood YES WE'RE OPEN so as not to lose business.

Where do you live? she asked.

There, I said pointing up to the third floor.

You live *there*?

There. I had to look to where she pointed—the third floor, the paint peeling, wooden bars Papa had nailed on the windows so we wouldn't fall out. You live *there*? The way she said it made me feel like nothing. *There*. I lived *there*. I nodded.

I knew then I had to have a house. A real house. One I could point to. But this isn't it. The house on Mango Street isn't it. For the time being, Mama says. Temporary, says Papa. But I know how those things go.

Chanclas

It's me—Mama, Mama said. I open up and she's there with bags and big boxes, the new clothes and, yes, she's got the socks and a new slip with a little rose on it and a pink-and-white striped dress. What about the shoes? I forgot. Too late now. I'm tired. Whew!

Six-thirty already and my little cousin's baptism is over. All day waiting, the door locked, don't open up for nobody, and I don't till Mama gets back and buys everything except the shoes.

Now Uncle Nacho is coming in his car, and we have to hurry to get to Precious Blood Church quick because that's where the baptism party is, in the basement rented for today for dancing and tamales and everyone's kids running all over the place.

Mama dances, laughs, dances. All of a sudden, Mama is sick. I fan her hot face with a paper plate. Too many tamales, but Uncle Nacho says too many this and tilts his thumb to his lips.

Everybody laughing except me, because I'm wearing the new dress, pink and white with stripes, and new underclothes and new socks and the old saddle shoes I wear to school, brown and white, the kind I get every September because they last long and they do. My feet scuffed and round, and the heels all crooked that look dumb with this dress, so I just sit.

Meanwhile that boy who is my cousin by first communion or something asks me to dance and I can't. Just stuff my feet under the metal folding chair stamped Precious Blood and pick on a wad of brown gum that's stuck beneath the seat. I shake my head no. My feet growing bigger and bigger.

Then Uncle Nacho is pulling and pulling my arm and it doesn't matter how new the dress Mama bought is because my feet are ugly until my uncle who is a liar says, You are the prettiest girl here, will you dance, but I believe him, and yes, we are dancing, my Uncle Nacho and me, only I don't want to at first. My feet swell big and heavy like plungers, but I drag them across the linoleum floor straight center where Uncle wants to show off the new dance we learned. And Uncle spins me, and my skinny arms bend the way he taught me, and my mother watches, and my little cousins watch, and the boy who is my cousin by first communion watches, and everyone says, wow, who are those two who dance like in the movies, until I forget that I am wearing only ordinary shoes, brown and white, the kind my mother buys each year for school.

And all I hear is the clapping when the music stops. My uncle and me bow and he walks me back in my thick shoes to my mother who is proud to be my mother. All night the boy who is a man watches me dance. He watched me dance.

The First Job

It wasn't as if I didn't want to work. I did. I had even gone to the social security office the month before to get my social security number. I needed money. The Catholic high school cost a lot, and Papa said nobody went to public school unless you wanted to turn out bad.

I thought I'd find an easy job, the kind other kids had, working in the dime store or maybe a hotdog stand. And though I hadn't started looking yet, I thought I might the week after next. But when I came home that afternoon, all wet because Tito had pushed me into the open water hydrant—only I had sort of let him—Mama called me in the kitchen before I could even go and change, and Aunt Lala was sitting there drinking her coffee with a spoon. Aunt Lala said she had found a job for me at the Peter Pan Photo Finishers on North Broadway where she worked, and how old was I, and to show up tomorrow saying I was one year older, and that was that.

So the next morning I put on the navy blue dress that made me look older and borrowed money for lunch and bus fare because Aunt Lala said I wouldn't get paid till the next Friday, and I went in and saw the boss of the Peter Pan Photo Finishers on North Broadway where Aunt Lala worked and lied about my age like she told me to and sure enough, I started that same day.

In my job I had to wear white gloves. I was supposed to match negatives with their prints, just look at the picture and look for the same one on the negative strip, put it in the envelope, and do the next one. That's all. I didn't know where these envelopes were coming from or where they were going. I just did what I was told.

It was real easy, and I guess I wouldn't have minded it except that you got tired after a while and I didn't know if I could sit down or not, and then I started sitting down only when the two ladies next to me did. After a while they started to laugh and came up to me and said I could sit when I wanted to, and I said I knew.

When lunchtime came, I was scared to eat alone in the company lunchroom with all those men and ladies looking, so I ate real fast standing in one of the washroom stalls and had lots of time left over, so I went back to work early. But then break time came, and not knowing where else to go, I went into the coatroom because there was a bench there.

I guess it was the time for the night shift or middle shift to arrive because a few people came in and punched the time clock, and an older Oriental man said hello and we talked for a while about my just starting, and he said we could be friends and next time to go in the lunchroom and sit with him, and I felt better. He had nice eyes and I didn't feel so nervous anymore. Then he asked if I knew what day it was, and when I said I didn't, he said it was his birthday and would I please give him a birthday kiss. I thought I would because he was so old and just as I was about to put my lips on his cheek, he grabs my face with both hands and kisses me hard on the mouth and doesn't let go.

MICHAEL CUNNINGHAM
(1952–)

Michael Cunningham spent his childhood in Cincinnati, Ohio, and received his undergraduate degree in English at Stanford University and an M.F.A. at the University of Iowa, where his early promise as a writer was acknowledged with a Michener Fellowship. He was awarded a National Endowment for the Arts Fellowship in 1988. His debut novel, *A Home at the End of the World* (1990), explored relationships in a nontraditional family consisting of two gay men and a woman. The year before, an excerpt from the novel, titled "The White Angel," appeared in *The New Yorker* and was chosen for inclusion in *Best American Short Stories 1989*. A second novel, *Flesh and Blood,* described as a domestic epic, appeared in 1995. Over the decade of the '90s, his work appeared in *The Atlantic Monthly*, *Redbook*, *Esquire*, *The Paris Review*, *The New Yorker*, *Vogue*, and *Metropolitan Home*. But it was in 1998 that Cunningham achieved his greatest success with the publication of *The Hours,* based on Virginia Woolf's *Mrs. Dalloway,* the book he credits with initiating him into the world of writing—it was literally thrown at him by a girl on whom he had a crush. *The Hours* received both a Pulitzer Prize and the PEN/Faulkner Award for Fiction. In 2002, it was made into a highly acclaimed film, starring Meryl Streep, Julianne Moore, and Nicole Kidman. His latest work is *Land's End: A Walk Through Provincetown* (2002), the first installment in Crown's travelogue series *Crown Journeys.*

---

from *A Home at the End of the World*

Bobby

We lived then in Cleveland, in the middle of everything. It was the sixties—our radios sang out love all day long. This of course is history. It happened before the city of Cleveland went broke, before its river caught fire. We were four. My mother and father, Carlton, and me. Carlton turned sixteen the year I turned nine. Between us were several brothers and sisters, weak flames quenched in our mother's womb. We are not a fruitful or many-branched line. Our family name is Morrow.

Our father was a high school music teacher. Our mother taught children called "exceptional," which meant that some could name the day Christmas would fall in the year 2000 but couldn't remember to drop their pants when they peed. We lived in a tract called Woodlawn—neat one- and two-story houses painted optimistic colors. Our tract bordered a cemetery. Behind our back yard was a gully choked with brush, and beyond that, the field of smooth, polished stones. I grew up with the cemetery, and didn't mind it. It could be beautiful. A single stone angel, small-breasted and determined, rose amid the more conservative markers close to our house. Farther away, in a richer section, miniature mosques and Parthenons spoke silently to Cleveland of man's enduring accomplishments. Carlton and I played in the cemetery as children and, with a little more age, smoked joints and drank Southern Comfort there. I was, thanks to Carlton, the most criminally advanced nine-year-old in my fourth-grade class. I was going places. I made no move without his counsel.

Here is Carlton several months before his death, in an hour so alive with snow that earth and sky are identically white. He labors among the markers and I run after, stung by snow, following the light of his red knitted cap. Carlton's hair is pulled back into a ponytail, neat and economical, a perfect pinecone of hair. He is thrifty, in his way.

We have taken hits of acid with our breakfast juice. Or rather, Carlton has taken a hit and I, considering my youth, have been allowed half. This acid is called windowpane. It is for clarity of vision, as Vicks is for decongestion of the nose. Our parents are at work, earning the daily bread. We have come out into the cold so that the house, when we reenter it, will shock us with its warmth and righteousness. Carlton believes in shocks.

"I think I'm coming on to it," I call out. Carlton has on his buckskin jacket, which is worn down to the shine. On the back, across his shoulder blades, his girlfriend has stitched an electric-blue eye. As we walk I speak into the eye. "I think I feel something," I say.

"Too soon," Carlton calls back. "Stay loose, Frisco. You'll know when the time comes."

I am excited and terrified. We are into serious stuff. Carlton has done acid half a dozen times before, but I am new at it. We slipped the tabs into our mouths at breakfast, while our mother paused over the bacon. Carlton likes taking risks.

Snow collects in the engraved letters on the headstones. I lean into the wind, trying to decide whether everything around me seems strange because of the drug, or just because everything truly is strange. Three weeks earlier, a family across town had been sitting at home, watching television, when a single-engine plane fell on them. Snow swirls around us, seeming to fall up as well as down.

Carlton leads the way to our spot, the pillared entrance to a society tomb. This tomb is a palace. Stone cupids cluster on the peaked roof, with stunted, frozen wings and matrons' faces. Under the roof is a veranda, backed by cast-iron doors that lead to the house of the dead proper. In summer this veranda is cool. In winter it blocks the wind. We keep a bottle of Southern Comfort there.

Carlton finds the bottle, unscrews the cap, and takes a good, long draw. He is studded with snowflakes. He hands me the bottle and I take a more conservative drink. Even in winter, the tomb smells mossy as a well. Dead leaves and a yellow M&M's wrapper, worried by the wind, scrape on the marble floor.

"Are you scared?" Carlton asks me.

I nod. I never think of lying to him.

"Don't be, man," he says. "Fear will screw you right up. Drugs can't hurt you if you feel no fear."

I nod. We stand sheltered, passing the bottle. I lean into Carlton's certainty as if it gave off heat.

"We can do acid all the time at Woodstock," I say.

"Right on. Woodstock Nation. Yow."

"Do people really *live* there?" I ask.

"Man, you've got to stop asking that. The concert's over, but people are still there. It's the new nation. Have faith."

I nod again, satisfied. There is a different country for us to live in. I am already a new person, renamed Frisco. My old name was Robert.

"We'll do acid all the time," I say.

"You better believe we will." Carlton's face, surrounded by snow and marble, is lit. His eyes are bright as neon. Something in them tells me he can see the future, a ghost that hovers over everybody's head. In Carlton's future we all get released from our jobs and schooling. Awaiting us all, and soon, is a bright, perfect simplicity. A life among the trees by the river.

"How are you feeling, man?" he asks me.

"Great," I tell him, and it is purely the truth. Doves clatter up out of a bare tree and turn at the same instant, transforming themselves from steel to silver in the snow-blown light. I know at that moment that the drug is working. Everything before me has become suddenly, radiantly itself. How could Carlton have known this was about to happen? "Oh," I whisper. His hand settles on my shoulder.

"Stay loose, Frisco," he says. "There's not a thing in this pretty world to be afraid of. I'm here."

I am not afraid. I am astonished. I had not realized until this moment how real everything is. A twig lies on the marble at my feet, bearing a cluster of hard brown berries. The broken-off end is raw, white, fleshly. Trees are alive.

"I'm here," Carlton says again, and he is.

Hours later, we are sprawled on the sofa in front of the television, ordinary as Wally and the Beav. Our mother makes dinner in the kitchen. A pot lid clangs. We are undercover agents. I am trying to conceal my amazement.

Our father is building a grandfather clock from a kit. He wants to have something to leave us, something for us to pass along. We can hear him in the basement, sawing and pounding. I know what is laid out on his sawhorses—a long raw wooden box, onto which he glues fancy moldings. A single pearl of sweat meanders down his forehead as he works. Tonight I have discovered my ability to see every room of the house at once, to know every single thing that goes on. A mouse nibbles inside the wall. Electrical wires curl behind the plaster, hidden and patient as snakes.

"Shhh," I say to Carlton, who has not said anything. He is watching television through his splayed fingers. Gunshots ping. Bullets raise chalk dust on a concrete wall. I have no idea what we are watching.

"Boys?" our mother calls from the kitchen. I can, with my new ears, hear her slap hamburger into patties. "Set the table like good citizens," she calls.

"Okay, Ma," Carlton replies, in a gorgeous imitation of normality. Our father hammers in the basement. I can feel Carlton's heart ticking. He pats my hand, to assure me that everything's perfect.

We set the table, spoon fork knife, paper napkins triangled to one side. We know the moves cold. After we are done I pause to notice the dining-room wallpaper: a golden farm, backed by mountains. Cows graze, autumn trees cast golden shade. This scene repeats itself three times, on three walls.

"Zap," Carlton whispers. "Zzzzzoom."

"Did we do it right?" I ask him.

"We did everything perfect, little son. How are you doing in there, anyway?" He raps lightly on my head.

"Perfect, I guess." I am staring at the wallpaper as if I were thinking of stepping into it.

"You guess. You guess? You and I are going to other planets, man. Come over here."

"Where?"

"Here. Come here." He leads me to the window. Outside the snow skitters, nervous and silver, under streetlamps. Ranch-style houses hoard their warmth, bleed light into the gathering snow. It is a street in Cleveland. It is our street.

"You and I are going to fly, man," Carlton whispers, close to my ear. He opens the window. Snow blows in, sparking on the carpet. "Fly," he says, and we do. For a moment we strain up and out, the black night wind blowing in our faces—we raise ourselves up off the cocoa-colored deep-pile wool-and-polyester carpet by a sliver of an inch. Sweet glory. The secret of flight is this—you have to do it immediately, before your body realizes it is defying the laws. I swear it to this day.

We both know we have taken momentary leave of the earth. It does not strike either of us as remarkable, any more than does the fact that airplanes sometimes fall from the sky, or that we have always lived in these rooms and will soon leave them. We settle back down. Carlton touches my shoulder.

"You wait, Frisco," he says. "Miracles are happening. Fucking miracles."

I nod. He pulls down the window, which reseals itself with a sucking sound. Our own faces look back at us from the cold, dark glass. Behind us, our mother drops the hamburgers sizzling into the skillet. Our father bends to his work under a hooded lightbulb, preparing the long box into which he will lay clockworks, pendulum, a face. A plane drones by overhead, invisible in the clouds. I glance nervously at Carlton. He smiles his assurance and squeezes the back of my neck.

March. After the thaw. I am walking through the cemetery, thinking about my endless life. One of the beauties of living in Cleveland is that any direction feels like progress. I've memorized the map. We are by my calculations three hundred and fifty miles shy of Woodstock, New York. On this raw new day I am walking east, to the place where Carlton and I keep our bottle. I am going to have an early nip, to celebrate my bright future.

When I get to our spot I hear low moans coming from behind the tomb. I freeze, considering my choices. The sound is a long-drawn-out agony with a whip at the end, a final high C, something like "ooooooOw." A wolf's cry run backward. What decides me on investigation rather than flight is the need to make a story. In the stories my brother likes best, people always do the foolish, risky thing. I find I can reach decisions this way, by thinking of myself as a character in a story told by Carlton.

I creep around the side of the monument, cautious as a badger, pressed up close to the marble. I peer over a cherub's girlish shoulder. What I find is Carlton on the ground with his girlfriend, in an uncertain jumble of clothes and bare flesh. Carlton's jacket, the one with the embroidered eye, is draped over the stone, keeping watch.

I hunch behind the statue. I can see the girl's naked arms, and the familiar bones of Carlton's spine. The two of them moan together in the dry winter grass. Though I can't make out the girl's expression, Carlton's face is twisted and grimacing, the cords of his neck pulled tight. I had never thought the experience might be painful. I watch, trying to learn. I hold on to the cherub's cold wings.

It isn't long before Carlton catches sight of me. His eyes rove briefly, ecstatically skyward, and what do they light on but his brother's small head, sticking up next to a cherub's. We lock eyes and spend a moment in mutual decision. The girl keeps on clutching at Carlton's skinny back. He decides to smile at me. He decides to wink.

I am out of there so fast I tear up divots. I dodge among the stones, jump the gully, clear the fence into the swing-set-and-picnic-table sanctity of the back yard. Something about that wink. My heart beats fast as a sparrow's.

I go into the kitchen and find our mother washing fruit. She asks what's going on. I tell her nothing is. Nothing at all.

She sighs over an apple's imperfection. The curtains sport blue teapots. Our mother works the apple with a scrub brush. She believes they come coated with poison.

"Where's Carlton?" she asks.

"Don't know," I tell her.

"Bobby?"

"Huh?"

"What exactly is going on?"

"Nothing," I say. My heart works itself up to a hummingbird's rate, more buzz than beat.

"I think something is. Will you answer a question?"

"Okay."

"Is your brother taking drugs?"

I relax a bit. It is only drugs. I know why she's asking. Lately police cars have been browsing our house like sharks. They pause, take note, glide on. Some neighborhood crackdown. Carlton is famous in these parts.

"No," I tell her.

She faces me with the brush in one hand, an apple in the other. "You wouldn't lie to me, would you?" She knows something is up. Her nerves run through this house. She can feel dust settling on the tabletops, milk starting to turn in the refrigerator.

"No," I say.

"Something's going on," she sighs. She is a small, efficient woman who looks at things as if they give off a painful light. She grew up on a farm in Wisconsin and spent her girlhood tying up bean rows, worrying over the sun and rain. She is still trying to overcome her habit of modest expectations.

I leave the kitchen, pretending sudden interest in the cat. Our mother follows, holding her brush. She means to scrub the truth out of me. I follow the cat, his erect black tail and pink anus.

"Don't walk away when I'm talking to you," our mother says.

I keep walking, to see how far I'll get, calling, "Kittykittykitty." In the front hall, our father's homemade clock chimes the half hour. I make for the clock. I get as far as the rubber plant before she collars me.

"I told you not to walk away," she says, and cuffs me a good one with the brush. She catches me on the ear and sets it ringing. The cat is out of there quick as a quarter note.

I stand for a minute, to let her know I've received the message. Then I resume walking. She hits me again, this time on the back of the head, hard enough to make me see colors. "Will you *stop*?" she screams. Still, I keep walking. Our house runs west to east. With every step I get closer to Yasgur's farm.

Carlton comes home whistling. Our mother treats him like a guest who's overstayed. He doesn't care. He is lost in optimism. He pats her cheek and calls her "Professor." He treats her as if she were harmless, and so she is.

She never hits Carlton. She suffers him the way farm girls suffer a thieving crow, with a grudge so old and endless it borders on reverence. She gives him a scrubbed apple, and tells him what she'll do if he tracks mud on the carpet.

I am waiting in our room. He brings the smell of the cemetery with him, its old snow and wet pine needles. He rolls his eyes at me, takes a crunch of his apple. "What's happening, Frisco?" he says.

I have arranged myself loosely on my bed, trying to pull a Dylan riff out of my harmonica. I have always figured I can bluff my way into wisdom. I offer Carlton a dignified nod.

He drops onto his own bed. I can see a crushed crocus, the first of the year, stuck to the black rubber sole of his boot.

"Well, Frisco," he says. "Today you are a man."

I nod again. Is that all there is to it?

"*Yow*," Carlton says. He laughs, pleased with himself and the world. "That was so perfect."

I pick out what I can of "Blowin' in the Wind."

Carlton says, "Man, when I saw you out there spying on us I thought to myself, *yes*. Now *I'm* really here. You know what I'm saying?" He waves his apple core.

"Uh-huh," I say.

"Frisco, that was the first time her and I ever did it. I mean, we'd talked. But when we finally got down to it, there you were. My brother. Like you *knew*."

I nod, and this time for real. What happened was an adventure we had together. All right. The story is beginning to make sense.

"Aw, Frisco," Carlton says. "I'm gonna find you a girl, too. You're nine. You been a virgin too long."

"Really?" I say.

"*Man*. We'll find you a woman from the sixth grade, somebody with a little experience. We'll get stoned and all make out under the trees in the boneyard. I want to be present at your deflowering, man. You're gonna need a brother there."

I am about to ask, as casually as I can manage, about the relationship between love and bodily pain, when our mother's voice cuts into the room. "You did it," she screams. "You tracked mud all over the rug."

A family entanglement follows. Our mother brings our father, who comes and stands in the doorway with her, taking in evidence. He is a formerly handsome man. His face has been worn down by too much patience. He has lately taken up some sporty touches—a goatee, a pair of calfskin boots.

Our mother points out the trail of muddy half-moons that lead from the door to Carlton's bed. Dangling over the foot of the bed are the culprits themselves, voluptuously muddy, with Carlton's criminal feet still in them.

"You see?" she says. "You see what he thinks of me?"

Our father, a reasonable man, suggests that Carlton clean it up. Our mother finds that too small a gesture. She wants Carlton not to have done it in the first place. "I don't ask for much," she says. "I don't ask where he goes. I don't ask why the police are suddenly so interested in our house. I ask that he not track mud all over the floor. That's all." She squints in the glare of her own outrage.

"Better clean it right up," our father says to Carlton.

"And that's it?" our mother says. "He cleans up the mess, and all's forgiven?"

"Well, what do you want him to do? Lick it up?"

"I want some consideration," she says, turning helplessly to me. "That's what I want." I shrug, at a loss. I sympathize with our mother, but am not on her team.

"All right," she says. "I just won't bother cleaning the house anymore. I'll let you men handle it. I'll sit and watch television and throw my candy wrappers on the floor."

She starts out, cutting the air like a blade. On her way she picks up a jar of pencils, looks at it and tosses the pencils on the floor. They fall like fortune-telling sticks, in pairs and crisscrosses.

Our father goes after her, calling her name. Her name is Isabel. We can hear them making their way across the house, our father calling, "Isabel, Isabel, Isabel," while our mother, pleased with the way the pencils had looked, dumps more things onto the floor.

"I hope she doesn't break the TV," I say.

"She'll do what she needs to do," Carlton tells me.

"I hate her," I say. I am not certain about that. I want to test the sound of it, to see if it's true.

"She's got more balls than any of us, Frisco," he says. "Better watch what you say about her."

I keep quiet. Soon I get up and start gathering pencils, because I prefer that to lying around trying to follow the shifting lines of allegiance. Carlton goes for a sponge and starts in on the mud.

"You get shit on the carpet, you clean it up," he says. "Simple."

The time for all my questions about love has passed, and I am not so unhip as to force a subject. I know it will come up again. I make a neat bouquet of pencils. Our mother rages through the house.

Later, after she has thrown enough and we three have picked it all up, I lie on my bed thinking things over. Carlton is on the phone to his girlfriend, talking low. Our mother, becalmed but still dangerous, cooks dinner. She sings as she cooks, some slow forties number that must have been all over the jukes when her first husband's plane went down in the Pacific. Our father plays his clarinet in the basement. That is where he goes to practice, down among his woodworking tools, the neatly hung hammers and awls that throw oversized shadows in the light of the single bulb. If I put my ear to the floor I can hear him, pulling a long low tomcat moan out of that horn. There is some strange comfort in pressing my ear to the carpet and hearing our father's music leaking up through the floorboards. Lying down, with my ear to the floor, I join in on my harmonica.

That spring our parents have a party to celebrate the sun's return. It has been a long, bitter winter and now the first wild daisies are poking up on the lawns and among the graves.

Our parents' parties are mannerly affairs. Their friends, schoolteachers all, bring wine jugs and guitars. They are Ohio hip. Though they hold jobs and meet mortgages, they think of themselves as independent spirits on a spying mission. They have agreed to impersonate teachers until they write their novels, finish their dissertations, or just save up enough money to set themselves free.

Carlton and I are the lackeys. We take coats, fetch drinks. We have done this at every party since we were small, trading on our precocity, doing a brother act. We know the moves. A big, lipsticked woman who has devoted her maidenhood to ninth-grade math calls me Mr. Right. An assistant vice principal in a Russian fur hat asks us both whether we expect to vote Democratic or Socialist. By sneaking sips I manage to get myself semi-crocked.

The reliability of the evening is derailed halfway through, however, by a half dozen of Carlton's friends. They rap on the door and I go for it, anxious as a carnival sharp to see who will step up next and swallow the illusion that I'm a kindly, sober nine-year-old child. I'm expecting callow adults and who do I find but a pack of young outlaws, big-booted and wild-haired. Carlton's girlfriend stands in front, in an outfit made up almost entirely of fringe.

"Hi, Bobby," she says confidently. She comes from New York, and is more than just locally smart.

"Hi," I say. I let them all in despite a retrograde urge to lock the door and phone the police. Three are girls, four boys. They pass me in a cloud of dope smoke and sly-eyed greeting.

What they do is invade the party. Carlton is standing on the far side of the rumpus room, picking the next album, and his girl cuts straight through the crowd to his side. She has the bones and the loose, liquid moves some people consider beautiful. She walks through that room as if she'd been sent to teach the whole party a lesson.

Carlton's face tips me off that this was planned. Our mother demands to know what's going on here. She is wearing a long dark-red dress that doesn't interfere with her shoulders. When she dresses up you can see what it is about her, or what it was. She is responsible for Carlton's beauty. I have our father's face.

Carlton does some quick talking. Though it's against our mother's better judgment, the invaders are suffered to stay. One of them, an Eddie Haskell for all his leather and hair, tells her she is looking good. She is willing to hear it.

So the outlaws, house-sanctioned, start to mingle. I work my way over to Carlton's side, the side unoccupied by his girlfriend. I would like to say something ironic and wised-up, something that will band Carlton and me against every other person in the room. I can feel the shape of the comment I have in mind but, being a tipsy nine-year-old, can't get my mouth around it. What I say is, "Shit, man."

Carlton's girl laughs at me. She considers it amusing that a little boy says "shit." I would like to tell her what I have figured out about her, but I am nine, and three-quarters gone on Tom Collinses. Even sober, I can only imagine a sharp-tongued wit.

"Hang on, Frisco," Carlton tells me. "This could turn into a real party."

I can see by the light in his eyes what is going down. He has arranged a blind date between our parents' friends and his own. It's a Woodstock move—he is plotting a future in which young and old have business together. I agree to hang on, and go to the kitchen, hoping to sneak a few knocks of gin.

There I find our father leaning up against the refrigerator. A line of butterfly-shaped magnets hovers around his head. "Are you enjoying this party?" he asks, touching his goatee. He is still getting used to being a man with a beard.

"Uh-huh."

"I am, too," he says sadly. He never meant to be a high school music teacher. The money question caught up with him.

"What do you think of this music?" he asks. Carlton has put the Stones on the turntable. Mick Jagger sings "19th Nervous Breakdown." Our father gestures in an openhanded way that takes in the room, the party, the whole house—everything the music touches.

"I like it," I say.

"So do I." He stirs his drink with his finger, and sucks on the finger.

"I *love* it," I say, too loud. Something about our father leads me to raise my voice. I want to grab handfuls of music out of the air and stuff them into my mouth.

"I'm not sure I could say I love it," he says. "I'm not sure if I could say that, no. I would say I'm friendly to its intentions. I would say that if this is the direction music is going in, I won't stand in its way."

"Uh-huh," I say. I am already anxious to get back to the party, but don't want to hurt his feelings. If he senses he's being avoided he can fall into fits of apology more terrifying than our mother's rages.

"I think I may have been too rigid with my students," our father says. "Maybe over the summer you boys could teach me a few things about the music people are listening to these days."

"Sure," I say, loudly. We spend a minute waiting for the next thing to say.

"You boys are happy, aren't you?" he asks. "Are you enjoying this party?"

"We're having a great time," I say.

"I thought you were. I am, too."

I have by this time gotten myself to within jumping distance of the door. I call out, "Well, goodbye," and dive back into the party.

Something has happened in my small absence. The party has started to roll. Call it an accident of history and the weather. Carlton's friends are on decent behavior, and our parents' friends have decided to give up some of their wine-and-folk-song propriety to see what they can learn. Carlton is dancing with a vice principal's wife. Carlton's friend Frank, with his ancient-child face and IQ in the low sixties, dances with our mother. I see that our father has followed me out of the kitchen. He positions himself at the party's edge; I jump into its center. I invite the fuchsia-lipped math teacher to dance. She is only too happy. She is big and graceful as a parade float, and I steer her effortlessly out into the middle of everything. My mother, who is known around school for Sicilian discipline, dances freely, which is news to everybody. There is no getting around her beauty.

The night rises higher and higher. A wildness sets in. Carlton throws new music on the turntable—Janis Joplin, the Doors, the Dead. The future shines for everyone, rich with the possibility of more nights exactly like this. Even our father is pressed into dancing, which he does like a flightless bird, all flapping arms and potbelly. Still, he dances. Our mother has a kiss for him.

Finally I nod out on the sofa, blissful under the drinks. I am dreaming of flight when our mother comes and touches my shoulder. I smile up into her flushed, smiling face.

"It's hours past your bedtime," she says, all velvet motherliness. I nod. I can't dispute the fact.

She keeps on nudging my shoulder. I am a moment or two apprehending the fact that she actually wants me to leave the party and go to bed. "No," I tell her.

"Yes," she smiles.

"No," I say cordially, experimentally. This new mother can dance, and flirt. Who knows what else she might allow?

"Yes." The velvet motherliness leaves her voice. She means business, business of the usual kind. I get myself out of there and no excuses this time. I am exactly nine and running from my bedtime as I'd run from death.

I run to Carlton for protection. He is laughing with his girl, a sweaty question mark of hair plastered to his forehead. I plow into him so hard he nearly goes over.

"Whoa, Frisco," he says. He takes me up under the arms and swings me a half-turn. Our mother plucks me out of his hands and sets me down, with a good farm-style hold on the back of my neck.

"Say good night, Bobby," she says. She adds, for the benefit of Carlton's girl, "He should have been in bed before this party started."

"*No*," I holler. I try to twist loose, but our mother has a grip that could crack walnuts.

Carlton's girl tosses her hair and says, "Good night, baby." She smiles a victor's smile. She smooths the stray hair off Carlton's forehead.

"*No*," I scream again. Something about the way she touches his hair. Our mother calls our father, who comes and scoops me up and starts out of the room with me, holding me like the live bomb I am. Before I go I lock eyes with Carlton. He shrugs and says, "Night, man." Our father hustles me out. I do not take it bravely. I leave flailing, too furious to cry, dribbling a slimy thread of horrible-child's spittle.

Later I lie alone on my narrow bed, feeling the music hum in the coiled springs. Life is cracking open right there in our house. People are changing. By tomorrow, no one will be quite the same. How can they let me miss it? I dream up revenge against our parents, and worse for Carlton. He is the one who could have saved me. He could have banded with me against them. What I can't forgive is his shrug, his mild-eyed "Night, man." He has joined the adults. He has made himself bigger, and taken size from me. As the Doors thump "Strange Days," I hope something awful happens to him. I say so to myself.

Around midnight, dim-witted Frank announces he has seen a flying saucer hovering over the back yard. I can hear his deep, excited voice all the way in my room. He says it's like a blinking, luminous cloud. I hear half the party struggling out through the sliding glass door in a disorganized, whooping knot. By that time everyone is so delirious a flying saucer would be just what was expected. That much celebration would logically attract an answering happiness from across the stars.

I get out of bed and sneak down the hall. I will not miss alien visitors for anyone, not even at the cost of our mother's wrath or our father's disappointment. I stop at the end of the hallway, though, embarrassed to be in pajamas. If there really are aliens, they will think I'm the lowest member of the house. While I hesitate over whether to go back to my room to change, people start coming back inside, talking about a trick of the mist and an airplane. People resume their dancing.

Carlton must have jumped the back fence. He must have wanted to be there alone, singular, in case they decided to take somebody with them. A few nights later I will go out and stand where he would have been standing. On the far side of the gully, now a river swollen with melted snow, the cemetery will gleam like a lost city. The moon will be full. I will hang around just as Carlton must have, hypnotized by the silver light on the stones, the white angel raising her arms up across the river.

According to our parents the mystery is why he ran back to the house full tilt. Something in the graveyard may have scared him, he may have needed to break its spell, but I think it's more likely that when he came back to himself he just couldn't wait to get back to the music and the people, the noisy disorder of continuing life.

Somebody has shut the sliding glass door. Carlton's girlfriend looks lazily out, touching base with her own reflection. I look, too. Carlton is running toward the house. I hesitate. Then I figure he can bump his nose. It will be a good joke on him. I let him keep coming. His girlfriend sees him through her own reflection, starts to scream a warning just as Carlton hits the glass.

It is an explosion. Triangles of glass fly brightly through the room. I think for him it must be more surprising than painful, like hitting water from a great height. He stands blinking for a moment. The whole party stops, stares, getting its bearings. Bob Dylan sings "Just Like a Woman." Carlton reaches up curiously to take out the shard of glass that is stuck in his neck, and that is when the blood starts. It shoots out of him. Our mother screams. Carlton steps forward into his girlfriend's arms and the two of them fall together. Our mother throws herself down on top of him and the girl. People shout their accident wisdom. Don't lift him. Call an ambulance. I watch from the hallway. Carlton's blood spurts, soaking into the carpet, spattering people's clothes. Our mother and father both try to plug the wound with their hands, but the blood just shoots between their fingers. Carlton looks more puzzled than anything, as if he can't quite follow this turn of events. "It's all right," our father tells him, trying to stop the blood. "It's all right, just don't move, it's all right." Carlton nods, and holds our father's hand. His eyes take on an astonished light. Our mother screams, "Is anybody *doing* anything?" What comes out of Carlton grows darker, almost black. I watch. Our father tries to get a hold on Carlton's neck while Carlton keeps trying to take his hand. Our mother's hair is matted with blood. It runs down her face. Carlton's girl holds him to her breasts, touches his hair, whispers in his ear.

He is gone by the time the ambulance gets there. You can see the life drain out of him. When his face goes slack our mother wails. A part of her flies wailing through the house, where it will wail and rage forever. I feel our mother pass through me on her way out. She covers Carlton's body with her own.

He is buried in the cemetery out back. Years have passed—we are living in the future, and it's turned out differently from what we'd planned. Our mother has established her life of separateness behind the guest-room door. Our father mutters his greetings to the door as he passes.

One April night, almost a year to the day after Carlton's accident, I hear cautious footsteps shuffling across the living-room floor after midnight. I run out eagerly, thinking of ghosts, but find only our father in moth-colored pajamas. He looks unsteadily at the dark air in front of him.

"Hi, Dad," I say from the doorway.

He looks in my direction. "Yes?"

"It's me. Bobby."

"Oh, Bobby," he says. "What are you doing up, young man?"

"Nothing," I tell him. "Dad?"

"Yes, son."

"Maybe you better come back to bed. Okay?"

"Maybe I had," he says. "I just came out here for a drink of water, but I seem to have gotten turned around in the darkness. Yes, maybe I better had."

I take his hand and lead him down the hall to his room. The grandfather clock chimes the quarter hour.

"Sorry," our father says.

I get him into bed. "There," I say. "Okay?"

"Perfect. Could not be better."

"Okay. Good night."

"Good night. Bobby?"

"Uh-huh?"

"Why don't you stay a minute?" he says. "We could have ourselves a talk, you and me. How would that be?"

"Okay," I say. I sit on the edge of his mattress. His bedside clock ticks off the minutes.

I can hear the low rasp of his breathing. Around our house, the Ohio night chirps and buzzes. The small gray finger of Carlton's stone pokes up among the others, within sight of the angel's blank white eyes. Above us, airplanes and satellites sparkle. People are flying even now toward New York or California, to take up lives of risk and invention.

I stay until our father has worked his way into a muttering sleep.

Carlton's girlfriend moved to Denver with her family a month before. I never learned what it was she'd whispered to him. Though she'd kept her head admirably during the accident, she lost her head afterward. She cried so hard at the funeral that she had to be taken away by her mother—an older, redder-haired version of her. She started seeing a psychiatrist three times a week. Everyone, including my parents, talked about how hard it was for her, to have held a dying boy in her arms at that age. I'm grateful to her for holding my brother while he died, but I never once heard her mention the fact that though she had been through something terrible, at least she was still alive and going places. At least she had protected herself by trying to warn him. I can appreciate the intricacies of her pain. But as long as she was in Cleveland, I could never look her straight in the face. I couldn't talk about the wounds she suffered. I can't even write her name.

F. SCOTT FITZGERALD
(1896—1940)

Born in St. Paul, Minnesota, F. Scott Fitzgerald was related on his father's side to the author of the "Star-Spangled Banner." He was able to attend St. Paul Academy, the Newman School in Hackensack, New Jersey, and Princeton University because of gifts from his mother's wealthy relatives. He left Princeton without earning a degree, partly because he expended so much time writing for the College's *Nassau Literary Magazine,* the Triangle Club, and *The Tiger* that his grades suffered. In 1917, he enlisted in the army and while stationed at Camp Sheridan in Montgomery, Alabama, he met Zelda Sayre, a beautiful and lively debutante. During the time that they were engaged to be married, Fitzgerald feared he would lose Zelda because he was not wealthy enough to provide the kind of lifestyle she demanded. Upon publication of his first novel, *This Side of Paradise* (1920), Zelda traveled to New York, where she and Scott were married in the rectory of St. Patrick's Cathedral. During the next decade, the era Fitzgerald named "The Jazz Age," the couple lived at various times in New York and Paris and on the Riviera. His stories of flappers and romantic young men commanded high prices at magazines, such as the *Saturday Evening Post* and *Smart Set,* but he was often in debt because of the extravagant way of life Zelda and he adopted. He published *The Beautiful and Damned* (1922), *The Great Gatsby* (1925), and *Tender Is the Night* (1934), and left the unfinished manuscript of *The Last Tycoon,* which was edited by Edmund Wilson and published in 1941. Among Fitzgerald's story collections are: *Flappers and Philosophers* (1921), *Tales of the Jazz Age* (1922), *All the Sad Young Men* (1926), and *Taps at Reveille* (1935).

Bernice Bobs Her Hair

After dark on Saturday night one could stand on the first tee of the golf-course and see the country-club windows as a yellow expanse over a very black and wavy ocean. The waves of this ocean, so to speak, were the heads of many curious caddies, a few of the more ingenious chauffeurs, the golf professional's deaf sister—and there were usually several stray, diffident waves who might have rolled inside had they so desired. This was the gallery.

The balcony was inside. It consisted of the circle of wicker chairs that lined the wall of the combination clubroom and ballroom. At these Saturday-night dances it was largely feminine; a great babel of middle-aged ladies with sharp eyes and icy hearts behind lorgnettes and large bosoms. The main function of the balcony was critical. It occasionally showed grudging admiration, but never approval, for it is well known among ladies over thirty-five that when the younger set dance in the summer-time it is with the very worst intentions in the world, and if they are not bombarded with stony eyes stray couples will dance weird barbaric interludes in the corners, and the more popular, more dangerous, girls will sometimes be kissed in the parked limousines of unsuspecting dowagers.

But, after all, this critical circle is not close enough to the stage to see the actors' faces and catch the subtler byplay. It can only frown and lean, ask questions and make satisfactory deductions from its set of postulates, such as the one which states that every young man with a large income leads the life of a hunted partridge. It never really appreciates the drama of the shifting, semicruel world of adolescence. No; boxes, orchestra-circle, principals, and chorus are represented by the medley of faces and voices that sway to the plaintive African rhythm of Dyer's dance orchestra.

From sixteen-year-old Otis Ormonde, who has two more years at Hill School, to G. Reece Stoddard, over whose bureau at home hangs a Harvard law diploma; from little Madeleine Hogue, whose hair still feels strange and uncomfortable on top of her head, to Bessie MacRae, who has been the life of the party a little too long—more than ten years—the medley is not only the centre of the stage but contains the only people capable of getting an unobstructed view of it.

With a flourish and a bang the music stops. The couples exchange artificial, effort-less smiles, facetiously repeat "*la*-de-*da-da* dum-*dum*," and then the clatter of young feminine voices soars over the burst of clapping.

A few disappointed stags caught in midfloor as they had been about to cut in sub-sided listlessly back to the walls, because this was not like the riotous Christmas dances— these summer hops were considered just pleasantly warm and exciting, where even the younger marrieds rose and performed ancient waltzes and terrifying fox trots to the tolerant amusement of their younger brothers and sisters.

Warren McIntyre, who casually attended Yale, being one of the unfortunate stags, felt in his dinner-coat pocket for a cigarette and strolled out onto the wide, semidark ve-randa, where couples were scattered at tables, filling the lantern-hung night with vague words and hazy laughter. He nodded here and there at the less absorbed and as he passed each couple some half-forgotten fragment of a story played in his mind, for it was not a large city and every one was Who's Who to every one else's past. There, for example, were Jim Strain and Ethel Demorest, who had been privately engaged for three years. Every one knew that as soon as Jim managed to hold a job for more than two months she would marry him. Yet how bored they both looked, and how wearily Ethel regarded Jim sometimes, as if she wondered why she had trained the vines of her affection on such a wind-shaken poplar.

Warren was nineteen and rather pitying with those of his friends who hadn't gone East to college. But, like most boys, he bragged tremendously about the girls of his city when he was away from it. There was Genevieve Ormonde, who regularly made the rounds of dances, house-parties, and football games at Princeton, Yale, Williams, and Cornell; there was black-eyed Roberta Dillon, who was quite as famous to her own generation as Hiram Johnson or Ty Cobb; and, of course, there was Marjorie Harvey, who besides having a fairylike face and a dazzling, bewildering tongue was already justly celebrated for having turned five cart-wheels in succession during the past pump-and-slipper dance at New Haven.

Warren, who had grown up across the street from Marjorie, had long been "crazy about her." Sometimes she seemed to reciprocate his feeling with a faint gratitude, but she had tried him by her infallible test and informed him gravely that she did not love him. Her test was that when she was away from him she forgot him and had affairs with other boys. Warren found this discouraging, especially as Marjorie had been making little trips all summer, and for the first two or three days after each arrival home he saw great heaps of mail on the Harveys' hall table addressed to her in various masculine handwritings. To make matters worse, all during the month of August she had been visited by her cousin Bernice from Eau Claire, and it seemed impossible to see her alone. It was always necessary to hunt round and find some one to take care of Bernice. As August waned this was becoming more and more difficult.

Much as Warren worshipped Marjorie, he had to admit that Cousin Bernice was sorta dopeless. She was pretty, with dark hair and high color, but she was no fun on a party. Every Saturday night he danced a long arduous duty dance with her to please Marjorie, but he had never been anything but bored in her company.

"Warren"—a soft voice at his elbow broke in upon his thoughts, and he turned to see Marjorie, flushed and radiant as usual. She laid a hand on his shoulder and a glow settled almost imperceptibly over him.

"Warren," she whispered, "do something for me—dance with Bernice. She's been stuck with little Otis Ormonde for almost an hour."

Warren's glow faded.

"Why—sure," he answered half-heartedly.

"You don't mind, do you? I'll see that you don't get stuck."

"'Sall right."

Marjorie smiled—that smile that was thanks enough.

"You're an angel, and I'm obliged loads."

With a sigh the angel glanced round the veranda, but Bernice and Otis were not in sight. He wandered back inside, and there in front of the women's dressing-room he found Otis in the centre of a group of young men who were convulsed with laughter. Otis was brandishing a piece of timber he had picked up, and discoursing volubly.

"She's gone in to fix her hair," he announced wildly. "I'm waiting to dance another hour with her."

Their laughter was renewed.

"Why don't some of you cut in?" cried Otis resentfully. "She likes more variety."

"Why, Otis," suggested a friend, "you've just barely got used to her."

"Why the two-by-four, Otis?" inquired Warren, smiling.

"The two-by-four? Oh, this? This is a club. When she comes out I'll hit her on the head and knock her in again."

Warren collapsed on a settee and howled with glee.

"Never mind, Otis," he articulated finally. "I'm relieving you this time."

Otis simulated a sudden fainting attack and handed the stick to Warren.

"If you need it, old man," he said hoarsely.

No matter how beautiful or brilliant a girl may be, the reputation of not being frequently cut in on makes her position at a dance unfortunate. Perhaps boys prefer her company to that of the butterflies with whom they dance a dozen times an evening, but youth in this jazz-nourished generation is temperamentally restless, and the idea of fox-trotting more than one full fox trot with the same girl is distasteful, not to say odious. When it comes to several dances and the intermissions between she can be quite sure that a young man, once relieved, will never tread on her wayward toes again.

Warren danced the next full dance with Bernice, and finally, thankful for the intermission, he led her to a table on the veranda. There was a moment's silence while she did unimpressive things with her fan.

"It's hotter here than in Eau Claire," she said.

Warren stifled a sigh and nodded. It might be for all he knew or cared. He wondered idly whether she was a poor conversationalist because she got no attention or got no attention because she was a poor conversationalist.

"You going to be here much longer?" he asked, and then turned rather red. She might suspect his reasons for asking.

"Another week," she answered, and stared at him as if to lunge at his next remark when it left his lips.

Warren fidgeted. Then with a sudden charitable impulse he decided to try part of his line on her. He turned and looked at her eyes.

"You've got an awfully kissable mouth," he began quietly.

This was a remark that he sometimes made to girls at college proms when they were talking in just such half dark as this. Bernice distinctly jumped. She turned an ungraceful red and became clumsy with her fan. No one had ever made such a remark to her before.

"Fresh!"—the word had slipped out before she realized it, and she bit her lip. Too late she decided to be amused, and offered him a flustered smile.

Warren was annoyed. Though not accustomed to have that remark taken seriously, still it usually provoked a laugh or a paragraph of sentimental banter. And he hated to be called fresh, except in a joking way. His charitable impulse died and he switched the topic.

"Jim Strain and Ethel Demorest sitting out as usual," he commented.

This was more in Bernice's line, but a faint regret mingled with her relief as the subject changed. Men did not talk to her about kissable mouths, but she knew that they talked in some such way to other girls.

"Oh, yes," she said, and laughed. "I hear they've been mooning round for years without a red penny. Isn't it silly?"

Warren's disgust increased. Jim Strain was a close friend of his brother's, and anyway he considered it bad form to sneer at people for not having money. But Bernice had had no intention of sneering. She was merely nervous.

II

When Marjorie and Bernice reached home at half after midnight they said good night at the top of the stairs. Though cousins, they were not intimates. As a matter of fact Marjorie had no female intimates—she considered girls stupid. Bernice on the contrary all through this parent-arranged visit had rather longed to exchange those confidences flavored with giggles and tears that she considered an indispensable factor in all feminine intercourse. But in this respect she found Marjorie rather cold; felt somehow the same difficulty in talking to her that she had in talking to men. Marjorie never giggled, was never frightened, seldom embarrassed, and in fact had very few of the qualities which Bernice considered appropriately and blessedly feminine.

As Bernice busied herself with tooth-brush and paste this night she wondered for the hundredth time why she never had any attention when she was away from home. That her family were the wealthiest in Eau Claire; that her mother entertained tremendously, gave little dinners for her daughter before all dances and bought her a car of her own to drive round in, never occurred to her as factors in her home-town social success. Like most girls she had been brought up on the warm milk prepared by Annie Fellows Johnston and on novels in which the female was beloved because of certain mysterious womanly qualities, always mentioned but never displayed.

Bernice felt a vague pain that she was not at present engaged in being popular. She did not know that had it not been for Marjorie's campaigning she would have danced the entire evening with one man; but she knew that even in Eau Claire other girls with less position and less pulchritude were given a much bigger rush. She attributed this to something subtly unscrupulous in those girls. It had never worried her, and if it had her mother would have assured her that the other girls cheapened themselves and that men really respected girls like Bernice.

She turned out the light in her bathroom, and on an impulse decided to go in and chat for a moment with her aunt Josephine, whose light was still on. Her soft slippers bore her noiselessly down the carpeted hall, but hearing voices inside she stopped near the partly opened door. Then she caught her own name, and without any definite intention of eavesdropping lingered—and the thread of the conversation going on inside pierced her consciousness sharply as if it had been drawn through with a needle.

"She's absolutely hopeless!" It was Marjorie's voice. "Oh, I know what you're going to say! So many people have told you how pretty and sweet she is, and how she can cook! What of it? She has a bum time. Men don't like her."

"What's a little cheap popularity?"

Mrs. Harvey sounded annoyed.

"It's everything when you're eighteen," said Marjorie emphatically. "I've done my best. I've been polite and I've made men dance with her, but they just won't stand being bored. When I think of that gorgeous coloring wasted on such a ninny, and think what Martha Carey could do with it—oh!"

"There's no courtesy these days."

Mrs. Harvey's voice implied that modern situations were too much for her.

When she was a girl all young ladies who belonged to nice families had glorious times.

"Well," said Marjorie, "no girl can permanently bolster up a lame-duck visitor, because these days it's every girl for herself. I've even tried to drop her hints about clothes and things, and she's been furious—given me the funniest looks. She's sensitive enough to know she's not getting away with much, but I'll bet she consoles herself by thinking that she's very virtuous and that I'm too gay and fickle and will come to a bad end. All unpopular girls think that way. Sour grapes! Sarah Hopkins refers to Genevieve and Roberta and me as gardenia girls! I'll bet she'd give ten years of her life and her European education to be a gardenia girl and have three or four men in love with her and be cut in on every few feet at dances."

"It seems to me," interrupted Mrs. Harvey rather wearily, "that you ought to be able to do something for Bernice. I know she's not very vivacious."

Marjorie groaned.

"Vivacious! Good grief! I've never heard her say anything to a boy except that it's hot or the floor's crowded or that she's going to school in New York next year. Sometimes she asks them what kind of car they have and tells them the kind she has. Thrilling!"

There was a short silence, and then Mrs. Harvey took up her refrain:

"All I know is that other girls not half so sweet and attractive get partners. Martha Carey, for instance, is stout and loud, and her mother is distinctly common. Roberta Dillon is so thin this year that she looks as though Arizona were the place for her. She's dancing herself to death."

"But, mother," objected Marjorie impatiently, "Martha is cheerful and awfully witty and an awfully slick girl, and Roberta's a marvellous dancer. She's been popular for ages!"

Mrs. Harvey yawned.

"I think it's that crazy Indian blood in Bernice," continued Marjorie. "Maybe she's a reversion to type. Indian women all just sat round and never said anything."

"Go to bed, you silly child," laughed Mrs. Harvey. "I wouldn't have told you that if I'd thought you were going to remember it. And I think most of your ideas are perfectly idiotic," she finished sleepily.

There was another silence, while Marjorie considered whether or not convincing her mother was worth the trouble. People over forty can seldom be permanently convinced of anything. At eighteen our convictions are hills from which we look; at forty-five they are caves in which we hide.

Having decided this, Marjorie said good night. When she came out into the hall it was quite empty.

III

While Marjorie was breakfasting late next day Bernice came into the room with a rather formal good morning, sat down opposite, stared intently over and slightly moistened her lips.

"What's on your mind?" inquired Marjorie, rather puzzled.

Bernice paused before she threw her hand-grenade.

"I heard what you said about me to your mother last night."

Marjorie was startled, but she showed only a faintly heightened color and her voice was quite even when she spoke.

"Where were you?"

"In the hall. I didn't mean to listen—at first."

After an involuntary look of contempt Marjorie dropped her eyes and became very interested in balancing a stray cornflake on her finger.

"I guess I'd better go back to Eau Claire—if I'm such a nuisance." Bernice's lower lip was trembling violently and she continued on a wavering note: "I've tried to be nice, and—and I've been first neglected and then insulted. No one ever visited me and got such treatment."

Marjorie was silent.

"But I'm in the way, I see. I'm a drag on you. Your friends don't like me." She paused, and then remembered another one of her grievances. "Of course I was furious last week when you tried to hint to me that that dress was unbecoming. Don't you think I know how to dress myself?"

"No," murmured Marjorie less than half-aloud.

"What?"

"I didn't hint anything," said Marjorie succinctly. "I said, as I remember, that it was better to wear a becoming dress three times straight than to alternate it with two frights."

"Do you think that was a very nice thing to say?"

"I wasn't trying to be nice." Then after a pause: "When do you want to go?"

Bernice drew in her breath sharply.

"Oh!" It was a little half-cry.

Marjorie looked up in surprise.

"Didn't you say you were going?"

"Yes, but——"

"Oh, you were only bluffing!"

They stared at each other across the breakfast-table for a moment. Misty waves were passing before Bernice's eyes, while Marjorie's face wore that rather hard expression that she used when slightly intoxicated undergraduates were making love to her.

"So you were bluffing," she repeated as if it were what she might have expected.

Bernice admitted it by bursting into tears. Marjorie's eyes showed boredom.

"You're my cousin," sobbed Bernice. "I'm v-v-visiting you. I was to stay a month, and if I go home my mother will know and she'll wah-wonder——"

Marjorie waited until the shower of broken words collapsed into little sniffles.

"I'll give you my month's allowance," she said coldly, "and you can spend this last week anywhere you want. There's a very nice hotel——"

Bernice's sobs rose to a flute note, and rising of a sudden she fled from the room.

An hour later, while Marjorie was in the library absorbed in composing one of those non-committal, marvellously elusive letters that only a young girl can write, Bernice reappeared, very red-eyed and consciously calm. She cast no glance at Marjorie but took a book at random from the shelf and sat down as if to read. Marjorie seemed absorbed in her letter and continued writing. When the clock showed noon Bernice closed her book with a snap.

"I suppose I'd better get my railroad ticket."

This was not the beginning of the speech she had rehearsed upstairs, but as Marjorie was not getting her cues—wasn't urging her to be reasonable; it's all a mistake— it was the best opening she could muster.

"Just wait till I finish this letter," said Marjorie without looking round. "I want to get it off in the next mail."

After another minute, during which her pen scratched busily, she turned round and relaxed with an air of "at your service." Again Bernice had to speak.

"Do you want me to go home?"

"Well," said Marjorie, considering, "I suppose if you're not having a good time you'd better go. No use being miserable."

"Don't you think common kindness——"

"Oh, please don't quote 'Little Women'!" cried Marjorie impatiently. "That's out of style."

"You think so?"

"Heavens, yes! What modern girl could live like those inane females?"

"They were the models for our mothers."

Marjorie laughed.

"Yes, they were—not! Besides, our mothers were all very well in their way, but they know very little about their daughters' problems."

Bernice drew herself up.

"Please don't talk about my mother."

Marjorie laughed.

"I don't think I mentioned her."

Bernice felt that she was being led away from her subject.

"Do you think you've treated me very well?"

"I've done my best. You're rather hard material to work with."

The lids of Bernice's eyes reddened.

"I think you're hard and selfish, and you haven't a feminine quality in you."

"Oh, my Lord!" cried Marjorie in desperation. "You little nut! Girls like you are responsible for all the tiresome colorless marriages; all those ghastly inefficiencies that pass as feminine qualities. What a blow it must be when a man with imagination marries the beautiful bundle of clothes that he's been building ideals round, and finds that she's just a weak, whining, cowardly mass of affectations!"

Bernice's mouth had slipped half open.

"The womanly woman!" continued Marjorie. "Her whole early life is occupied in whining criticisms of girls like me who really do have a good time."

Bernice's jaw descended farther as Marjorie's voice rose.

"There's some excuse for an ugly girl whining. If I'd been irretrievably ugly I'd never have forgiven my parents for bringing me into the world. But you're starting life without any handicap—" Marjorie's little fist clinched. "If you expect me to weep with you you'll be disappointed. Go or stay, just as you like." And picking up her letters she left the room.

Bernice claimed a headache and failed to appear at luncheon. They had a matinée date for the afternoon, but the headache persisting, Marjorie made explanations to a not very downcast boy. But when she returned late in the afternoon she found Bernice with a strangely set face waiting for her in her bedroom.

"I've decided," began Bernice without preliminaries, "that maybe you're right about things—possibly not. But if you'll tell me why your friends aren't—aren't interested in me I'll see if I can do what you want me to."

Marjorie was at the mirror shaking down her hair.

"Do you mean it?"

"Yes."

"Without reservations? Will you do exactly what I say?"

"Well, I——"

"Well nothing! Will you do exactly as I say?"

"If they're sensible things."

"They're not! You're no case for sensible things."

"Are you going to make—to recommend—"

"Yes, everything. If I tell you to take boxing lessons you'll have to do it. Write home and tell your mother you're going to stay another two weeks."

"If you'll tell me——"

"All right—I'll just give you a few examples now. First, you have no ease of manner. Why? Because you're never sure about your personal appearance. When a girl feels that she's perfectly groomed and dressed she can forget that part of her. That's charm. The more parts of yourself you can afford to forget the more charm you have."

"Don't I look all right?"

"No; for instance, you never take care of your eyebrows. They're black and lustrous, but by leaving them straggly they're a blemish. They'd be beautiful if you'd take care of them in one-tenth the time you take doing nothing. You're going to brush them so that they'll grow straight."

Bernice raised the brows in question.

"Do you mean to say that men notice eyebrows?"

"Yes—subconsciously. And when you go home you ought to have your teeth straightened a little. It's almost imperceptible, still——"

"But I thought," interrupted Bernice in bewilderment, "that you despised little dainty feminine things like that."

"I hate dainty minds," answered Marjorie. "But a girl has to be dainty in person. If she looks like a million dollars she can talk about Russia, ping-pong, or the League of Nations and get away with it."

"What else?"

"Oh, I'm just beginning! There's your dancing."

"Don't I dance all right?"

"No, you don't—you lean on a man; yes, you do—ever so slightly. I noticed it when we were dancing together yesterday. And you dance standing up straight instead of bending over a little. Probably some old lady on the sideline once told you that you looked so dignified that way. But except with a very small girl it's much harder on the man, and he's the one that counts."

"Go on." Bernice's brain was reeling.

"Well, you've got to learn to be nice to men who are sad birds. You look as if you'd been insulted whenever you're thrown with any except the most popular boys. Why, Bernice, I'm cut in on every few feet—and who does most of it? Why, those very sad birds. No girl can afford to neglect them. They're the big part of any crowd. Young boys too shy to talk are the very best conversational practice. Clumsy boys are the best dancing practice. If you can follow them and yet look graceful you can follow a baby tank across a barb-wire sky-scraper."

Bernice sighed profoundly, but Marjorie was not through.

"If you go to a dance and really amuse, say, three sad birds that dance with you; if you talk so well to them that they forget they're stuck with you, you've done something. They'll come back next time, and gradually so many sad birds will dance with you that the attractive boys will see there's no danger of being stuck—then they'll dance with you."

"Yes," agreed Bernice faintly. "I think I begin to see."

"And finally," concluded Marjorie, "poise and charm will just come. You'll wake up some morning knowing you've attained it, and men will know it too."

Bernice rose.

"It's been awfully kind of you—but nobody's ever talked to me like this before, and I feel sort of startled."

Marjorie made no answer but gazed pensively at her own image in the mirror.

"You're a peach to help me," continued Bernice.

Still Marjorie did not answer, and Bernice thought she had seemed too grateful.

"I know you don't like sentiment," she said timidly.

Marjorie turned to her quickly.

"Oh, I wasn't thinking about that. I was considering whether we hadn't better bob your hair."

Bernice collapsed backward upon the bed.

IV

On the following Wednesday evening there was a dinner-dance at the country club. When the guests strolled in Bernice found her place-card with a slight feeling of irritation. Though at her right sat G. Reece Stoddard, a most desirable and distinguished young bachelor, the all-important left held only Charley Paulson. Charley lacked height, beauty, and social shrewdness, and in her new enlightenment Bernice decided that his only qualification to be her partner was that he had never been stuck with her. But this feeling of irritation left with the last of the soup-plates, and Marjorie's specific instruction came to her. Swallowing her pride she turned to Charley Paulson and plunged.

"Do you think I ought to bob my hair, Mr. Charley Paulson?"

Charley looked up in surprise.

"Why?"

"Because I'm considering it. It's such a sure and easy way of attracting attention."

Charley smiled pleasantly. He could not know this had been rehearsed. He replied that he didn't know much about bobbed hair. But Bernice was there to tell him.

"I want to be a society vampire, you see," she announced coolly, and went on to inform him that bobbed hair was the necessary prelude. She added that she wanted to ask his advice, because she had heard he was so critical about girls.

Charley, who knew as much about the psychology of women as he did of the mental states of Buddhist contemplatives, felt vaguely flattered.

"So I've decided," she continued, her voice rising slightly, "that early next week I'm going down to the Sevier Hotel barber-shop, sit in the first chair, and get my hair bobbed." She faltered, noticing that the people near her had paused in their conversation and were listening; but after a confused second Marjorie's coaching told, and she finished her paragraph to the vicinity at large. "Of course I'm charging admission, but if you'll all come down and encourage me I'll issue passes for the inside seats."

There was a ripple of appreciative laughter, and under cover of it G. Reece Stoddard leaned over quickly and said close to her ear: "I'll take a box right now."

She met his eyes and smiled as if he had said something surpassingly brilliant.

"Do you believe in bobbed hair?" asked G. Reece in the same undertone.

"I think it's unmoral," affirmed Bernice gravely. "But, of course, you've either got to amuse people or feed 'em or shock 'em." Marjorie had culled this from Oscar Wilde. It was greeted with a ripple of laughter from the men and a series of quick, intent looks from the girls. And then as though she had said nothing of wit or moment Bernice turned again to Charley and spoke confidentially in his ear.

"I want to ask you your opinion of several people. I imagine you're a wonderful judge of character."

Charley thrilled faintly—paid her a subtle compliment by overturning her water.

Two hours later, while Warren McIntyre was standing passively in the stag line abstractedly watching the dancers and wondering whither and with whom Marjorie had disappeared, an unrelated perception began to creep slowly upon him—a perception that Bernice, cousin to Marjorie, had been cut in on several times in the past five minutes. He closed his eyes, opened them and looked again. Several minutes back she had been dancing with a visiting boy, a matter easily accounted for; a visiting boy would know no better. But now she was dancing with some one else, and there was Charley Paulson headed for her with enthusiastic determination in his eye. Funny—Charley seldom danced with more than three girls an evening.

Warren was distinctly surprised when—the exchange having been effected—the man relieved proved to be none other than G. Reece Stoddard himself. And G. Reece seemed not at all jubilant at being relieved. Next time Bernice danced near, Warren regarded her intently. Yes, she was pretty, distinctly pretty; and to-night her face seemed really vivacious. She had that look that no woman, however histrionically proficient, can successfully counterfeit—she looked as if she were having a good time. He liked the way she had her hair arranged, wondered if it was brilliantine that made it glisten so. And that dress was becoming—a dark red that set off her shadowy eyes and high coloring. He remembered that he had thought her pretty when she first came to town, before he had realized that she was dull. Too bad she was dull—dull girls unbearable—certainly pretty though.

His thoughts zigzagged back to Marjorie. This disappearance would be like other disappearances. When she reappeared he would demand where she had been—would be told emphatically that it was none of his business. What a pity she was so sure of him! She basked in the knowledge that no other girl in town interested him; she defied him to fall in love with Genevieve or Roberta.

Warren sighed. The way to Marjorie's affections was a labyrinth indeed. He looked up. Bernice was again dancing with the visiting boy. Half unconsciously he took a step out from the stag line in her direction, and hesitated. Then he said to himself that it was charity. He walked toward her—collided suddenly with G. Reece Stoddard.

"Pardon me," said Warren.

But G. Reece had not stopped to apologize. He had again cut in on Bernice.

That night at one o'clock Marjorie, with one hand on the electric-light switch in the hall, turned to take a last look at Bernice's sparkling eyes.

"So it worked?"

"Oh, Marjorie, yes!" cried Bernice.

"I saw you were having a gay time."

"I did! The only trouble was that about midnight I ran short of talk. I had to repeat myself—with different men of course. I hope they won't compare notes."

"Men don't," said Marjorie, yawning, "and it wouldn't matter if they did—they'd think you were even trickier."

She snapped out the light, and as they started up the stairs Bernice grasped the banister thankfully. For the first time in her life she had been danced tired.

"You see," said Marjorie at the top of the stairs, "one man sees another man cut in and he thinks there must be something there. Well, we'll fix up some new stuff to-morrow. Good night."

"Good night."

As Bernice took down her hair she passed the evening before her in review. She had followed instructions exactly. Even when Charley Paulson cut in for the eighth time she had simulated delight and had apparently been both interested and flattered. She had not talked about the weather or Eau Claire or automobiles or her school, but had confined her conversation to me, you, and us.

But a few minutes before she fell asleep a rebellious thought was churning drowsily in her brain—after all, it was she who had done it. Marjorie, to be sure, had given her

her conversation, but then Marjorie got much of her conversation out of things she read. Bernice had bought the red dress, though she had never valued it highly before Marjorie dug it out of her trunk—and her own voice had said the words, her own lips had smiled, her own feet had danced. Marjorie nice girl—vain, though—nice evening—nice boys—like Warren—Warren—Warren—what's-his-name—Warren——

She fell asleep.

V

To Bernice the next week was a revelation. With the feeling that people really enjoyed looking at her and listening to her came the foundation of self-confidence. Of course there were numerous mistakes at first. She did not know, for instance, that Draycott Deyo was studying for the ministry; she was unaware that he had cut in on her because he thought she was a quiet, reserved girl. Had she known these things she would not have treated him to the line which began "Hello, Shell Shock!" and continued with the bathtub story—"It takes a frightful lot of energy to fix my hair in the summer—there's so much of it—so I always fix it first and powder my face and put on my hat; then I get into the bathtub, and dress afterward. Don't you think that's the best plan?"

Though Draycott Deyo was in the throes of difficulties concerning baptism by immersion and might possibly have seen a connection, it must be admitted that he did not. He considered feminine bathing an immoral subject, and gave her some of his ideas on the depravity of modern society.

But to offset that unfortunate occurrence Bernice had several signal successes to her credit. Little Otis Ormonde pleaded off from a trip East and elected instead to follow her with a puppy-like devotion, to the amusement of his crowd and to the irritation of G. Reece Stoddard, several of whose afternoon calls Otis completely ruined by the disgusting tenderness of the glances he bent on Bernice. He even told her the story of the two-by-four and the dressing-room to show her how frightfully mistaken he and every one else had been in their first judgment of her. Bernice laughed off that incident with a slight sinking sensation.

Of all Bernice's conversation perhaps the best known and most universally approved was the line about the bobbing of her hair.

"Oh, Bernice, when you goin' to get the hair bobbed?"

"Day after to-morrow maybe," she would reply, laughing. "Will you come and see me? Because I'm counting on you, you know."

"Will we? You know! But you better hurry up."

Bernice, whose tonsorial intentions were strictly dishonorable, would laugh again.

"Pretty soon now. You'd be surprised."

But perhaps the most significant symbol of her success was the gray car of the hypercritical Warren McIntyre, parked daily in front of the Harvey house. At first the parlor-maid was distinctly startled when he asked for Bernice instead of Marjorie; after a week of it she told the cook that Miss Bernice had gotta holda Miss Marjorie's best fella.

And Miss Bernice had. Perhaps it began with Warren's desire to rouse jealousy in Marjorie; perhaps it was the familiar though unrecognized strain of Marjorie in Bernice's conversation; perhaps it was both of these and something of sincere attraction besides. But somehow the collective mind of the younger set knew within a week that Marjorie's most reliable beau had made an amazing face-about and was giving an indisputable rush to Marjorie's guest. The question of the moment was how Marjorie would take it. Warren called Bernice on the 'phone twice a day, sent her notes, and they were frequently seen together in his roadster, obviously engrossed in one of those tense, significant conversations as to whether or not he was sincere.

Marjorie on being twitted only laughed. She said she was mighty glad that Warren had at last found some one who appreciated him. So the younger set laughed, too, and guessed that Marjorie didn't care and let it go at that.

One afternoon when there were only three days left of her visit Bernice was waiting in the hall for Warren, with whom she was going to a bridge party. She was in rather a blissful mood, and when Marjorie—also bound for the party—appeared beside her and began casually to adjust her hat in the mirror, Bernice was utterly unprepared for anything in the nature of a clash. Marjorie did her work very coldly and succinctly in three sentences.

"You may as well get Warren out of your head," she said coldly.

"What?" Bernice was utterly astounded.

"You may as well stop making a fool of yourself over Warren McIntyre. He doesn't care a snap of his fingers about you."

For a tense moment they regarded each other—Marjorie scornful, aloof; Bernice astounded, half-angry, half-afraid. Then two cars drove up in front of the house and there was a riotous honking. Both of them gasped faintly, turned, and side by side hurried out.

All through the bridge party Bernice strove in vain to master a rising uneasiness. She had offended Marjorie, the sphinx of sphinxes. With the most wholesome and innocent intentions in the world she had stolen Marjorie's property. She felt suddenly and horribly guilty. After the bridge game, when they sat in an informal circle and the conversation became general, the storm gradually broke. Little Otis Ormonde inadvertently precipitated it.

"When you going back to kindergarten, Otis?" some one had asked.

"Me? Day Bernice gets her hair bobbed."

"Then your education's over," said Marjorie quickly. "That's only a bluff of hers. I should think you'd have realized."

"That a fact?" demanded Otis, giving Bernice a reproachful glance.

Bernice's ears burned as she tried to think up an effectual comeback. In the face of this direct attack her imagination was paralyzed.

"There's a lot of bluffs in the world," continued Marjorie quite pleasantly. "I should think you'd be young enough to know that, Otis."

"Well," said Otis, "maybe so. But gee! With a line like Bernice's——"

"Really?" yawned Marjorie. "What's her latest bon mot?"

No one seemed to know. In fact, Bernice, having trifled with her muse's beau, had said nothing memorable of late.

"Was that really all a line?" asked Roberta curiously.

Bernice hesitated. She felt that wit in some form was demanded of her, but under her cousin's suddenly frigid eyes she was completely incapacitated.

"I don't know," she stalled.

"Splush!" said Marjorie. "Admit it!"

Bernice saw that Warren's eyes had left a ukulele he had been tinkering with and were fixed on her questioningly.

"Oh, I don't know!" she repeated steadily. Her cheeks were glowing.

"Splush!" remarked Marjorie again.

"Come through, Bernice," urged Otis. "Tell her where to get off."

Bernice looked round again—she seemed unable to get away from Warren's eyes.

"I like bobbed hair," she said hurriedly, as if he had asked her a question, "and I intend to bob mine."

"When?" demanded Marjorie.

"Any time."

"No time like the present," suggested Roberta.

Otis jumped to his feet.

"Good stuff!" he cried. "We'll have a summer bobbing party. Sevier Hotel barbershop, I think you said."

In an instant all were on their feet. Bernice's heart throbbed violently.

"What?" she gasped.

Out of the group came Marjorie's voice, very clear and contemptuous.

"Don't worry—she'll back out!"

"Come on, Bernice!" cried Otis, starting toward the door.

Four eyes—Warren's and Marjorie's—stared at her, challenged her, defied her. For another second she wavered wildly.

"All right," she said swiftly, "I don't care if I do."

An eternity of minutes later, riding down-town through the late afternoon beside Warren, the others following in Roberta's car close behind, Bernice had all the sensations of Marie Antoinette bound for the guillotine in a tumbrel. Vaguely she wondered why she did not cry out that it was all a mistake. It was all she could do to keep from clutching her hair with both hands to protect it from the suddenly hostile world. Yet she did neither. Even the thought of her mother was no deterrent now. This was the test supreme of her sportsmanship; her right to walk unchallenged in the starry heaven of popular girls.

Warren was moodily silent, and when they came to the hotel he drew up at the curb and nodded to Bernice to precede him out. Roberta's car emptied a laughing crowd into the shop, which presented two bold plate-glass windows to the street.

Bernice stood on the curb and looked at the sign, Sevier Barber-Shop. It was a guillotine indeed, and the hangman was the first barber, who, attired in a white coat and smoking a cigarette, leaned nonchalantly against the first chair. He must have heard of her; he must have been waiting all week, smoking eternal cigarettes beside that portentous, too-often-mentioned first chair. Would they blindfold her? No, but they would tie a white cloth around her neck lest any of her blood—nonsense—hair—should get on her clothes.

"All right, Bernice," said Warren quickly.

With her chin in the air she crossed the sidewalk, pushed open the swinging screen-door, and giving not a glance to the uproarious, riotous row that occupied the waiting bench, went up to the first barber.

"I want you to bob my hair."

The first barber's mouth slid somewhat open. His cigarette dropped to the floor.

"Huh?"

"My hair—bob it!"

Refusing further preliminaries, Bernice took her seat on high. A man in the chair next to her turned on his side and gave her a glance, half lather, half amazement. One barber started and spoiled little Willy Schuneman's monthly haircut. Mr. O'Reilly in the last chair grunted and swore musically in ancient Gaelic as a razor bit into his cheek. Two bootblacks became wide-eyed and rushed for her feet. No, Bernice didn't care for a shine.

Outside a passer-by stopped and stared; a couple joined him; half a dozen small boys' noses sprang into life, flattened against the glass; and snatches of conversation borne on the summer breeze drifted in through the screen-door.

"Lookada long hair on a kid!"

"Where'd yuh get 'at stuff? 'At's a bearded lady he just finished shavin'."

But Bernice saw nothing, heard nothing. Her only living sense told her that this man in the white coat had removed one tortoise-shell comb and then another; that his fingers were fumbling clumsily with unfamiliar hairpins; that this hair, this wonderful hair of hers, was going—she would never again feel its long voluptuous pull as it hung in a dark-brown glory down her back. For a second she was near breaking down, and then the picture before her swam mechanically into her vision—Marjorie's mouth curling in a faint ironic smile as if to say:

"Give up and get down! You tried to buck me and I called your bluff. You see you haven't got a prayer."

And some last energy rose up in Bernice, for she clinched her hands under the white cloth, and there was a curious narrowing of her eyes that Marjorie remarked on to some one long afterward.

Twenty minutes later the barber swung her round to face the mirror, and she flinched at the full extent of the damage that had been wrought. Her hair was not curly, and now it lay in lank lifeless blocks on both sides of her suddenly pale face. It was ugly as sin—she had known it would be ugly as sin. Her face's chief charm had been a Madonna-like simplicity. Now that was gone and she was—well, frightfully mediocre—not stagy; only ridiculous, like a Greenwich Villager who had left her spectacles at home.

As she climbed down from the chair she tried to smile—failed miserably. She saw two of the girls exchange glances; noticed Marjorie's mouth curved in attenuated mockery—and that Warren's eyes were suddenly very cold.

"You see"—her words fell into an awkward pause—"I've done it."

"Yes, you've—done it," admitted Warren.

"Do you like it?"

There was a half-hearted "Sure" from two or three voices, another awkward pause, and then Marjorie turned swiftly and with serpent-like intensity to Warren.

"Would you mind running me down to the cleaners?" she asked. "I've simply got to get a dress there before supper. Roberta's driving right home and she can take the others."

Warren stared abstractedly at some infinite speck out the window. Then for an instant his eyes rested coldly on Bernice before they turned to Marjorie.

"Be glad to," he said slowly.

VI

Bernice did not fully realize the outrageous trap that had been set for her until she met her aunt's amazed glance just before dinner.

"Why, Bernice!"

"I've bobbed it, Aunt Josephine."

"Why, child!"

"Do you like it?"

"Why, Ber-nice!"

"I suppose I've shocked you."

"No, but what'll Mrs. Deyo think to-morrow night? Bernice, you should have waited until after the Deyos' dance—you should have waited if you wanted to do that."

"It was sudden, Aunt Josephine. Anyway, why does it matter to Mrs. Deyo particularly?"

"Why, child," cried Mrs. Harvey, "in her paper on 'The Foibles of the Younger Generation' that she read at the last meeting of the Thursday Club she devoted fifteen minutes to bobbed hair. It's her pet abomination. And the dance is for you and Marjorie!"

"I'm sorry."

"Oh, Bernice, what'll your mother say? She'll think I let you do it."

"I'm sorry."

Dinner was an agony. She had made a hasty attempt with a curling-iron, and burned her finger and much hair. She could see that her aunt was both worried and grieved, and her uncle kept saying, "Well, I'll be darned!" over and over in a hurt and faintly hostile tone. And Marjorie sat very quietly, intrenched behind a faint smile, a faintly mocking smile.

Somehow she got through the evening. Three boys called; Marjorie disappeared with one of them, and Bernice made a listless unsuccessful attempt to entertain the two others—sighed thankfully as she climbed the stairs to her room at half past ten. What a day!

When she had undressed for the night the door opened and Marjorie came in.

"Bernice," she said, "I'm awfully sorry about the Deyo dance. I'll give you my word of honor I'd forgotten all about it."

"'Sall right," said Bernice shortly. Standing before the mirror she passed her comb slowly through her short hair.

"I'll take you down-town to-morrow," continued Marjorie, "and the hairdresser'll fix it so you'll look slick. I didn't imagine you'd go through with it. I'm really mighty sorry."

"Oh, 'sall right!"

"Still it's your last night, so I suppose it won't matter much."

Then Bernice winced as Marjorie tossed her own hair over her shoulders and began to twist it slowly into two long blond braids until in her cream-colored negligee she looked like a delicate painting of some Saxon princess. Fascinated, Bernice watched the braids grow. Heavy and luxurious they were, moving under the supple fingers like restive snakes—and to Bernice remained this relic and the curling-iron and a to-morrow full of eyes. She could see G. Reece Stoddard, who liked her, assuming his Harvard manner and telling his dinner partner that Bernice shouldn't have been allowed to go to the movies so much; she could see Draycott Deyo exchanging glances with his mother and then being conscientiously charitable to her. But then perhaps by to-morrow Mrs. Deyo would have heard the news; would send round an icy little note requesting that she fail to appear—and behind her back they would all laugh and know that Marjorie had made a fool of her; that her chance at beauty had been sacrificed to the jealous whim of a selfish girl. She sat down suddenly before the mirror, biting the inside of her cheek.

"I like it," she said with an effort. "I think it'll be becoming."

Marjorie smiled.

"It looks all right. For heaven's sake, don't let it worry you!"

"I won't."

"Good night, Bernice."

But as the door closed something snapped within Bernice. She sprang dynamically to her feet, clinching her hands, then swiftly and noiselessly crossed over to her bed and from underneath it dragged out her suitcase. Into it she tossed toilet articles and a change of clothing. Then she turned to her trunk and quickly dumped in two drawerfuls of lingerie and summer dresses. She moved quietly, but with deadly efficiency, and in three-quarters of an hour her trunk was locked and strapped and she was fully dressed in a becoming new travelling suit that Marjorie had helped her pick out.

Sitting down at her desk she wrote a short note to Mrs. Harvey, in which she briefly outlined her reasons for going. She sealed it, addressed it, and laid it on her pillow. She glanced at her watch. The train left at one, and she knew that if she walked down to the Marborough Hotel two blocks away she could easily get a taxicab.

Suddenly she drew in her breath sharply and an expression flashed into her eyes that a practiced character reader might have connected vaguely with the set look she had worn in the barber's chair—somehow a development of it. It was quite a new look for Bernice—and it carried consequences.

She went stealthily to the bureau, picked up an article that lay there, and turning out all the lights stood quietly until her eyes became accustomed to the darkness. Softly she pushed open the door to Marjorie's room. She heard the quiet, even breathing of an untroubled conscience asleep.

She was by the bedside now, very deliberate and calm. She acted swiftly. Bending over she found one of the braids of Marjorie's hair, followed it up with her hand to the point nearest the head, and then holding it a little slack so that the sleeper would feel no pull, she reached down with the shears and severed it. With the pigtail in her hand she held her breath. Marjorie had muttered something in her sleep. Bernice deftly amputated the other braid, paused for an instant, and then flitted swiftly and silently back to her own room.

Down-stairs she opened the big front door, closed it carefully behind her, and feeling oddly happy and exuberant stepped off the porch into the moonlight, swinging her heavy grip like a shopping-bag. After a minute's brisk walk she discovered that her left hand still held the two blond braids. She laughed unexpectedly—had to shut her mouth hard to keep from emitting an absolute peal. She was passing Warren's house now, and on the impulse she set down her baggage, and swinging the braids like pieces of rope flung them at the wooden porch, where they landed with a slight thud. She laughed again, no longer restraining herself.

"Huh!" she giggled wildly. "Scalp the selfish thing!"

Then picking up her suitcase she set off at a half-run down the moonlit street.

ERNEST HEMINGWAY
(1899–1961)

The second of the six children of Grace Hall Hemingway, a singer and music teacher, and Clarence Edmonds Hemingway, a physician, Ernest Hemingway was born in Oak Park, Illinois. Upon graduating from Oak Park High School, he chose to begin working as a reporter for the *Kansas City Star* rather than to attend college. A volunteer Red Cross ambulance driver during WWI, he was severely wounded in both legs on the Italian front. During the early 1920s, he supported himself in Paris as a newspaper correspondent; he published his first volume, *Three Stories and Ten Poems,* in 1923. Two years later, he added nine stories and numerous miniature sketches to the original three stories to form *In Our Time,* a volume that received critical acclaim for originality of technique and subject matter. Arguably the most influential American writer of the twentieth century, he employed hard, spare prose to depict the disillusionment, changing values, and loss of faith experienced by many after WWI. Among his best-known novels are *The Sun Also Rises* (1926), the work that established his reputation; *A Farewell to Arms* (1929); *To Have and Have Not* (1937); *For Whom the Bell Tolls* (1940); *The Old Man and the Sea* (1952); and *Islands in the Stream* (1970). His short story collections include *Men Without Women* (1927), *Winner Take Nothing* (1933), and *The Nick Adams Stories* (1972), a compilation of sixteen previously published stories and eight stories discovered in manuscript that depict the childhood, adolescence, and young manhood of the same central character. In 1954, Hemingway won the Nobel Prize for literature.

Indian Camp

At the lake shore there was another rowboat drawn up. The two Indians stood waiting.

Nick and his father got in the stern of the boat and the Indians shoved it off and one of them got in to row. Uncle George sat in the stern of the camp rowboat. The young Indian shoved the camp boat off and got in to row Uncle George.

The two boats started off in the dark. Nick heard the oarlocks of the other boat quite a way ahead of them in the mist. The Indians rowed with quick choppy strokes. Nick lay back with his father's arm around him. It was cold on the water. The Indian who was rowing them was working very hard, but the other boat moved further ahead in the mist all the time.

"Where are we going, Dad?" Nick asked.

"Over to the Indian camp. There is an Indian lady very sick."

"Oh," said Nick.

Across the bay they found the other boat beached. Uncle George was smoking a cigar in the dark. The young Indian pulled the boat way up on the beach. Uncle George gave both the Indians cigars.

They walked up from the beach through a meadow that was soaking wet with dew, following the young Indian who carried a lantern. Then they went into the woods and followed a trail that led to the logging road that ran back into the hills. It was much lighter on the logging road as the timber was cut away on both sides. The young Indian stopped and blew out his lantern and they all walked on along the road.

They came around a bend and a dog came out barking. Ahead were the lights of the shanties where the Indian bark-peelers lived. More dogs rushed out at them. The two Indians sent them back to the shanties. In the shanty nearest the road there was a light in the window. An old woman stood in the doorway holding a lamp.

Inside on a wooden bunk lay a young Indian woman. She had been trying to have her baby for two days. All the old women in the camp had been helping her. The men had moved off up the road to sit in the dark and smoke out of range of the noise she made. She screamed just as Nick and the two Indians followed his father and Uncle George into the shanty. She lay in the lower bunk, very big under a quilt. Her head was turned to one side. In the upper bunk was her husband. He had cut his foot very badly with an ax three days before. He was smoking a pipe. The room smelled very bad.

Nick's father ordered some water to be put on the stove, and while it was heating he spoke to Nick.

"This lady is going to have a baby, Nick," he said.

"I know," said Nick.

"You don't know," said his father. "Listen to me. What she is going through is called being in labor. The baby wants to be born and she wants it to be born. All her muscles are trying to get the baby born. That is what is happening when she screams."

"I see," Nick said.

Just then the woman cried out.

"Oh, Daddy, can't you give her something to make her stop screaming?" asked Nick.

"No. I haven't any anaesthetic," his father said. "But her screams are not important. I don't hear them because they are not important."

The husband in the upper bunk rolled over against the wall.

The woman in the kitchen motioned to the doctor that the water was hot. Nick's father went into the kitchen and poured about half of the water out of the big kettle into a basin. Into the water left in the kettle he put several things he unwrapped from a handkerchief.

"Those must boil," he said, and began to scrub his hands in the basin of hot water with a cake of soap he had brought from the camp. Nick watched his father's hands scrubbing each other with the soap. While his father washed his hands very carefully and thoroughly, he talked.

"You see, Nick, babies are supposed to be born head first but sometimes they're not. When they're not they make a lot of trouble for everybody. Maybe I'll have to operate on this lady. We'll know in a little while."

When he was satisfied with his hands he went in and went to work.

"Pull back that quilt, will you, George?" he said. "I'd rather not touch it."

Later when he started to operate Uncle George and three Indian men held the woman still. She bit Uncle George on the arm and Uncle George said, "Damn squaw bitch!" and the young Indian who had rowed Uncle George over laughed at him. Nick held the basin for his father. It all took a long time. His father picked the baby up and slapped it to make it breathe and handed it to the old woman.

"See, it's a boy, Nick," he said. "How do you like being an interne?"

Nick said, "All right." He was looking away so as not to see what his father was doing.

"There. That gets it," said his father and put something into the basin.

Nick didn't look at it.

"Now," his father said, "there's some stitches to put in. You can watch this or not, Nick, just as you like. I'm going to sew up the incision I made."

Nick did not watch. His curiosity had been gone for a long time.

His father finished and stood up. Uncle George and the three Indian men stood up. Nick put the basin out in the kitchen.

Uncle George looked at his arm. The young Indian smiled reminiscently.

"I'll put some peroxide on that, George," the doctor said. He bent over the Indian woman. She was quiet now and her eyes were closed. She looked very pale. She did not know what had become of the baby or anything.

"I'll be back in the morning," the doctor said, standing up. "The nurse should be here from St. Ignace by noon and she'll bring everything we need."

He was feeling exalted and talkative as football players are in the dressing room after a game.

"That's one for the medical journal, George," he said. "Doing a Caesarian with a jack-knife and sewing it up with nine-foot, tapered gut leaders."

Uncle George was standing against the wall, looking at his arm.

"Oh, you're a great man, all right," he said.

"Ought to have a look at the proud father. They're usually the worst sufferers in these little affairs," the doctor said. "I must say he took it all pretty quietly."

He pulled back the blanket from the Indian's head. His hand came away wet. He mounted on the edge of the lower bunk with the lamp in one hand and looked in. The Indian lay with his face toward the wall. His throat had been cut from ear to ear. The blood had flowed down into a pool where his body sagged the bunk. His head rested on his left arm. The open razor lay, edge up, in the blankets.

"Take Nick out of the shanty, George," the doctor said.

There was no need of that. Nick, standing in the door of the kitchen, had a good view of the upper bunk when his father, the lamp in one hand, tipped the Indian's head back.

It was just beginning to be daylight when they walked along the logging road back toward the lake.

"I'm terribly sorry I brought you along, Nickie," said his father, all his post-operative exhilaration gone. "It was an awful mess to put you through."

"Do ladies always have such a hard time having babies?" Nick asked.

"No, that was very, very exceptional."

"Why did he kill himself, Daddy?"

"I don't know, Nick. He couldn't stand things, I guess."

"Do many men kill themselves, Daddy?"

"Not very many, Nick."

"Do many women?"

"Hardly ever."

"Don't they ever?"

"Oh, yes. They do sometimes."

"Daddy?"

"Yes."

"Where did Uncle George go?"

"He'll turn up all right."

"Is dying hard, Daddy?"

"No, I think it's pretty easy, Nick. It all depends."

They were seated in the boat, Nick in the stern, his father rowing. The sun was coming up over the hills. A bass jumped, making a circle in the water. Nick trailed his hand in the water. It felt warm in the sharp chill of the morning.

In the early morning on the lake sitting in the stern of the boat with his father rowing, he felt quite sure that he would never die.

KATHERINE L. HESTER

(1964–)

Born in Texas, Katherine L. Hester was raised in Athens, Georgia. She received a bachelor's degree in journalism from the University of Georgia and founded one of Athens's better literary and art magazines, *Blue Plate Special* (1988–90). She also completed an M.A. in English at the University of Texas at Austin and won a fellowship to the MacDowall Colony and a James A. Michener Fellowship in Writing. Her fiction is unmistakably Southern, focusing on the architecture and details of everyday life in her native Texas and Georgia. Typically, her characters are the overlooked, the ignored, and the snubbed living forlornly outside the reach of prosperity. According to Hester, her work is about "the tension between the romanticized America of sitcoms and of the 1950s, and the reality of life in America, which is very different from that idealized version." The inspiration for her highly acclaimed volume of short stories, *Eggs for Young America,* came from her job-hunting experiences after college, during the economic slump of the mid-80s. Her work has been published in *Prize Stories: The O. Henry Award* (1994), *American Short Fiction,* and other literary journals. *Eggs for Young America* (1996) won the first annual Bread Loaf Writers' Conference Literary Prize for fiction, called the Katherine Bakeless Nason Fiction prize. Her story "Going Down" was included in the collection *The Ex-Files: New Stories About Old Flames* (2000), edited by Blake Ferris.

Deadman's Float

Paula said the lake was haunted, and she'd been at camp since the summer started. Her corner of the tent looked more like the inside of someone's bedroom than it did the corner of a moldy-smelling tent off in the woods somewhere. She had boxes of M&M's hidden underneath the uniforms inside her suitcase and pictures torn from *Tiger Beat* Scotch-taped to the wall above her cot. When she started talking about the ghost, she looked at Leah because Leah was the one who'd mentioned she heard things at night.

"There's a girl who paddles across the lake nights when the moon is absolutely, completely full," Paula swore. It was early in the morning, before breakfast, and they were getting ready for the flag ceremony. Paula had remembered about the ghost because the girl's initials were carved into the Tent Four platform. She yanked her suitcase out from underneath her cot to prove it. The initials J.L.P. were gouged into the wood underneath.

"Her name was Juliette Lynn Parsons," Paula explained. She told them the girl was always dressed in white and she had drowned a long time ago. There wasn't a single ripple in the water after her canoe went past. If you saw her, it meant you would probably drown within a day or two.

Cordele looked over Paula's shoulder. She put her fingers on the letters. "Those look pretty new," she interrupted. "And anyhow, wouldn't she be going around in her Girl Scout uniform if she drowned here?" She poked a finger at Paula's green bermuda shorts. Paula slid the suitcase back under her cot and looked at Cordele as if it were all completely obvious, and Cordele was just too dumb to see it.

"I don't believe in ghosts, anyhow," Katie told them suddenly. "My mom says things like that are just the product of an overactive imagination." She touched her badge sash and yawned. "Is it straight?" she questioned Leah. She pirouetted in a circle.

Leah was impressed by Katie because during the year, Katie had explained to them, she took ballet. Her family had a boat on Lake Lanier. She knew how to water-ski. She looked like something from the Girl Scout catalog, with her beret tilted over her hair and the badge sash covered with embroidered disks flung across one shoulder.

"It's straight," Leah told her. She put her own sash on. It was limp and wrinkled because it wasn't new like Katie's, it was from the secondhand store. Her Girl Scout Trefoil and the pin she had gotten at the Juliette Low Birthplace the time she and her mother went to Savannah were almost the only things on it. "What about mine?" she asked, but she didn't look at Katie, she looked down at the floor. Cordele was sitting on the wooden rail outside the tent, and Leah could see Paula standing on the path, kicking rocks toward the tents further down the trail. Katie brushed her hair. She barely looked at Leah.

"Yeah," she said. "It's fine."

Back in the winter, Leah had tried to get the Housekeeping badge, which was on page 143 of the *Girl Scout Handbook*. She picked it because it was something Mrs. Fulton, the troop leader, had suggested. Housekeeping was not like Horsemanship or Water Sports. You could do it at home. It involved cleaning house and cooking meals. *Things every girl should know*, Mrs. Fulton told her brightly, after the third badge ceremony when everyone but Leah received a small white envelope with at least one badge in it. Leah's mother thought Housekeeping was a fine idea—she had just taped a chart she'd made to the front of the refrigerator showing the different days she wanted Leah and J.D. to cook supper. The chart was big, done in black Magic Marker. It also listed the days Leah should do laundry and when J.D. was supposed to work outside and mow the grass.

That chart was something the family counselor had suggested, the one time they had gone to see him. The family counselor had been a man with a large Adam's apple that bobbed slowly when he talked. When they walked into his office, J.D. chose the chair farthest away from him. He slouched into his jacket and stared at the sign on the counselor's desk that said NO SMOKING PLEASE. J.D. was *the identified patient* in the family, the counselor explained after a while. He was not really the problem. J.D. looked around the room and fumbled in his jacket pocket. He slowly lit a cigarette.

"Look at him," their mother said. "You mean to tell me *he* is not a problem?" J.D.

flicked ash onto the floor. The counselor's face slowly turned red. Leah noticed that even the tops of his ears were pink. She folded her knees up underneath her and moved around in her chair so she could see the street outside the window. A green car passed, and then a white one, and then a dirty, yellow pickup truck.

"Son," the counselor said, "would you mind putting that out?"

J.D. looked at the hot tip of the cigarette. He held it up and studied it.

"Fuck you," he told the counselor. He raised the cigarette up to his lips.

Leah had been very excited about the Housekeeping badge at first. It was a tiny milk bottle and an egg embroidered onto a blue background the color of the sky. Leah looked at her mother's *International Cookbook* before her nights to cook. She burned things in the bottoms of all the pans, trying to make strawberry crepes while her mother was in her bedroom with the lights off, resting after work.

"What is this shit?" J.D. said the first time Leah cooked, when she put the flabby, burnt-up ovals that were supposed to be crepes on his plate. J.D. still came home for supper then.

"It's food," their mother said. "Your sister worked very hard. You had better eat it." J.D. threw his napkin down. His eyes were glassy.

"We don't have a good crepe pan," Leah tried to explain to him. "That's why they stuck. But it's a real good recipe."

J.D. stood up and turned his back. "I'm going down to Dave's," he said. Dave's was the pizza place down at the corner. "I don't have to eat this crap."

For Leah to get the Housekeeping badge, they had to have family meetings once a month. "Maybe if we take votes on everything," she coaxed her mother, "J.D. will feel better." But when it was time for the first meeting J.D. refused to leave his room.

"I don't have the time for any of this dumb-ass Girl Scout shit," he said when she went up to his room to tell him they were waiting for him. He was lying on his bed with his Dingo boots planted against the wall and screechy music on his record player. He looked at Leah and dragged his feet down. A long black mark scratched across the paint.

On the chart taped to the refrigerator, it said J.D. would cook dinner twice a week. But he only did it once, and that time he didn't really cook because he came home with a pizza he had gotten at Dave's.

"Where are you getting the money to pay for this?" their mother asked. J.D. didn't answer.

"How much money do you have, James?" Her voice was quiet. They were standing in the kitchen and Leah was putting plates onto the table. She laid the silverware beside the napkins she had tried to pull into graceful shapes like swans. Their mother walked toward J.D. He gazed wildly over her shoulder.

"If this is a campaign to get me to send you to your father," she said suddenly, "*he* doesn't want you either."

J.D. looked at her and then he turned toward the sink and reached up to the magnetic knife holder hung above it. He yanked a knife down off it. It made a slippery noise when it slid across the magnet. He looked at her. His face was strained. He tossed the knife from one hand to the other. He was six foot two already.

"Why couldn't it be *you* who went away?" he screamed. That was the first night the police came.

J.D. told Leah he had *friends*. He had places he could go. It wasn't like he even *wanted* to be in their stupid white-bread house in their stupid neighborhood where their neighbors were always doing stupid things, like mowing their grass and playing their pianos and listening behind their doors so they could call the police the first minute they heard something. He didn't talk at all to their mother. He just came in late at night and went out early in the morning. It had been fall when their father left. It was winter when J.D. quit coming home from school until after it got dark. He'd throw his books down on the chair beside the living room door and stomp up to his room. His door would slam and Leah could hear the sound of one of his records on the turntable.

In the afternoons, when Leah was on the bus coming home from the middle school, she'd look out the window when it went down Warner Street, and that was where he'd be. Always with a bunch of other boys, their hands stuck deep into the pockets of their jackets, their shoulders hunched. They were always walking toward downtown, even though the high school didn't let out until three forty-five.

"Your brother looks like Jesus." People at school came up to Leah in the halls to tell her so. "He looks like John Lennon." And then they'd look at her. "Why does he act like *that*?" they'd ask. "Why is his hair so long?" *Their* older brothers were on the football team, *their* older sisters were cheerleaders. *They* said J.D. wasn't anything, besides a freak. He wore little wire-framed sunglasses, even inside school. Sometimes, when Leah saw him on the street, he looked like he was blind.

"I've been coming to Camp Columbus since *second grade*," Katie told them when they were walking to the flag ceremony, "and I've never, ever, seen anything that looked like it could be a ghost." Paula walked ahead of them, acting like she didn't care what they were saying. Her white uniform blouse gaped open in between the buttons, but she didn't seem to notice.

Leah didn't say anything to Katie although there *was* a bird off toward the lake that cried, at night. It was the only one. And every night the watchman marched up and down the trail, shining his flashlight underneath the tent platforms as he went by. Leah didn't know what he was looking for. "Tent Four," he always said. "You girls okay?" Then he was past their tent and they could hear his feet crunching through the leaves on the path. "Tent Five?" he'd say above the crickets, and it would be a second before Paula started talking again, telling some story about what-all it was that she had done in Columbus, with her flashlight in her lap, pointed upward at her chin so that it made her look like she had awful holes where her mouth and eyes should be.

*   *   *

Back in the winter, Leah's mother had said *their* house was haunted, but she was talking about a different kind of ghost—sometimes it seemed like Leah's father was still there. Still walking around. Sometimes Leah thought she could hear him slamming the front door, early in the morning before it was even light, going out to get the paper lying in the driveway. Sometimes at night, she thought she heard him in the kitchen, when she woke up and the kitchen light was falling through the doorway against the rug in the hall. But usually it was J.D., and once it was their mother. When Leah went in to see, she was at the kitchen table in her nightgown, and there was a single beer on the tabletop in front of her. Mascara was smudged around her eyes.

"Are you waiting up for J.D.?" Leah had asked.

Her mother looked right at her, but she didn't say anything. Leah went back to her bedroom and tried to think of something so that she would go to sleep. *Just think black,* her mother used to say when she was little. *Just think black and then you'll fall asleep.* But thinking black was like thinking about being dead. It made Leah think of the two cats they'd had that had gotten hit by cars and were buried in the backyard. The window above her bed opened up onto the dark backyard. Cold air slid around the edges of the glass. There was the sound of the kitchen light being turned off, and later, when Leah had finally almost gone to sleep, there was a bumping noise upstairs, like J.D. had finally come home and was taking off his boots.

If they dropped the flag down in the dirt, they were supposed to burn it.

"So what," Paula said. They were walking to the ragged, half-mowed clearing in the trees with the flagpole in the middle of it, where everyone was waiting for the flag ceremony to start. The night before, Paula and Leah had been the color guard, which meant they were the ones who took the flag down before it got dark. When they unhooked it from the chain, Paula had let her end droop into the dirt. Leah hadn't said anything.

Today, Leah was the one who was the flag bearer. She carried the triangle that was the folded flag carefully in her hands. She made sure the stars were facing *up,* the point of the triangle was facing *forward.* She marched toward the clearing. Cordele and Paula were the color guard behind her, Katie behind them.

"Leah's walking like she thinks she's in the army," Paula observed, and Leah was embarrassed. She had just been thinking about something else. She stopped lifting her feet so high off the ground and let them shuffle through the dirt.

She stopped abruptly in front of the flagpole and then turned around. Katie and Cordele and Paula whirled around behind her. They stared out at everybody else, standing in a horseshoe shape in front of them. "Attention," Katie shrieked. She was the only who knew all of the flag ceremony's words, so she was always the commander. The second-graders' end of the horseshoe was ragged. Most of the counselors were at that end. Some of the little girls didn't have complete uniforms. They wore their badge sashes over the muddy-green tie-dyed shirts they'd made in Crafts. Most of the Brownies' uniforms were a mouse-colored sort of brown. They looked like they'd been wadded up in suitcases. Katie started the Girl Scout oath. Leah stared at the ragged line of pines around the edges of the clearing. They looked like fingers pointing toward the sky. She looked down at the ground, at the tiny flat sheets of mica that winked back at her. Katie poked her in the back. There was a solemn hush. She and Cordele and Katie started unfolding the flag. Everyone was quiet while they hooked it to the chain and raised it up. There wasn't any wind. The flag hung there like a piece of laundry and everybody just looked at it for a minute.

"They treat us like slaves," Paula announced. It was after breakfast and they had just checked the list tacked up outside the dining hall to see what chores they had. They had latrine duty again, which meant they had to scrub the toilets in the bathhouse. Every morning, the counselors made up a roster—every tent was supposed to have a different duty. The Brownies were not very good at cleaning toilets. Katie and Cordele and Paula and Leah—Tent Four—were the oldest girls. They almost always had latrine duty.

"I don't know why we even look at that piece of paper," Paula said. "We already *know* what it is we have to do." Earlier, she had pointed out the fact that the counselors never gave themselves any of the chores. The counselors had it way too easy, Paula said. They had their own tent, up next to the dining hall. It even had electricity. When Tent Four woke up in the mornings, they could hear the radio the counselors had up there, playing "Muskrat Love" or "Goodbye Yellow Brick Road." The sound was loud, slipping down toward the lake from between the trees.

"Why did you even come here?" Cordele asked Paula abruptly. She was down on her knees scrubbing at the toilet. She looked up. Her face was red. "If it's so awful, why don't you just *leave*?" Paula looked at her. Her mouth was open. She turned her head and looked out through the door toward the lake. Then she turned back around and put her hands on her hips.

"I could go anywhere," she told them. "I could have gone to Six Flags if I wanted."

Cordele flushed the toilet. She stood up. "I think you're here because there's nobody that wants you."

"You're just jealous," Paula said. She cleared her throat. "My sister's coming to see me today," she said. "While you-all are at Swimming. She's going to take me out to eat. Maybe to McDonald's. I was going to try to bring you something, but I don't guess I really can."

The first day of Leah's camp session, the bus her mother put her on had jerked to a stop in Columbus, where Leah waited patiently underneath a drooping paper banner with CAMP COLUMBUS written on it for the counselors to drive up with the camp van. The inside of the bus station stank like exhaust, which always made her feel like she was getting carsick.

Two counselors came to pick her up. They both were very tan. They kept leaning over the front seat to look back at her. She was the only person waiting underneath the sagging banner. "Most people's parents drive them to the camp," one of the counselors told her. The other counselor turned the radio up, and Leah just looked out the window at the telephone pole–straight pine trees flashing past them and the patches of blood-colored dirt.

At Camp Columbus, there was a dock down by the water, and a twisted nylon rope hung down with aqua and white floats that marked off the little beach beside it. Up the hill where the counselor had parked the van, there was the bathhouse and the dining hall and the huge charred-up fire ring where they all sang, "Make new friends but keep the old" at the end of every one-week session, when the girls who were leaving cried and the ones who were staying through the summer acted like they didn't care at all, that leaving was a bad thing and not what almost everybody wanted.

The tents curved in a wiggly arc around one end of the lake. In the daylight, Leah could see them through the trees, bright yellow through the blackberries and poison ivy. At night, before it got too late, she would stand outside Tent Four, and if she squinted hard enough, she could see the light from someone's flashlight glowing against the yellow canvas of one of the other tents or bobbing through the trees along the path that led up to the bathroom. She could never hear what was going on in the other tents, but it was good, she thought, to know that they were there. At night, right after the campfire, when they came back down the hill to go to bed, the watchman was always sitting on the dock eating his lunch. Sometimes Leah could smell his cigarettes and see their red glow when he threw them toward the water. They reminded her of her father and the way, before he left, sometimes he sat on the back steps of the house at night and smoked, one cigarette after the other, staring out at the backyard. Leah watched him through her open bedroom window. He held himself very still. Leah's eyes would start to close and finally she would lie down on the bed and fall asleep.

The first night Leah was at Camp Columbus, Katie had sworn there had never been a watchman at Camp Columbus before, but that year they had three.

"It's to keep the boys out," Paula said. They were lying in their sleeping bags on their cots. Paula and Katie had gotten the best ones because they'd been at Camp Columbus since the very beginning of the summer—they had gotten to switch cots after the two girls who had been there for the first three sessions left.

"They don't want us to have any sort of social contact whatsoever," Paula explained to Cordele and Leah, who were new. She paused. "Although there's a cute boy who washes dishes at the dining hall. He looks like Scott Baio."

"Yuck," Cordele commented.

Paula ignored her. "He's probably going to ask me out," she told them.

None of them wanted to go to sleep. Leah felt strange, lying in a sleeping bag out in the middle of the woods with these three girls she didn't even know. The sleeping bag she'd brought had been J.D.'s; it even smelled like him, like cigarettes and the incense he was always burning in his room, although Leah wasn't sure when he'd last slept in it. He didn't care much about the woods anymore.

"I'm sure he won't mind if you take it," their mother had told her. In May, J.D. had gotten caught taking money out of the cash register at his job, and now he was out at

Beaverdam, the juvenile detention center. Leah hadn't seen him since the summer started. The inside of his sleeping bag was soft red flannel printed with a pattern of flying ducks and Irish setters. J.D. had had his sleeping bag a long time, since back when he and Leah had played like they were camping in the backyard, and that had been when Leah was a Brownie and he was a Webelo. The next year after that might have been the year he decided things like Boy Scouts were stupid.

That first night, Katie and Paula had their flashlights on. Katie sat cross-legged on her cot, picking through a box of candy her mother had sent from home, holding pieces up to her flashlight to see if she could tell if they were creams or toffees. Outside, the night watchman's boots scraped on the gravel of the path. His footsteps stopped outside the tent. "Tent Four?" he said. His voice slid in between the tent flaps. "Everything okay?"

Paula stopped talking. Leah could hear the chink of his keys when he walked past.

"Do you-all know?" she said after a minute. She lowered her voice and looked around like she was checking to make sure they all were listening. "Do you-all know what a *blow job* is?"

"Yeah, sure," Cordele said. "Of course. Big deal." Her voice was edgy.

Leah was quiet.

"Like going to third base?" Katie asked. She didn't seem that interested.

"What do *you* think, Leah?" Paula asked. Leah didn't say anything.

"Of course *Leah* doesn't know," Paula answered herself. "Because she's such a baby." She pointed her flashlight at each one of them in turn.

"This is what it is," she told them. "You take his *thing* and do like this."

"You mean you put it in your *mouth*?" Leah said it before she even thought. She looked around. Paula lowered her flashlight from her face.

"It's true," she said.

Cordele's face was disgusted. "Nuh-uh," she said. "That's gross."

Even Katie seemed surprised. "How do you know?" she said. "My mother never told me *that*."

"My brother-in-law told me." Paula looked at them smugly. They'd already heard all about Paula's sister and her husband and the little baby her sister had. How Paula lived with them instead of with her mother. How Paula's brother-in-law was a *hunk*, cuter even than Shaun Cassidy. He drove a bright red Thunderbird. "T-bird," Paula said importantly. It was one of the first things she had told them. Her brother-in-law took her to Baskin-Robbins for ice cream while her sister was at home with the baby. "My sister used to be a fox," Paula had explained, "but after the baby she got kind of blubbery." She cocked her head as if she was listening to something someone else was saying. Her sister, she said firmly, was a drag.

She ran her flashlight beam over the canvas of the tent. Everyone was quiet. "You're making that up," Cordele said finally. Leah slid down in her sleeping bag and put her pillow over her ears.

* * *

In March, Leah's mother had started bringing home brochures for places she called *luxury communities*. Luxury communities were all on the east side of town. They had recreation rooms and swimming pools and saunas and shag carpeting.

"We're just two little old peas in a great big pod, aren't we, Leah-Bird?" her mother said. Her mother hadn't called her Leah-Bird since she was little, and Leah didn't think that they should move because someday J.D. would be coming back. He wasn't always going to live in the little apartment their father had driven over from Birmingham to help him find the month before. He wasn't always going to work at Long John Silver's, which was the only place he could find a job where they wouldn't make him get a haircut.

Her mother sat at the dining room table with a pen and the brochures spread out around her.

"This one has a recreation center," she said. "Leah, honey, how'd you like to live in *this*?" Her pen tapped against a photograph of a row of brick buildings flanked by a kidney bean–shaped pool. Leah liked the room she had, the way she'd gotten to pick out the frilly curtains and help paint all the dresser drawers. She didn't want to have to move and start going to the other middle school where there were lots of rednecks and everyone dressed bad and lived way out somewhere in the country.

"Who cares?" she said, under her breath. "Who cares?" But all her mother said was *What, honey?* She picked up a pen and drew a careful circle around a phone number on one of the brochures.

"I'll call them in the morning," she told Leah.

The part of the day at Camp Columbus Leah hated most was Swimming, which came an hour after lunch. She hated Swimming more than anything else they did because before it they had to change into their swimsuits in front of one another. In the mornings, when they first got up, it was easy for her to get dressed huddled down inside her sleeping bag. She just pretended she was cold. But in the middle of the afternoon it wasn't like she could just jump back into her sleeping bag. And Paula always noticed if she turned her back. Paula would look at Leah's itchy training bra and say, *So where did you get that? K-Mart?* Paula's bras looked like the kind Leah's mother wore. She left them lying on her cot, right there in plain view. Cordele swore to Leah that Paula *wanted* them to see them. Paula claimed that at her school in Columbus, her nickname was Boom-Boom. If they wanted, she said, looking at them, they were free to call her that. She tossed back her hair and stuck out her chest.

Leah tried to get her swimsuit on without taking her T-shirt all the way off. It was getting all stretched out, from the way she yanked it up over her shoulders. Paula sat on her cot, stuffing things into her knapsack. It was, she told them airily, her time of the month—she had gotten special permission to miss Swimming. Her sister was driving out from Columbus to visit, to take her out to dinner at the McDonald's on the interstate.

"You're going to miss the certification," Cordele told her. Paula shrugged her shoulders.

"I got permission to go," she said in a loud voice. "My sister's taking me out to dinner and then we'll go out to a movie. At my sister's, I can do whatever I feel like. We'll have potato chips, and Cokes, whatever."

"Would you sneak something back?" Katie asked her.

"Maybe," Paula said, but then she looked at Cordele. "I don't know," she said.

"If you're gone today," Leah reminded her, "you can't get your junior lifesaving certificate. Then you can't be a lifeguard."

"Who wants to be a lifeguard?" Paula said. She shoved a hot-pink pair of sunglasses into her bag. "I sure don't. You dummies are brainwashed."

The bottom of the lake was slimy reddish clay. From the very first day, Leah had hated the way it squished underneath her feet when she tried to touch bottom.

"Okay," Melissa, the swimming counselor, told them. She held a clipboard and a piece of paper out in front of her. A whistle dangled around her neck, hanging from a chain. Melissa's face was red and the skin on her nose was peeling. She squinted. Leah and Cordele and Katie were lined up on the dock in front of her. The littler girls, the Brownies, were running up and down the beach behind them, singing something stupid. It sounded like "Little Bunny Foo-foo," a song they all had to sing at the sing-alongs after dinner, around the campfire. "Little Bunny Foo-foo" was such a retarded song, the second-graders loved it. After the first night, Leah and Cordele had quit even moving their lips.

"Okay," Melissa said. "Today we're doing the test to see if y'all can get your junior lifesaving certification." She looked down at her piece of paper. "Today we'll do the water part. Tomorrow I'll test you on the lifesaving, the mouth-to-mouth."

"Gross," Cordele said and made a kissing sound. Melissa stood in front of them with her hands on her hips.

"Today, what we're going to do is this," she continued firmly. "First, you're going to tread water in your clothes for five minutes. A shirt and a pair of pants. With your swimsuit underneath. When I blow the whistle, you'll throw your clothes up on the dock and swim across the lake. You can use any stroke you want, except dog paddle. I'll be right behind in the canoe."

"This is retarded," Cordele said. "Why do we have to do it?"

"Because this is junior lifesaving. What would happen if you fell off a boat? You have to be able to swim in your clothes. They're heavier." Melissa looked at them severely. "You girls are *Girl Scouts,* remember? The little girls are watching. You-all are the oldest." She paused and wrinkled up her nose. "You're supposed to be the best." Leah looked at Cordele and Katie. They both looked bored.

"I *can't* do this," she whispered suddenly. Katie shrugged and moved away from her, lining up her feet at the edge of the dock so that when Melissa blew the whistle she could make a perfect dive.

* * *

Their clothes *were* heavier. Although Katie and Cordele didn't seem to notice. They bobbed up and down in the water solemnly, and behind them, Leah could see the aqua and white weights that cordoned off the shallow water. Leah's pants dragged against her legs like they were coated with cement. The water was warm, and it had started going up her nose. She flailed her arms and bicycled her legs. No one said anything. There was just the sound of churning water and the little girls giggling and splashing in the shallow water. Melissa stood on the dock, looking at her stopwatch.

"How long?" Leah gasped, trying to tilt her head up so that she could see her.

Melissa was silent. She stared at the stopwatch. "One minute," she intoned.

Leah's arms and legs felt heavy. They sliced slowly through the water, as if it were a wind pushing against her, bending her bones back. It was harder and harder to keep her head above the water. The lake was dark and smelled like mud. It was impossible to see the bottom. Melissa had said that at its deepest, the lake was only ten feet deep. Leah's legs churned slowly. She squinted, staring down through the water, but all she saw was the flash of her own legs. Like silver, darting fish. It didn't even seem that they belonged to her. The dark water gaped. No matter how far Leah sank, her toes would never touch the bottom.

"How long now?" she shrieked, spitting out the water that had gotten in her mouth.

"Three minutes," Melissa said and yawned.

Leah's legs felt like they were made of wood. She looked across the water at Cordele. Her face was expressionless. She methodically moved her legs up and down.

"Okay," Melissa said finally. "Throw your clothes up here."

Leah struggled with her Camp Columbus T-shirt. It was soggy and stretched out and she realized that when she tried to pull it over her head, she would be completely underwater, unable to move her arms. She wondered how far she would sink before she pulled it off. The T-shirt felt like gauze, and her hands were tangled in it. She yanked it over her head and slung it toward the dock. Katie and Cordele had already started swimming. Melissa was in the canoe, holding her paddle across her legs, looking back at Leah.

"You can swim faster than that, Leah," she shouted.

Leah started with the backstroke because she didn't want to put her face into the water. She lay against the surface of the water and the blue sky and the pine trees jerked in front of her while she tried to catch her breath. She hadn't ever been very good at the backstroke and her arms felt like someone had pulled at them, the way when she was little, she and J.D. pulled at wishbones until they cracked. She kept stopping to tread water so she could see how far off course she had gotten. Katie and Cordele were far in front of her, Melissa in the canoe a few feet ahead.

"You'll never finish," Melissa finally shouted to her, "if you keep with the backstroke. You need to do the crawl."

Leah turned over and lowered her face into the water. When she tilted it to get air, she caught a glimpse of sky and shore and dirty water. Her breath was ragged.

Every swimming lesson since Leah had started camp, Melissa had taught them something. First it was mouth-to-mouth, how to do it on a baby or a grown-up. How to brace your body on the shore and pull someone who was floundering and panicked in. Different ways to float. Melissa told them stories about people who had waited in the water for hours before anyone could get to them. One of the ways to rest while you were waiting was the deadman's float. Leah thought of something white and heavy floating in some scummy water like a log. The deadman's float was perfect if you were out on a boat that started sinking and you were waiting to be rescued.

They'd never had to do the deadman's float, really. It was just something it was good to know about, in case of an emergency. All they had to do was lie facedown in the water with their arms stretched out, then turn their heads barely to the side, for air.

Leah was treading water. She felt so tired. Katie and Cordele were almost at the opposite shore. She didn't think she could catch up with them. She didn't think that she could breathe. She remembered about the deadman's float. She stretched her arms up and put her face into the water. She couldn't float at all. Her legs pulled her downward. She was underwater; she could see the brownish, silty water. It was the color of tea; everything was quiet underneath it. Leah's hair waved back and forth in front of her face, like grass, like leaves, like there was a wind to move it.

Paula claimed you could even see the girl who drowned in daylight. Was she still drifting underwater, her hair moving like mud-colored seaweed? Paula had told them the girl was just their age; she had drowned the summer before she started seventh grade. The water seemed dark and warm and peaceful. Leah pushed herself back up to the surface.

"Please let me in the boat," she shouted to Melissa. "I can't go any farther."

"Nope," Melissa said. "You don't have far to go." Her voice was firm, the same way Coach Fredricks's would be during the year, at school, when Leah was running track in P.E., when the coach would yell, It hurts so good while someone threw up on the grass beside the bleachers.

"Let me in the boat," she said. She treaded water beside it.

"You can do it," Melissa said. She started paddling faster.

"I can't," Leah shouted. "I don't want to anymore. Please let me in," she begged. The water around her swirled in tiny perfect whirlpools where Melissa had just pushed her paddle through it. Leah could barely keep her head above the water enough to see that Melissa wasn't going to turn the canoe around and come back.

Paula got back after supper, after the campfire, after the rest of them had already straggled down the hill in the half-dark and gotten into their sleeping bags. Leah was so tired she could barely stay awake.

"I found out why there are security guards this year," Paula announced to them importantly as soon as she came in. She pulled on the Camp Columbus T-shirt and the shorts she slept in. She climbed into her sleeping bag.

"Why?" Katie asked.

"I don't know if I should say. My sister said I shouldn't even know." Paula's flashlight beam was turned toward the ceiling and she looked up at it coyly.

"What?" Cordele said. "You have to tell."

"It's this," she said. She lowered her voice to a whisper. "There's this man . . ."

It had been in all the papers. The Atlanta TV crews had been in Columbus—it had been on the news. They hadn't heard anything because they were at camp. Even though Columbus was so close. But everybody else knew. There was a curfew in Columbus.

The man had killed six women. He drove up and down the streets of Columbus, Paula said theatrically, in a beat-up Chevrolet. There had been an artist's drawing of what the police thought he looked like in the Columbus paper. That was what Paula had seen that made her ask her sister what it was all about.

Paula said the picture looked like Charles Manson, hair out around his face like *this*. She measured with her hands around her head. The man had little-bitty eyes, the way Charles Manson did in *Helter Skelter*, which had been on TV the spring before. Leah had not been supposed to watch *Helter Skelter*, but her mother had had a date that night and hadn't known.

"He wraps a panty hose around their necks," Paula told them. "He pulls tighter and tighter until they're dead. He climbs in through their bedroom windows."

Everyone was quiet. "He does something to them, after they're dead," Paula said. "My sister wouldn't tell me what. I think," she said slowly, "he does something with his thing, after they're dead."

"You're a liar," Leah screamed suddenly. She jumped off her cot. Her sleeping bag slid onto the floor. Her arms were flailing. She lunged toward Paula and started shaking her. "You think you know everything, but you really don't know nothing," she yelled. The watchman pulled the tent flap back. His flashlight was so bright it hurt their eyes.

"What's all this?" he said. Leah pulled her sleeping bag up off the floor and straightened it on her cot.

"Just playing a game," Katie said after a minute.

"I'll send a counselor in here if I hear another thing," he said. He let the tent flap drop back down.

Paula turned her flashlight off. No one said anything.

"You're just *white trash*." Cordele's voice was soft in the sudden darkness. "All you are is trash," she said to Paula.

"You cheerleader piece of shit," Paula said back. She paused. "You fucking baby," she hissed toward Leah's cot. None of them could believe the words that hung there in the air.

Leah woke up abruptly, not knowing where she was. It was dark, really dark, like her head was underneath her sleeping bag. Her heart beat hard. She was standing up.

"Cordele?" she whispered. "Paula? Are you there?" Her eyes were open wide.

She felt leaves underneath her feet. She could hear the creaking of tree limbs and the wind. There was a little light now, faint, from the sky, above the branches. Somehow, she was outside the tent beside the wooden platform. She put out her hand and touched it. She listened hard. She could hear the watchman, whistling. His flashlight beam played over the bushes.

* * *

The first time she'd walked in her sleep had been right after she and her mother moved into the new apartment. Her mother told her she'd been sitting in the living room when Leah walked out of her bedroom. She walked through the living room and out the unlocked door. Her mother had read that it was dangerous to wake someone who was sleepwalking so she just followed behind Leah, watching closely. Leah walked toward the swimming pool. Her eyes were open. Her mother said, *Leah?* But she kept on. Her mother was afraid she would drown. She shook her by the shoulder.

That was when Leah woke up. The swimming pool was a blue shimmery disk, curved in a shape like a pin her grandmother had worn once. The underwater lights were on. She could hear the cars down on the highway, going past.

"Where were you going?" her mother asked her. Leah didn't know. She didn't even know how she had gotten there. She was still half-asleep.

"Home," she told her mother.

It was cold; Leah heard the sound of the watchman's feet crunching on the path. She was just in the clothes she slept in, a white T-shirt and panties. The T-shirt was faded; it brushed against her thighs. She tried to yank it further down her legs. The watchman's feet got closer. She leapt up the two stairs to the tent and ducked inside.

She lay awake for a long time. She put out her hand and touched the thin canvas walls of the tent. She didn't feel any safer than she had waking up out in the dark, half-asleep, her bare feet on the ground. The watchman walked past again. He was whistling a song her mother used to sing. Leah could hear the jingle of his keys, the creak of the leather holster she knew he wore across one shoulder. There were goose bumps on her arms and she pulled them under the sleeping bag. Katie turned over on the cot across from her. Out on the lake a bird made one sharp cry. Paula's pictures torn from magazines stared down from the walls. There was a splash, but Leah knew there was no way that it could be a person, not even someone drowning.

"Who's there?" the watchman called, and Leah held herself quiet in the rustling sleeping bag. Waiting for an answer, but she knew from hikes and woodcraft that the trees outside the tent were straight and leaned toward each other densely. Brambles spilled down into the deep ravines and vines of poison ivy, thick as snakes, twined up and down the trees. If there was someone out there, he wasn't going to answer. She pushed herself down into her sleeping bag. She heard the sound of Paula's sigh. Some nights, Paula talked in her sleep, but when they sat up in the dark and questioned her, she wouldn't say a thing. Paula had been the one who convinced Leah to lie down on the floor, the night they'd planned to have the séance. She vowed she knew a way that they could lift her, just with their fingertips. She held her index finger against Leah's side. Katie and Cordele stood at her head and feet. Paula said the magic word but nothing ever happened. Leah felt immovable as stone.

"Think about air," Katie had cried, and Leah closed her eyes. *Think black,* she had told herself. She wished she was asleep.

ALICE HOFFMAN

(1952–)

Born in New York City, Alice Hoffman was raised in a working-class neighborhood on Long Island. When she was eight years old, her parents divorced, and her mother, unlike most mothers at that time, began to work. She received a B.A. from Adelphi University, where she majored in English and anthropology. Awarded a Mirrellees Fellowship to the Stanford University Creative Writing Center, she earned an M.A. in creative writing in 1974. A well-known professor at Stanford, Albert Guerard, and his wife, Maclin, helped Hoffman to publish her first story in *Fiction* magazine, which quickly led to the publication of a selection from *Property Of*, a first novel in progress, in *American Review*. She has published fifteen novels; *Local Girls* (1999), a collection of interrelated short stories; and five books for children. With her husband, Tom Martin, she has coauthored more than fifty screenplays; she is the author of the screenplay for *Independence Day* (1983), a film that starred Dianne Wiest and Kathleen Quinlan. Her novel *Practical Magic* (1995) was made into a film that featured Sandra Bullock and Nicole Kidman. Among her other novels are *Fortune's Daughter* (1985), *Illumination Night* (1987), *At Risk* (1988), *Seventh Heaven* (1990), *Turtle Moon* (1993), *Second Nature* (1994), *Here on Earth* (1997), *Blue Diary* (2001), and *The Probable Future* (2003). Her essays and short stories have been published in *The New York Times, The Boston Globe Magazine, Redbook,* and *The Kenyon Review* among others. Hoffman donated her royalty advance from *At Risk* to AIDS research and that from *Local Girls* to breast cancer research and breast cancer care centers.

Flight

Eugene Kessler was supposed to be my brother's best friend, but he and I actually had a lot more in common. It wasn't so much that Eugene and I liked each other, or that there was any possibility of romance between us. It was more that we both despised Franconia, the suburb where we were doomed to live. In Franconia, no one's imagination was working overtime, that much was evident from the moment you first walked through town, where you could find the Franconia High School, the Franconia Mall, the Franconia Diner, and, for special occasions—proms, for instance, or extramarital trysts—the Franconia Steak House, which Eugene and I called Marie's, not only because Marie Fortuna's husband caught her there, eating antipasto with her boyfriend, who happened to be the soccer coach at the high school, but because we couldn't stand to hear the word Franconia used one more time.

Eugene and I were in business together, earning money for our escape from town by selling term papers, and June was our busiest time of the year. By the end of the month, however, we were no longer doing our best work. The pressure was on, the stupid among us had panicked, and I was writing all night. In part, I kept odd hours because my brother strongly disapproved of our venture, and Jason was so honest and good that a single look from him could make a person feel sordid and corrupt. But the real reason I was writing three or more papers at a time was that Eugene was in charge of the division of labor, and he'd divided it so that two thirds of the labor was mine. After all, he had started the business, so it was only fair that he administered everything, including our finances, which were kept in a joint savings account. Or at least, this was Eugene's line every time I complained. And when I really considered my situation, it wasn't so difficult to accept the deal he offered and keep my mouth shut. In August, Eugene would be leaving—he and my brother had done what no one in our town had ever managed before and had both gotten into Harvard—at which point the business would be all mine.

So I kept cranking out term papers. I went through the great religions of the world, then turned to literature—Shakespeare's comedies for the juniors, tragedies for the seniors. I wrote dream journals and essays about my various families, some so moving I brought myself to tears. At least, writing these papers kept my mind off the heat, which was nearly unbearable that June. I had a lot not to think about back then, including the horrible noise the cicadas made all day and night, an echo that could lead you to believe little bombs were going off on your neighbors' front lawns. I certainly didn't want to dwell on the fact that I'd probably ruined my hair for good. I had dyed it black and cut the front much too short, using a dull nail scissors, so that I now looked as though I were in a constant state of shock. Well, maybe I was, and maybe I had good reason to be. Not long ago my father had moved out and now my mother barely left her room. Even our dog, a Labrador retriever known to do little but sleep, had attacked Mrs. Fisher's cat across the street and now, instead of roaming the neighborhood, he was chained up in our yard, eating cicadas, making himself sick.

Through it all, the heat just kept getting worse. At school, people fainted during homeroom. There were fights in the parking lot of the Franconia Mall, real fights that were bloody and unforgiving and hot. After a while, all anyone could hear were those horrible cicadas and the whirring of air conditioners. It got so that I hated everyone— not Jason of course, who was too pure to hate, just everyone else who lived and breathed inside the Franconia town limits.

The only one who seemed to understand me at that point in time was Eugene Kessler, and this notion was just about as scary as any I'd ever had. On truly hot nights, when the air was so humid and thick it was a triumph to draw a deep breath, I would sometimes see Eugene out in his yard. Somehow, I knew how alone he felt, and it gave me the shivers to think that alienation could be a shared experience. Eugene had found a great horned owl at a rest area on the parkway two summers earlier. Now, on nights when everyone else was at home with the air conditioner turned on high, Eugene would let the owl fly free. He'd been informed by a lieutenant down at the police department that he'd better keep the owl caged at all times, because of an incident involving a toy poodle that had been carried off, but Eugene had his own view of natural selection. He figured that the Yorkie who lived on the corner, and the Chihuahua who snarled from behind a fence over on Maple, had better run for cover when they spied the owl's shadow above them. In Eugene's opinion, their fate was in their own paws.

Jason was different. He wasn't like Eugene, and he certainly wasn't like me. He always played by the rules. My brother was so serious and straitlaced that teenage girls were constantly after him. Several had spent all year attempting to seduce him, but Jason had other things on his mind. He'd devoted every free minute to his senior science thesis. Twenty hamsters were kept in cages in his bedroom. Ten had been given a balanced diet of seeds and grains, but the other ten had eaten nothing but Twinkies. My brother hoped to finish his research before leaving for college, although to me it already seemed obvious that the Twinkie ten were not only fatter but far more intelligent. As soon as they heard my brother's bedroom door open, they ran to their feeding stations, while the grain and nut hamsters just went on running on their wheels, making the same hopeless circles they spun every night.

Maybe Jason would have finished his research if Eugene had remembered to write Joey Jergens's history paper, but Eugene was too busy planning his future, plotting his imminent escape, to pay much attention to our schedule. Eugene had missed the delivery date and Joey was outraged when he called me. I had to soothe him with promises of ten pages on the Salem witch trials by eight the following morning.

"Don't be mad," Eugene said as soon as he saw me the next day.

We were in the field behind the high school and Joey was headed straight for us. Of course, I refused to speak to Eugene. I had slept for two hours. I was in no mood for this.

"I'll do the *Romeo and Juliet* for Sue Greco," Eugene vowed. He knew I dreaded Shakespeare papers, and had one of my own past due. "The Industrial Revolution for Horowitz?" Eugene whispered. "Consider it done."

By now, Joey Jergens was upon us. "Got my paper?"

Joey was not a conversationalist, but it was enough that he had taken fifteen dollars out of his jeans pocket. I started to hand over the opus I'd written, but Eugene grabbed for it. "Let me check for typos," he said.

"No way," I said. "Who sat up all night with this thing? This paper's mine."

"Be careful with that," Joey Jergens warned me, and maybe I was clutching on too tightly. But Eugene was trying to pry my hard work away, and I wouldn't let him, and that was how Mr. Prospero, the vice principal, found us, struggling over a report neither of us cared about, enmeshed in a battle that would only cause us grief.

By nine-fifteen we were all suspended. Joey Jergens had been expecting to go to summer school, so it didn't matter much to him, but now Eugene wouldn't graduate. Maybe he stood there for a while, staring at the high school, and maybe he didn't. I don't know. I immediately headed for home. I was thinking about myself and no one else. I had just lost the summer, after all. Other people would be having a life, I'd be reading *Romeo and Juliet* in a classroom hot enough to bake bread on the desks.

Naturally, my brother blamed me for everything. He didn't care that Eugene had started the business and had practically drafted me.

"He can still go to Cambridge with you," I told my brother, even though I knew it wasn't true. You couldn't enroll for more than two classes in the summer, and Eugene would be missing four credits.

My brother phoned Eugene, ready to let him have it for throwing his future away for fifteen lousy dollars, but when Jason came back into the living room he didn't seem mad anymore. Eugene had already been to the bank and withdrawn our entire joint savings. Then he'd gone home and left a note for his mother in which he swore he would pay me back someday, although I certainly wasn't about to hold my breath. Eugene had also informed his mother that he was buying a plane ticket and by the time she read his note he'd already be on his way to San Francisco. Maybe I should have been angry about working all year for nothing, but I wasn't. I went over and let Mrs. Kessler tell me about the way Eugene had taught himself to read the dictionary when he was two and a half, even though I'd heard the story about a million times before. Mrs. Kessler had a weird look on her face, and it made me think of my mother, just after my father had left her. It made me think that summer would never be the same, not now and not ever.

I guess deep inside I did believe everything that had happened was my fault. I must have, because sometime between the moment when I got to the Kesslers' and the moment when I left, I told Eugene's mother I'd be glad to take care of the owl until Eugene returned. Of course, Mrs. Kessler was delighted to get rid of the owl. She got down on her knees and helped me coax it into its cage. I walked home carefully, trying not to jostle the owl, but as soon as I set the cage down on our living room floor, I realized my mistake. Somehow, the owl looked much bigger in our house. Its feet were as big as our Labrador retriever's. I couldn't even stand to be in the same room as Eugene's horrible pet. I went to the kitchen and telephoned everyone I knew to announce my suspension from school, but it wasn't the same as talking to Eugene. Still, I talked for a long time, long enough so that Jason was the one who discovered that the owl had killed every one of his hamsters. Either the cage had been left open or the owl knew some tricks I wasn't aware of. Frankly, its method of escape didn't matter. By the time Jason walked into his bedroom, the owl was sitting on the air conditioner, distressed and thwarted, its feathers ruffled; although it had managed to kill all the hamsters, it still couldn't get to them through the meshing of their cages.

My brother had hoped to finish his experiment before leaving for college; now he didn't have to worry. It was over. If the owl hadn't belonged to Eugene, I think Jason would have killed it. Instead, he went out and bought six live chicks at the pet store. But the owl wouldn't eat. We watched over it for days and then weeks, but the owl never really recovered. Maybe the heat was what caused its feathers to drop out, one by one, as it perched on the air conditioner. Or maybe it was only longing for someone who wasn't afraid to let it fly above the poplars and crab apples, searching backyards, a streak of lightning in our dark sky.

DAVID LEAVITT
(1961–)

Born in Pittsburgh, Pennsylvania, David Leavitt grew up in Palo Alto, California. In 1982, while still a Yale undergraduate, he published his first short story, "Territory," in *The New Yorker.* At Yale, where he earned a B.A., he was awarded the Willets Prize for fiction. In 1984, he published *Family Dancing: Stories,* which was nominated for a National Book Critics Circle Award and for the PEN/Faulkner Award for best fiction. He received a National Endowment for the Arts Fellowship (1984) and a Guggenheim Fellowship (1990). *The Lost Language of Cranes* (1986), his first novel, was adapted for a BBC television movie. His novel *While England Sleeps* (1993)—based on *World Within World,* the 1951 memoir of British poet Stephen Spender—became the center of a controversy when the poet threatened a lawsuit, causing the book to be withdrawn. Among Leavitt's other works are the story collections *A Place I've Never Been* (1990) and *The Marble Quilt* (2001), and the novels *Equal Affections* (1989), *The Page Turner* (1998), and *Martin Bauman: Or, a Sure Thing* (2000). With Mark Mitchell, he coedited *The Penguin Book of Gay Short Stories* (1994) and the *Penguin Book of International Gay Writing* (1996), and coauthored *Italian Pleasures* (1996). Currently, he is a professor of creative writing at the University of Florida.

Danny in Transit

Danny's cousins, Greg and Jeff, are playing catch. A baseball arcs over the green lawn between them, falls into the concavity of each glove with a soft thump, and flies again. They seem to do nothing but lift their gloves into the ball's path; it moves of its own volition.

Danny is lying facedown on the diving board, his hands and feet dangling over the sides, watching the ball. Every few seconds he reaches out his hands, so that his fingers brush the surface of the pool. He is trying to imagine the world extending out from where he lies: the Paper Palace, and the place he used to live, and the Amboys, Perth and South. Then Elizabeth. Then West New York. Then New York, Long Island, Italy. He listens to the sucking noise of the wind the ball makes, as it is softly swallowed. He listens to his cousins' voices. And then he takes tight hold of the diving board and tries to will it into flight, imagining it will carry him away from this backyard. But the sounds persist. He isn't going anywhere.

The huge backyard is filled with chilly New Jersey light, elegant as if it were refracted off the surface of a pearl. Carol and Nick, his aunt and uncle, sip tomato juice under an umbrella. Nearby, but separate, Elaine, Danny's mother, stares at nothing, her lips slightly parted, her mouth asleep, her eyes taking account. All that is between them is a plate of cheese.

"We went to a new restaurant, Elaine," Carol says. She is rubbing Noxzema between her palms. "Thai food. Peanut sauce and—oh, forget it."

"Keep that pitch steady, buddy," Nick calls to his sons. "Good wrist action, remember, that's the key." Both of the boys are wearing T-shirts which say *Coca-Cola* in Arabic.

"What can I do?" Carol asks.

"She's not going to talk. I don't see why we have to force her." Nick turns once again to admire his children.

"Greg, Jeff, honey, why don't you let Danny play with you?" Carol calls to her sons. They know Danny too well to take her request seriously, and keep throwing. "Come on, Danny," Carol says. "Wouldn't you like to play?"

"No, no, no, no, no," Danny says. He is roaring, but his mouth is pressed so tightly against the diving board that his voice comes out a hoarse yowl. Such an outburst isn't hard for Danny to muster. He is used to bursting into tears, into screams, into hysterical fits at the slightest inclination.

Nick gives Carol a wearied look and says, "Now you've done it." Danny bolts up from the diving board and runs into the house.

Carol sighs, takes out a Kleenex, and swats at her eyes. Nick looks at Elaine, whose expression has not changed.

"He's your son," Nick says.

"What?" says Elaine, touching her face like a wakened dreamer.

Carol rocks her face in her hands.

Belle, Danny's grandmother, is in the kitchen, pulling burrs from the dog and cooking lunch, when Danny runs by. "Danny! What's wrong?" she shouts, but he doesn't answer, and flies through the door at the back of the kitchen into the room where he lives. Once inside, he dives into the big pink bed, with its fancy dust ruffle and lace-trimmed pillows; he breathes in the clean smell of the linen. It is Belle's room, the maid's quarters made over for her widowhood, and it is full of photographs of four generations of champion Labrador retrievers. When Danny arrived he was supposed to live with Greg and Jeff in their room, but he screamed so loudly that Belle—exhausted—said he could sleep in her room, and she would sleep with her other grandsons—at least for the time being. It has been two months, and Danny has not relented.

Belle is pulling burrs from her pants suit. "I'm coming in, Danny," she says, and he buries his face—hard—in the pillow. He has learned that he can usually make himself cry by doing this, even when he is actually feeling happy. The trick is to clench your eyes until a few drops of water squeeze out. And then it just happens.

Danny feels hot breath on his hair, and a soft body next to his on the bed. Belle crawls and eases her way around him, making the bed squeak, until her wet mouth is right at his ear. "What's wrong, sweetie pie?" she whispers, but he doesn't answer, only moans into his pillow.

Belle gets up abruptly. "Oh, Danny," she says, "things would be so much easier if you'd just be nice. What happened to the old Danny I used to know? Don't you know how much happier everyone else would be if you'd just be happy?"

"I hate baseball," Danny says.

Danny is an only child and he looks like the perfect combination of his two parents. His eyes are round and blue, like his mother's, his mouth small and pouting, like his father's, and his wavy brown hair halfway between Elaine's, which is red and packed in tight curls, and Allen's, which is black and straight and dense. Growing up, Danny rarely saw his parents together, and so he doesn't know the extent to which he resembles them. He remembers that his father would come home from work and insist that Danny not disturb him. In those days Allen believed that when a man got back to the house in the evening he deserved time alone with his wife as a reward for his labors. Every night Elaine ate two dinners—Spaghetti-Os or Tater Tots with Danny, at six, and later, after Danny had gone to bed, something elaborate and romantic, by candlelight, with Allen. She would usually talk about the later dinners with Danny during the earlier ones. "Your father's very demanding," she said once, proudly. "He has strict notions of what a wife should do. Tonight I'm making chicken cacciatore." Danny knows that both he and his mother must have been very young when she said this, because he remembers the dreamy deliberateness with which Elaine pronounced "cacciatore," as if it were a magical incantation.

Sometimes, before Elaine put Danny to bed, Allen would pick him up and twirl him around and make sounds like an airplane. Danny slept. Through the open crack in his bedroom door he could see the candles flickering.

As he grew up Danny got to know his mother better. Starting when he was six or seven she lost her enthusiasm for dinner. "I can't manage you, Danny," she'd grumble to him. "I can't manage children. I'm unfit." Danny thought of how she always wrote DANNY G. on his lunchbag (and would continue to do so, even when he entered middle school, where last names matter). He thought of the way she made his lunch each day—peanut butter sandwich, apple, bag of cheese puffs, paper napkin. The candlelit dinners stopped, and Danny, who had never attended any of them, probably missed the ritual more than either of his parents. The three of them ate together, now, usually in silence. In those days, Elaine had a habit of staring darkly at Allen when he wasn't looking. Danny remembers Allen's anxious looks back, when he caught her face full of questions, before she shifted her eyes and changed the subject. In retrospect, Danny knows that his mother was trying to guess something, and that his father was trying to figure out how much she already knew. "I still wanted to cover my tracks," Allen recently told his son. "I knew it was futile. I knew there was no going back. I don't think I even wanted to go back. But I still covered my tracks. It becomes a habit when you do it your whole life."

One day Danny's mother did not show up to pick him up at day camp. It was getting dark, and he was the only one left. The counselor who had stayed behind began to grow impatient. Watching the sky darken, Danny felt more embarrassment than fear.

He was worried that Elaine would be misconstrued as the neglectful mother she believed herself to be, and he knew her not to be.

He lied. "Oh, I forgot," he said. "She had a doctor's appointment. She said I should ask you to drive me home."

"Drive you home?" the counselor said. "Why didn't she send a note?"

"I guess she just thought you would," Danny said.

The counselor looked at him, her face full of confusion, and the beginnings of pity. Perhaps she would call child welfare. Perhaps he would be taken away. But nothing happened. She drove him home. His mother offered no explanation for what she had done, but she did not forget to pick him up again. Danny was relieved. He had feared that she would break down, sobbing, and say to the counselor, "I'm an unfit mother. Take him away."

Somehow they survived the winter. One night at dinner, a few days before spring vacation, Elaine stood up and said, "This is a sham." Then she sat down again and continued eating. Allen looked at her, looked at Danny, looked at his plate. A few nights later she picked up the top of a ceramic sugar bowl which Danny had made her for Christmas and threw it overhand at Allen. It missed him, and shattered against the refrigerator door. Danny jumped, and fought back tears.

"See what I can do?" she said. "See what you've driven me to?"

Allen did not answer her. He quietly put on his jacket, and without a word walked out the back door. He was not home for dinner the next night. When Danny asked Elaine where he'd gone, she threw down her fork and started to cry. "Danny," she said, "there have been a lot of lies in this house."

The next day was the first Monday of vacation, and when Danny came home from playing his mother was still in bed.

"It's O.K., Danny," she said. "I just decided to take the day off. Lie in bed all day, since it's something I've never done before. Don't worry about me. Go ahead and play."

Danny did as she said. That night, at dusk, when he got home, she was asleep, the lights in her room all turned out. He was frightened, and he kept the house lights on even after he'd gone to bed. In the morning he knew that his father was really gone. Only his mother was in the bed when he gently pushed open the door. "I'm not getting up again," she said. "Are you all right, honey? Can you go to the Kravitzes' for dinner?"

"Don't you want anything to eat?" Danny asked.

"I'm not hungry. Don't worry about me."

Danny had dinner with the Kravitzes. Later, returning home, he heard her crying, but he couldn't hear her after he turned on *Star Trek*.

Every afternoon for a week he stood in the threshold of her doorway and asked if she wanted to get up, or if she wanted something to eat. He bought Spaghetti-Os and Doritos with the money in the jar at the back of the pantry he was not supposed to know about. He never asked where his father was. Her room was musty from the closed windows, and even in the morning full of that five o'clock light which is darker than darkness, and in which the majority of car accidents happen. "Leave me alone," she would call out from the dark now. "I'm tired. For Christ's sake, just let me get some sleep. Go play or something."

Then he would close the door and make himself some Campbell's soup and watch forbidden TV all night—variety shows and detective shows and reruns after eleven. Elaine had always allotted him three hours of TV per day; when she came home from shopping she'd feel the TV to see if it was warm, if he'd been cheating. Now there were no rules.

The first day of school—a week after Elaine had gone to bed—Danny woke up to hear her screaming. He ran to her bedroom, and found her sitting up on the bed, streaked in light. She had ripped the curtains open, and the bared morning sun, through the shutters, bisected her face, the mat of her unwashed hair, the nightgown falling over her shoulders. She sat there and screamed, over and over again, and Danny rushed in, shouting, "What's wrong? What's wrong?"

And then she grabbed the ends of her hair and began tearing at them, and grinding her teeth together, and wailing. Finally she collapsed, in tears, onto the bed. She turned to look at Danny and she screamed, "I can't change! Don't you see, no matter how much I want to, I just can't change!"

Danny got Mrs. Kravitz. She came over and hoisted Elaine out of bed and began marching her around the hall. "One, two, three, let's go, let's go," Mrs. Kravitz said. "Danny, go look in the bathroom for empty pill bottles, sweetheart, your mommy's going to be just fine."

Danny didn't find any empty pill bottles, and when he came out of the bathroom some paramedics were coming through the kitchen with a stretcher. "I can't stand up," Elaine was telling Mrs. Kravitz. "I'll be sick."

"Just lie down now," Mrs. Kravitz said. Danny remembered that today was the first day of school, and he wondered whether he should go to his homeroom class or not, but when he looked at the clock, he saw that it was already eight o'clock. School had started.

Danny spent the night at the Kravitzes' house, and the next day he went to Nick and Carol's. This was in a different school district, but nobody talked about school. That night, when his cousins wanted to watch a different television show from Danny, he threw his first fit.

A few days later, while he was eating his cereal at the kitchen table, Danny's father arrived. Danny didn't say hello. He continued to spoon the sweet milk into his mouth, though the cereal was gone. Belle, who was making pancakes, turned the burner off and quietly slunk out of the room. Allen sat down across from Danny, holding a cup of coffee. He had a new short haircut, and was growing a stubbly beard. They were alone in the room.

"I know you're angry," Allen said. "I know you wonder where I've been and why your mother got sick. I don't know where to begin, and I don't expect instant forgiveness, but I do want you to hear me out. Will you do that for me? I know you'll have a lot of questions, and I'm prepared to answer them. Just give me a chance."

Danny looked at his father and didn't say anything.

* * *

On weekends Danny went to visit his father in the city. Allen was living with a man named Gene in an apartment in Greenwich Village, and though he had quit being a stockbroker, he continued to live off his own investments. Each Friday Danny rode the train up, past the fast-food franchises thrown up around the railroad stations, the muddy Amboys, the rows of tenements in Elizabeth. Allen took him to museums, to the theater, to restaurants. On Sunday he saw his son off at Penn Station. "I used to ride this train every day," he told Danny, as they waited on the platform. "I used to play cards with Uncle Nick on this train. It seems like hundreds of years."

"That was when you and Mom had dinner by candlelight," Danny said, remembering how his father twirled him in the air, how his mother pronounced the word "cacciatore"—slowly, and with such relish.

"We were innocent," Allen said. "Your mother and I believed in something that was wrong for us. Wrong for me, I should say."

Danny looked away from his father, toward the train which was now moving into the station.

"You probably think your mother's getting sick is the result of my being gay," Allen said, putting his hand on his son's shoulder. "But that's only partially true. It goes much further, much deeper than that, Danny. You know your mother hasn't been well for a long time."

From where he's lying, his face against the pillow, Danny hears the harsh sound of tires against gravel, and bolts up in bed. Through his window he sees a taxi in the driveway, and Allen, dressed in blue jeans and a lumberjack shirt, fighting off Belle's furious barking dog. Elaine, seeing Allen, has crawled up on her haunches, and is hugging her knees. When Allen sees Elaine, he turns to rehail the taxi, but it is already out of the driveway.

"Now, Allen, don't be upset," Nick says, walking out onto the gravel, taking Allen's shoulder in one hand, the dog in the other.

"You didn't tell me she was going to be here," Allen says.

"That's because you wouldn't have come out," says Carol, joining them. "You two have to talk. We're sorry to do this, but it's the only way. Someone's got to take some responsibility."

As if he is a child about to ride a bicycle for the first time without training wheels, Allen is literally pushed by Carol toward his wife.

"What's going on? What's happening here?" shouts Belle. When she sees Allen, she stops dead in her tracks.

"You didn't tell him?" Belle asks.

Allen begins to move uncertainly toward Elaine, who is still rearing, and Carol and Nick push Belle into the kitchen. Danny jumps out of his bed and kneels next to the door.

They whisper. Nick nods and walks outdoors. "Relax, Mom," says Carol. "They've got to talk. They've got to make some decisions."

"Elaine's hospitalized." Belle announces this known fact in a low voice, and looks toward the door to her room.

"She's been hiding her whole life. She's got to face up to facts. I can't take this much longer." Carol lights a cigarette, and rubs her eyes.

Belle looks away. "He's just a child," she says.

"Their child," Carol says. "Not ours."

"Not so loudly!" Belle says, and points to the bedroom door. "Have some sympathy. She's been through a personal hell."

"I know things were hard," Carol says. "But to commit herself! I'm sorry, Mom, but as far as I'm concerned, that's just self-dramatizing. No one commits themselves these days. You see a psychiatrist on Central Park West once a week. You continue your life, and you deal with your problem."

"Her problem is worse than that," Belle says. "She needs help. All my life I never said so, but I knew she was—not strong. And now I have to admit, knowing she's taken care of, I feel relieved."

"But it's not like she's crazy!" Carol says. "It's not like she's a raving lunatic, or schizophrenic, or anything. She's basically just fine, isn't she? She just needs some help, doesn't she?"

Belle doesn't answer. Carol sits down, lays her head on the kitchen table, and starts to cry.

"Oh, my poor girl," Belle says, and strokes her daughter's hair. "I know you're worried about your sister. And she is fine. She'll be fine."

"Then why can't she just check herself out of that hospital and take her kid and start seeing a goddamned shrink once a week?" Carol says, lifting up her head and turning to face her mother. "I'll pay for it, if that's what she needs."

"Keep your voice down!" Belle whispers loudly. "Let's talk outside."

She pulls Carol out of her chair, and out the screen door. As soon as they've left the kitchen, Danny makes a run for the stairs. He sneaks into his cousins' room, which is full of baseball cards and Star Wars toys, closes the door, and perches on the window seat, which overlooks the swimming pool. Below him, he can see his parents arguing in one corner, while in another, Belle and Carol continue their discussion. Belle is trying to explain that Elaine cannot take care of a household, and this is her problem, and Carol is shaking her head. As for Nick, he has moved out onto the lawn, where he is playing baseball with Greg and Jeff.

Danny can just barely make out his parents' voices. "They arranged this," he hears Elaine saying. "They think Danny's a pain in the ass."

"You know I'd take him if I could," Allen answers.

"I thought you were leading such a model life!"

"There's nothing about my life which would create an unhealthy atmosphere for Danny. I'm just not ready for him yet."

"Good," Elaine says. "He can come live with me."

Danny closes the window. He knows to cover up his tracks. Then he runs back downstairs, through the kitchen, and out the screen door. He runs alongside the pool, past his parents, and toward the woods. Allen catches his eye, and waves. Danny waves back, keeps running.

When Danny first arrived at Nick and Carol's, everything was alien: the extra bed in Greg and Jeff's room which pulled out from under, the coloration of the television set, the spaghetti sauce. They were so indulgent toward him, in his unhappiness, that he wondered if perhaps he had leukemia, and they weren't telling him. And then he realized that he did not have leukemia. He was merely the passive victim of a broken home. For months he had held back his own fear and anger for the sake of his mother. Now she had betrayed him. She *was* unfit. He *had* been taken away, as had she. There was no reason to be good anymore.

What Danny didn't count on was Carol and Nick's expectation that somehow he would change, shape himself to their lives. No child with leukemia would be asked to change. Danny decided to become a child with leukemia—a sick child, a thwarted child, a child to be indulged. Nick and Carol asked him if he wouldn't maybe consider trading places with his grandmother and moving into his cousins' room, which would be fun for all three, like camp. Danny threw his biggest fit ever. They never asked him again. They gave him wearied looks, when he refused to eat, when he demanded to watch what he wanted to watch, when he wouldn't talk to company. They lost patience, and he in turn lost patience: Didn't they understand? He was a victim. And certainly he had only to mention his mother's name, and his own stomach would sink, and Carol's eyes would soften, and suddenly she would become like his grandmother—maternal and embracing. He made himself need her to be maternal and embracing.

The night his mother went to bed forever, Danny learned two things: to be silent was to be crazy, and to be loud was also to be crazy. It seemed to him that he did not have a choice. He knew no way of living that did not include morose silences and fits of fury. When Carol asked him why he wouldn't just enjoy the life he had, he felt a fierce resistance rise in his chest. He was not going to give himself up.

Now, running from his crazy parents, Danny arrives at a place in the woods—a patch of dry leaves sheltered by an old sycamore—which he has designated his own. Only a few feet away, the neighborhood children are playing Capture the Flag in the cul-de-sac, and he can hear their screams and warnings through the trees. He turns around once, circling his territory, and then he begins. Today he will invent an episode of *The Perfect Brothers Show,* the variety show on his personal network. He has several other series in the works, including *Grippo,* a detective drama, and *Pierre!* set in the capital city of South Dakota.

He begins. He does all the voices, and makes the sound of applause by driving his tongue against the roof of his mouth. "And now," he says, "for your viewing pleasure, another episode of *The Perfect Brothers Show!*"

The orchestra plays a fanfare. In another voice, Danny sings:

> *A perfect night for comedy!*
> *For fun and musicality!*

We'll change you!
Rearrange you!
Just you wait and see!
Welcome to The Perfect Brothers Show*!*

He is in the midst of inventing a comic skit, followed by a song from this week's guest star, Loni Anderson, when Jeff—the younger and more persistently good-natured of the brothers—appears from between the trees. "Can I play?" he asks.

Danny, to his own surprise, doesn't throw a fit. "Yes," he says. "We'll do a comedy skit. You're the housewife and I'm Superman."

"I want to be Superman," Jeff says.

"All right, all right." Now Danny begins to give instructions for the skit, but halfway through Jeff interrupts and says, "This is boring. Let's play baseball."

"If you want to play something like *that,*" Danny says, "go play Capture the Flag." He throws up his hands in disgust.

"There are girls playing," Jeff says. "Well, if you won't play, I'll play baseball with my dad!"

"Good," says Danny. "Leave me alone."

Jeff runs off towards the house. Part of the way there, he turns once. "You're weird," he says.

Danny ignores him. He is halfway through his skit—playing both parts—when he is interrupted again. This time it is his father. "How are you, old man?" Allen asks. "Want to go to the Paper Palace?"

For a moment Danny's eyes widen, and then he remembers how unhappy he is. "All right," he says.

They take Carol's station wagon, and drive to the Paper Palace, a huge pink cement structure in the middle of an old shopping center. The shopping center is near Danny's old house.

"You've loved the Paper Palace—how long?" Allen asks. "I think you were four the first time I brought you here. You loved it. Remember what I bought you?"

"An origami set and a Richie Rich comic book," Danny says. He rarely gets to the Paper Palace anymore; Carol shops in the more elegant mall near her house.

"When we lived here, all I wanted to do was to get into Carol and Nick's neighborhood. A year ago today. Just think. All I could think about was getting a raise and buying a house. I might have bought the house next door to Carol and Nick's. I wanted you to grow up in that area. All those trees. The fresh air. The great club."

"I am anyhow, I guess," Danny says.

"Don't let it fool you," Allen says. "It all seems so perfect. It all looks so perfect. But soon enough the paint chips, there are corners bitten by the dog, you start sweeping things under the bed. Believe me, under the beds, there's as much dust in Nick and Carol's house as there was in ours."

"Carol has a maid," Danny says.

"Just never trust cleanness. All the bad stuff—the really bad stuff—happens in clean houses, where everything's tidy and nobody says anything more than good morning."

"Our house wasn't like that," Danny says.

Allen looks at him. But now they are in the parking lot of the shopping center, and the colorful promise of the Paper Palace takes both of them over. They rush inside. Danny browses ritualistically at stationery and comic books, reads through the plot synopses in the soap opera magazines, scrupulously notes each misspelling of a character's name. Allen lags behind him. They buy a copy of *Vogue* for Elaine. In front of them in line, a fat, balding man upsets a box of candy on the sales counter as he purchases a copy of *Playgirl*. His effort to avoid attention has backfired, and drawn the complicated looks of all around him. Danny avoids looking at Allen, but Allen's eyes shoot straight to Danny, whose face has a pained, embarrassed expression on it. They do not mention the fat man as they walk out of the store.

Years ago, when Danny was only six or seven, he found a magazine. He was playing in the basement, dressing up in some old clothes of Allen's which he had found in a cardboard box. The magazine was at the bottom of the box. When Elaine came down to check what Danny was up to, she found him sitting on a trunk, examining a series of pictures of young, dazed-looking men posed to simulate various acts of fornication. Elaine grabbed the magazine away from Danny and demanded to know where he'd gotten it. He told her that he had found it, and he pointed to the box.

Elaine looked again at the magazine, and then at the box. She thumbed through the pages, looking at the photographs. Then she put the magazine down on top of the box and wrapped her arms around herself.

"Danny," she said, "for God's sake, don't lie about this. You don't have to. You can tell me the truth. Are you sure that's where you got this thing?"

"Swear to God and hope to die, stick a needle in my eye," Danny said.

"Get upstairs," said Elaine.

"Do you want a Velamint?" Allen asks Danny in the car, as they drive back from the Paper Palace. They are riding down a wide, dark road, lined with sycamores. Danny takes the small blue wafer from his father, without saying anything. He opens the window, sticks his hand out into the breeze.

"You know, Danny, I've been thinking," Allen says. "I know this fantastic place, this school, in New Hampshire. It's great—really innovative—and it's specially for bright, motivated kids like you."

Danny doesn't answer. When Allen turns to look at him, he sees that his son is clutching the armrest so hard his knuckles have turned white, and biting his lip to hold back tears.

"Danny," Allen says. "Danny, what's wrong?"

"I know I've been a problem," Danny says. "But I've decided to change. Today. I've decided to be happy. Please. I'll make them want me to stay."

Allen is alarmed by Danny's panic. "Danny," he says, "this school isn't punishment. It's a great place. You deserve to go there."

"I played with Jeff today!" Danny says. His voice is at its highest register. He is staring at Allen, his face flushed, a look of pure pleading in his eyes.

Allen puts his hand over his mouth and winces. When they reach a stop sign, he turns to Danny and says, as emphatically as he can, "Danny, don't worry, no one's going to *make* you go anywhere. But, Danny, I don't know if I *want* you to stay with Nick and Carol. After fifteen years in that world, I don't know if I want my son to be hurt by it like I was."

"I won't become a stockbroker. I won't sweep the dust under the bed. But, please, don't send me away."

"Danny, I thought you didn't like it here," Allen says.

"I'm not unfit."

They are still at the stop sign. Behind them, a car is honking, urging them to move on. Danny's eyes are brimming with tears.

Allen shakes his head, and reaches for his son.

They go to Carvel's for ice cream. Ahead of them in line a flustered-looking woman buys cones for ten black children who stand in pairs, holding hands. Two of the girls are pulling violently at each other's arms, while a boy whose spiral of soft-serve ice cream has fallen off his cone cries loudly, and demands reparations. Allen orders two chocolate cones with brown bonnets, and he and Danny sit down in chairs with tiny desks attached to them, like the chairs in Danny's elementary school. There are red lines from tears on Danny's face, but he doesn't really cry—at least, he doesn't make any of the crying noises, the heaves and stuttering wails. He picks off the chocolate coating of the brown bonnet and eats it in pieces before even touching the actual ice cream.

"I'm glad you haven't lost your appetite," Allen says.

Danny nods weakly, and continues to eat. The woman marches the ten children out the door, and into a small pink van. "Danny," Allen says, "what can I say? What do you want me to say?"

Danny bites off the bottom of his cone. Half-melted ice cream plops onto the little desk. "Jesus Christ," Allen mutters, and rubs his eyes.

When they get back to the house, Allen joins Nick and Carol under the umbrella on the patio. Elaine is still lying on the chaise, her eyes closed. Danny gets out of the car after his father, walks a circle around the pool, biting his thumbnail, and resumes his position on the diving board. Nearby, Greg and Jeff are again playing catch. "Hey, Danny, want to throw the ball?" Allen shouts. He does not hear Carol hiss her warning, "No!" But Danny neither does nor says anything.

"Danny!" Allen shouts again. "Can you hear me?"

Very slowly Danny hoists himself up, crawls off the diving board and walks back toward the house.

"Oh, Christ," Carol says, taking off her sunglasses. "This is more than I can take."

Now Belle appears at the kitchen door, waving a batter-caked spatula. "What happened?" she asks.

"The same story," Carol says.

"I'll see to him," Allen says. He casts a parting glance at Elaine, and walks into the kitchen. "The same thing happened this morning," Belle tells him as they walk toward Danny's room.

But this time, the door is wide open, instead of slammed shut, and Danny is lying on his back on the bed, his face blank, his eyes tearless.

At first Belle thinks he is sick. "Honey, are you all right?" she asks, feeling his head. "He's cool," she tells Allen.

Allen sits down on the bed and arcs his arms over Danny's stomach. "Danny, what's wrong?" he asks.

Danny turns to look at his father, his face full of a pain too strong for a child to mimic.

"I can't change," he says. "I can't change. I can't change."

In the kitchen, Belle is wrathful. She does not keep her voice down; she does not seem to care that Danny can hear every word she is saying. "I see red when I look at you people," she tells her children. "In my day, people didn't just abandon everything to gratify themselves. In my day, people didn't abandon their children. You're so selfish, all you think about is yourselves."

"What do you want from me?" Allen answers. "What kind of father could I have been? I was living a lie."

"See what I mean?" Belle says. "Selfish. You assume I'm talking about you. But I'm talking about all of you. And you, too, Carol."

"For Christ's sake, Mother, he's not my son!" Carol says. "And he's wrecking my sons' lives. And my life."

Elaine has been fingering her hair. But now she suddenly slams her hand against the table and lets out a little moan. "He really said that?" she says. "Oh, Christ, he really said that."

"I've had it up to here with all of you," Belle announces. "It's unspeakable. I've heard enough."

She turns from them all, as if she has seen enough as well. Allen and Elaine and Nick look down at the table, like ashamed children. But Carol gets up, and walks very deliberately to face her mother. "Now just one minute," she says, her lips twitching with anger. "Just one minute. It's easy for you to just stand there and rant and rave. But I have to live with it, day in and day out, I have to take care of him and put up with his crap. And I have to listen to my kids say, 'What's with that Danny? When's he going away?' Well, maybe I am selfish. I've worked hard to raise my kids well. And now, just because Elaine screws everything up for herself, suddenly I'm expected to bear the brunt of it, take all the punishment. And everything I've been working for is going down the tubes because she can't take care of her own kid! Well, then, I will be selfish. I am selfish. I have had enough of this."

"Now just a minute, Carol," Allen says.

"You take him," Carol says, turning around to confront him. "You take him home, or don't say a word to me. There's not one word you have a right to say to me."

"Damn it!" Allen says. "Doesn't anybody understand? I'm doing my best."

"You've had two months," Nick says.

Belle, her arms wrapped around her waist, begins to cry softly. Sitting at the table, Elaine cries as well, though more loudly, and with less decorum.

Then, with a small click, the door to Danny's bedroom opens, and he walks into the kitchen. Allen and Nick stand up, nearly knocking their chairs over in the process. "Danny!" Carol says. Her voice edges on panic. "Are you all right?"

"Yes, thank you," Danny says.

Elaine lifts her head from the table. "Danny," she says. "Danny, I—" She moves her lips, struggling to form words. But nothing comes out. Danny looks down at her, his eyes full of a frightening, adult pity. Then he turns away and walks outside.

Everyone jumps up at once to follow him. But Allen holds up his hand. "I'll go," he says. He scrambles out the door, and after Danny, who is marching past the swimming pool, toward the patch of woods where he likes to play. When he gets there, he stops and waits, his back to his father.

"Danny," Allen says, coming up behind him. "You heard everything. I don't know what to say. I wish I did."

Danny has his arms crossed tightly over his chest. "I've thought about it," he says. "I've decided."

"What?" Allen says.

"About the school," Danny says. "I've decided I'll go."

A few days later, Danny boards the train which snakes along the Jersey coast to New York. He is riding to visit his father. An old couple is sitting across the way from him, a gnarled little man and his taller, white-haired wife, her white-gloved hands clasped calmly around each other. Like Danny, the couple is not reading the paper, but looking out the green-tinted windows at yellow grass, small shops, warehouses.

"You'd better get your things together," the husband says. "We're almost there."

"No," the wife says. "We don't want South Amboy. We want Perth Amboy." The husband shakes his head no. "South Amboy. I'm sure she said South Amboy."

The wife is quiet for a few seconds, until the conductor shouts, "South Amboy, South Amboy next!" Now she cannot control herself. "I'm *sure* it's Perth Amboy," she says. The husband is buttoning his jacket, reaching for his hat. "Will you listen to me for once?" he says. "It's South Amboy." The wife shakes her head. "I'm sure," she says. "I'm sure."

Gradually, and then with a sudden grind, the train comes to a halt. The husband lumbers down the aisle, knocking past Danny, shaking his head. "I'm getting off," he says. "Are you coming?" The wife stands, hesitates, sits down. "It's not this stop," she says. He makes a violent motion with his hand, and walks out the door, onto the station platform. She stands to follow him, but the doors close suddenly. His fist appears, as if disembodied, rapping on the window. Then the train is moving again.

For a moment, she just stands there, shocked. Then the train's lurching forces her to sit down. A look comes over her face first of indignation, then of fear and confusion, then finally, of weariness—with her husband, with the train, with their lives which will go on like this. She bends over and pulls herself into the corner of her seat, as if trying to make herself as small as possible, and picks at a loose thread of her dress with one of her white-gloved hands.

Then she comes to consciousness. She realizes that she is not alone on the train. Her eyes narrow, and focus on Danny. Late afternoon, almost dark. He is singing a song about comedy and fun and musicality. He tells her it's going to be a perfect night.

JACK LONDON
(1876–1916)

The illegitimate son of a father who was a traveling astrologer and spiritualist and a mother who performed as a medium, Jack London experienced poverty and deprivation from his earliest days. Beginning as an adolescent, he took jobs wherever he could find them, at various times working as an ice-wagon driver, pin-boy in a bowling alley, oyster pirate on a San Francisco ship, factory worker, and longshoreman. He traveled throughout the country riding in railroad boxcars as well as sailing to Japan as a crew member of a sealing ship. In 1897, he traveled to the Klondike in search of gold. In that year, he began to publish his stories. His first collection of stories, *The Son of the Wolf*, appeared in 1900. Although he never completed his freshman year at the University of California, London read widely and was particularly influenced by the works of Darwin, Marx, and Nietzsche. Among the fifty volumes of stories, novels, and essays he published during a highly successful writing career are the novels *The Call of the Wild* (1903), *The Sea-Wolf* (1904), *The Game* (1905), *White Fang* (1906), *Martin Eden* (1909), *Adventure* (1911), *The Mutiny of the Elsinore* (1914), and *The Star Rover* (1915). Some of his stories are collected in *Love of Life* (1906) and *When God Laughs and Other Stories* (1911).

The Apostate

> Now I wake me up to work;
> I pray the Lord I may not shirk.
> If I should die before the night,
> I pray the Lord my work's all right.
> —Amen.

"If you don't git up, Johnny, I won't give you a bite to eat!"

The threat had no effect on the boy. He clung stubbornly to sleep, fighting for its oblivion as the dreamer fights for his dream. The boy's hands loosely clenched themselves, and he made feeble, spasmodic blows at the air. These blows were intended for his mother, but she betrayed practiced familiarity in avoiding them as she shook him roughly by the shoulder.

"Lemme 'lone!"

It was a cry that began, muffled, in the deeps of sleep, that swiftly rushed upward, like a wail, into passionate belligerence, and that died away and sank down into an inarticulate whine. It was a bestial cry, as of a soul in torment, filled with infinite protest and pain.

But she did not mind. She was a sad-eyed, tired-faced woman, and she had grown used to this task, which she repeated every day of her life. She got a grip on the bed-clothes and tried to strip them down; but the boy, ceasing his punching, clung to them desperately. In a huddle, at the foot of the bed, he still remained covered. Then she tried dragging the bedding to the floor. The boy opposed her. She braced herself. Hers was the superior weight, and the boy and bedding gave, the former instinctively following the latter in order to shelter against the chill of the room that bit into his body.

As he toppled on the edge of the bed it seemed that he must fall headfirst to the floor. But consciousness fluttered up in him. He righted himself and for a moment perilously balanced. Then he struck the floor on his feet. On the instant his mother seized him by the shoulders and shook him. Again his fists struck out, this time with more force and directness. At the same time his eyes opened. She released him. He was awake.

"All right," he mumbled.

She caught up the lamp and hurried out, leaving him in darkness.

"You'll be docked," she warned back to him.

He did not mind the darkness. When he had got into his clothes, he went out into the kitchen. His tread was very heavy for so thin and light a boy. His legs dragged with their own weight, which seemed unreasonable because they were such skinny legs. He drew a broken-bottomed chair to the table.

"Johnny!" his mother called sharply.

He arose as sharply from the chair and, without a word, went to the sink. It was a greasy, filthy sink. A smell came up from the outlet. He took no notice of it. That a sink should smell was to him part of the natural order, just as it was a part of the natural order that the soap should be grimy with dishwater and hard to lather. Nor did he try very hard to make it lather. Several splashes of the cold water from the running faucet completed the function. He did not wash his teeth. For that matter he had never seen a toothbrush, nor did he know that there existed beings in the world who were guilty of so great a foolishness as tooth washing.

"You might wash yourself wunst a day without bein' told," his mother complained.

She was holding a broken lid on the pot as she poured two cups of coffee. He made no remark, for this was a standing quarrel between them, and the one thing upon which his mother was hard as adamant. "Wunst" a day it was compulsory that he should wash his face. He dried himself on a greasy towel, damp and dirty and ragged, that left his face covered with shreds of lint.

"I wish we didn't live so far away," she said, as he sat down. "I try to do the best I can. You know that. But a dollar on the rent is such a savin', an' we've more room here. You know that."

He scarcely followed her. He had heard it all before, many times. The range of her thought was limited, and she was ever harking back to the hardship worked upon them by living so far from the mills.

"A dollar means more grub," he remarked sententiously. "I'd sooner do the walkin' an' git the grub."

He ate hurriedly, half chewing the bread and washing the unmasticated chunks down with coffee. The hot and muddy liquid went by the name of coffee. Johnny thought it was coffee—and excellent coffee. That was one of the few of life's illusions that remained to him. He had never drunk real coffee in his life.

In addition to the bread, there was a small piece of cold pork. His mother refilled his cup with coffee. As he was finishing the bread, he began to watch if more was forthcoming. She intercepted his questioning glance.

"Now, don't be hoggish, Johnny," was her comment. "You've had your share. Your brothers an' sisters are smaller'n you."

He did not answer the rebuke. He was not much of a talker. Also, he ceased his hungry glancing for more. He was uncomplaining, with a patience that was as terrible as the school in which it had been learned. He finished his coffee, wiped his mouth on the back of his hand, and started to rise.

"Wait a second," she said hastily. "I guess the loaf kin stand you another slice—a thin un."

There was legerdemain in her actions. With all the seeming of cutting a slice from the loaf for him, she put loaf and slice back in the bread box and conveyed to him one of her own two slices. She believed she had deceived him, but he had noted her sleight of hand. Nevertheless, he took the bread shamelessly. He had a philosophy that his mother, what of her chronic sickliness, was not much of an eater anyway.

She saw that he was chewing the bread dry, and reached over and emptied her coffee cup into his.

"Don't set good somehow on my stomach this morning," she explained.

A distant whistle, prolonged and shrieking, brought both of them to their feet. She glanced at the tin alarm clock on the shelf. The hands stood at half-past five. The rest of the factory world was just arousing from sleep. She drew a shawl about her shoulders, and on her head put a dingy hat, shapeless and ancient.

"We've got to run," she said, turning the wick of the lamp and blowing down the chimney.

They groped their way out and down the stairs. It was clear and cold, and Johnny shivered at the first contact with the outside air. The stars had not yet begun to pale in the sky, and the city lay in blackness. Both Johnny and his mother shuffled their feet as they walked. There was no ambition in the leg muscles to swing the feet clear of the ground.

After fifteen silent minutes, his mother turned off to the right.

"Don't be late," was her final warning from out of the dark that was swallowing her up.

He made no response, steadily keeping on his way. In the factory quarter, doors were opening everywhere, and he was soon one of a multitude that pressed onward through the dark. As he entered the factory gate the whistle blew again. He glanced at the east. Across a ragged skyline of housetops a pale light was beginning to creep. This much he saw of the day as he turned his back upon it and joined his work gang.

He took his place in one of many long rows of machines. Before him, above a bin filled with small bobbins, were large bobbins revolving rapidly. Upon these he wound the jute twine of the small bobbins. The work was simple. All that was required was celerity. The small bobbins were emptied so rapidly, and there were so many large bobbins that did the emptying, that there were no idle moments.

He worked mechanically. When a small bobbin ran out, he used his left hand for a brake, stopping the large bobbin and at the same time, with thumb and forefinger, catching the flying end of twine. Also, at the same time, with his right hand, he caught up the loose twine end of a small bobbin. These various acts with both hands were performed simultaneously and swiftly. Then there would come a flash of his hands as he looped the weaver's knot and released the bobbin. There was nothing difficult about weaver's knots. He once boasted he could tie them in his sleep. And for that matter, he sometimes did, toiling centuries long in a single night at tying an endless succession of weaver's knots.

Some of the boys shirked, wasting time and machinery by not replacing the small bobbins when they ran out. And there was an overseer to prevent this. He caught Johnny's neighbor at the trick, and boxed his ears.

"Look at Johnny there—why ain't you like him?" the overseer wrathfully demanded.

Johnny's bobbins were running full blast, but he did not thrill at the indirect praise. There had been a time . . . but that was long ago, very long ago. His apathetic face was expressionless as he listened to himself being held up as a shining example. He was the perfect worker. He knew that. He had been told so, often. It was a commonplace, and besides it didn't seem to mean anything to him any more. From the perfect worker he had evolved into the perfect machine. When his work went wrong, it was with him as with the machine, due to faulty material. It would have been as possible for a perfect nail die to cut imperfect nails as for him to make a mistake.

And small wonder. There had never been a time when he had not been in intimate relationship with machines. Machinery had almost been bred into him, and at any rate he had been brought up on it. Twelve years before, there had been a small flutter of excitement in the loom room of this very mill. Johnny's mother had fainted. They stretched her out on the floor in the midst of the shrieking machines. A couple of elderly women were called from their looms. The foreman assisted. And in a few minutes there was one more soul in the loom room than had entered by the doors. It was Johnny, born with the pounding, crashing roar of the looms in his ears, drawing with his first breath the warm, moist air that was thick with flying lint. He had coughed that first day in order to rid his lungs of the lint; and for the same reason he had coughed ever since.

The boy alongside of Johnny whimpered and sniffed. The boy's face was convulsed with hatred for the overseer who kept a threatening eye on him from a distance; but every bobbin was running full. The boy yelled terrible oaths into the whirling bobbins before him; but the sound did not carry half a dozen feet, the roaring of the room holding it in and containing it like a wall.

Of all this Johnny took no notice. He had a way of accepting things. Besides, things grow monotonous by repetition, and this particular happening he had witnessed many times. It seemed to him as useless to oppose the overseer as to defy the will of a machine. Machines were made to go in certain ways and to perform certain tasks. It was the same with the overseer.

But at eleven o'clock there was excitement in the room. In an apparently occult way the excitement instantly permeated everywhere. The one-legged boy who worked on the other side of Johnny bobbed swiftly across the floor to a bin truck that stood empty. Into this he dived out of sight, crutch and all. The superintendent of the mill was coming along, accompanied by a young man. He was well dressed and wore a starched shirt—a gentleman, in Johnny's classification of men, and also, "the Inspector."

He looked sharply at the boys as he passed along. Sometimes he stopped and asked questions. When he did so, he was compelled to shout at the top of his lungs, at which moments his face was ludicrously contorted with the strain of making himself heard. His quick eye noted the empty machine alongside of Johnny's, but he said nothing. Johnny also caught his eye, and he stopped abruptly. He caught Johnny by the arm to draw him back a step from the machine; but with an exclamation of surprise he released the arm.

"Pretty skinny," the superintendent laughed anxiously.

"Pipe stems," was the answer. "Look at those legs. The boy's got the rickets—incipient, but he's got them. If epilepsy doesn't get him in the end, it will be because tuberculosis gets him first."

Johnny listened, but did not understand. Furthermore he was not interested in future ills. There was an immediate and more serious ill that threatened him in the form of the inspector.

"Now, my boy, I want you to tell me the truth," the inspector said, or shouted, bending close to the boy's ear to make him hear. "How old are you?"

"Fourteen," Johnny lied, and he lied with the full force of his lungs. So loudly did he lie that it started him off in a dry, hacking cough that lifted the lint which had been settling in his lungs all morning.

"Looks sixteen at least," said the superintendent.

"Or sixty," snapped the inspector.

"He's always looked that way."

"How long?" asked the inspector, quickly.

"For years. Never gets a bit older."

"Or younger, I dare say. I suppose he's worked here all those years?"

"Off and on—but that was before the new law was passed," the superintendent hastened to add.

"Machine idle?" the inspector asked, pointing at the unoccupied machine beside Johnny's, in which the part-filled bobbins were flying like mad.

"Looks that way." The superintendent motioned the overseer to him and shouted in his ear and pointed at the machine. "Machine's idle," he reported back to the inspector.

They passed on, and Johnny returned to his work, relieved in that the ill had been averted. But the one-legged boy was not so fortunate. The sharp-eyed inspector haled him out at arm's length from the bin truck. His lips were quivering, and his face had all the expression of one upon whom was fallen profound and irremediable disaster. The overseer looked astounded, as though for the first time he had laid eyes on the boy, while the superintendent's face expressed shock and displeasure.

"I know him," the inspector said. "He's twelve years old. I've had him discharged from three factories inside the year. This makes the fourth."

He turned to the one-legged boy. "You promised me, word and honor, that you'd go to school."

The one-legged boy burst into tears. "Please, Mr. Inspector, two babies died on us, and we're awful poor."

"What makes you cough that way?" the inspector demanded, as though charging him with crime.

And as in denial of guilt, the one-legged boy replied: "It ain't nothin'. I jes' caught a cold last week, Mr. Inspector, that's all."

In the end the one-legged boy went out of the room with the inspector, the latter accompanied by the anxious and protesting superintendent. After that, monotony settled down again. The long morning and the longer afternoon wore away and the whistle blew for quitting time. Darkness had already fallen when Johnny passed out through the factory gate. In the interval the sun had made a golden ladder of the sky, flooded the world with its gracious warmth, and dropped down and disappeared in the west behind a ragged skyline of housetops.

Supper was the family meal of the day—the one meal at which Johnny encountered his younger brothers and sisters. It partook of the nature of an encounter, to him, for he was very old, while they were distressingly young. He had no patience with their excessive and amazing juvenility. He did not understand it. His own childhood was too far behind him. He was like an old and irritable man, annoyed by the turbulence of their young spirits that was to him arrant silliness. He glowered silently over his food, finding compensation in the thought that they would soon have to go to work. That would take the edge off of them and make them sedate and dignified—like him. Thus it was, after the fashion of the human, that Johnny made of himself a yardstick with which to measure the universe.

During the meal, his mother explained in various ways and with infinite repetition that she was trying to do the best she could; so that it was with relief, the scant meal ended, that Johnny shoved back his chair and arose. He debated for a moment between bed and the front door, and finally went out the latter. He did not go far. He sat down on the stoop, his knees drawn up and his narrow shoulders drooping forward, his elbows on his knees and the palms of his hands supporting his chin.

As he sat there, he did no thinking. He was just resting. So far as his mind was concerned, it was asleep. His brothers and sisters came out, and with other children played noisily about him. An electric globe on the corner lighted their frolics. He was peevish and irritable, that they knew, but the spirit of adventure lured them into teasing him. They joined hands before him, and, keeping time with their bodies, chanted in his face weird and uncomplimentary doggerel. At first he snarled curses at them—curses he had learned from the lips of various foremen. Finding this futile, and remembering his dignity, he relapsed into dogged silence.

His brother Will, next to him in age, having just passed his tenth birthday, was the ringleader. Johnny did not possess particularly kindly feelings toward him. His life had early been embittered by continual giving over and giving way to Will. He had a definite feeling that Will was greatly in his debt and was ungrateful about it. In his own playtime, far back in the dim past, he had been robbed of a large part of that playtime by being compelled to take care of Will. Will was a baby then, and then, as now, their mother had spent her days in the mills. To Johnny had fallen the part of little father and little mother as well.

Will seemed to show the benefit of the giving over and the giving way. He was well built, fairly rugged, as tall as his elder brother and even heavier. It was as though the lifeblood of the one had been diverted into the other's veins. And in spirits it was the same. Johnny was jaded, worn out, without resilience, while his younger brother seemed bursting and spilling over with exuberance.

The mocking chant rose louder and louder. Will leaned closer as he danced, thrusting out his tongue. Johnny's left arm shot out and caught the other around the neck. At the same time he rapped his bony fist to the other's nose. It was a pathetically bony fist, but that it was sharp to hurt was evidenced by the squeal of pain it produced. The other children were uttering frightened cries, while Johnny's sister, Jennie, had dashed into the house.

He thrust Will from him, kicked him savagely on the shins, then reached for him and slammed him face downward in the dirt. Nor did he release him till the face had been rubbed into the dirt several times. Then the mother arrived, an anemic whirlwind of solicitude and maternal wrath.

"Why can't he leave me alone?" was Johnny's reply to her upbraiding. "Can't he see I'm tired?"

"I'm as big as you." Will raged in her arms, his face a mess of tears, dirt, and blood. "I'm as big as you now, an' I'm goin' to git bigger. Then I'll lick you—see if I don't."

"You ought to be to work, seein' how big you are," Johnny snarled. "That's what's the matter with you. You ought to be to work. An' it's up to your ma to put you to work."

"But he's too young," she protested. "He's only a little boy."

"I was younger'n him when I started to work."

Johnny's mouth was open, further to express the sense of unfairness that he felt, but the mouth closed with a snap. He turned gloomily on his heel and stalked into the house and to bed. The door of his room was open to let in warmth from the kitchen. As he undressed in the semidarkness he could hear his mother talking with a neighbor woman who had dropped in. His mother was crying, and her speech was punctuated with spiritless sniffles.

"I can't make out what's gittin' into Johnny," he could hear her say. "He didn't used to be this way. He was a patient little angel."

"An' he *is* a good boy," she hastened to defend. "He's worked faithful, an' he did go to work too young. But it wasn't my fault. I do the best I can, I'm sure."

Prolonged sniffling from the kitchen, and Johnny murmured to himself as his eyelids closed down, "You betcher life I've worked faithful."

The next morning he was torn bodily by his mother from the grip of sleep. Then came the meager breakfast, the tramp through the dark, and the pale glimpse of day across the housetops as he turned his back on it and went in through the factory gate. It was another day, of all the days, and all the days were alike.

And yet there had been variety in his life—at the times he changed from one job to another, or was taken sick. When he was six, he was little mother and father to Will and the other children still younger. At seven he went into the mills—winding bobbins. When he was eight, he got work in another mill. His new job was marvelously easy. All he had to do was to sit down with a little stick in his hand and guide a stream of cloth that flowed past him. This stream of cloth came out of the maw of a machine, passed over a hot roller, and went on its way elsewhere. But he sat always in the one place, beyond the reach of daylight, a gas jet flaring over him, himself part of the mechanism.

He was very happy at that job, in spite of the moist heat, for he was still young and in possession of dreams and illusions. And wonderful dreams he dreamed as he watched the steaming cloth streaming endlessly by. But there was no exercise about the work, no call upon his mind, and he dreamed less and less, while his mind grew torpid and drowsy. Nevertheless, he earned two dollars a week, and two dollars represented the difference between acute starvation and chronic underfeeding.

But when he was nine, he lost his job. Measles was the cause of it. After he recovered, he got work in a glass factory. The pay was better, and the work demanded skill. It was piecework, and the more skillful he was, the bigger wages he earned. Here was incentive. And under this incentive he developed into a remarkable worker.

It was simple work, the tying of glass stoppers into small bottles. At his waist he carried a bundle of twine. He held the bottles between his knees so that he might work with both hands. Thus, in a sitting position and bending over his own knees, his narrow shoulders grew humped and his chest was contracted for ten hours each day. This was not good for the lungs, but he tied three hundred dozen bottles a day.

The superintendent was very proud of him, and brought visitors to look at him. In ten hours three hundred dozen bottles passed through his hands. This meant that he had attained machinelike perfection. All waste movements were eliminated. Every motion of his thin arms, every movement of a muscle in the thin fingers, was swift and accurate. He worked at high tension, and the result was that he grew nervous. At night his muscles twitched in his sleep, and in the daytime he could not relax and rest. He remained keyed up and his muscles continued to twitch. Also he grew sallow and his lint cough grew worse. Then pneumonia laid hold of the feeble lungs within the contracted chest, and he lost his job in the glassworks.

Now he had returned to the jute mills where he had first begun with winding bobbins. But promotion was waiting for him. He was a good worker. He would next go on the starcher, and later he would go into the loom room. There was nothing after that except increased efficiency.

The machinery ran faster than when he had first gone to work, and his mind ran slower. He no longer dreamed at all, though his earlier years had been full of dreaming. Once he had been in love. It was when he first began guiding the cloth over the hot roller, and it was with the daughter of the superintendent. She was much older than he, a young woman, and he had seen her at a distance only a paltry half-dozen times. But that made no difference. On the surface of the cloth stream that poured past him, he pictured radiant futures wherein he performed prodigies of toil, invented miraculous machines, won to the mastership of the mills, and in the end took her in his arms and kissed her soberly on the brow.

But that was all in the long ago, before he had grown too old and tired to love. Also, she had married and gone away, and his mind had gone to sleep. Yet it had been a wonderful experience, and he used often to look back upon it as other men and women look back upon the time they believed in fairies. He had never believed in fairies nor Santa Claus; but he had believed implicitly in the smiling future his imagination had wrought into the steaming cloth stream.

He had become a man very early in life. At seven, when he drew his first wages, began his adolescence. A certain feeling of independence crept up in him, and the relationship between him and his mother changed. Somehow, as an earner and breadwinner, doing his own work in the world, he was more like an equal with her. Manhood, full-blown manhood, had come when he was eleven, at which time he had gone to work on the night shift for six months. No child works on the night shift and remains a child.

There had been several great events in his life. One of these had been when his mother bought some California prunes. Two others had been the two times when she cooked custard. Those had been events. He remembered them kindly. And at that time his mother had told him of a blissful dish she would sometime make—"floating island," she had called it, "better than custard." For years he had looked forward to the day when he would sit down to the table with floating island before him, until at last he had relegated the idea of it to the limbo of unattainable ideals.

Once he found a silver quarter lying on the sidewalk. That, also, was a great event in his life, withal a tragic one. He knew his duty on the instant the silver flashed on his eyes, before even he had picked it up. At home, as usual, there was not enough to eat, and home he should have taken it as he did his wages every Saturday night. Right conduct in this case was obvious; but he never had any spending of his money, and he was suffering from candy hunger. He was ravenous for the sweets that only on red-letter days he had ever tasted in his life.

He did not attempt to deceive himself. He knew it was sin, and deliberately he sinned when he went on a fifteen-cent candy debauch. Ten cents he saved for a future orgy; but not being accustomed to the carrying of money, he lost the ten cents. This occurred at the time when he was suffering all the torments of conscience, and it was to him an act of divine retribution. He had a frightened sense of the closeness of an awful and wrathful God. God had seen, and God had been swift to punish, denying him even the full wages of sin.

In memory he always looked back upon that event as the one great criminal deed of his life, and at the recollection his conscience always awoke and gave him another twinge. It was the one skeleton in his closet. Also, being so made and circumstanced, he looked back upon the deed with regret. He was dissatisfied with the manner in which he had spent the quarter. He could have invested it better and, out of his later knowledge of the quickness of God, he would have beaten God out by spending the whole quarter at one fell swoop. In retrospect he spent the quarter a thousand times, and each time to better advantage.

There was one other memory of the past, dim and faded, but stamped into his soul everlasting by the savage feet of his father. It was more like a nightmare than a remembered vision of a concrete thing—more like the race memory of man that makes him fall in his sleep and that goes back to his arboreal ancestry.

This particular memory never came to Johnny in broad daylight when he was wide awake. It came at night, in bed, at the moment that his consciousness was sinking down and losing itself in sleep. It always aroused him to frightened wakefulness, and for the moment, in the first sickening start, it seemed to him that he lay crosswise on the foot of the bed. In the bed were the vague forms of his father and mother. He never saw what his father looked like. He had but one impression of his father, and that was that he had savage and pitiless feet.

His earlier memories lingered with him, but he had no late memories. All days were alike. Yesterday or last year were the same as a thousand years—or a minute. Nothing ever happened. There were no events to mark the march of time. Time did not march. It stood always still. It was only the whirling machines that moved, and they moved nowhere—in spite of the fact that they moved faster.

When he was fourteen, he went to work on the starcher. It was a colossal event. Something had at last happened that could be remembered beyond a night's sleep or a week's payday. It marked an era. It was a machine Olympiad, a thing to date from. "When I went to work on the starcher," or, "after," or "before I went to work on the starcher," were sentences often on his lips.

He celebrated his sixteenth birthday by going into the loom room and taking a loom. Here was an incentive again, for it was piecework. And he excelled, because the clay of him had been molded by the mills into the perfect machine. At the end of three months he was running two looms, and, later, three and four.

At the end of his second year at the looms he was turning out more yards than any other weaver, and more than twice as much as some of the less skillful ones. And at home things began to prosper as he approached the full stature of his earning power. Not, however, that his increased earnings were in excess of need. The children were growing up. They ate more. And they were going to school, and schoolbooks cost money. And somehow, the faster he worked, the faster climbed the prices of things. Even the rent went up, though the house had fallen from bad to worse disrepair.

He had grown taller; but with his increased height he seemed leaner than ever. Also, he was more nervous. With the nervousness increased his peevishness and irritability. The children had learned by many bitter lessons to fight shy of him. His mother respected him for his earning power, but somehow her respect was tinctured with fear.

There was no joyousness in life for him. The procession of the days he never saw.

The nights he slept away in twitching unconsciousness. The rest of the time he worked, and his consciousness was machine consciousness. Outside this his mind was a blank. He had no ideals, and but one illusion; namely, that he drank excellent coffee. He was a workbeast. He had no mental life whatever; yet deep down in the crypts of his mind, unknown to him, were being weighed and sifted every hour of his toil, every movement of his hands, every twitch of his muscles, and preparations were making for a future course of action that would amaze him and all his little world.

It was in the late spring that he came home from work one night aware of unusual tiredness. There was a keen expectancy in the air as he sat down to the table, but he did not notice. He went through the meal in moody silence, mechanically eating what was before him. The children um'd and ah'd and made smacking noises with their mouths. But he was deaf to them.

"D'ye know what you're eatin'?" his mother demanded at last, desperately.

He looked vacantly at the dish before him and vacantly at her.

"Floatin' island," she announced triumphantly.

"Oh," he said.

"Floating island," the children chorused loudly.

"Oh," he said. And after two or three mouthfuls, he added, "I guess I ain't hungry tonight."

He dropped the spoon, shoved back his chair, and arose wearily from the table.

"An' I guess I'll go to bed."

His feet dragged more heavily than usual as he crossed the kitchen floor. Undressing was a Titan's task, a monstrous futility, and he wept weakly as he crawled into bed, one shoe still on. He was aware of a rising, swelling something inside his head that made his brain thick and fuzzy. His lean fingers felt as big as his wrist, while in the ends of them was a remoteness of sensation vague and fuzzy like his brain. The small of his back ached intolerably. All his bones ached. He ached everywhere. And in his head began the shrieking, pounding, crashing, roaring of a million looms. All space was filled with flying shuttles. They darted in and out, intricately, amongst the stars. He worked a thousand looms himself, and ever they speeded up, faster and faster, and his brain unwound, faster and faster, and became the thread that fed the thousand flying shuttles.

He did not go to work next morning. He was too busy weaving colossally on the thousand looms that ran inside his head. His mother went to work, but first she sent for the doctor. It was a severe attack of the grippe, he said. Jennie served as nurse and carried out his instructions.

It was a very severe attack, and it was a week before Johnny dressed and tottered feebly across the floor. Another week, the doctor said, and he would be fit to return to work. The foreman of the loom room visited him on Sunday afternoon, the first day of his convalescence. The best weaver in the room, the foreman told his mother. His job would be held for him. He could come back to work a week from Monday.

"Why don't you thank 'im, Johnny?" his mother asked anxiously.

"He's ben that sick he ain't himself yet," she explained apologetically to the visitor.

Johnny sat hunched up and gazing steadfastly at the floor. He sat in the same position long after the foreman had gone. It was warm outdoors, and he sat on the stoop in the afternoon. Sometimes his lips moved. He seemed lost in endless calculations.

Next morning, after the day grew warm, he took his seat on the stoop. He had pencil and paper this time with which to continue his calculations, and he calculated painfully and amazingly.

"What comes after millions?" he asked at noon, when Will came home from school. "An' how d'ye work 'em?"

That afternoon finished his task. Each day, but without paper and pencil, he returned to the stoop. He was greatly absorbed in the one tree that grew across the street. He studied it for hours at a time, and was unusually interested when the wind swayed its branches and fluttered its leaves. Throughout the week he seemed lost in a great communion with himself. On Sunday, sitting on the stoop, he laughed aloud, several times, to the perturbation of his mother, who had not heard him laugh in years.

Next morning, in the early darkness, she came to his bed to rouse him. He had had his fill of sleep all week, and awoke easily. He made no struggle, nor did he attempt to hold on to the bedding when she stripped it from him. He lay quietly, and spoke quietly.

"It ain't no use, ma."

"You'll be late," she said, under the impression that he was still stupid with sleep.

"I'm awake, ma, an' I tell you it ain't no use. You might as well lemme alone. I ain't goin' to git up."

"But you'll lose your job!" she cried.

"I ain't goin' to git up," he repeated in a strange, passionless voice.

She did not go to work herself that morning. This was sickness beyond any sickness she had ever known. Fever and delirium she could understand; but this was insanity. She pulled the bedding up over him and sent Jennie for the doctor.

When that person arrived, Johnny was sleeping gently, and gently he awoke and allowed his pulse to be taken.

"Nothing the matter with him," the doctor reported. "Badly debilitated, that's all. Not much meat on his bones."

"He's always been that way," his mother volunteered.

"Now go 'way, ma, an' let me finish my snooze."

Johnny spoke sweetly and placidly, and sweetly and placidly he rolled over on his side and went to sleep.

At ten o'clock he awoke and dressed himself. He walked out into the kitchen, where he found his mother with a frightened expression on her face.

"I'm goin' away, ma," he announced, "an' I jes' want to say good-by."

She threw her apron over her head and sat down suddenly and wept. He waited patiently.

"I might a-known it," she was sobbing.

"Where?" she finally asked, removing the apron from her head and gazing up at him with a stricken face in which there was little curiosity.

"I don't know—anywhere."

As he spoke, the tree across the street appeared with dazzling brightness on his inner vision. It seemed to lurk just under his eyelids, and he could see it whenever he wished.

"An' your job?" she quavered.

"I ain't never goin' to work again."

"My God, Johnny!" she wailed, "don't say that!"

What he had said was blasphemy to her. As a mother who hears her child deny God, was Johnny's mother shocked by his words.

"What's got into you, anyway?" she demanded, with a lame attempt at imperativeness.

"Figures," he answered. "Jes' figures. I've ben doin' a lot of figurin' this week, an' it's most surprisin'."

"I don't see what that's got to do with it," she sniffled.

Johnny smiled patiently, and his mother was aware of a distinct shock at the persistent absence of his peevishness and irritability.

"I'll show you," he said. "I'm plum' tired out. What makes me tired? Moves. I've ben movin' ever since I was born. I'm tired of movin', an' I ain't goin' to move any more. Remember when I worked in the glasshouse? I used to do three hundred dozen a day. Now I reckon I made about ten different moves to each bottle. That's thirty-six thousan' moves a day. Ten days, three hundred an' sixty thousan' moves a day. One month, one million an' eighty thousan' moves. Chuck out the eighty thousan'—" he spoke with the complacent beneficence of a philanthropist—"chuck out the eighty thousan', that leaves a million moves a month—twelve million moves a year.

"At the looms I'm movin' twic'st as much. That makes twenty-five million moves a year, an' it seems to me I've ben a movin' that way 'most a million years.

"Now this week I ain't moved at all. I ain't made one move in hours an' hours. I tell you it was swell, jes' settin' there, hours an' hours, an' doin' nothin'. I ain't never ben happy before. I never had any time. I've ben movin' all the time. That ain't no way to be happy. An' I ain't goin' to do it any more. I'm jes' goin' to set, an' set, an' rest, an' rest, and then rest some more."

"But what's goin' to come of Will an' the children?" she asked despairingly.

"That's it, 'Will an' the children,'" he repeated.

But there was no bitterness in his voice. He had long known his mother's ambition for the younger boy, but the thought of it no longer rankled. Nothing mattered any more. Not even that.

"I know, ma, what you've ben plannin' for Will—keepin' him in school to make a bookkeeper out of him. But it ain't no use, I've quit. He's got to go to work."

"An' after I have brung you up the way I have," she wept, starting to cover her head with the apron and changing her mind.

"You never brung me up," he answered with sad kindliness. "I brung myself up, ma, an' I brung up Will. He's bigger'n me, an' heavier, an' taller. When I was a kid, I reckon I didn't git enough to eat. When he come along an' was a kid, I was workin' an' earnin' grub for him too. But that's done with. Will can go to work, same as me, or he can go to hell, I don't care which. I'm tired. I'm goin' now. Ain't you goin' to say good-by?"

She made no reply. The apron had gone over her head again, and she was crying. He paused a moment in the doorway.

"I'm sure I done the best I knew how," she was sobbing.

He passed out of the house and down the street. A wan delight came into his face at the sight of the lone tree. "Jes' ain't goin' to do nothin'," he said to himself, half aloud, in a crooning tone. He glanced wistfully up at the sky, but the bright sun dazzled and blinded him.

It was a long walk he took, and he did not walk fast. It took him past the jute mill. The muffled roar of the loom room came to his ears, and he smiled. It was a gentle, placid smile. He hated no one, not even the pounding, shrieking machines. There was no bitterness in him, nothing but an inordinate hunger for rest.

The houses and factories thinned out and the open spaces increased as he approached the country. At last the city was behind him, and he was walking down a leafy lane beside the railroad track. He did not walk like a man. He did not look like a man. He was a travesty of the human. It was a twisted and stunted and nameless piece of life that shambled like a sickly ape, arms loose-hanging, stoop-shouldered, narrow-chested, grotesque and terrible.

He passed by a small railroad station and lay down in the grass under a tree. All afternoon he lay there. Sometimes he dozed, with muscles that twitched in his sleep. When awake, he lay without movement, watching the birds or looking up at the sky through the branches of the tree above him. Once or twice he laughed aloud, but without relevance to anything he had seen or felt.

After twilight had gone, in the first darkness of the night, a freight train rumbled into the station. When the engine was switching cars on to the sidetrack, Johnny crept along the side of the train. He pulled open the side door of an empty boxcar and awkwardly and laboriously climbed in. He closed the door. The engine whistled. Johnny was lying down, and in the darkness he smiled.

BHARATI MUKHERJEE
(1940–)

Mukherjee was born in Calcutta, the second of three daughters in a wealthy family headed by a Hindu father of the highest caste (Brahmin) who was a pharmaceutical chemist. She was raised in a large house that accommodated her extended family, including uncles, aunts, and cousins. She attended the universities of Calcutta and Baroda, earning a master's degree in English and Ancient Indian Culture. In 1961, she came to America to study at the University of Iowa's Writers' Workshop, where she received a master's in fine arts degree followed by a Ph.D. in English from that university. She taught at McGill University in Montreal for fourteen years and is currently a professor of English at the University of California at Berkeley. In 1988, she became an American citizen. Mukherjee often depicts the situation of immigrants from India, particularly women, who find themselves thrust into an American setting with problems about relationships and a lifestyle for which their traditional upbringing and values have not prepared them. Her collection *The Middleman and Other Stories* (1988) won the National Book Critics Circle Award in 1989. Among her other works of fiction are *The Tiger's Daughter* (1971); *Wife* (1975); *Jasmine* (1989); *The Holder of the World,* a *New York Times* Notable Book (1993); *Leave It to Me* (1997); and *Desirable Daughters* (2002). In collaboration with her husband, Clark Blaise, she has also published two nonfiction works: *Days and Nights in Calcutta* (1977) and *The Sorrow and the Terror* (1987).

Danny's Girls

I was thirteen when Danny Sahib moved into our building in Flushing. That was his street name, but my Aunt Lini still called him Dinesh, the name he'd landed with. He was about twenty, a Dogra boy from Simla with slicked-back hair and coppery skin. If he'd worked on his body language, he could have passed for Mexican, which might have been useful. Hispanics are taken more seriously, in certain lines of business, than Indians. But I don't want to give the wrong impression about Danny. He wasn't an enforcer, he was a charmer. No one was afraid of him; he was a merchant of opportunity. I got to know him because he was always into ghetto scams that needed junior high boys like me to pull them off.

He didn't have parents, at least none that he talked about, and he boasted he'd been on his own since he was six. I admired that, I wished I could escape my family, such as it was. My parents had been bounced from Uganda by Idi Amin, and then barred from England by some parliamentary trickery. Mother's sister—Aunt Lini—sponsored us in the States. I don't remember Africa at all, but my father could never forget that we'd once had servants and two Mercedes-Benzes. He sat around Lini's house moaning about the good old days and grumbling about how hard life in America was until finally the women organized a coup and chucked him out. My mother sold papers in the subway kiosks, twelve hours a day, seven days a week. Last I heard, my father was living with a Trinidad woman in Philadelphia, but we haven't seen him or talked about him for years. So in Danny's mind I was an orphan, like him.

He wasn't into the big-money stuff like drugs. He was a hustler, nothing more. He used to boast that he knew some guys, Nepalese and Pakistanis, who could supply him with anything—but we figured that was just talk. He started out with bets and scalping tickets for Lata Mangeshkar or Mithun Chakravorty concerts at Madison Square Garden. Later he fixed beauty contests and then discovered the marriage racket.

Danny took out ads in papers in India promising "guaranteed Permanent Resident status in the U.S." to grooms willing to proxy-marry American girls of Indian origin. He arranged quite a few. The brides and grooms didn't have to live with each other, or even meet or see each other. Sometimes the "brides" were smooth-skinned boys from the neighborhood. He used to audition his brides in our apartment and coach them—especially the boys—on keeping their faces low, their saris high, and their arms as glazed and smooth as caramel. The immigration inspectors never suspected a thing. I never understood why young men would pay a lot of money—I think the going rate was fifty thousand rupees—to come here. Maybe if I remembered the old country I might feel different. I've never even visited India.

Flushing was full of greedy women. I never met one who would turn down gold or a fling with the money market. The streets were lousy with gold merchants, more gold emporia than pizza parlors. Melt down the hoarded gold of Jackson Heights and you could plate the Queensboro Bridge. My first job for Danny Sahib was to approach the daughters in my building for bride volunteers and a fifty-buck fee, and then with my sweet, innocent face, sign a hundred-dollar contract with their mothers.

Then Danny Sahib saw he was thinking small. The real money wasn't in rupees and bringing poor saps over. It was in selling docile Indian girls to hard-up Americans for real bucks. An Old World wife who knew her place and would breed like crazy was worth at least twenty thousand dollars. To sweeten the deal and get some good-looking girls for his catalogues, Danny promised to send part of the fee back to India. No one in India could even imagine *getting* money for the curse of having a daughter. So he expanded his marriage business to include mail-order brides, and he offered my smart aunt Lini a partnership. My job was to put up posters in the Laundromats and pass out flyers on the subways.

Aunt Lini was a shrewd businesswoman, a widow who'd built my uncle's small-time investor service for cautious Gujarati gentlemen into a full-scale loan-sharking operation that financed half the Indian-owned taxi medallions in Queens. Her rates were simple: double the prime, no questions asked. Triple the prime if she smelled a risk, which she usually did. She ran it out of her kitchen with a phone next to the stove. She could turn a thousand dollars while frying up a *bhaji*.

Aunt Lini's role was to warehouse the merchandise, as she called the girls, that couldn't be delivered to its American destination (most of those American fiancés had faces a fly wouldn't buzz). Aunt Lini had spare rooms she could turn into an informal S.R.O. hotel. She called the rooms her "pet shop" and she thought of the girls as puppies in the window. In addition to the flat rate that Danny paid her, she billed the women separately for bringing gentlemen guests, or shoppers, into the room. This encouraged a prompt turnover. The girls found it profitable to make an expeditious decision.

The summer I was fifteen, Aunt Lini had a paying guest, a Nepalese, a real looker. Her skin was white as whole milk, not the color of tree bark I was accustomed to. Her lips were a peachy orange and she had high Nepalese cheekbones. She called herself "Rosie" in the mail-order catalogue and listed her age as sixteen. Danny wanted all his girls to be sixteen and most of them had names like Rosie and Dolly. I suppose when things didn't work out between her and her contract "fiancé" she saw no reason to go back to her real name. Or especially, back to some tubercular hut in Katmandu. Her parents certainly wouldn't take her back. They figured she was married and doing time in Toledo with a dude named Duane.

Rosie liked to have me around. In the middle of a sizzling afternoon she would send me to Mr. Chin's store for a pack of Kents, or to Ranjit's liquor store for gin. She was a good tipper, or maybe she couldn't admit to me that she couldn't add. The money came from Danny, part of her "dowry" that he didn't send back to Nepal. I knew she couldn't read or write, not even in her own language. That didn't bother me—guaranteed illiteracy is a big selling point in the mail-order bride racket—and there was nothing abject about her. I'd have to say she was a proud woman. The other girls Danny brought over were already broken in spirit; they'd marry just about any freak Danny brought around. Not Rosie—she'd throw some of them out, and threaten others with a cobra she said she kept in her suitcase if they even thought of touching her. After most of my errands, she'd ask me to sit on the bed and light me a cigarette and pour me a weak drink. I'd fan her for a while with the newspaper.

"What are you going to be when you finish school?" she'd ask me and blow rings, like kisses, that wobbled to my face and broke gently across it. I didn't know anyone who blew smoke rings. I thought they had gone out with black-and-white films. I became a staunch admirer of Nepal.

What I wanted to be in those days was someone important, which meant a freedom like Danny's but without the scams. Respectable freedom in the bigger world of America, that's what I wanted. Growing up in Queens gives a boy ambitions. But I didn't disclose them. I said to Rosie what my ma always said when other Indians dropped by. I said I would be going to Columbia University to the Engineering School. It was a story ma believed because she'd told it so often, though I knew better. Only the Indian doctors' kids from New Jersey and Long Island went to Columbia. Out in Flushing we got a different message. Indian boys were placed on earth to become accountants and engineers. Even old *Idi Amin* was placed on earth to force Indians to come to America to become accountants and engineers. I went through high school scared, wondering what there was in my future if I hated numbers. I wondered if Pace and Adelphi had engineering. I didn't want to turn out like my aunt Lini, a ghetto money-lender, and I didn't want to suffer like my mother, and I hated my father with a passion. No wonder Danny's world seemed so exciting. My mother was knocking herself out at a kiosk in Port Authority, earning the minimum wage from a guy who convinced her he was doing her a big favor, all for my mythical Columbia tuition. Lini told me that in America grades didn't count; it was all in the test scores. She bought me the SAT workbooks and told me to memorize the answers.

"Smashing," Rosie would say, and other times, "Jolly good," showing that even in the Himalayan foothills, the sun hadn't yet set on the British Empire.

Some afternoons Rosie would be doubled over in bed with leg pains. I know now she'd had rickets as a kid and spent her childhood swaying under hundred-pound sacks of rice piled on her head. By thirty she'd be hobbling around like an old football player with blown knees. But at sixteen or whatever, she still had great, hard, though slightly bent legs, and she'd hike her velour dressing gown so I could tightly crisscross her legs and part of her thighs with pink satin hair ribbons. It was a home remedy, she said, it stopped circulation. I couldn't picture her in that home, Nepal. She was like a queen ("The Queen of Queens," I used to joke) to me that year. Even India, where both my parents were born, was a mystery.

Curing Rosie's leg pains led to some strong emotions, and soon I wanted to beat on the gentlemen callers who came, carrying cheap boxes of candy and looking her over like a slave girl on the auction block. She'd tell me about it, nonchalantly, making it funny. She'd catalogue each of their faults, imitate their voices. They'd try to get a peek under the covers or even under the clothing, and Danny would be there to cool things down. I wasn't allowed to help, but by then I would have killed for her.

I was no stranger to the miseries of unrequited love. Rosie was the unavailable love in the room upstairs who talked to me unblushingly of sex and made the whole transaction seem base and grubby and funny. In my Saturday morning Gujarati class, on the other hand, there was a girl from Syosset who called herself "Pammy Patel," a genuine Hindu-American Princess of the sort I had never seen before, whose skin and voice and eyes were as soft as clouds. She wore expensive dresses and you could tell she'd spent hours making herself up just for the Gujarati classes in the Hindu temple. Her father was a major surgeon, and he and Pammy's brothers would stand outside the class to protect her from any contact with boys like me. They would watch us filing out of the classroom, looking us up and down and smirking the way Danny's catalogue brides were looked at by their American buyers.

I found the whole situation achingly romantic. In the Hindi films I'd see every Sunday, the hero was always a common man with a noble heart, in love with an unattainable beauty. Then she'd be kidnapped and he'd have to save her. Caste and class would be overcome and marriage would follow. To that background, I added a certain American equality. I grew up hating rich people, especially rich Indian immigrants who didn't have the problems of Uganda and a useless father, but otherwise were no better than I. I never gave them the deference that Aunt Lini and my mother did.

With all that behind me, I had assumed that real love *had* to be cheerless. I had assumed I wouldn't find a girl worth marrying, not that girls like Pammy could make me happy. Rosie was the kind of girl who could make me happy, but even I knew she was not the kind of girl I could marry. It was confusing. Thoughts of Rosie made me want to slash the throats of rivals. Thoughts of Pammy made me want to wipe out her whole family.

One very hot afternoon Rosie, as usual, leaned her elbows on the windowsill and shouted to me to fetch a six-pack of tonic and a lemon. I'd been sitting on the stoop, getting new tips from Danny on scalping for an upcoming dance recital—a big one, Lincoln Center—but I leaped to attention and shook the change in my pockets to make sure I had enough for Mr. Chin. Rosie kept records of her debts, and she'd pay them off, she said, just as soon as Danny arranged a green card to make her legit. She intended to make it here without getting married. She exaggerated Danny's power. To her, he was some kind of local bigwig who could pull off anything. None of Danny's girls had tried breaking a contract before, and I wondered if she'd actually taken it up with him.

Danny pushed me back so hard I scraped my knee on the stoop. "You put up the posters," he said. After taping them up, I was to circulate on the subway and press the pictures on every lonely guy I saw. "I'll take care of Rosie. You report back tomorrow."

"After I get her tonic and a lemon," I said.

It was the only time I ever saw the grown-up orphan in Danny, the survivor. If he'd had a knife or a gun on him, he might have used it. "I give the orders," he said, "you follow." Until that moment, I'd always had the implicit sense that Danny and I were partners in some exciting enterprise, that together we were putting something over on India, on Flushing, and even on America.

Then he smiled, but it wasn't Danny's radiant, conspiratorial, arm-on-the-shoulder smile that used to warm my day. "You're making her fat," he said. "You're making her drunk. You probably want to diddle her yourself, don't you? Fifteen years old and never been out of your auntie's house and you want a real woman like Rosie. But she thinks you're her errand boy and you just love being her smiley little *chokra*-boy, don't you?" Then the smile froze on his lips, and if he'd ever looked Mexican, this was the time. Then he said something in Hindi that I barely understood, and he laughed as he watched me repeat it, slowly. Something about eunuchs not knowing their place. "Don't ever go up there again, *hijra*-boy."

I was starting to take care of Danny's errands quickly and sloppily as always, and then, at the top of the subway stairs, I stopped. I'd never really thought what a strange, pimpish thing I was doing, putting up pictures of Danny's girls, or standing at the top of the subway stairs and passing them out to any lonely-looking American I saw—what kind of joke was this? How dare he do this, I thought, how dare he make me a part of this? I couldn't move. I had two hundred sheets of yellow paper in my hands, descriptions of Rosie and half a dozen others like her, and instead of passing them out, I threw them over my head and let them settle on the street and sidewalk and filter down the paper-strewn, garbage-littered steps of the subway. How dare he call me *hijra*, eunuch?

I got back to Aunt Lini's within the hour. She was in her kitchen charring an eggplant. "I'm making a special *bharta* for you," she said, clapping a hand over the receiver. She was putting the screws on some poor Sikh, judging from the stream of coarse Punjabi I heard as I tore through the kitchen. She shouted after me, "Your ma'll be working late tonight." More guilt, more Columbia, more engineering.

I didn't thank Aunt Lini for being so thoughtful, and I didn't complain about Ma not being home for me. I was in a towering rage with Rosie and with everyone who ever slobbered over her picture.

"Take your shoes off in the hall," Lini shouted. "You know the rules."

I was in the mood to break rules. For the first time I could remember, I wasn't afraid of Danny Sahib. I wanted to liberate Rosie, and myself. From the hall stand I grabbed the biggest, sturdiest, wood-handled umbrella—gentlemen callers were always leaving behind souvenirs—and in my greasy high-tops I clumped up the stairs two at a time and kicked open the door to Rosie's room.

Rosie lay in bed, smoking. She'd propped a new fan on her pillow, near her face. She sipped her gin and lime. *So,* I thought in my fit of mad jealousy, he's bought her a fan. And now suddenly she likes limes. Damn him, *damn* him. She won't want me and my newspapers, she won't want my lemons. I wouldn't have cared if Danny and half the bachelors in Queens were huddled around that bed. I was so pumped up with the enormity of love that I beat the mattress in the absence of rivals. Whack! Whack! Whack! went the stolen umbrella, and Rosie bent her legs delicately to get them out of the way. The fan teetered off the pillow and lay there beside her on the wilted, flopping bed, blowing hot air at the ceiling. She held her drink up tight against her nose and lips and stared at me around the glass.

"So, you want me, do you?" she said.

Slowly, she moved the flimsy little fan, then let it drop. I knelt on the floor with my head on the pillow that had pressed into her body, smelling flowers I would never see in Flushing and feeling the tug on my shoulder that meant I should come up to bed and for the first time I felt my life was going to be A-Okay.

NONFICTION

RUSSELL BAKER
(1925–)

Russell Baker was born in Loudoun County in rural Virginia. He graduated from Johns Hopkins University, where he majored in English. For the next seven years he worked as a reporter for *The Baltimore Sun,* advancing from police reporter to London correspondent to White House reporter. In 1954, he joined *The New York Times* as a Washington correspondent, covering the White House, the Congress, the State Department, and the political scene. In 1962 he started the "Observer" column for the *Times* op-ed page, which he continued to write for the next thirty-six years. In his final column in 1998, he estimated that he had written at least three million words. Baker has won two Pulitzer Prizes, one in 1979 for his commentary and a second in 1983 for his memoir *Growing Up.* He has served as a member of the Pulitzer Prize Board and the American Academy of Arts and Letters and is a fellow of the American Academy of Arts and Sciences. In 1993, he replaced Alistair Cooke as host of *Masterpiece Theatre* on PBS. He has returned to his Virginia roots, to Leesburg, the town he referred to over the years as Burgville in his columns. In addition to *Growing Up,* Baker has written a second memoir, *The Good Times* (1989), addressing his adult life. He has written or edited more than a dozen other books, among them *City on the Potomac* (1958), *An American in Washington* (1961), *No Cause for Panic* (1964), *All Things Considered* (1965), *Our Next President* (1968), *Poor Russell's Almanac* (1972), *The Upside-Down Man* (1977), *So This Is Depravity* (1980), *The Rescue of Miss Yaskall* (1983), *There's a Country in My Cellar* (1990), *Russell Baker's Book of American Humor* (1993), and *Looking Back* (2002).

---

from *Growing Up*

I began working in journalism when I was eight years old. It was my mother's idea. She wanted me to "make something" of myself and, after a levelheaded appraisal of my strengths, decided I had better start young if I was to have any chance of keeping up with the competition.

The flaw in my character which she had already spotted was lack of "gumption." My idea of a perfect afternoon was lying in front of the radio rereading my favorite Big Little Book, *Dick Tracy Meets Stooge Viller.* My mother despised inactivity. Seeing me having a good time in repose, she was powerless to hide her disgust. "You've got no more gumption than a bump on a log," she said. "Get out in the kitchen and help Doris do those dirty dishes."

My sister Doris, though two years younger than I, had enough gumption for a dozen people. She positively enjoyed washing dishes, making beds, and cleaning the house. When she was only seven she could carry a piece of short-weighted cheese back to the A&P, threaten the manager with legal action, and come back triumphantly with the full quarter-pound we'd paid for and a few ounces extra thrown in for forgiveness. Doris could have made something of herself if she hadn't been a girl. Because of this defect, however, the best she could hope for was a career as a nurse or schoolteacher, the only work that capable females were considered up to in those days.

This must have saddened my mother, this twist of fate that had allocated all the gumption to the daughter and left her with a son who was content with Dick Tracy and Stooge Viller. If disappointed, though, she wasted no energy on self-pity. She would make me make something of myself whether I wanted to or not. "The Lord helps those who help themselves," she said. That was the way her mind worked.

She was realistic about the difficulty. Having sized up the material the Lord had given her to mold, she didn't overestimate what she could do with it. She didn't insist that I grow up to be President of the United States.

Fifty years ago parents still asked boys if they wanted to grow up to be President, and asked it not jokingly but seriously. Many parents who were hardly more than paupers still believed their sons could do it. Abraham Lincoln had done it. We were only sixty-five years from Lincoln. Many a grandfather who walked among us could remember Lincoln's time. Men of grandfatherly age were the worst for asking if you wanted to grow up to be President. A surprising number of little boys said yes and meant it.

I was asked many times myself. No, I would say, I didn't want to grow up to be President. My mother was present during one of these interrogations. An elderly uncle, having posed the usual question and exposed my lack of interest in the Presidency, asked, "Well, what *do* you want to be when you grow up?"

I loved to pick through trash piles and collect empty bottles, tin cans with pretty labels, and discarded magazines. The most desirable job on earth sprang instantly to mind. "I want to be a garbage man," I said.

My uncle smiled, but my mother had seen the first distressing evidence of a bump budding on a log. "Have a little gumption, Russell," she said. Her calling me Russell was a signal of unhappiness. When she approved of me I was always "Buddy."

When I turned eight years old she decided that the job of starting me on the road toward making something of myself could no longer be safely delayed. "Buddy," she said one day, "I want you to come home right after school this afternoon. Somebody's coming and I want you to meet him."

When I burst in that afternoon she was in conference in the parlor with an executive of the Curtis Publishing Company. She introduced me. He bent low from the waist and shook my hand. Was it true as my mother had told him, he asked, that I longed for the opportunity to conquer the world of business?

My mother replied that I was blessed with a rare determination to make something of myself.

"That's right," I whispered.

"But have you got the grit, the character, the never-say-quit spirit it takes to succeed in business?"

My mother said I certainly did.

"That's right," I said.

He eyed me silently for a long pause, as though weighing whether I could be trusted to keep his confidence, then spoke man-to-man. Before taking a crucial step, he said, he wanted to advise me that working for the Curtis Publishing Company placed enormous responsibility on a young man. It was one of the great companies of America. Perhaps the greatest publishing house in the world. I had heard, no doubt, of the *Saturday Evening Post?*

Heard of it? My mother said that everyone in our house had heard of the *Saturday Post* and that I, in fact, read it with religious devotion.

Then doubtless, he said, we were also familiar with those two monthly pillars of the magazine world, the *Ladies' Home Journal* and the *Country Gentleman*.

Indeed we were familiar with them, said my mother.

Representing the *Saturday Evening Post* was one of the weightiest honors that could be bestowed in the world of business, he said. He was personally proud of being a part of that great corporation.

My mother said he had every right to be.

Again he studied me as though debating whether I was worthy of a knighthood. Finally: "Are you trustworthy?"

My mother said I was the soul of honesty.

"That's right," I said.

The caller smiled for the first time. He told me I was a lucky young man. He admired my spunk. Too many young men thought life was all play. Those young men would not go far in this world. Only a young man willing to work and save and keep his face washed and his hair neatly combed could hope to come out on top in a world such as ours. Did I truly and sincerely believe that I was such a young man?

"He certainly does," said my mother.

"That's right," I said.

He said he had been so impressed by what he had seen of me that he was going to make me a representative of the Curtis Publishing Company. On the following Tuesday, he said, thirty freshly printed copies of the *Saturday Evening Post* would be delivered at our door. I would place these magazines, still damp with the ink of the presses, in a handsome canvas bag, sling it over my shoulder, and set forth through the streets to bring the best in journalism, fiction, and cartoons to the American public.

He had brought the canvas bag with him. He presented it with reverence fit for a chasuble. He showed me how to drape the sling over my left shoulder and across the chest so that the pouch lay easily accessible to my right hand, allowing the best in journalism, fiction, and cartoons to be swiftly extracted and sold to a citizenry whose happiness and security depended upon us soldiers of the free press.

The following Tuesday I raced home from school, put the canvas bag over my shoulder, dumped the magazines in, and, tilting to the left to balance their weight on my right hip, embarked on the highway of journalism.

We lived in Belleville, New Jersey, a commuter town at the northern fringe of

Newark. It was 1932, the bleakest year of the Depression. My father had died two years before, leaving us with a few pieces of Sears, Roebuck furniture and not much else, and my mother had taken Doris and me to live with one of her younger brothers. This was my uncle Allen. Uncle Allen had made something of himself by 1932. As salesman for a soft-drink bottler in Newark, he had an income of $30 a week; wore pearl-gray spats, detachable collars, and a three-piece suit; was happily married; and took in threadbare relatives.

With my load of magazines I headed toward Belleville Avenue. That's where the people were. There were two filling stations at the intersection with Union Avenue, as well as an A&P, a fruit stand, a bakery, a barber shop, Zuccarelli's drugstore, and a diner shaped like a railroad car. For several hours I made myself highly visible, shifting position now and then from corner to corner, from shop window to shop window, to make sure everyone could see the heavy black lettering on the canvas bag that said THE SATURDAY EVENING POST. When the angle of the light indicated it was suppertime, I walked back to the house.

"How many did you sell, Buddy?" my mother asked.

"None."

"Where did you go?"

"The corner of Belleville and Union Avenues."

"What did you do?"

"Stood on the corner waiting for somebody to buy a *Saturday Evening Post*."

"You just stood there?"

"Didn't sell a single one."

"For God's sake, Russell!"

Uncle Allen intervened. "I've been thinking about it for some time," he said, "and I've about decided to take the *Post* regularly. Put me down as a regular customer." I handed him a magazine and he paid me a nickel. It was the first nickel I earned.

Afterwards my mother instructed me in salesmanship. I would have to ring doorbells, address adults with charming self-confidence, and break down resistance with a sales talk pointing out that no one, no matter how poor, could afford to be without the *Saturday Evening Post* in the home.

I told my mother I'd changed my mind about wanting to succeed in the magazine business.

"If you think I'm going to raise a good-for-nothing," she replied, "you've got another think coming." She told me to hit the streets with the canvas bag and start ringing doorbells the instant school was out next day. When I objected that I didn't feel any aptitude for salesmanship, she asked how I'd like to lend her my leather belt so she could whack some sense into me. I bowed to superior will and entered journalism with a heavy heart.

My mother and I had fought this battle almost as long as I could remember. It probably started even before memory began, when I was a country child in northern Virginia and my mother, dissatisfied with my father's plain workman's life, determined that I would not grow up like him and his people, with calluses on their hands, overalls on their backs, and fourth-grade educations in their heads. She had fancier ideas of life's possibilities. Introducing me to the *Saturday Evening Post,* she was trying to wean me as early as possible from my father's world where men left with their lunch pails at sunup, worked with their hands until the grime ate into the pores, and died with a few sticks of mail-order furniture as their legacy. In my mother's vision of the better life there were desks and white collars, well-pressed suits, evenings of reading and lively talk, and perhaps—if a man were very, very lucky and hit the jackpot, really made something important of himself—perhaps there might be a fantastic salary of $5,000 a year to support a big house and a Buick with a rumble seat and a vacation in Atlantic City.

And so I set forth with my sack of magazines. I was afraid of the dogs that snarled behind the doors of potential buyers. I was timid about ringing the doorbells of strangers, relieved when no one came to the door, and scared when someone did. Despite my mother's instructions, I could not deliver an engaging sales pitch. When a door opened I simply asked, "Want to buy a *Saturday Evening Post?*" In Belleville few persons did. It was a town of 30,000 people, and most weeks I rang a fair majority of its doorbells. But I rarely sold my thirty copies. Some weeks I canvassed the entire town for six days and still had four or five unsold magazines on Monday evening; then I dreaded the coming of Tuesday morning, when a batch of thirty fresh *Saturday Evening Post*s was due at the front door.

"Better get out there and sell the rest of those magazines tonight," my mother would say.

I usually posted myself then at a busy intersection where a traffic light controlled commuter flow from Newark. When the light turned red I stood on the curb and shouted my sales pitch at the motorists.

"Want to buy a *Saturday Evening Post?*"

One rainy night when car windows were sealed against me I came back soaked and with not a single sale to report. My mother beckoned to Doris.

"Go back down there with Buddy and show him how to sell these magazines," she said.

Brimming with zest, Doris, who was then seven years old, returned with me to the corner. She took a magazine from the bag, and when the light turned red she strode to the nearest car and banged her small fist against the closed window. The driver, probably startled at what he took to be a midget assaulting his car, lowered the window to stare, and Doris thrust a *Saturday Evening Post* at him.

"You need this magazine," she piped, "and it only costs a nickel."

Her salesmanship was irresistible. Before the light changed half a dozen times she disposed of the entire batch. I didn't feel humiliated. To the contrary. I was so happy I decided to give her a treat. Leading her to the vegetable store on Belleville Avenue, I bought three apples, which cost a nickel, and gave her one.

"You shouldn't waste money," she said.

"Eat your apple." I bit into mine.

"You shouldn't eat before supper," she said. "It'll spoil your appetite."

Back at the house that evening, she dutifully reported me for wasting a nickel. Instead of a scolding, I was rewarded with a pat on the back for having the good sense to buy fruit instead of candy. My mother reached into her bottomless supply of maxims and told Doris, "An apple a day keeps the doctor away."

By the time I was ten I had learned all my mother's maxims by heart. Asking to stay up past normal bedtime, I knew that a refusal would be explained with, "Early to bed and early to rise, makes a man healthy, wealthy, and wise." If I whimpered about having to get up early in the morning, I could depend on her to say, "The early bird gets the worm."

The one I most despised was, "If at first you don't succeed, try, try again." This was the battle cry with which she constantly sent me back into the hopeless struggle whenever I moaned that I had rung every doorbell in town and knew there wasn't a single potential buyer left in Belleville that week. After listening to my explanation, she handed me the canvas bag and said, "If at first you don't succeed . . ."

Three years in that job, which I would gladly have quit after the first day except for her insistence, produced at least one valuable result. My mother finally concluded that I would never make something of myself by pursuing a life in business and started considering careers that demanded less competitive zeal.

One evening when I was eleven I brought home a short "composition" on my summer vacation which the teacher had graded with an A. Reading it with her own schoolteacher's eye, my mother agreed that it was top-drawer seventh-grade prose and complimented me. Nothing more was said about it immediately, but a new idea had taken life in her mind. Halfway through supper she suddenly interrupted the conversation.

"Buddy," she said, "maybe you could be a writer."

I clasped the idea to my heart. I had never met a writer, had shown no previous urge to write, and hadn't a notion how to become a writer, but I loved stories and thought that making up stories must surely be almost as much fun as reading them. Best of all, though, and what really gladdened my heart, was the ease of the writer's life. Writers did not have to trudge through the town peddling from canvas bags, defending themselves against angry dogs, being rejected by surly strangers. Writers did not have to ring doorbells. So far as I could make out, what writers did couldn't even be classified as work.

I was enchanted. Writers didn't have to have any gumption at all. I did not dare tell anybody for fear of being laughed at in the schoolyard, but secretly I decided that what I'd like to be when I grew up was a writer.

ART BUCHWALD

(1920–)

Born in Mount Vernon, New York, Arthur Buchwald was the fourth child and only son of Jewish immigrant parents. His mother's severe chronic depression and paranoia necessitated that, shortly after his birth, she be sent, first, to a private mental hospital and, later, because of the cost, to a New York State hospital. Buchwald never knew her. Instead, he lived in a household for sickly children (he suffered from rickets) run by nurses who were Seventh-Day Adventists and later—from the ages of six to fifteen—he was in a series of foster homes arranged by the Hebrew Orphan Asylum. Though his father, whose floundering business consisted of making and hanging drapes and curtains, was unable to support his children, Buchwald describes him as "a devoted father," a caring man who arranged to visit with his children every Sunday and who was involved in all decisions concerning them. At the age of seventeen, Art enlisted in the marines, serving during WWII as an ordnance man assigned to marine corps aviation on Engebi, a coral atoll in the Marshall Islands. While living in Paris after the war, he began to write about Paris nightlife and restaurants for the European edition of *The New York Herald Tribune,* and within a few years, his columns were syndicated by hundreds of American newspapers. An often-quoted humorist, he is the author of thirty-two books, among them two autobiographical works, *Leaving Home* (1993) and *I'll Always Have Paris* (1996), as well as *I Think I Don't Remember* (1987), *Whose Rose Garden Is It Anyway?* (1989), *We'll Laugh Again* (2002), and the novel *Stella in Heaven* (2000). In 1982, he received the Pulitzer Prize for "Outstanding Commentary," and in 1986, he was elected to membership in the American Academy of Arts and Letters.

---

from *Leaving Home*

Flossie and the Marines

The infamous attack at Pearl Harbor on December 7, 1941, came as a shock to Forest Hills. A group of us, including Bob Markay, George Hankoff, Arnie Alperstein, and Dick Zimmerman, were in the bowling alley on Austin Street when the news flashed over the radio. First there was disbelief, followed by serious discussion of what would happen next. We were all sixteen years old—and we were certain of everything.

Arnie said, "We'll beat the hell out of them in two weeks."

Bob Markay agreed. "Our fleet will sink the bastards and then they can kiss our ass."

Everyone at the bowling alley was certain of the brevity and outcome of the war, and fearful that it would be over before we could serve our country.

Let me state that most of the ethnic references about the Japanese and the Emperor used at the time would not be considered politically correct today. But in those days after Pearl Harbor, it was permissible to call the Japanese anything you wanted to.

Our group was not too well informed about Japan, except that their soldiers were very short, had gold teeth, and raped Chinese women. We knew that they owed their allegiance to the Emperor and didn't give a damn about their own lives, preferring at the slightest excuse to slit their stomachs open if they thought they had disgraced their country in any way. Before the war they had made very cheap toys that always fell apart and, therefore, we concluded that if their war equipment was of the same quality they were doomed to defeat.

Our knowledge of the Germans was much better. Those of us raised in Jewish homes had been briefed by the adults about what a butcher Adolf Hitler was. Throughout our lives, we were told to pray that he and his supporters should die a thousand deaths while being eaten by wild dogs.

One of the things that has puzzled me all my life is that every Jewish family in America knew what Hitler was doing to their relatives—but President Roosevelt didn't appear to know and neither did anyone else in the government. Was it a question of not believing what they heard or was Hitler one of those pre-war embarrassments?

Forest Hills was angry. While my friends were discussing Pearl Harbor as the country's problem, I took it personally. It dawned on me that the Japanese attack could be my ticket out of high school. The country needed manpower, and the call to arms was resounding over the airwaves every half hour. I was prepared to lie for my country and say I was eighteen so I could avenge the treachery of Pearl Harbor. No one ever mentioned it, but thousands of men welcomed World War II as a way to escape their humdrum lives rather than a chance to fight for God and country.

The next morning, on December 8, bright and early, I went down to the Naval recruiting station in lower Manhattan. The line wound three times around the block. It was a sight to behold. There were men in double-breasted suits and young recruits in overalls. Every color of skin was represented. There was an excitement in the air. The enemy had struck the first blow—now the men in line were prepared to reply in kind.

I stood in front of two boys from Brooklyn.

One said, "They say thousands were killed at Pearl."

The other one responded, "Roosevelt will never tell us, because he blew it."

"I hope I get on a submarine," I told them. "You sink a lot more ships on a submarine than you do on the surface."

The first Brooklyn boy said, "My brother's in the Navy and he says he gets more fuzz than he can handle. Women are crazy about sailors and they're not going to refuse you when you're prepared to die for your country."

Now this interested me very much. "How do you get your pants off in the Navy?" I asked. "They all have funny buttons on them."

"You learn that the first week. My brother is stationed in San Diego, and he has to beat the dames off with a broom."

Then I said, "Maybe with a war on, they'll keep the women away from us."

He shook his head. "No chance. Things will be even better than before Pearl Harbor for servicemen. I know a girl in Brooklyn who told me that if I come back in uniform, she'll go all the way as soon as I walk in the door."

"Be careful," his buddy warned. "Those are the kind that will make you marry them."

Unfortunately, the line moved at a snail's pace. An Army recruiting sergeant moved up and down the line shouting, "No waiting to get into the Army—no waiting to get into the Army." The third time, I bit, and followed him to the Army recruiting station, which was down the block.

I filled out the papers, lied about my age, and was sent into a classroom to take a test designed to find out if I could read and write or had any emotional problems. The men surrounding me were not too bright and they kept asking me for the answers to the questions, which I was happy to supply.

I helped three recruits pass the tests, with flying colors. I am certain that they were the ones who captured Omaha Beach on D day, and were given battlefield promotions to the rank of colonel on the spot. After the test, I moved on into another wing of the recruiting station for a physical exam.

It was the first time that I had appeared naked in front of so many other men, and I was embarrassed. The Army was not too thorough about the physical, although one of the doctors called me on the carpet for biting my fingernails. He said that he didn't think he could take me unless I promised not to bite them. I agreed, but, frankly, I couldn't understand how you could be shot at with live bullets *without* biting your nails.

I passed everything and was informed that a letter would be sent to my parents requesting them to sign the forms permitting their son to join the service.

I wasn't quite certain how to handle the problem, but the next morning I stole the key to the apartment mailbox from my sister's purse. I intended to open the box before she got home and forge my father's name to the papers.

Sadly, my sister was sick that day and stayed home from work. She couldn't find her key for the mail, so she asked the superintendent to open the box. There she found the letter from the War Department (in those days you named things for what they were) and promptly went on a crying jag. When my sister Alice came home, she went on one also. My father didn't cry, but raged. He was so mad that when I walked in the door, he shouted, "You came by accident and you'll go by accident."

I have remembered that line all my life. It confirmed something that I had often suspected during my childhood. I really wasn't wanted.

I'm sure that my father said it in anger, but if there hadn't been some truth to it, he would not have said it at all.

It was a frosty gathering in the living room that December 9. Everyone started to yell at me at once. If patriotism is the last refuge of the scoundrel, then I was the biggest scoundrel in Forest Hills.

"Someone has to fight Hitler," I declared.

"Not children," Alice retorted.

"I am a man, and my country has been attacked by the Japanese. Do you expect me to stand by and do nothing?"

My father tore up the permission papers, and my last words to him that evening were, "I'll do it again."

With the war on, it was more difficult than ever for me to concentrate on high school. I cut classes all the time. I attended early matinees of war films and was completely inspired by the U.S. Marine movies starring John Wayne and Victor McLaglen. I wanted to be a leatherneck more than anything in the world and come back in Marine blues to Queens and show everyone what a real hero looked like.

That brings us to the "Summer of '42," which had a tremendous effect on my life. There was a resort hotel in New Hampshire called the Mount Washington Hotel, located (not surprisingly) at the base of Mt. Washington, on 10,000 acres of land known as Bretton Woods. In 1944, it would become famous when the economic geniuses of the world met there to decide what everybody's money was worth.

I was hired as a bellboy, thanks to my experience at the Nassau Hotel the previous summer. There were no questions asked about my race, creed, or religion, which was surprising. Not long after I arrived at the hotel, I discovered that the Mount Washington did not take Jewish guests. I can't be too sure how they felt about Jewish employees, although as the summer wore on I suspected that I was under heavy suspicion of being "one of them."

The reality of a restricted hotel was brought home very brutally to me one day, when a man arrived by taxi and I was sent out to carry in his bags. The manager on duty gave him a registration form, which he signed with a Jewish name. The manager blanched and said, "I'm sorry, Mr. Kaplan, I made a mistake. There are no rooms."

I knew that there were, and I sensed the problem was the man's name. He realized he was in the "wrong" place and asked, "Could you call me a taxi?"

The manager replied, "I'm sorry, but all our phones are tied up."

"I'll get you a taxi," I said. I went to the phone at the bell captain's desk and called for one. Then I stood with the man on the porch in the heat for an hour, waiting for it to arrive. He told me that he was a salesman passing through, and that it was the first time something like this had happened to him. I was too ashamed to say I was Jewish, too. The brave thing would have been for me to have left with him. I didn't. I expected to get fired, but the owners of the hotel liked me, and it was hard for the manager to do anything except be nasty to me for the rest of the summer.

The hotel guests were very fancy people, including American oil tycoons such as the Sun Oil Pew Family, and the president of Tiffany's, and assorted blue bloods who preferred the mountains to Southampton.

I was very uncomfortable about my situation, but I didn't have the guts to call it quits. I liked wearing a uniform and I enjoyed the people I worked with very much. I particularly enjoyed the company of a waitress named Flossie Starling. She was a student at the University of North Carolina at Greensboro, and she drove me mad with her Southern accent. There was no place to go at night except the woods or the hotel golf course. The boys and girls slept in separate dormitories and the rules were, you couldn't enter one if you didn't live there.

Flossie and I got into heavy petting on our first date. It took place on the eighteenth hole of the golf course, only several inches from the cup. Flossie would not give me any sexual favors, but it didn't matter because I fell in love, and since I knew that we would someday marry I could wait for her most precious gift. At Mount Washington, I claimed to be a freshman at Columbia University, which was the only reason Flossie would have anything to do with me. The other reason was that there were twenty-five boys and seventy-five girls working at the hotel, and the one-to-three ratio played in my favor.

We climbed Mt. Washington by moonlight, splashed under waterfalls, and picked wildflowers in the meadows. By day I wore a dashing uniform, and Flossie was dressed in an immaculate waitress outfit that could not camouflage her glorious body.

Some guests were easy to get along with and some were impossible. We could deal with the latter if they tipped well—usually they didn't. The help seemed like family. We had students from Gallaudet, the school for the deaf in Washington, D.C., working as dishwashers. One day the Gallaudet students taught sign language to several of the boys. We then spoke to each other using our hands, which made the girls furious. So they learned it, too, and in no time the deaf students became part of the gang.

I was checking the rich high society in, enjoying the role of a Columbia freshman and in love with an older woman who made me gulp every time she said in her Southern accent, "Would you please pass the meat loaf?"

The summer went by, and before we knew it, it was time to go back to where we'd come from. Flossie and I parted in an embrace, vowing that no matter what happened we would always love each other. I don't recall if there were tears or not, but the message we whispered to each other was clear. This was the beginning—not the end.

So I went back to Forest Hills, no longer a Columbia freshman, but a high school senior disgusted with every phase of my life and constantly thinking of Flossie. In October, a few weeks before my seventeenth birthday, I decided to take action. I planned to run away from home and join the U.S. Marine Corps. I was not just going to join the Marines—I was going to make it into a movie scene. I chose to head South to North Carolina and say good-bye to Flossie, just as I imagined it would happen if I directed it for the silver screen. Flossie (played in the film by Jennifer Jones) would beg me not to go. But I would tell her somebody had to stop the yellow peril and their craven ally, Benito Mussolini, as well as the U-boats that sank ships loaded with innocent people and vital war cargo.

The script called for Flossie to say I had to choose between her and the Marine Corps, and I would reply, "My country, right or wrong."

At the end of the fantasy, I would be standing on the train with my head out the window. The train's whistle would sound as we pulled out of the station. Suddenly, Flossie would be running along the platform. She'd yell to me, "I love you, my darling Arthur. Come back alive." Then she would disappear in the swirling steam from the engine. Cut. That's the way I planned my entrance into the Corps.

I started hitchhiking South, leaving word on the kitchen table that I was going to enlist in the Army. When I passed near Fort Dix, I mailed a postcard to my family which said, "Well, I got in. I love you." My intention was for them to look for me only in the Army, which would keep them away from the Marines.

As I was on the road, my sisters launched a search for me. My trick worked. The Army was where they were trying to find me. Alice told me that she called Fort Dix and they turned her over to a sergeant. She was panicky—he was calm. He made her spell my name, then came back and asked, "Is he colored?"

She burst into tears. Alice quickly discovered that the military couldn't care less about underage boys joining up. They took them gladly and kept them, unless someone made a fuss about it.

I arrived in Durham with enough money to rent a room in a boardinghouse. It was six dollars a week, which included breakfast. The boardinghouse also came with a voluptuous owner's daughter who had never bundled with a Yankee before, and although her mother didn't know it, she included herself in the price of the room. In true Southern style, the breakfasts were banquets. It was the only serious meal I had all day. There were meats, grits, eggs, waffles, jams, and Southern biscuits. These breakfasts were in a class with any meals I have eaten in Paris.

To earn some money, I took a job in a meatpacking plant. I was stationed in the refrigerator. They put a very, very heavy overcoat on me and assigned me to a butcher's block. My job was to scrape meat off bones, which was sold for stew.

The fridge was freezing and my fingers immediately went numb, so while I scraped the bones I noticed pools of blood on the block. It didn't take long for me to realize that it was my blood.

By the fourth day, all my fingers were bandaged. At the end of the week, I concluded scraping meat off bones was not what it was cracked up to be. I had enough money to keep moving and said good-bye to Durham.

I never wavered from my goal, which was Greensboro, North Carolina, where Flossie was attending the university, which at that time was an all-girls' school. It was a Friday afternoon when I arrived at Flossie's dormitory. My surprise was complete. She couldn't believe that I would show up without notifying her.

I was wearing a leather jacket and a dirty shirt and all my fingers were bandaged. I hadn't intended to look that bad, but I assumed Flossie would feel sorry for me. She demanded to know what I was doing there. I told her that I hitchhiked all the way from New York to say good-bye to her before enlisting in the Marines.

"Did it ever occur to you I might have other plans?" she asked.

It hadn't.

"A boy from VMI is coming down this weekend for the Fall Hop, and I am going out with him."

"Don't those nights on the eighteenth hole of the golf course mean anything to you?" I asked.

"That was summer," she replied, in an exasperated voice. Then she said, "Do you want to go to the dance with my roommate?"

"I don't have a tuxedo."

"Pete d'Angelo, the orchestra leader from Mount Washington, left his with me."

Later on, while I was overseas, it dawned on me that something was going on between Pete and Flossie. Otherwise how did the tuxedo get in Flossie's room?

I was so desperate to be near her that I agreed to go to the dance. I had one more problem besides the fact that the tux didn't fit very well. I had no black shoes. I took five dollars and went to a secondhand store in Greensboro and bought a pair. That left me just about enough money to pay my bill at the YMCA.

The night of the dance, Flossie breezed into the ballroom as gorgeous as I had ever seen her, with the VMI cadet in dress uniform at her side. I, on the other hand, was fighting to keep Pete's tux on. It was too big for me and I kept getting lost in it. There were a few close moments when I thought I would lose my pants. Flossie's roomie liked me just as much as I liked her, which communicated itself in stony silence. I never heard a word she said, because my eyes were always on Flossie. No one has ever accused me of being Fred Astaire, so I couldn't even put the VMI guy to shame with my jitterbugging.

The dance ended and we went to a roadhouse for hamburgers and milk shakes. There were about three other couples with us. The VMI twit had a convertible, and my date and I piled into the backseat. I sat on a pint of liquor. Feeling its shape with my hand, I made up my mind that Flossie's lips would never touch the bottle and I placed it where I could steal it when I left the car.

At the roadhouse, everyone was polite but cold. Along with everything else I had to worry about—I had no money to pay for my share of the food. I had spent my last five dollars for the black shoes. When the check came, all the men threw in their share. I sat—a block of cement with a red face—looking into my glass. They all stared and then someone quietly threw in my share. Flossie was furious and my date was humiliated. And so we rode back to the YMCA in silence. It was then I committed my final despicable act of the evening. I put the pint of whiskey under my shirt and, without saying good night, walked to the YMCA doors.

The next morning, which was Saturday, I woke and realized that I had no choice but to enlist in the Marines, and the sooner the better. I knew the recruiting office was at the post office, so I arrived at nine.

A tough Marine Corps sergeant was sitting behind his desk.

"I want to join the Marine Corps," I said.

"How old are you?"

"Seventeen."

"You have to get your parent's permission."

"No problem," I assured him. "Dad's in town now buying feed for the farm. Just give it to me and I'll see that it gets signed."

"It has to be notarized."

"No problem," I told him. "I'll see to that."

He gave me the papers and then growled, "We close at noon on Saturdays."

I was out in the street on Skid Row trying to work this one out in my head when a tiny, grizzled man stopped me. "Would you give me a dime so I can get a drink?" he whined.

"I'll do better than that," I said. "I'll give you a pint of whiskey."

"What do I have to do?" he asked suspiciously.

"I'm trying to get into the Marines and my dad won't let me. If you become my father for just thirty minutes, I'll give you the whiskey."

The old man's bloodshot eyes crinkled up and he said, "Why, that's patriotic."

Someone steered me to a notary and I said, "Can I talk to you privately?" He took me into the other room.

"My dad's been drunk for a month and I'm trying to get into the Marine Corps. Would you have any objection if I steadied his hand while he signed the papers?"

"I'll do anything for someone going into the Marines," he said.

We went back and I held the drunk's shaking hand so that the signature read, "Joseph Buchwald."

Racing against the clock, I ran back to the YMCA and gave the old man his pint of whiskey. Then I ran down to the post office and at five of twelve delivered the papers to the sergeant.

"How long do you need to get things in order?"

"I am ready to go this minute."

He shrugged, swore me in, and gave me a bus ticket to Raleigh, food coupons for two days, and a voucher for a seedy hotel.

I called Flossie. "Flossie, I'm at the bus terminal and I'm leaving for Parris Island to fight for my country."

Flossie said, "You behaved terribly last night. I've never been so ashamed in my life. You also stole Fred's bottle of liquor. I don't ever want to speak to you again."

I could tell that she was mad and that she had no intention of coming down to the bus station to see me off. In spite of it, I hung my head out the window as the bus pulled away from Greensboro, hoping that at the last moment Flossie would come running alongside and crying, "I'll wait for you." And that is the true story of how one of America's fine young men wound up in the U.S. Marine Corps.

There is a happy ending to this story.

Years later, I received a call from the University of North Carolina at Greensboro, which was coed by then, asking me to speak at their commencement. They were unaware of my previous connection with the school.

I said that I would love to be their speaker. Instead of giving the boilerplate pabulum, my entire talk was about my 1942 adventure at the school. I spoke of Flossie with warm affection and of my drunken "father" with great nostalgia. I described everything just as I have here. The audience was transfixed. It was unlike any school speech they had heard before. I was assured afterward by several graduating students that the story of Flossie would inspire them in their future life. The faculty thanked me for making the commencement one to remember. No runaway had ever had the opportunity to return to the scene of one of his greatest humiliations and be received with such acclaim.

There is a second happy ending to this story. I heard from Flossie the other day and she's not mad at me anymore. She asked for my forgiveness.

I replied to her letter saying, "Nothing new on the war front. The Japanese lost Midway and Guadalcanal and are now begging for mercy. The war should be over soon. You're forgiven."

VERONICA CHAMBERS
(1970–)

Born on a United States army base in Panama to a Panamanian mother and a father who had emigrated to America from the Dominican Republic, Veronica Chambers was raised in Brooklyn from the age of five. As her parents' relationship deteriorated, Veronica, her younger brother, and her mother were abused by her father, who left the family when she was ten years old. Early on in her public school education, she was identified as a talented and gifted student, but Chambers was frustrated and hurt by her mother's seeming indifference to her scholarly achievements and intellectual ability. When her mother remarried and relocated, she had a brief nightmarish experience of gangs and guns in Los Angeles. She entered Simon's Rock College of Band in Massachusetts with early admission at the end of her junior year of high school and graduated summa cum laude with a B.A. in literary studies. At Columbia University, Chambers was awarded a Freedom Forum Fellowship. Her career as a journalist began midway through her sophomore year of college, when she arranged for an internship for herself at a new teen magazine titled *Sassy,* followed by internships at *Seventeen* and *Essence* magazines. Now the executive editor of *Savoy* magazine, she has held various editorial positions at *Newsweek, The New York Times Magazine, Premiere,* and *Essence.* Her memoir *Mama's Girl,* published in 1996, was a Book-of-the-Month Club selection and became an American Library Association Best Book of 1996. Chambers coauthored *Poetic Justice: Filmmaking South Central Style* with John Singleton (1991) and has published a number of children's and young adult books, including *Amistad Rising: A Story of Freedom* (1998), *Marisol and Magdalena: The Sound of Our Sisterhood* (1998), *Double Dutch: A Celebration of Jump Rope, Rhyme, and Sisterhood* (2000), and *Quinceañera Means Sweet 15* (2001). In 2003, she published *Having It All: Black Women and Success.*

---

from *Mama's Girl*

Ten years before Air Jordans, I learned to fly. It's like the way brothers pimp-walk to a basketball hoop with a pumped-up ball and throw a few shots, hitting each one effortlessly. Like a car idling before a drag race, there is an invitation, perhaps even a threat, in the way their sneakers soft-shoe the pavement and the ball rolls around in their hands.

As double-dutch girls, we had our own prance. Three of us and a couple of ropes. It had to be at least three girls—two to turn, one to jump. We knew the corners where you could start a good game. Like guys going up for a layup, we started turning nice and slow. Before jumping in, we would rock back and forth, rocking our knees in order to propel ourselves forward; rocking our hips just to show how cute we were. It wasn't a question of whether we'd make it in, we'd conquered that years before. The challenge was to prove how long we could jump. The tricks we would do—pop-ups, mambo, around the world—were just for show, just to work the other girls' nerves. The real feat was longevity. So when we picked the corner where we were going to double dutch, we came with ropes and patience.

There is a space between the concrete and heaven where the air is sweeter and your heart beats faster. You drop down and then you jump up again and you do it over and over until the rope catches on your foot or your mother calls you home. You keep your arms to your sides, out of the way, so they don't get tangled in the rope. Your legs feel powerful and heavy as they beat the ground. When you mambo back and forth, it's like dancing. When you do around the world, it's like a ballet dancer's pirouette. In the rope, if you're good enough, you can do anything and be anything you want.

> *Beverly Road go swinging,*
> *Beverly Road go swing-ing,*
> *Beverly Road go swinging,*
> *Beverly Road go swing-ing.*

On my side of the street is where we jumped rope because Drena, who lived by me, had the best rope, and like cattle, we followed the rope. The best kind of jumping rope was telephone wire because it was light, yet sturdy, and it hit the sidewalk with a steady rhythm—tat tat tat. The telephone wire that connected your phone to the jack was not long enough. The only way to get telephone rope was from someone who worked for the telephone company. Drena's uncle was a telephone repairman so she always had rope.

The worst kind of rope was the kind you bought in the store—cloth ropes with red plastic handles that came in plastic packages with pictures of little blonde girls on them. First of all, they were too short. It would take two or three to make one side of a good double-dutch rope. Second, the ropes were too soft for serious jumping (which only made sense because everybody knew that white girls were no kind of competition when it came to jumping rope). But in a clutch, you could run a soft rope under a hose and get it good and wet to make it heavier. The only problem was keeping it wet.

> *Miss Mary Mack-Mack-Mack*
> *All dressed in black-black-black*
> *With silver buttons-buttons-buttons*
> *All down her back-back-back*

We would split into teams. Only two positions: jumper and turner. You had to be good at both. No captain, just Shannon with her big mouth and Lisa, who really couldn't jump, but talked a lot of junk. With two people turning and one person jumping and everybody else sitting around, waiting for their turn, it wasn't hard to start a fight.

"Pick your feet up! *Pick your feet up!*"

"I hear you."

"Well then, act like it."

"You just mind your business, okay."

Sometimes when I was jumping, I would catch someone on my team yanking the rope so she could call a time-out. Usually, it was Drena because it was her rope and she thought that meant she didn't have to play fair.

"Uh-huh. Start over. Jeanine is turning double-handed," Drena would say. To us, double-handed was something like being crippled or blind. When a double-handed person turned, the ropes would hit against each other, spiraling in lopsided arcs. It not only messed up our jumping, it looked ugly, shaky, and uneven. A good double-dutch rope looked like a wire eggbeater in motion.

"It's okay. It's fine," I would say.

Drena wouldn't be swayed. "Veronica, don't try to cover up. Everybody on the block knows Jeanine is double-handed."

"I am not," Jeanine would mumble.

If there wasn't someone to take Jeanine's place, Drena would wrap up the rope and declare the game over. Then we'd go back to her house and watch TV. Drena was the only girl on the block to have her own room, plus a canopy bed, a dressing table, a TV, and a stereo. Staring blankly at *Gilligan's Island*, I would ask Drena, "Why'd you mess up the game? You know Jeanine is not double-handed."

She would roll her eyes. "I'm so sick of those girls. I was just trying to get us out of there." But other times, she would stick to her story and refuse to budge. "You *know* that girl is double-handed. Shut up and pass the Munchos."

> *Ooh, she thinks she's bad.*
> *Baby, I* know *I'm bad.*
> *Ooh, she thinks she's cool.*
> *Cool enough to steal your dude.*

We'd meet at about 3:30, after we'd changed from our school clothes into our play clothes. Then we'd jump until the parents started coming home. Most of our parents worked nine to five in Manhattan and it took them about an hour to get home. We knew it was coming up on six o'clock when we saw the first grown-up in business clothes walking down the hill from the Utica Avenue bus stop.

Sometimes a grown-up woman, dressed in the stockings and sneakers that all our mothers wore for the long commute home, would jump in—handbag and all—just to show us what she could do. She usually couldn't jump for very long. These women had no intention of sweating their straightened hair into kinkiness anyway. But we always gave them props for being able to get down. Secretly, I loved the way they clutched their chests, as if bras were useless in double dutch, and the way their bosoms rose and fell in the up-and-down rhythm of the rope. I longed for the day I would jump double dutch and have something round and soft to hang on to.

Around this time, I would start looking out for my mother. I could usually spot her from two blocks away. In the spring, she wore her tan raincoat. In the fall, she wore the same raincoat with the liner buttoned underneath. I knew the purses she carried and the way she walked. If I hadn't made up my bed or if I was jumping in my good school clothes, I could usually dash into the house before she got there and do what I was supposed to do. If I was not in trouble, I'd try to make my turn last long enough so that my mother could see me jump.

"Wait, Mom, watch me jump!" I would say. Even though I knew she'd say no.

"I've got to start dinner," she'd say. "And I've seen you jump before."

"But I've learned a new trick!" I'd try not to sound like a baby in front of my friends.

But she wouldn't even turn around. She'd be carrying a plastic shopping bag that held her work shoes and the *Daily News*.

"Some other time," she'd say, closing the gate behind her.

There's so much I can do. So much stuff she doesn't know. But it's always some other time with her.

Here is what I wish she knew: There is a space between the two ropes where nothing is better than being a black girl. The helix encircles you and protects you and there you are strong. I wish she'd let me show her. I could teach her how it feels.

■ ■ ■ ■ ■

My father is seeing another woman. I know because I hear my mother telling one of her friends over the phone. My father travels everywhere with his beeper. Like the props in his act, it's one of his gadgets. It's become his exit line, "I'm gone. Beep me."

Every Saturday morning, my mother would do a thorough cleaning of the house. She'd clean the oven and the refrigerator, mop the bathroom, and vacuum the living room. One morning, I get up from the cartoons I've been watching and go into the living room to ask my mother if we are going to visit my cousins today. My mother has been cleaning the glass coffee table. The bottle of Windex and a roll of paper towels are on the floor. My father's beeper is on the table. My mother is holding a hammer above her head, ready to smash the beeper and the table to pieces. All of a sudden my father appears and sees what she's about to do. He runs over to her screaming, "What, are you crazy? Do you know how much that beeper cost me?" Then he grabs the hammer from her hand and swings it at her head. He hits her with one sure stroke, like he is John Henry and my mother's head is a railroad spike. I am mute. I don't cry.

I think I am dead. I must be dead and I must be in hell. Where else would I see something like this? He will kill her, but all I think about is: She can't leave me alone with him. I love her, but I do not help her. It all happens so fast. The hammer is pure steel and it does not take long to do its cruel work. If it was something else, something softer he was hitting her with, maybe I would have run downstairs to the neighbors. Maybe I would have called 911. It is a moment I will play over and over in my mind. I know now that faced with calamity, I am ineffective.

When the hammer connects, my mother doesn't scream. Her head is gouged. My father sits in the burgundy reclining chair as if he is about to watch his favorite television show. He raises the footrest and crosses his legs. My mother sees me watching and tells me to go to my room, she is going to the hospital. She says it in a calm, grown-up, don't worry voice. But I'm not a fool. I can see the blood. I refuse to move. My father does not offer to drive her. At last I find my voice and beg my mother to take me with her to the hospital. I don't want to be alone with my father. He could kill me while she's gone. She tells me again to go to my room.

Instead, I follow her to the bathroom where she grabs a towel. She presses the towel against the hole in her head. The towel is white, which she isn't thinking about as she bleeds into the snowy terry cloth. The blood seeps through slowly and the towel turns red in a wavy circle that extends beyond my mother's hand. My mother grabs her purse off the kitchen table and goes out the front door. She's bleeding so much, but she doesn't cry. I run into my grandmother's room and look out the window. I watch my mother walk down the steps. She opens and closes the gate and then she walks away. I watch her for blocks until she turns a corner and then she is gone. I pray harder than I have ever prayed that she comes back, that she isn't so fed up that she turns the corner and keeps on walking.

Just after my mother leaves, my father becomes affectionate. He calls to me from his reclining chair, "Come over and give me a kiss." I look at my father and I meet hate for the first time. By showing me his very worst side, my father introduces me to the worst in myself. Before, I was always scared and helpless because I was a little girl. Now I want to kill him and though I know I can't do it, the desire to hurt him makes me feel stronger. I do not give him a kiss. I go into the bedroom and watch cartoons with my brother.

The first Saturday after my father left, my mother woke me and my brother early. It was the day before New Year's Eve. "Let's go," she said, as she led us each into the shower. "I've got some errands to run."

My brother scrunched up his face while standing firmly in place. "Errands?" he said, doubtfully. "Like what?"

My mother started to look vexed, but then smiled. "I'm the mother and you're the child. I don't have to answer your questions. I'm going out. Period. If you want to stay home, stay home."

Inside I was doing somersaults. If Malcolm wanted to stay home and watch TV with Flora, all the better for me. I hardly ever got to go anywhere alone with my mom. Even errands sounded thrilling. Something had happened after my father left. As sad as my mother had been, as scared as she still was, there was suddenly space and light in our house. It was like anything could happen because my father wasn't there. All the rules had changed.

My mother and I got dressed. Before we left, my mother went into the bedroom to talk to Flora. She started speaking quickly in Spanish so I couldn't understand. I walked over to the television where my brother was sitting, two inches from the screen. I took a big bite out of the apple I was eating, then opened my mouth so my brother could see the chewed-up food inside.

"Bleeeeech," I growled, pretending like I was about to throw up all over him.

"Maaaaa!!!" my brother screamed. "Vicki is chewing up her food and . . ."

My mother turned around and rolled her eyes. "Enough already," she said to my brother. Then, to me: "Come on, little girl. Let's go."

The minute we got out the door, I asked my mother where we were going. "To the grocery store?" I asked. "To the butcher? To the fish market?"

"Flatbush Avenue" was all she would say.

"But Flatbush Avenue is the biggest street in Brooklyn!" I said, pressing for more details.

"I know," my mother said with a grin. "Now let it rest."

We walked for what felt like miles. I kept thinking I would see one of my friends from school and I could introduce them to my mom, but it was too early in the morning. The only people out were women doing their morning shopping and really little babies being pushed in strollers. Still, I was happy to be hanging out with my mom. Even if it was nine o'clock in the morning.

"This is it," my mother said, stopping in front of what looked like an old Hallmark store.

"A card store?" I asked. "We came all this way to buy a birthday card? They sell cards right down the block from our house. . . ."

"Veronica," my mother said, using the name she reserved for putting me in check. "Shut up."

I walked into the store and surveyed the three or four racks of dusty old cards. There wasn't much of a selection. Why did we come all this way when there were better cards right down our street? I turned to ask my mother, but she had walked to the back of the store where an old Puerto Rican woman sat behind a counter.

"May I help you?" the woman said in English with a heavy accent.

"Estoy buscando algo para limpiar la casa," my mother replied.

Immediately, the woman relaxed. It was a scene I had witnessed many times before. Latinos would look at my mother's black skin and brush her off. Then, when she began speaking Spanish, their attitude would change. I knew, from my little Spanish, that *"limpiar la casa"* meant "clean the house," but why had my mother come to a card store for Mop & Glo?

I walked up to the counter and looked around. There were all kinds of candles in every color—red candles with hearts on them and the word "Amor" printed across them, white candles and orange candles, rainbow candles and black candles with skulls and crossbones on them like a poison label. There were bottles of different-colored oils, and as the woman began pouring some into little bottles for my mother, I fell in love with the smells. I read the names on the little bottles and they all seemed exotic and exciting: Sage, Roses, Success, Prosperity, Almond, Showers of Gold. By the time we left, my mother had a big shopping bag full of things.

"What do you do with all this stuff?" I asked.

"You'll see," she said.

That afternoon, I watched my mother "clean house" for the first time. She burned incense—frankincense and myrrh. As I read the label I could hardly believe that this was the same frankincense and myrrh I'd read about in the Bible with the three Wise Men. I watched my mother mix up the oils in the bucket and mop the whole house until the scent of incense and oil filled every room. There was a deliberate way in her motions that made me think that even though she saw me, she didn't really see me. She was in her own world. Then it occurred to me that it was like that shampoo commercial, "I'm going to wash that man right out of my hair." My mother was mopping my father right out of the house.

The next night was New Year's Eve and we were all going to a party at one of my mother's friends. But before we went to the party, my mother told us we each had to take a bath. Immediately, my brother started crying. He was going through a big anti-water phase.

"Here we go," my mother said, sighing. "Let's get this over with."

But when my mother stepped toward him, my brother made a mad dash for the living room. My mother ran after him. They stood, facing each other down on either side of the glass coffee table. My mother couldn't reach across and grab him, the coffee table was too wide. She'd always warn us not to play near the table or the glass top might cut us or fall off and break. But now my brother was walking around the coffee table, slowly. My mother started following him, slowly. Then he started to run. She started to run, too. They had gone around two or three times when my mother burst out laughing. Malcolm and I started laughing, too.

"*Fine then!*" she said, laughing harder than I'd ever seen before. "*Stink* up the whole party if you want to."

Then she turned to me. "Come on, Vicki. You first."

I was surprised when my mother followed me into the bathroom. "I can take my own bath," I said, feeling like she was invading my privacy.

"I know," my mother said. "Just call me when you're about to get out of the water."

I filled the tub with water, so hot I could barely stand it, and poured six capfuls of bubble bath instead of the two that the package said I should use. I lay back into the suds and promptly began daydreaming about all the things I would do in the new year. Before long, there was a knock on the door.

"Are you ready?" my mother said.

"I guess so," I answered, with just a little bit of attitude.

My mother didn't notice. She came into the bathroom with a silver basin filled with a mixture of the same water and oils she had used to mop the floor.

"That didn't come from the bucket you used on the floor, I hope," I said, scornfully.

"No," she said, shaking her head. "Why would I do something like that?"

I hadn't noticed the plastic bag in my mother's left hand. But when I saw it, I couldn't figure out why she was bringing a bouquet of white daisies into the bathroom.

"What's that for?" I said, pointing at the bag.

"You'll see." Then she proceeded to pick the petals off the flowers and throw them into the basin. It was like seeing my mother as a little girl for the first time, sitting on the bathroom floor, making daisy chains.

"Ooh, let me have one!" I said, reaching for a daisy. "I want to do He loves me, He loves me not."

Again, she gave me a curious stare. "That's not what I'm doing." She knelt next to the tub. "These oils are for a New Year's blessing. The white flowers are for purification, cleansing. Do you understand?"

Then she began to cup the mixture with her hand and pour it over my head. I jumped at the coolness of the water, but I didn't say a word. For once, I had nothing to say. It felt like I was being baptized, even though I was ten years old. It felt like I was sitting under a waterfall in Hawaii, even though I was just sitting in an old tub in Brooklyn. I felt the water run down my shoulders and back, and as she poured the mixture over me, petals stuck in my hair. I had petals all over my arms and chest. It was strange and amazing and fun.

"Wow," I said, swirling the petals around my bathwater.

My mother got up and turned around to leave. "Don't be long," she said. "Whether he likes it or not, that little boy is going to bathe."

I sat there for a few more minutes with a bouquet of daisy petals blooming like water lilies around me. Although I did not really understand what the bath was about, I did know that things were going to be okay without my father. My mother, as mysterious as she was, would take care of me. I flicked the petals off me, one by one. She loves me. She loves me.

(1936–)

Born in New York City, Frank Conroy saw little of his father, who stopped living with his wife when Conroy was three or four and who spent considerable time in rest homes for the mentally ill. His parents divorced when Conroy was eleven years old, and a year later, his father died of cancer. His mother's divorce and second marriage impoverished the family, which included Conroy, his older sister, and a half sister born to his mother and stepfather. Conroy spent most of his childhood living in an apartment on East Eighty-sixth Street in Manhattan, and aside from two years between the ages of nine and eleven at an experimental Pennsylvania boarding school, he attended P.S. 6 and Stuyvesant High School in the city. After his parents' divorce, despite being a voracious reader and an intelligent adolescent, Frank became a poor student who often cut classes, a problem child who was often difficult. At the age of seventeen, he left an unhappy home life behind by traveling to Denmark, where he studied at the International Folk High School of Elsinore and visited his maternal grandparents. Then he was accepted by Haverford College, where his talent as a writer was encouraged. In 1967, Conroy published his first book, *Stop-Time,* breaking with the long-established precedent that autobiographies were published by famous movie stars, politicians, or writers toward the end of their careers. His story collection *Midair* was published in 1985, followed by the novel *Body & Soul* in 1993 and *Dogs Bark but the Caravan Rolls On* (a collection of nonfiction works that have appeared in magazines) in 2002. He edited *The Iowa Award: The Best Stories from Twenty Years* (1991) and *The Eleventh Draft: Craft and the Writing Life from the Iowa Writers' Workshop* (1991). He has received fellowships from the Guggenheim and Rockefeller foundations and the National Council for the Arts, and presently serves as director of the University of Iowa Writers' Workshop.

---

from *Stop-Time*

I was twelve when my father died. From the ages of nine to eleven I was sent to an experimental boarding school in Pennsylvania called Freemont. I wasn't home more than a few days during these years. In the summer Freemont became a camp and I stayed through.

The headmaster was a big, florid man named Teddy who drank too much. It was no secret, and even the youngest of us were expected to sympathize with his illness and like him for it—an extension of the attitude that forbade the use of last names to make everyone more human. All of us knew, in the mysterious way children pick things up, that Teddy had almost no control over the institution he'd created, and that when decisions were unavoidable his wife took over. This weakness at the top might have been the key to the wildness of the place.

Life at Freemont was a perpetual semihysterical holiday. We knew there were almost no limits in any direction. A situation of endless, dreamlike fun, but one that imposed a certain strain on us all. Classes were a farce, you didn't have to go if you didn't want to, and there were no tests. Freedom was the key word. The atmosphere was heavy with the perfume of the nineteen-thirties—spurious agrarianism, group singing of proletarian chants from all countries, sexual freedom (I was necking at the age of nine), sentimentalism, naïveté. But above all, filtering down through the whole school, the excitement of the *new thing,* of the experiment—that peculiar floating sensation of not knowing what's going to happen next.

One warm spring night we staged a revolution. All the Junior boys, thirty or forty of us, spontaneously decided not to go to bed. We ran loose on the grounds most of the night, stalked by the entire faculty. Even old Ted was out, stumbling and crashing through the woods, warding off the nuts thrown from the trees. A few legitimate captures were made by the younger men on the staff, but there was no doubt most of us could have held out indefinitely. I, for one, was confident to the point of bravado, coming out in the open three or four times just for the fun of being chased. Can there be anything as sweet for a child as victory over authority? On that warm night I touched heights I will never reach again—baiting a thirty-year-old man, getting him to chase me over my own ground in the darkness, hearing his hard breath behind me (ah, the *word- lessness* of the chase, no words, just action), and finally leaping clean, leaping effortlessly over the brook at exactly the right place, knowing he was too heavy, too stupid as an animal, too old, and too tired to do what I had done. Oh God, my heart burst with joy when I heard him fall, flat out, in the water. Lights flashed in my brain. The chase was over and I had won. I was untouchable. I raced across the meadow, too happy to stop running.

Hours later, hidden in a bower, I heard the beginning of the end. A capture was made right below me. Every captured boy was to join forces with the staff and hunt the boys still out. My reaction was outrage. Dirty pool! But outrage dulled by recognition— "Of course. What else did you expect? They're clever and devious. Old people, with cold, ignorant hearts." The staff's technique didn't actually work as planned, but it spread confusion and broke the lovely symmetry of us against them. The revolution was no longer simple and ran out of gas. To this day I'm proud that I was the last boy in, hours after the others. (I paid a price though—some inexplicable loss to my soul as I crept around all that time in the dark, looking for another holdout.)

We went through a fire period for a couple of weeks one winter. At two or three in the morning we'd congregate in the huge windowless coatroom and set up hundreds of birthday candles on the floor. They gave a marvelous eerie light as we sat around telling horror stories. Fire-writing became the rage—paint your initials on the wall in airplane glue and touch a flame to it. At our most dramatic we staged elaborate takeoffs on religious services, complete with capes and pseudo-Latin. We were eventually discovered by our bug-eyed counselor—a homosexual, I recognize in retrospect, who had enough problems caring for thirty-five boys at the brink of puberty. As far as I know he never touched anyone.

Teddy announced a punishment that made the hair rise on the backs of our necks. After pointing out the inadequacies of the fire-escape system he decreed that each of us would be forced to immerse his left hand in a pot of boiling water for ten seconds, the sentence to be carried out two days hence. Frightened, morbidly excited, we thought about nothing else, inevitably drawn to the image of the boiling water with unhealthy fascination. We discussed the announcement almost lovingly till all hours of the night, recognizing a certain beauty in the phrasing, the formal specification of the "left hand," the precision of "immersed for ten seconds"—it had a medieval flavor that thrilled us.

But Teddy, or his wife (it was done in her kitchen), lost his nerve after the screams and tears of the first few boys. The flame was turned off under the pot and by the time my turn came it didn't hurt at all.

The only successful bit of discipline I remember was their system to get us to stop smoking. We smoked corn silk as well as cigarettes. (The preparation of corn silk was an important ritual. Hand-gathered in the field from only the best ears, it was dried in the sun, rubbed, aged, and rolled into pipe-sized pellets. We decimated Freemont's corn crop, ineptly tended in the first place, by leaving ten stripped ears rotting on the ground for every one eventually harvested. No one seemed to mind. Harvest day, in which we all participated, was a fraudulent pastoral dance of symbolic rather than economic significance.) With rare decisiveness Teddy got organized about the smoking. The parents of the only non-scholarship student in the school, a neat, well-to-do Chinese couple, removed him without warning after a visit. The faculty believed it was the sight of students lounging around the public rooms with cigarettes hanging expertly from their rosy lips, while we maintained it was the toilet-paper war. The parents had walked through the front door when things were reaching a crescendo—endless white rolls streaming down the immense curved stairway, cylindrical bombs hurtling down the stairwell from the third-floor balcony to run out anticlimactically a few feet from the floor, dangling like exhausted white tongues. The withdrawal of the only paying student was a catastrophe, and the smoking would have to stop.

Like a witch doctor, some suburban equivalent of the rainmaker, Mr. Kleinberg arrived in his mysterious black panel truck. Members of the staff were Teddy, George, or Harry, but this outsider remained Mr. Kleinberg, a form of respect to which it turned out he was entitled. We greeted him with bland amusement, secure in the knowledge that no one could do anything with us. A cheerful realist with a big smile and a pat on the shoulder for every boy in reach, he was to surprise us all.

The procedure was simple. He packed us into a small, unventilated garage, unloaded more cigarettes than the average man will see in a lifetime, passed out boxes of kitchen matches, and announced that any of us still smoking after ten packs and five cigars was excluded from the new, heavily enforced ban on smoking. None of us could resist the challenge.

He sat behind his vast mound with a clipboard, checking off names as we took our first, fresh packs. Adjusting his glasses eagerly and beaming with friendliness, he distributed his fantastic treasure. The neat white cartons were ripped open, every brand was ours for the asking—Old Gold, Pall Mall (my brand), Chesterfields, Wings, Camels, Spud, Caporals, Lucky Strike (*Loose Sweaters Mean Floppy Tits*), Kools, Benson & Hedges. He urged us to try them all. "Feel free to experiment, boys, it may be your last chance," he said, exploding with benevolent laughter.

I remember sitting on the floor with my back against the wall. Bruce, my best friend, was next to me.

"We're supposed to get sick," he said.

"I know."

We lighted up a pair of fat cigars and surveyed the scene. Forty boys puffed away in every corner of the room, some of them lined up for supplies, keeping Mr. Kleinberg busy with his paperwork. The noise was deafening. Gales of nervous laughter as someone did an imitation of John Garfield, public speeches as so-and-so declared his intention to pass out rather than admit defeat, or his neighbor yelled that he'd finished his fourth pack and was still by God going strong. One had to scream through the smoke to be heard. It wasn't long before the first boys stumbled out, sick and shamefaced, to retch on the grass. There was no way to leave quietly. Every opening of the door sent great shafts of sunlight across the smoky room, the signal for a derisive roar—boos, hoots, whistles, razzberries—from those sticking it out. I felt satisfaction as an enemy of mine left early, when the crowd was at its ugliest.

The rest of us followed eventually, of course, some taking longer than others, but all poisoned. Mr. Kleinberg won and smoking ended at Freemont. With dazed admiration we watched him drive away the next day in his black truck, smiling and waving, a panetela clamped between his teeth.

A rainy day. All of us together in the big dorm except a fat boy named Ligget. I can't remember how it started, or if any one person started it. A lot of talk against Ligget, building quickly to the point where talk was not enough. When someone claimed to have heard him use the expression "nigger-lipping" (wetting the end of a cigarette), we decided to act. Ligget was intolerable. A boy was sent to find him.

I didn't know Ligget. He had no friends even though he'd been at school longer than the rest of us. There was some vagueness about his origins, probably his parents were dead and relatives cared for him. We knew he was in the habit of running away. I remember waking up one night to see three men, including a policeman, carrying him back to his bed. He fought with hysterical strength, although silently, as if he were afraid to wake the rest of us. All three had to hold him down for the hypodermic.

On this rainy day he didn't fight. He must have known what was up the moment he walked through the door, but he didn't try to run. The two boys assigned to hold his arms were unnecessary. Throughout the entire trial he stood quite still, only his eyes, deep in the pudgy face, swiveling from side to side as he followed the speakers. He didn't say anything.

The prosecutor announced that first of all the trial must be fair. He asked for a volunteer to conduct Ligget's defense. When it became clear no one wanted the job a boy named Herbie was elected by acclamation. It seemed the perfect choice: Herbie was colorless and dim, steady if not inspired.

"I call Sammy as a witness," said the prosecutor. There was a murmur of approval. Sammy was something of a hero to us, as much for his experiences in reform school as for his fabulous condition. (An undescended testicle, which we knew nothing about. To us he had only one ball.) "The prisoner is charged with saying 'nigger-lip.' Did you hear him say it?"

"Yes. He said it a couple of days ago. We were standing over there in front of the window." Sammy pointed to the end of the room. "He said it about Mark Schofield." (Schofield was a popular athletic star, a Senior, and therefore not in the room.)

"You heard him?"

"Yes. I got mad and told him not to talk like that. I walked away. I didn't want to hear him."

"Okay. Now it's your turn, Herbie."

Herbie asked only one question. "Are you sure he said it? Maybe he said something else and you didn't hear him right."

"He said it, all right." Sammy looked over at Ligget. "He said it."

"Okay," said the prosecutor, "I call Earl." Our only Negro stepped forward, a slim, good-looking youth, already vain. (A sin so precocious we couldn't even recognize it.) He enjoyed the limelight, having grown used to it in the large, nervous, and visit-prone family that had spoiled him so terribly. He got a package every week, and owned a bicycle with gears, unheard of before his arrival.

"What do you know about this?" asked the prosecutor.

"What do you mean?"

"Did you ever hear him say what he said?"

"If he ever said that around me I'd kill him."

"Have you noticed anything else?"

"What?"

"I mean, well, does he avoid you or anything?"

Herbie suddenly yelled, "But he avoids everybody!" This was more than we had expected from old Herbie. He was shouted down immediately.

"I don't pay him no mind," said Earl, lapsing uncharacteristically into the idiom of his people.

The trial must have lasted two hours. Witness after witness came forward to take a stand against race prejudice. There was an interruption when one of the youngest boys, having watched silently, suddenly burst into tears.

"Look, Peabody's crying."

"What's wrong, Peabody?" someone asked gently.

Confused, overwhelmed by his emotions, Peabody could only stammer, "I'm sorry, I'm sorry, I don't know what's the matter. . . . It's so horrible, how could he . . ."

"What's horrible?"

"Him saying that. How could he say that? I don't understand," the boy said, tears falling from his eyes.

"It's all right, Peabody, don't worry."

"I'm sorry, I'm sorry."

Most of the testimony was on a high moral plane. Children are swept away by morality. Only rarely did it sink to the level of life. From the boy who slept next to Ligget: "He smells."

We didn't laugh. We weren't stupid boys, nor insensitive, and we recognized the seriousness of such a statement.

"His bed smells, and his clothes, and everything he has. He's a smelly, fat slob and I won't sleep next to him. I'm going to move my bed."

Sensing impatience in the room, the prosecutor called the prisoner himself. "Do you have anything to say?"

Ligget stood stock-still, his hidden eyes gleaming. He was pale.

"This is your last chance, you better take it. We'll all listen, we'll listen to your side of it." The crowd voiced its agreement, moved by an instant of homage to fair play, and false sympathy. "Okay then, don't say you didn't have a chance."

"Wait a second," said Herbie. "I want to ask him something. Did you say 'nigger-lip' to Sammy?"

It appeared for a moment that Ligget was about to speak, but he gave up the effort. Shaking his head slowly, he denied the charge.

The prosecutor stepped forward. "All those who find him guilty say aye." A roar from forty boys. "All those who find him innocent say nay." Silence. (In a certain sense the trial was a parody of Freemont's "town meetings" in which rather important questions of curriculum and school policy were debated before the students and put to a vote.)

The punishment seemed to suggest itself. We lined up for one punch apiece.

Although Ligget's beating is part of my life (past, present, and future coexist in the unconscious, says Freud), and although I've worried about it off and on for years, all I can say about it is that brutality happens easily. I learned almost nothing from beating up Ligget.

There was a tremendous, heart-swelling excitement as I waited. The line moved slowly, people were taking their time. You got only one punch and you didn't want to waste it. A ritual of getting set, measuring the distance, perhaps adjusting the angle of his jaw with an index finger—all this had to be done before you let go. A few boys had fluffed already, only grazing him. If you missed completely you got another chance.

It wasn't hurting Ligget that was important, but rather the unbelievable opportunity to throw a clean, powerful punch completely unhindered, and with none of the sloppiness of an actual fight. Ligget was simply a punching bag, albeit the best possible kind of punching bag, one in human form, with sensory equipment to measure the strength of your blows.

It was my turn. Ligget looked at me blankly. I picked a spot on his chin, drew back my arm, and threw as hard a punch as I could muster. Instant disappointment. I hadn't missed, there was a kind of snapping sound as my fist landed, and his head jerked back, but the whole complex of movements was too fast, somehow missing the exaggerated movie-punch finality I had anticipated. Ligget looked at the boy behind me and I stepped away. I think someone clapped me on the back.

"Good shot."

Little Peabody, tearstained but sober, swung an awkward blow that almost missed, grazing Ligget's mouth and bringing a little blood. He moved away and the last few boys took their turns.

Ligget was still on his feet. His face was swollen and his small eyes were glazed, but he stood unaided. He had kept his hands deep in his pockets to prevent the reflex of defense. He drew them out and for a moment there was silence, as if everyone expected him to speak.

Perhaps it was because we felt cheated. Each boy's dreams-of-glory punch had been a shade off center, or not quite hard enough, or thrown at the wrong angle, missing perfection by a maddeningly narrow margin. The urge to try again was strong. Unconsciously we knew we'd never have another chance. This wild freedom was ours once only. And perhaps among the older boys there were some who harbored the dream of throwing one final, superman punch, the knock-out blow to end all knock-out blows. Spontaneously, the line formed again.

After three or four blows Ligget collapsed. He sank to the floor, his eyes open and a dark stain spreading in his crotch. Someone told him to get up but it became clear he couldn't understand. Eventually a boy was sent to get the nurse. He was taken to the hospital in an ambulance.

X rays revealed that Ligget's jaw was broken in four places. We learned this the day after the beating, all of us repentant, sincerely unable to understand how it had happened. When he was well enough we went to visit him in the hospital. He was friendly, and accepted our apologies. One could tell he was trying, but his voice was thin and stiff, without a person behind it, like a bad actor reading lines. He wouldn't see us alone, there had to be an adult sitting by him.

No disciplinary action was taken against us. There was talk for a while that Sammy was going to be expelled, but it came to nothing. Ligget never returned.

MARY CROW DOG

(1953–)

Mary Crow Dog (née Mary Brave Bird) was born on the Rosebud Sioux Reservation in South Dakota and raised in a one-room cabin without electricity or running water. Sent to an oppressive Catholic boarding school where attempts were made to "Americanize" her, she was abused and beaten but learned to fight back. She left school only to be caught up in a cycle of urban poverty, drinking, shoplifting, and random sex. In 1971, she encountered the American Indian Movement (AIM), then sweeping through Native American communities, "like a tornado," according to Brave Bird. She participated in the occupation of the BIA building in Washington, DC, as well as in the second siege of Wounded Knee in 1973, during which her first child was born. She married Leonard Crow Dog, a Lakota medicine man and spiritual leader of AIM, who revived the outlawed Ghost Dance. Her contact with AIM and Crow Dog helped radicalize her and strengthen her involvement with tribal ways, but she and Crow Dog eventually divorced. *Lakota Woman,* cowritten with Richard Erdoes, was published in 1990 and recounts her experiences up to 1977. A national bestseller, it won an American Book Award. In 1993, she published *Ohitika Woman* (*ohitika* means *brave* in Lakota), which she also cowrote with Erdoes, using her birth name, Brave Bird. The latter volume chronicles her continuing dedication to her people and their struggles as well as her own troubled personal life. With Percy Bullchild, she wrote the introduction to *American Indian Genesis: The Story of Creation* (1998).

---

from *Lakota Woman*

Grandpa and Grandma Moore were good to us, raising us ever since we were small babies. Grandfather Noble Moore was the only father I knew. He took responsibility for us in his son's place. He gave us as good a home as he could. He worked as a janitor in the school and had little money to take care of a large family, his own and that of his son. Nine people in all plus always some poor relatives with no jobs. I don't know how he managed, but somehow he did.

The old couple raised us way out on the prairie near He-Dog in a sort of home-made shack. We had no electricity, no heating system, no plumbing. We got our water from the river. Some of the things which even poor white or black ghetto people take for granted we did not even know existed. We knew little about the outside world, having no radio and no TV. Maybe that was a blessing.

Our biggest feast was Thanksgiving because then we had hamburgers. They had a wonderful taste to them which I still remember. Grandpa raised us on rabbits, deer meat, ground squirrels, even porcupines. They never seemed to have money to buy much food. Grandpa Moore and two of his brothers were hunting all the time. It was the only way to put some fresh, red meat on the table, and we Sioux are real tigers when it comes to meat. We can't do without it. A few times Grandpa came back from fishing with a huge mud turtle and threw it in the pot. That was a feast for him. He said one could taste seven different kinds of meat flavors in a turtle stew—chicken, pork, beef, rabbit, deer, wild duck, antelope, all these. We also got the usual commodities after OEO came in.

Our cabin was small. It had only one room which served as our kitchen, living room, dining room, parlor, or whatever. At night we slept there, too. That was our home—one room. Grandma was the kind of woman who, when visitors dropped in, immediately started to feed them. She always told me: "Even if there's not much left, they gonna eat. These people came a long ways to visit us, so they gonna eat first. I don't care if they come at sunrise or at sundown, they gonna eat first. And whatever is left after they leave, even if it's only a small dried-up piece of fry bread, that's what we eat." This my grandmother taught me. She was Catholic and tried to raise us as whites, because she thought that was the only way for us to get ahead and lead a satisfying life, but when it came to basics she was all Sioux, in spite of the pictures of Holy Mary and the Sacred Heart on the wall. Whether she was aware of how very Indian she had remained, I cannot say. She also spoke the Sioux language, the real old-style Lakota, not the modern slang we have today. And she knew her herbs, showing us how to recognize the different kinds of Indian plants, telling us what each of them was good for. She took us to gather berries and a certain mint for tea. During the winter we took chokecherries, the skin and the branches. We boiled the inside layers and used the tea for various sorts of sicknesses. In the fall she took us to harvest chokecherries and wild grapes. These were the only sweets we had. I never discovered candy until much later when I was in school. We did not have the money for it and only very seldom went to town.

We had no shoes and went barefoot most of the time. I never had a new dress. Once a year we would persuade somebody to drive us to the Catholic mission for a basement rummage sale. Sometimes we found something there to put on our feet before it got cold, and maybe a secondhand blouse or skirt. That was all we could afford. We did not celebrate Christmas, at least not the kind of feast white people are used to. Grandma would save a little money and when the time came she bought some crystal sugar—it looked like small rocks of glass put on a string—some peanuts, apples, and oranges. And she got some kind of cotton material, sewing it together, making little pouches for us, and in each put one apple, one orange, a handful of peanuts, and some of that crystal sugar which took forever to melt in one's mouth. I loved it. That was Christmas and it never changed.

I was too small to know about racism then. When I was in third grade some relative took me to Pine Ridge and I went into a store. It was not very big, a small country grocery. One of my teachers was inside. I went right to the vegetable and fruit bins where I saw oranges just like the one I always got on Christmas. I sure wanted one of them. I picked the biggest one. An uncle had given me a nickel to go on a wild spree with and I wanted to use it paying for the orange. The store owner told me, "A nickel ain't enough to pay for one of them large Sunkist navel oranges, the only ones I got. Put it back." I still remember that. I had to put that damned orange back. Next to me, the wasičun teacher saw me do it and she made a face saying out loud, so that everyone in the store could hear it: "Why can't those dirty Indians keep their hands off this food? I was going to buy some oranges, but they put their dirty hands on them and now I must try to find some oranges elsewhere. How disgusting!" It made a big impression on me, even though I could not understand the full meaning of this incident.

Grandma told me: "Whatever you do, don't go into white people's homes. 'Cause when they come into our homes they make fun of us, because we are poor." When we were growing up at He-Dog there were a few Indian shacks and the garage for buses and the filling station and that was totally it. Then the government started to move us to Parmelee where they put up new OEO houses, small, matchstick structures without cellars which the people called "poverty houses." A school was also built and a few white teachers moved there. I made friends with a little white girl. She said, "Come to my house." I answered, "No, I ain't supposed to go to nobody's house." She said, "My ma ain't home. She's visiting neighbors. Just come!" So I sneaked over there without Grandma knowing it. The white girl had many toys, dolls, a dollhouse. All the things I used to admire in the Sears, Roebuck catalogue which I always studied in the outhouse. She had everything. She said, "Sit down and play with my toys." I did. I thought she was my friend. Suddenly I heard the door banging, banging, banging. It was the little girl's mother and she was yelling, "You open this door! You got some nerve coming into my home. You locked me out." She was screaming and I was shaking. I did not know what to do. I told her, "I did not lock you out. I did not even know that door was locked." She yelled, "Where is my whip?" She went into the hallway and got hold of a big, thick leather belt. She said, "Get over here!"

I ran as fast as I could back to my grandmother's house. I told her, "That white woman is going to whip me."

"What did you do?"

"Nothing. I just went into her house and she wants to whip me. Her little girl got me into trouble. I didn't do nothing. Hide me, Grandma!" I was so scared.

By about that time the lady was coming. Grandma told me, "You stay in here!" Then she got her big butcher knife. She went out standing in the doorway and told that woman, "You goddam white trash, you coming any closer and I'll chop your ears off." I never saw anybody run as fast as did that white lady.

In South Dakota white kids learn to be racists almost before they learn to walk. When I was about seven or eight years old, I fought with the school principal's daughter. We were in the playground. She was hanging on the monkey bar saying, "Come on, monkey, this thing is for you." She also told me that I smelled and looked like an Indian. I grabbed her by the hair and yanked her down from the monkey bar. I would have done more, but I saw the principal coming.

As I said, grandma spoke Sioux fluently. So does my mother. But we were not allowed to speak it and we were not taught. Many times I asked my grandmother, "Why don't you teach me the language?" Her answer always was: "'Cause we want you to get an education, to live a good life. Not have a hard time. Not depend on nobody. Times coming up are going to be real hard. You need a white man's education to live in this world. Speaking Indian would only hold you back, turn you the wrong way."

She thought she was helping me by not teaching me Indian ways. Her being a staunch Catholic also had something to do with it. The missionaries had always been repeating over and over again: *"You must kill the Indian in order to save the man!"* That was part of trying to escape the hard life. The missions, going to church, dressing and behaving like a wasičun—that for her was the key which would magically unlock the door leading to the good life, the white life with a white-painted cottage, and a carpet on the floor, a shiny car in the garage, and an industrious, necktie-wearing husband who was not a wino. Examples abounded all around her that it was the wrong key to the wrong door, that it would not change the shape of my cheekbones, or the slant of my eyes, the color of my hair, or the feelings inside me. She had only to open her eyes to see, but could not or would not. Her little dream was nourished and protected by the isolation in which she lived.

Grandma had been to mission school and that had influenced her to abandon much of our traditional ways. She gave me love and a good home, but if I wanted to be an Indian I had to go elsewhere to learn how to become one. To Grandma's older sister, Mary, for instance, the one who is married to Charlie Little Dog. I call them Grandfather and Grandmother, too, after the Sioux manner. He is a hundred and four years old now and Grandma Little Dog about ninety-eight. They are very traditional people, faithful to the ancient rituals. They still carry their water from the river. They still chop wood. They still live like the Sioux of a hundred years ago. When Charlie Little Dog talks, he still uses the old words. You have to be at least sixty or seventy years old to understand what he is talking about—the language has changed that much. So I went to them if I wanted to hear the old tales of warriors and spirits, the oral history of our people.

I also went to Grand-Uncle Dick Fool Bull, the flute maker, who took me to my first peyote meeting, and to people like the Bear Necklaces, the Brave Birds, Iron Shells, Hollow Horn Bears, and Crow Dogs. One woman, Elsie Flood, a niece of Grandma's, had a big influence upon me. She was a turtle woman, a strong, self-reliant person, because a turtle stands for strength, resolution, and long life. A turtle heart beats and beats for days, long after the turtle itself is dead. It keeps on beating all by itself. In traditional families a beaded charm in the shape of a turtle is fastened to a newborn child's cradle. The baby's navel cord is put inside this turtle charm, which is believed to protect the infant from harm and bad spirits. The charm is also supposed to make the child live to a great old age. A turtle is a strength of mind, a communication with the thunder.

I loved to visit Aunt Elsie Flood to listen to her stories. With her high cheekbones she looked like Grandma. She had a voice like water bubbling, talking with a deep, throaty sound. And she talked fast, mixing Indian and English together. I had to pay strict attention if I wanted to understand what she told me. She always paid her bills, earning a living by her arts and crafts, her beautiful work with beads and porcupine quills—what she called "Indian novelties." She was also a medicine woman. She was an old-time woman carrying her pack on her back. She would not let a man or younger woman carry her burden. She carried it herself. She neither asked nor accepted help from anybody, being proud of her turtle strength. She used turtles as her protection. Wherever she went, she always had some little live turtles with her and all kinds of things made out of tortoiseshell, little charms and boxes. She had a little place in Martin, halfway between Rosebud and Pine Ridge, and there she lived alone. She was very independent but always glad to have me visit her. Once she came to our home, trudging along as usual with the heavy pack on her back and two shopping bags full of herbs and strange things. She also brought a present for me—two tiny, very lively turtles. She had painted Indian designs on their shells and their bottoms. She communicated with them by name. One she called "Come" and the other "Go." They always waddled over to her when she called them to get their food. She had a special kind of feed for them, leaving me whole bags of it. These small twin turtles stayed tiny. They never grew. One day the white principal's son came over and smashed them. Simply stomped them to death. When she heard it my aunt said that this was an evil sign for her.

The turtle woman was afraid of nothing. She was always hitchhiking, constantly on the road thumbing her way from one place to the other. She was a mystery to some. The Indians held her in great respect, saying that she was "wakan," that she was some sort of holy person to whom turtles had given their powers. In the summer of 1976 she was found beaten to death in her home. She was discovered under the bed, face-down and naked, with weeds in her hair. She had never hurt anyone or done an unkindness to anybody, only helped people who needed it. No Indian would have touched a single hair on her head. She died that way. I still grieve for her. Her death has never been investigated. The life of an Indian is not held in great value in the state of South Dakota. There is no woman like her anymore.

■ ■ ■ ■ ■

I lived the simple life at He-Dog until I had to go to boarding school. We kids did not suffer from being poor, because we were not aware of it. The few Indians nearby lived in the same kind of want, in the same kind of dilapidated shacks or one-room log cabins with dirt floors. We had nothing to compare our life to. We existed in a vacuum of our own. We were not angry because we did not know that somewhere there was a better, more comfortable life. To be angry, poverty has to rub shoulders with wealth, as for instance ghetto people in squalid tenements living next door to the rich in their luxury apartments as I have seen during my visits to New York. TV has destroyed the innocence, broken through the wall that separates the rich whites from the poor non-whites. The "boob tube" brainwashes people, but if they are poor and nonwhite, it also makes them angry seeing all those things advertised that they can never hope to have—the fancy homes and cars, the dishwashers and microwaves, the whole costly junk of affluent America. I wonder whether the advertisers who spend a hundred thousand dollars on a commercial are aware of broadcasting a revolutionary message.

As we had no electricity we also had no "idiot box" and therefore felt no envy. Except for that one incident in the white lady's home, I had not yet encountered racism in its varied forms, and that one event I had not fully comprehended. It left me afraid of white people, though, that and some stories I had heard. As I hardly met any white people, they did not bother me. I liked the food I got; I did not know any other, and hunger is a good cook. I liked our shack. Its being overcrowded only meant womblike security to me. Again, except for that white lady's house, I only knew the kind that looked like ours, except for the filling station, but that was not a home. I had food, love, a place to sleep, and a warm, potbellied, wood-fed stove to sit near in the winter. I needed nothing more. Finally, I had something white kids don't usually have—horses to ride. No matter how poor we Sioux are, there are always a few ponies around. When I was a small girl you could buy a nice-looking pinto for ten dollars. So I was riding from as early an age as I can remember. I liked the feel of a horse under me, a feeling of mastery, of freedom, of wildness, of being Indian. It is a feeling shared by everybody on the reservation. Even the most white-manized Sioux is still half horse. I never particularly wished for anything during my earlier childhood except to own an Appaloosa, because I had seen a picture of one in a magazine and fell in love with it. Maybe one day, if I live, I'll get my wish.

Grandfather Moore died in 1972. He passed away peacefully in his sleep. I was glad he had such an easy death. He was a good, loving man, a hardworking janitor. I miss him. I miss Grandma. They protected us as long as they were able, but they could not protect us from being taken away to boarding school.

■ ■ ■ ■ ■

The mission school at St. Francis was a curse for our family for generations. My grandmother went there, then my mother, then my sisters and I. At one time or other every one of us tried to run away. Grandma told me once about the bad times she had experienced at St. Francis. In those days they let students go home only for one week every year. Two days were used up for transportation, which meant spending just five days out of three hundred and sixty-five with her family. And that was an improvement. Before Grandma's time, on many reservations they did not let the students go home at all until they had finished school. Anybody who disobeyed the nuns was severely punished. The building in which my grandmother stayed had three floors, for girls only. Way up in the attic were little cells, about five by five by ten feet. One time she was in church and instead of praying she was playing jacks. As punishment they took her to one of those little cubicles where she stayed in darkness because the windows had been boarded up. They left her there for a whole week with only bread and water for nourishment. After she came out she promptly ran away, together with three other girls. They were found and brought back. The nuns stripped them naked and whipped them. They used a horse buggy whip on my grandmother. Then she was put back into the attic—for two weeks.

My mother had much the same experiences but never wanted to talk about them, and then there I was, in the same place. The school is now run by the BIA—the Bureau of Indian Affairs—but only since about fifteen years ago. When I was there, during the 1960s, it was still run by the Church. The Jesuit fathers ran the boys' wing and the Sisters of the Sacred Heart ran us—with the help of the strap. Nothing had changed since my grandmother's days. I have been told recently that even in the '70s they were still beating children at that school. All I got out of school was being taught how to pray. I learned quickly that I would be beaten if I failed in my devotions or, God forbid, prayed the wrong way, especially prayed in Indian to Wakan Tanka, the Indian Creator.

The girls' wing was built like an F and was run like a penal institution. Every morning at five o'clock the sisters would come into our large dormitory to wake us up, and immediately we had to kneel down at the sides of our beds and recite the prayers. At six o'clock we were herded into the church for more of the same. I did not take kindly to the discipline and to marching by the clock, left-right, left-right. I was never one to like being forced to do something. I do something because I feel like doing it. I felt this way always, as far as I can remember, and my sister Barbara felt the same way. An old medicine man once told me: "Us Lakotas are not like dogs who can be trained, who can be beaten and keep on wagging their tails, licking the hand that whipped them. We are like cats, little cats, big cats, wildcats, bobcats, mountain lions. It doesn't matter what kind, but cats who can't be tamed, who scratch if you step on their tails." But I was only a kitten and my claws were still small.

Barbara was still in the school when I arrived and during my first year or two she could still protect me a little bit. When Barb was a seventh-grader she ran away together with five other girls, early in the morning before sunrise. They brought them back in the evening. The girls had to wait for two hours in front of the mother superior's office. They were hungry and cold, frozen through. It was wintertime and they had been running the whole day without food, trying to make good their escape. The mother superior asked each girl, "Would you do this again?" She told them that as punishment they would not be allowed to visit home for a month and that she'd keep them busy on work details until the skin on their knees and elbows had worn off. At the end of her speech she told each girl, "Get up from this chair and lean over it." She then lifted the girls' skirts and pulled down their underpants. Not little girls either, but teenagers. She had a leather strap about a foot long and four inches wide fastened to a stick, and beat the girls, one after another, until they cried. Barb did not give her that satisfaction but just clenched her teeth. There was one girl, Barb told me, the nun kept on beating and beating until her arm got tired.

I did not escape my share of the strap. Once, when I was thirteen years old, I refused to go to Mass. I did not want to go to church because I did not feel well. A nun grabbed me by the hair, dragged me upstairs, made me stoop over, pulled my dress up (we were not allowed at the time to wear jeans), pulled my panties down, and gave me what they called "swats"—twenty-five swats with a board around which Scotch tape had been wound. She hurt me badly.

My classroom was right next to the principal's office and almost every day I could hear him swatting the boys. Beating was the common punishment for not doing one's homework, or for being late to school. It had such a bad effect upon me that I hated and mistrusted every white person on sight, because I met only one kind. It was not until much later that I met sincere white people I could relate to and be friends with. Racism breeds racism in reverse.

The routine at St. Francis was dreary. Six A.M., kneeling in church for an hour or so; seven o'clock, breakfast; eight o'clock, scrub the floor, peel spuds, make classes. We had to mop the dining room twice every day and scrub the tables. If you were caught taking a rest, doodling on the bench with a fingernail or knife, or just rapping, the nun would come up with a dish towel and just slap it across your face, saying, "You're not supposed to be talking, you're supposed to be working!" Monday mornings we had cornmeal mush, Tuesday oatmeal, Wednesday rice and raisins, Thursday cornflakes, and Friday all the leftovers mixed together or sometimes fish. Frequently the food had bugs or rocks in it. We were eating hot dogs that were weeks old, while the nuns were dining on ham, whipped potatoes, sweet peas, and cranberry sauce. In winter our dorm was icy cold while the nuns' rooms were always warm.

I have seen little girls arrive at the school, first-graders, just fresh from home and to-tally unprepared for what awaited them, little girls with pretty braids, and the first thing the nuns did was chop their hair off and tie up what was left behind their ears. Next they would dump the children into tubs of alcohol, a sort of rubbing alcohol, "to get the germs off." Many of the nuns were German immigrants, some from Bavaria, so that we sometimes speculated whether Bavaria was some sort of Dracula country inhabited by monsters. For the sake of objectivity I ought to mention that two of the German fathers were great linguists and that the only Lakota-English dictionaries and grammars which are worth anything were put together by them.

At night some of the girls would huddle in bed together for comfort and reassur-ance. Then the nun in charge of the dorm would come in and say, "What are the two of you doing in bed together? I smell evil in this room. You girls are evil incarnate. You are sinning. You are going to hell and burn forever. You can act that way in the devil's fry-ing pan." She would get them out of bed in the middle of the night, making them kneel and pray until morning. We had not the slightest idea what it was all about. At home we slept two and three in a bed for animal warmth and a feeling of security.

The nuns and the girls in the two top grades were constantly battling it out physi-cally with fists, nails, and hair-pulling. I myself was growing from a kitten into an undersized cat. My claws were getting bigger and were itching for action. About 1969 or 1970 a strange young white girl appeared on the reservation. She looked about eighteen or twenty years old. She was pretty and had long, blond hair down to her waist, patched jeans, boots, and a backpack. She was different from any other white person we had met before. I think her name was Wise. I do not know how she man-aged to overcome our reluctance and distrust, getting us into a corner, making us lis-ten to her, asking us how we were treated. She told us that she was from New York. She was the first real hippie or Yippie we had come across. She told us of people called the Black Panthers, Young Lords, and Weathermen. She said, "Black people are get-ting it on. Indians are getting it on in St. Paul and California. How about you?" She also said, "Why don't you put out an underground paper, mimeograph it. It's easy. Tell it like it is. Let it all hang out." She spoke a strange lingo but we caught on fast.

Charlene Left Hand Bull and Gina One Star were two full-blood girls I used to hang out with. We did everything together. They were willing to join me in a Sioux uprising. We put together a newspaper which we called the *Red Panther*. In it we wrote how bad the school was, what kind of slop we had to eat—slimy, rotten, blackened potatoes for two weeks—the way we were beaten. I think I was the one who wrote the worst article about our principal of the moment, Father Keeler. I put all my anger and venom into it. I called him a goddam wasičun son of a bitch. I wrote that he knew nothing about Indians and should go back to where he came from, teaching white children whom he could relate to. I wrote that we knew which priests slept with which nuns and that all they ever could think about was filling their bellies and buying a new car. It was the kind of writing which foamed at the mouth, but which also lifted a great deal of weight from one's soul.

On Saint Patrick's Day, when everybody was at the big powwow, we distributed our newspapers. We put them on windshields and bulletin boards, in desks and pews, in dorms and toilets. But someone saw us and snitched on us. The shit hit the fan. The three of us were taken before a board meeting. Our parents, in my case my mother, had to come. They were told that ours was a most serious matter, the worst thing that had ever happened in the school's long history. One of the nuns told my mother, "Your daughter really needs to be talked to." "What's wrong with my daughter?" my mother asked. She was given one of our *Red Panther* newspapers. The nun pointed out its name to her and then my piece, waiting for Mom's reaction. After a while she asked, "Well, what have you got to say to this? What do you think?"

My mother said, "Well, when I went to school here, some years back, I was treated a lot worse than these kids are. I really can't see how they can have any complaints, because we was treated a lot stricter. We could not even wear skirts halfway up our knees. These girls have it made. But you should forgive them because they are young. And it's supposed to be a free country, free speech and all that. I don't believe what they done is wrong." So all I got out of it was scrubbing six flights of stairs on my hands and knees, every day. And no boy-side privileges.

The boys and girls were still pretty much separated. The only time one could meet a member of the opposite sex was during free time, between four and five-thirty, in the study hall or on benches or the volleyball court outside, and that was strictly supervised. One day Charlene and I went over to the boys' side. We were on the ball team and they had to let us practice. We played three extra minutes, only three minutes more than we were supposed to. Here was the nuns' opportunity for revenge. We got twenty-five swats. I told Charlene, "We are getting too old to have our bare asses whipped that way. We are old enough to have babies. Enough of this shit. Next time we fight back." Charlene only said, "Hoka-hay!"

We had to take showers every evening. One little girl did not want to take her panties off and one of the nuns told her, "You take those underpants off—or else!" But the child was ashamed to do it. The nun was getting her swat to threaten the girl. I went up to the sister, pushed her veil off, and knocked her down. I told her that if she wanted to hit a little girl she should pick on me, pick one her own size. She got herself transferred out of the dorm a week later.

In a school like this there is always a lot of favoritism. At St. Francis it was strongly tinged with racism. Girls who were near-white, who came from what the nuns called "nice families," got preferential treatment. They waited on the faculty and got to eat ham or eggs and bacon in the morning. They got the easy jobs while the skins, who did not have the right kind of background—myself among them—always wound up in the laundry room sorting out ten bushel baskets of dirty boys' socks every day. Or we wound up scrubbing the floors and doing all the dishes. The school therefore fostered fights and antagonism between whites and breeds, and between breeds and skins. At one time Charlene and I had to iron all the robes and vestments the priests wore when saying Mass. We had to fold them up and put them into a chest in the back of the church. In a corner, looking over our shoulders, was a statue of the crucified Savior, all bloody and beaten up. Charlene looked up and said, "Look at that poor Indian. The pigs sure worked him over." That was the closest I ever came to seeing Jesus.

I was held up as a bad example and didn't mind. I was old enough to have a boyfriend and promptly got one. At the school we had an hour and a half for ourselves. Between the boys' and the girls' wings were some benches where one could sit. My boyfriend and I used to go there just to hold hands and talk. The nuns were very uptight about any boy-girl stuff. They had an exaggerated fear of anything having even the faintest connection with sex. One day in religion class, an all-girl class, Sister Bernard singled me out for some remarks, pointing me out as a bad example, an example that should be shown. She said that I was too free with my body. That I was holding hands, which meant that I was not a good example to follow. She also said that I wore unchaste dresses, skirts which were too short, too suggestive, shorter than regulations permitted, and for that I would be punished. She dressed me down before the whole class, carrying on and on about my unchastity.

I stood up and told her, "You shouldn't say any of those things, miss. You people are a lot worse than us Indians. I know all about you, because my grandmother and my aunt told me about you. Maybe twelve, thirteen years ago you had a water stoppage here in St. Francis. No water could get through the pipes. There are water lines right under the mission, underground tunnels and passages where in my grandmother's time only the nuns and priests could go, which were off-limits to everybody else. When the water backed up they had to go through all the water lines and clean them out. And in those huge pipes they found the bodies of newborn babies. And they were white babies. They weren't Indian babies. At least when our girls have babies, they don't do away with them that way, like flushing them down the toilet, almost.

"And that priest they sent here from Holy Rosary in Pine Ridge because he molested a little girl. You couldn't think of anything better than dump him on us. All he does is watch young women and girls with that funny smile on his face. Why don't you point him out for an example?"

Charlene and I worked on the school newspaper. After all we had some practice. Every day we went down to Publications. One of the priests acted as the photographer, doing the enlarging and developing. He smelled of chemicals which had stained his hands yellow. One day he invited Charlene into the darkroom. He was going to teach her developing. She was developed already. She was a big girl compared to him, taller too. Charlene was nicely built, not fat, just rounded. No sharp edges anywhere.

All of a sudden she rushed out of the darkroom, yelling to me, "Let's get out of here! He's trying to feel me up. That priest is nasty." So there was this too to contend with—sexual harassment. We complained to the student body. The nuns said we just had a dirty mind.

We got a new priest in English. During one of his first classes he asked one of the boys a certain question. The boy was shy. He spoke poor English, but he had the right answer. The priest told him, "You did not say it right. Correct yourself. Say it over again." The boy got flustered and stammered. He could hardly get out a word. But the priest kept after him: "Didn't you hear? I told you to do the whole thing over. Get it right this time." He kept on and on.

I stood up and said, "Father, don't be doing that. If you go into an Indian's home and try to talk Indian, they might laugh at you and say, 'Do it over correctly. Get it right this time!'"

He shouted at me, "Mary, you stay after class. Sit down right now!"

I stayed after class, until after the bell. He told me, "Get over here!" He grabbed me by the arm, pushing me against the blackboard, shouting, "Why are you always mocking us? You have no reason to do this."

I said, "Sure I do. You were making fun of him. You embarrassed him. He needs strengthening, not weakening. You hurt him. I did not hurt you."

He twisted my arm and pushed real hard. I turned around and hit him in the face, giving him a bloody nose. After that I ran out of the room, slamming the door behind me. He and I went to Sister Bernard's office. I told her, "Today I quit school. I'm not taking any more of this, none of this shit anymore. None of this treatment. Better give me my diploma. I can't waste any more time on you people."

Sister Bernard looked at me for a long, long time. She said, "All right, Mary Ellen, go home today. Come back in a few days and get your diploma." And that was that. Oddly enough, that priest turned out okay. He taught a class in grammar, orthography, composition, things like that. I think he wanted more respect in class. He was still young and unsure of himself. But I was in there too long. I didn't feel like hearing it. Later he became a good friend of the Indians, a personal friend of myself and my husband. He stood up for us during Wounded Knee and after. He stood up to his superiors, stuck his neck way out, became a real people's priest. He even learned our language. He died prematurely of cancer. It is not only the good Indians who die young, but the good whites, too. It is the timid ones who know how to take care of themselves who grow old. I am still grateful to that priest for what he did for us later and for the quarrel he picked with me—or did I pick it with him?—because it ended a situation which had become unendurable for me. The day of my fight with him was my last day in school.

LAURA SHAINE CUNNINGHAM
(1947–)

Born only a few blocks from Yankee Stadium in the Bronx, Laura Shaine Cunningham was raised by two loving bachelor uncles, Len and Gabe, after the death of her mother, Rosie, when Laura was eight years old. She describes herself as "a child of a romance," because she was born as the result "of a love affair, not a marriage." During her earliest years, Laura and her mother made their home with a series of relatives. She has vividly depicted her coming of age in the somewhat eccentric family household created by her uncles in a Bronx apartment house. A graduate of New York University, she has worked as a journalist (winning an award for a 1984 *Newsday* cover story), novelist, playwright, and author of two highly acclaimed memoirs, *Sleeping Arrangements* (1989)—described by a *New York Times* reviewer as a "wonderfully vivid chronicle of a young girl's coming-of-age . . . funny, sad, irreverent, and generous"—and *A Place in the Country* (2000)—described by a *BookPage* reviewer as combining "autobiographical accounting with near-poetic turns of phrase . . . [that] cohere through an understanding of the importance of place in general, and of the sanctity of a home." She was awarded a fellowship by the New York Foundation of the Arts as well as a grant by the National Endowment for the Arts. Among her novels are *Beautiful Bodies* (2002), about the problems and character traits of six very different women friends, and *Dreams of Rescue* (2003), which depicts a film star confronting the end of her marriage. She has published fiction and nonfiction in *The New Yorker, The Atlantic Monthly, The New York Times, Harper's Bazaar,* and *Vogue.* Her plays include *Bang, I Love You, Two* ("Where She Went, What She Did" and "The Man at the Door"), *Cruisin' Close to Crazy, The Wives,* and *The Fall of the House of Glass.* She divides her time between an upstate New York farm and New York City.

---

from *A Place in the Country*

In the weeks following the loss of my mother, a turn of fate sent me north to true country for the first time. Where we had planned to go together, I now went alone—to a camp high in the mountains. This period formed an interval between two lives—the life I had shared with Rosie and the life I would live in the care of her two bachelor brothers, my uncles Len and Gabe.

My uncles had materialized in 3M almost as soon as my mother had disappeared into the hospital, but it was decided two weeks after her death that I should join my friend and neighbor Susan for the summer at the camp where she had just started the season. I had campaigned to join her—more than campaigned, I begged and threatened in the relentless way of an eight-year-old—until one morning, I found myself on board a bus, heading to the mountains a hundred miles north of the city.

Camp Ava was situated in the Catskills, in a dark, forested mountainscape that must have been reminiscent of the "old country" to the Polish and Russian Jews who had set up the camp there. The area was already popular with Jewish groups. Some rambling hotels and bungalow colonies had been established by working-class New York Jews and refugees from the not-so-distant war in Europe. There, they created a seasonal way of life that celebrated their liberation (from the city, from the war) yet still recalled the hardships of life as they had known it. The children's camps were poor places, set on rough terrain: Camp Ava, for example, occupied a mountainside so Bavarian in character that the sun set on it an hour before light faded from nearby pastures and the local village of Upper Cragsdale. I, at eight, knew none of this, of course—I had a clear image in my mind of the Camp Ava I wanted: a series of Hansel-and-Gretel cottages set into misted meadows afire with wildflowers, bisected by babbling brooks. I pictured a "fairy-tale" woodland, and, with the magical thinking experienced by children in my situation, it seemed not impossible that somehow Rosie was waiting for me there.

I boarded the bus with my uncle Gabe, Rosie's youngest brother, a bachelor who even at thirty-eight seemed suspended in permanent boyhood. He wore sneakers and, like my boy cousins, liked to bounce a basketball against walls. Gabe had come to mind me while my mother was in the hospital, and I had grown accustomed to his strangeness. Gabe was many things, most of them contradictory—he was a grown-up, but he played like a child. He chased me around the parks, in a game he invented, called Birdie and the Giant. He seemed to enjoy the chase as much as I did, and we would collapse, laughing, gasping at the conclusion, when I'd be cornered under full-blooming forsythia. Like me, Gabe loved nature. He was a poet and a songwriter, and he claimed to find inspiration at every turn of the footpath. He actually wrote on his notepad while leaning against a tree. An Orthodox Jew, he had somehow combined his faith with a love of black gospel singing and set many of his poems to a soulful rhythm. Gabe sang as we explored the mini-forest of the Cement Park.

I had another uncle, Uncle Len, who was more mysterious. Len was two years older and a head taller than Gabe, his kid brother. At six feet, six inches, Len towered over everyone, but, despite his size, managed to be elusive. Len had no permanent address. He costumed himself in trench coats and slouch hats and alluded to secret missions, as if he were a CIA agent. Complicating his image, Len often referred to Abraham Lincoln, whom he somewhat resembled. He was a Lincoln buff and could recite many of the late president's most famous speeches. Other than the Lincoln speeches, Len maintained significant silences. When asked a direct question, he replied with an indirect answer. "That remains to be seen," was his favored response. Len, too, had appeared in 3M, but briefly; when I would see him again "remained to be seen." It was left to Gabe to prepare me for the trip to summer camp.

We bought the requisite camp T-shirts and green shorts and had name tags sewn in by a tailor. At last, a week behind my friend Susan, I headed for camp on an ancient bus that seemed to splutter exhaust at the thought of climbing the mountainous road to Upper Cragsdale.

The city we left behind was sweltering. We slept in the blast of floor fans that sent our bedsheets billowing. Some nights, the heat could not be defeated indoors, and entire families slept on fire escapes or rooftops. We needed *Luft,* and *Luft* was scarce in the city summers. Among many families, it was customary to send the children to the country; often, the mothers went, too. "Summer bachelors" were a common sight: men who trudged alone to and from work through July and August. They suffered the subways—rumbling rides through hell. But the spirit of self-sacrifice was considered normal. "All is for the children" was the saying, and the threat of polio was not distant enough to relax the precautions: even I knew a boy at school whose leg dragged in a clanking brace. It was considered healthy, desirable to depart for the mountains if one could possibly escape. For the first time, I was part of the seasonal exodus.

The bus pulled out of the Bronx on a memorably muggy day—there seemed little difference between the air and the exhaust. A vapor rose from the softening asphalt. As the old bus backfired, rudely passing more black gases, I had the sensation I was getting out of town just in time. The minute we hit the open road, my uncle Gabe began to suffer from motion sickness. Although he often wrote and sang songs that celebrated travel, he vomited at fifteen-minute intervals throughout the trip. I saw more margins of greenery as the bus pulled over so that my uncle could alight and retch. Between incidents, he commented on the scenery as I scanned the roadside for my longed-for caves and haunted houses. The last leg, the vertiginous climb to Camp Ava, was taken by taxi. We pulled up at dusk.

What I saw should have warned me: the camp was situated on a slope so steep that it seemed as if the bunkhouses could slide down the mountain. Everything listed to the left, including the Camp Ava sign. This tilt reflected the camp politics—it had been founded by socialist labor union leaders.

We arrived in the rosiness of sunset. Uncle Gabe was dispatched to the infirmary, where his nausea did not abate but gained recognition as a chronic condition. He was put under observation. Gabe loved the country, but he was, in fact, allergic to it. He suffered hay fever, sinus irritation, and skin rashes. Even a minor bug bite ballooned into a deforming lump. Insects seemed to seek him out. "I have the sweet skin," he said. Nothing diminished his pleasure: "I'm so glad to get out in the fresh air," he wheezed on his way to the infirmary.

Gabe would spend the better part of the summer in that camp shack, where, the single adult patient, he recuperated. Whenever he came out, he'd gaze at the mountains in rapture and sing country songs: "Oh, my darling, oh my darling, oh my darling Clementine/You are lost but not forgotten, oh my darling Clementine."

Meanwhile, I was left on my own to check out the camp. At the height of the season, the place appeared abandoned. Even the crabgrass had died. The center playing field was denuded. The advertised swimming pool turned out to be a slime pit, dammed by concrete, that leached turquoise paint chips.

Of course, I could not take all this in at first sight. As night fell, throwing the silhouettes of the hemlock trees into relief, I stood in the main field, holding my clothes, packed into a pillowcase (my uncles' substitution for a suitcase).

I could not quite grasp that this was the real Camp Ava. I had envisioned the camp so completely that I was certain that my notion of it had to exist somewhere—maybe on the other side of the mountain. The weeks that followed were an encapsulated version of my future country experiences: I went into "nature shock"—stung by bugs, inflamed by rashes, and more susceptible to fear than delight when I found myself alone in the longed-for wilderness. But I would also find what I sought—solace in a sylvan setting. I had arrived a week late in a ten-week season—I might as well have arrived in the next century. In the abbreviated social time span, the week I missed could never be made up. Friendships had formed, rivalries flared. Bunks were divided, and the bunk wars had begun.

Camp Ava had advertised swimming, nature hikes, horseback riding, but the actual activities at camp were diarrhea, masturbation, stripping, and attempted escape. During my nine-week stay, I would experience most of the highlights, with a few personal detours.

Later, I discovered that the camp fee was one hundred dollars—ten dollars a week. A collection had been taken up at Rosie's office to finance my expedition. Special entrée had been gained by my friend Susan's father. All these good intentions came to naught only minutes after my arrival, when the camp managers, Ava and Manny, greeted me with bad news. Ava told me, "There is no bed." There had been a mistake.

Although they were probably middle-aged, Manny and Ava appeared ancient. They had seemingly exchanged sexes—Ava, though dressed in gypsy skirts and a ruffled blouse, had chin whiskers and barked commands in a deep voice. Manny had softened, with breasts drooping onto the ledge of his belly. He spoke in a high, piping voice, squeaking out double negatives. He knew nothing about registration "procedures" we had followed down in the city. There was no bed for me at Camp Ava. They had not been prepared. Every bunk was filled.

A blue light suffused the clearing in the forest. A white mist, an extension of the sugared-looking needles of the spruce trees, infiltrated the air. It was a warm night, but low white clouds settled like an out-of-season frost. The night song of the woods began; crickets sang and insects chittered. The children joined in, with a halfhearted rendition of "Michael, Row the Boat Ashore." The campfire sputtered and died. It was too late to return to the city. I was left in the care of Ava herself, who, gypsy skirt swinging, led me to her cabin, "just for tonight."

My first-ever night in the country. Ava snapped open a canvas cot covered with Rorschach-suggestible stains and positioned it next to an open window. She pointed out the window to a cherry tree hung with ripe fruit. "You will want to reach out and pick those cherries," she predicted. "Don't do it. I know how many are there." The minute Ava fell asleep, I leaned out and plucked those cherries. And, of course, they were the most juicy cherries I had ever tasted, their flavor enhanced by their being nothing less than forbidden fruit.

I could not sleep in such strange surroundings, far from my familiar city. I passed my first country night in near delirium, a fevered semiconsciousness in which dreams and reality were confused.

Ava awoke at dawn—this was something people did in nature, I assumed, rather than ducking under the covers to postpone the day, as you did at home. Here, there were no high-rise barriers to the sun. Light slashed through the windows sooner than I was accustomed to seeing it. Ava crooked her finger—"Follow me"—and led me from the cabin to the still-dark woods. The grass felt wet, and I saw my first dew—diamonds sparkling on each spare blade of grass. I followed Ava on a narrow footpath that seemed to retravel a dream I had had, down to a pond, hidden far below camp. Rabbits hopped past. Apparently, this was the time to spot wild animals. They got up early, too. We reached the lower end of the pond, draped in mist. Ava stepped onto a rough wooden deck and dropped her clothes. I couldn't believe it. Except for my mother, I had never seen a woman in the nude. Ava was older, more angular—her bones supported her skin, which was like a leather casing. Her breasts dangled empty, twin sacks that had once held something more. Her buttocks were shriveled, too, and reflected the droop of her breasts. Despite her lack of muscle tone, Ava assumed the perfect diver's pose, then disappeared beneath the fog.

When she emerged, Ava said that I could swim, but I declined. I loved to swim, but without a bathing suit and in this fogged, exotic atmosphere, I could not imagine myself imitating Ava—stripping and jumping into that unseen water.

Nudity became a theme of the "torture vacation," as I came to regard my stay at Camp Ava. I was kept constantly on the run by the older girls, who pursued the younger campers with intent to strip them. I ended up living a semiferal existence on the edges of the camp. I was having a memorably miserable time, save for two events that redeemed the summer—and, possibly, my soul.

After much debate, Manny and Ava let me stay in a bunkhouse for my age group, the eight-year-old Bluebells. I had only one goal in life—to be reunited with my friend Susan. Susan was ten years old and in an off-limits bunkhouse for older girls; she was a Dandelion. Susan had not exactly forgotten me, her little friend from AnaMor Towers, but she seemed a bit vague and very uncommitted to having me in her bunkhouse. She had already made a new friend—Roberta, plump and pink as a piglet, stuffed into her Camp Ava T-shirt and bermudas. Susan's lack of interest did nothing to dissuade me; I waged a campaign to get into her bunkhouse, which ended in a sit-in on the basketball court one July night. I reached a stalemate with Manny and Ava: they would not let me join Susan's bunk, and I would not go to bed with the baby Bluebells. The moon was rising, the mosquitoes were whining, and no one knew what to do.

My uncle Len was summoned and arrived by Checker cab from Manhattan. He emerged as if he were attending a spy convention, in complete costume—fedora, trench coat, and carrying a single piece of luggage: a manila envelope. Uncle Len disembarked from the taxi and strode onto the basketball court. He was the ultimate in urban style: he had never even contemplated driving.

Wearing his oxblood lace-up shoes, Len walked slowly with purpose to where I sat cross-legged, glaring at Manny and Ava. He loomed large and cast an even longer shadow. With the moon rising at his back, Uncle Len appeared at least nine feet tall. "I must remonstrate with you," he addressed Ava and Manny. They conferred under the hoop. He spoke of "détente" and the "possibilities of negotiation." Manny and Ava argued—if they gave in to me, all the campers would want the same thing. Uncle Len suggested that they must make a single exception. "After all," he pointed out, "we are dealing with special circumstances here. We are talking about a child who lost her mother two weeks ago." Could they declare an exception, in this one case? No, they couldn't. Voices were raised (although not Len's—like a great actor, he knew that lowering his voice would command more attention). He spoke in his gravest, most Lincolnesque manner: "We are gathered here tonight on this basketball court to decide the fate of one small girl." Still, they resisted. Len offered his urban solution to the problem—check into a hotel.

I lay down on the court—the asphalt had rippled, resisting the thrust of the earth beneath it. "No," I said. "I'm not going anywhere except into Susan's bunkhouse."

A boy counselor appeared, cajoling: "Do it for me. I taught you how to swim and dive."

"I knew how to swim and dive before I met you!" I spit back.

"Negotiations," as Uncle Len would express it, broke down. Manny and Ava retired to their respective rotting bungalows, leaving me on the basketball court to "freeze my tushie off" if that's what I wanted. Of course, it was not what I wanted, and the shadows of the night forest were already encroaching. After a few minutes, when the campers dispersed to their bunks, all that stood between me and the wilderness was the tall form of Uncle Len.

Len had warned Ava and Manny that their actions were ill-advised and there would be "serious repercussions." I didn't know what repercussions were, but I liked the sound of them. But how long, realistically, could I last out here in this alien dark and cold? Already, there were rustlings in the woods, the distant howl of a coyote. The mountain air chilled fast; soon the radiant heat left the asphalt court. I started to shiver.

Uncle Len took off his trench coat and covered me. Then, in a surprise move, he lay down on the court, too. "They are a tough bunch," he told me, but we would prevail. He quoted my remark to the boy counselor: "I knew how to swim and dive before I met you." We laughed together.

That night was my introduction to the true outdoors. The moon rose and stars sequined the sky, in sequence. As Uncle Len pointed out the constellations, I began to grasp the "big picture"—where we were in the solar system. Back in the Bronx, the stadium lights and the urban glow had blanched out the heavens.

For the first time since losing my mother, I dared voice the questions that haunted me: Was it possible that when people died, they didn't entirely vanish but went to other planets? Could souls soar free in space? I imagined my mother among the stars, or living on Mars with a duplicate daughter. Uncle Len and I lost ourselves in these speculations, lost our sense of time, but not of place. With my back to the ground, I felt a part of the globe, turning toward the next day. I had the feeling of being at once diminished and enhanced, part of the glittering infinite above me.

We were brought up sharp to the reality of our situation when Ava and Manny, emissaries from the land of the gross and ordinary, clomped out in flapping bedroom slippers to announce an end to the standoff. They didn't need lawsuits if we got pneumonia. They would break with precedent: I would be allowed to join Susan in the older girls' bunkhouse.

Uncle Len rose and led me to the plank steps of Dandelion House. I inhaled the scent of honeysuckle and listened to the crickets, night critters who, I now knew, chirped by rubbing their hairy legs together.

I tiptoed into the bunkhouse and took my place on a cot beside the sleeping Susan. When I took a final look out the bunkhouse window, I saw Uncle Len, walking backward across the basketball court. He waved his fedora.

His diplomatic mission completed, Uncle Len vanished as he had appeared—in a Checker cab. That left my other uncle, Uncle Gabe, "incapacitated," as he would say, in the children's infirmary. Uncle Gabe recuperated among the children with sprained ankles, poison ivy rashes, and infected wasp bites. His illness was complicated by its cure: the refugee camp doctor turned out not to be a doctor at all. He was a dentist. "He made up the part about the medical degree," Manny and Ava admitted. But the man was a Holocaust survivor, and it was deemed acceptable to allow him to practice whatever he could.

By the time Gabe tottered out of the infirmary, the camp season was nearing conclusion. He emerged with a classic case of city-person-in-the-country euphoria. He sang full-out in the meadows and under the pines. "Oh, love is a river, flowing forever, while by your side, I stumble a-long." In his striped pajamas, Gabe looked like an inmate, which, in a sense, he was, as he "stumbled a-long" on his daily nature hike to build up his strength. He made a point of pausing every few steps to gulp the fresh air—inhaling the ragweed that aggravated his sinuses. He seemed to overdose on *Luft*, keeling over and reeling back to bed.

Gabe fit in well at Camp Ava, socializing with the adult camp counselors and the talent adviser. The grown-ups at Camp Ava, led by Ava herself, had imported familiar city foods and customs. The menu leaned heavily on tuna fish, caraway-seeded rye bread, challah, sardines, and a steady supply of bagels and deli food driven up each weekend by visitors who nourished the Catskills colony. If we had traditional camp events, such as cookouts, the campfire featured Hebrew National hot dogs—definitely not *trafe*. And no marshmallow was speared without a search on the plastic sack for its kosher "U" rating and its "P" for "pareve." The meals were served in accordance with Orthodox procedure: one did not mix "meat" (*fleishig*) with dairy (*milchig*), which led to incongruous rules at our rests: on Indian Day, the braves and squaws were forbidden to have their ice cream until six hours after the *fleischdekeh* lunch.

Many of the parents and visitors brought signs of the city with them: Roberta's father, a shoe manufacturer, actually peddled his wares from an open car trunk. Mr. Zolotow took sandal orders one weekend and returned with the shoes for his junior clientele a few weeks later. He was supposed to have complicated relationships with Ava and Manny and was later accused of skimming sandal profit. Meanwhile, union leaders had frequent flare-ups over who would get the contract for the next season's T-shirts.

If the city-country combination evolved into a climactic experience, it occurred on Talent Night, when adults and campers competed in the social hall, displaying a variety of gifts. Uncle Gabe belted out his Jewish gospel, the lone spotlight glaring off his eyeglasses: "Oh, how did Moses ever know, Over ten thousand years ago. About love and charity, clean living with so much clarity." He won second prize: a pressure cooker.

Like Hans Castorp in *The Magic Mountain,* Uncle Gabe evenly divided the remainder of his time at camp into daily hikes to promote strength and sessions of suffering. I began to slip away from my bunk to walk with Gabe. I taught him the camp songs as I learned them. He sang full-out, charging along a footpath lined with daisies.

Uncle Gabe ultimately left Camp Ava, too, following in Uncle Len's large footsteps. Gabe said they would be setting up a new home for me for when I returned to the city.

I spent what time remained at camp delving deeper into the actual woods and also into my alter ego, Deer Girl. Whenever possible, I darted away from the group to explore on my own: this was the forest I pictured. If the camp itself fell short, the terrain did not. There was a great granite outcropping whose shadows, I was sure, hid caves and forests so dark, the green appeared black.

Hearing the echo of my own last dare to my mother—"I'm off to the happy hunting grounds"—I set forth to explore in earnest and one afternoon wandered farther than I ever had before, inching along a rock crevice—my belly against the stone, my back to a gorge spiked with evergreen trees.

I felt the cold breath of the cave before I saw it. Sideways, I wedged myself into the crevice. Once inside, I saw that I stood on a natural balcony. I looked down at a full cavern, complete with permanent icicles and a conical pile of ash at its center. I caught my breath and lowered myself, inch by inch, down the side of the cave, using the creases in the rock as sneakerholds. My heart beat against my T-shirt. *This was it,* what I had been searching for.

It was freezing inside, and I was shaking from the cold by the time I reached what must have been an ancient campfire site. I reached down and touched the conical pile—it turned to finer dust at my touch. I bent to examine what I was holding and saw traces of color on beads that disintegrated between my fingers. Indian beads? I tried to collect a few, but each time I touched one, it turned to powder. Then, in the midst of the pile I felt something firmer. It was made of metal, silver perhaps—I looked—it was a bracelet. I slipped it on my wrist and knew that I would not take it off for a long time.

The discovery of the Indian cave and the bracelet led to two new pleasures—I wrote down the details of my discovery in my first short story, "The Bracelet," and I also began to confide in my first true boyfriend, a kindred spirit named Frankie who had also broken from the pack and whom I encountered in the shadowy world of my forbidden walks to the cave.

One hot afternoon, I led him down to the secret crevice and showed him how to hold his breath and slide inside the cavern. He gasped—from the chill as well as from wonder. Inside, we held hands, and he gave me my first sweetheart kiss.

We were both eight years old. It would be many years before I knew such perfect love again. I soon returned to the city, to start my new life with my uncles. We lived in the same building, AnaMor Towers, but moved up in the floors and in the hierarchy. While my mother and I had shared the simplest accommodation, a studio, with Gabe and Len I moved into a junior four.

7G was located on the top floor. The next flight of stairs led to the roof. I would climb those stairs and open the fire door to step out onto the tarred roof of the building. From there, I could see the roofscape of the South Bronx, across Grand Concourse to the straight rows of more apartment buildings and the squares of greenery that were our parks. It would be ten years before my next interlude in what I think of as true country. But I often stared up at the night skies, trying to discern the constellations that I now knew were up there. In the insomniac violet glow cast by Yankee Stadium, only one or two of the brightest stars could ever prevail. From that year onward, however, I knew the configurations of the heavens, however hidden, and the greener glades and rock gorges that lay just north of the city. I had the sense of a great unexplored territory that waited and ultimately held a place for me.

BEVERLY DONOFRIO
(1950–)

Born in Wallingford, Connecticut, into a working-class Italian-American family with limited expectations for her future, Donofrio became a rebellious teenager in the '60s, especially against her policeman father. Her involvement with drugs and casual promiscuity led her to become pregnant before she graduated from high school. While caring for her infant son, she attended Middlesex Community College, where her grades paved the way for admission to Wesleyan University. After college, she took her young son to New York City, where she earned an M.F.A. at Columbia University and became a freelance journalist and regular contributor to National Public Radio. Her memoir, *Riding in Cars with Boys: Confessions of a Bad Girl Who Makes Good* (1990), is her best-known work; it was made into a motion picture starring Drew Barrymore and James Woods in 2001. With Rosalie Bonanno, Donofrio cowrote *Mafia Marriage* (1990), about the union of two powerful Mafia families. Most recently Donofrio, who describes herself as a lapsed Catholic, but who regularly collected statues of Mary from garage sales, worked on a radio documentary about sightings of the Virgin Mary, traveling as far as Fatima and Medjugorja in search of material. The project became a personal one for her and led to the publication in 2000 of *Looking for Mary: Or, the Blessed Mother and Me* about her own faith journey. She currently lives in Mexico.

---

from *Riding in Cars with Boys*

Trouble began in 1963. I'm not blaming it on President Kennedy's assassination or its being the beginning of the sixties or the Vietnam War or the Beatles or the make-out parties in the fallout shelters all over my hometown of Wallingford, Connecticut, or my standing in line with the entire population of Dag Hammarskjold Junior High School and screaming when a plane flew overhead because we thought it was the Russians. These were not easy times, it's true. But it's too convenient to pin the trouble that would set me on the path of most resistance on the times.

The trouble I'm talking about was my first real trouble, the age-old trouble. The getting in trouble as in "Is she in Trouble?" trouble. As in pregnant. As in the girl who got pregnant in high school. In the end that sentence for promiscuous behavior, that penance (to get Catholic here for a minute, which I had the fortune or misfortune of being, depending on the way you look at it)—that kid of mine, to be exact—would turn out to be a blessing instead of a curse. But I had no way of knowing it at the time and, besides, I'm getting ahead of myself.

By 1963, the fall of the eighth grade, I was ready. I was hot to trot. My hair was teased to basketball dimensions, my 16 oz. can of Miss Clairol hairspray was tucked into my shoulder bag. Dominic Mezzi whistled between his teeth every time I passed him in the hallway, and the girls from the project—the ones with boys' initials scraped into their forearms, then colored with black ink—smiled and said hi when they saw me. I wore a padded bra that lifted my tits to inches below my chin, and my father communicated to me only through my mother. "Mom," I said. "Can I go to the dance at the Y on Friday?"

"It's all right with me, but you know your father."

Yes. I knew my father. Mr. Veto, the Italian cop, who never talked and said every birthday, "So, how old're you anyway? What grade you in this year?" It was supposed to be a joke, but who could tell if he really knew or was just covering? I mean, the guy stopped looking at me at the first appearance of my breasts, way back in the fifth grade.

In the seventh grade, I began to suspect he was spying on me, when I had my run-in with Danny Dempsey at Wilkinson's Theater. Danny Dempsey was a high school dropout and a hood notorious in town for fighting. I was waiting in the back of the seats after the lights dimmed for my best friend, Donna Wilhousky, to come back with some candy when this Danny Dempsey sidled up to me and leaned his shoulder into mine. Then he reached in his pocket and pulled out a knife, which he laid in the palm of his hand, giving it a little tilt so it glinted in the screen light. I pressed my back against the wall as far away from the knife as I could, and got goosebumps. Then Donna showed up with a pack of Banana Splits and Mint Juleps, and Danny Dempsey backed away. For weeks, every time the phone rang I prayed it was Danny Dempsey. That was about the time my father started acting suspicious whenever I set foot out of his house. He was probably just smelling the perfume of budding sexuality on me and was acting territorial, like a dog. Either that or maybe his buddy Skip Plotkin, the official cop of Wilkinson's Theater, had filed a report on me.

Which wasn't a bad idea when I think of it, because I was what you call boy crazy. It probably started with Pat Boone when I was four years old. I went to see him in the movie where he sang "Bernadine" with his white bucks thumping and his fingers snapping, and I was in love. From that day on whenever "Bernadine" came on the radio, I swooned, spun around a couple of times, then dropped in a faked-dead faint. I guess my mother thought this was cute because she went out and bought me the forty-five. Then every day after kindergarten, I ran straight to the record player for my dose, rocked my head back and forth, snapped my fingers like Pat Boone, then when I couldn't stand it another second, I swooned, spun around, and dropped in a faked-dead faint.

I was never the type of little girl who hated boys. Never. Well, except for my brother. I was just the oldest of three girls, while he was the Oldest, plus the only boy in an Italian family, and you know what that means: golden penis. My father sat at one end of the table and my brother sat at the other, while my mother was on the sidelines with us girls. You could say I resented him a little. I had one advantage though—the ironclad rule. My brother, because he was a boy, was not allowed to lay one finger on us girls. So when his favorite show came on the TV, I stood in front of it. And when he said, "Move," I said, "Make me," which he couldn't.

But other boys could chase me around the yard for hours dangling earthworms from their fingers, or call me Blackie at the bus stop when my skin was tanned dirt-brown after the summer, or forbid me to set foot in their tent or play in their soft-, kick-, or dodgeball games. They could chase me away when I tried to follow them into the woods, their bows slung over their shoulders and their hatchets tucked into their belts. And I still liked them, which is not to say I didn't get back at them. The summer they all decided to ban girls, meaning me and Donna, from their nightly softball games in the field behind our houses, Donna and I posted signs on telephone poles announcing the time of the inoculations they must receive to qualify for teams. On the appointed day they stood in line at Donna's cellar door. Short ones, tall ones, skinny and fat, they waited their turn, then never even winced when we pricked their skin with a needle fashioned from a pen and a pin.

By the summer of 1963, my boy craziness had reached such a pitch that I was prepared to sacrifice the entire summer to catch a glimpse of Denny Winters, the love of my and Donna's life. Donna and I walked two miles to his house every day, then sat under a big oak tree across the street, our transistor radio between us, and stared at his house, waiting for some movement, a sign of life, a blind pulled up or down, a curtain shunted aside, a door opening, a dog barking. Anything. Denny's sister, who was older and drove a car, sometimes drove off and sometimes returned. But that was it. In an entire summer of vigilance, we never saw Denny Winters arrive or depart. Maybe he had mononucleosis; maybe he was away at camp. We never saw him mow the lawn or throw a ball against the house for practice.

What we did see was a lot of teenage boys sitting low in cars, cruising by. Once in a while, a carload would whistle, flick a cigarette into the gutter at our feet, and sing, "Hello, girls." Whenever they did that, Donna and I stuck our chins in the air and turned our heads away. "Stuck up," they hollered.

But we knew the cars to watch for: the blue-and-white Chevy with the blond boy driving, the forest-green Pontiac with the dark boy, the white Rambler, the powder-blue Camaro, the yellow Falcon. I decided that when I finally rode in a car with a boy, I wouldn't sit right next to him like I was stuck with glue to his armpit. I'd sit halfway there—just to the right of the radio, maybe.

My father, however, had other ideas. My father forbade me to ride in cars with boys until I turned sixteen. That was the beginning.

"I hate him," I cried to my mother when my father was out of the house.

"Well, he thinks he's doing what's best for you," she said.

"What? Keeping me prisoner?"

"You know your father. He's suspicious. He's afraid you'll get in trouble."

"What kind of trouble?"

"You'll ruin your reputation. You're too young. Boys think they can take advantage. Remember what I told you. If a boy gets fresh, just cross your legs."

It was too embarrassing. I changed the subject. "I hate him," I repeated.

By the time I turned fourteen, the next year, I was speeding around Wallingford in crowded cars with guys who took corners on two wheels, flew over bumps, and skidded down the road to get me screaming. Whenever I saw a cop car, I lay down on the seat, out of sight.

While I was still at Dag Hammarskjold Junior High School, I got felt up in the backseat of a car, not because I wanted to exactly, but because I was only fourteen and thought that when everybody else was talking about making out, it meant they got felt up. That was the fault of two girls from the project, Penny Calhoun and Donna DiBase, who were always talking about their periods in front of boys by saying their *friend* was staying over for a week and how their *friend* was a *bloody mess*. They told me that making out had three steps: kissing, getting felt up, and then Doing It. Next thing I knew, I was at the Church of the Resurrection bazaar and this cute little guy with a Beatles haircut sauntered up and said, "I've got a sore throat. Want to go for a ride to get some cough drops?" I hesitated. I didn't even know his name, but then the two girls I was with, both sophomores in high school, said, "Go! Are you crazy? That's Skylar Barrister, the president of the sophomore class." We ended up with two other couples parked by the dump. My face was drooly with saliva (step one) when "A Hard Day's Night" came on the radio and Sky placed a hand on one of my breasts (step two). Someone must've switched the station, because "A Hard Day's Night" was on again when his hand started moving up the inside of my thigh. I crossed my legs like my mother said, but he uncrossed them. Lucky for me, there was another couple in the backseat and Sky Barrister either was too afraid or had good enough manners not to involve them in the loss of my virginity or I really would've been labeled a slut. Not that my reputation wasn't ruined anyway, because sweetheart Sky broadcast the news that Beverly Donofrio's easy—first to his friends at the country club and then, exponentially, to the entire town. Hordes of boys called me up after that. My father was beside himself. I was grounded. I couldn't talk on the phone for more than a minute. My mother tried to intervene. "Sonny," she said. "You have to trust her."

"I know what goes on with these kids. I see it every day, and you're going to tell me?"

"What's talking on the phone going to hurt?" my mother asked.

"You heard what I said. I don't want to hear another word about it. You finish your phone call in a minute, miss, or I hang it up on you. You hear me?"

I heard him loud and clear, and it was okay with me—for a while, anyway, because my love of boys had turned sour. Sophomore year in high school, my English class was across the hall from Sky Barrister's and every time I walked by, there was a disturbance— a chitter, a laugh—coming from the guys he stood with. My brother was the captain of the football team and I wished he was the type who'd slam Sky Barrister against a locker, maybe knock a couple of his teeth out, but not my brother. My brother was the type who got a good-citizenship medal for never missing a single day of high school.

Meanwhile, his sister began to manifest definite signs of being a bad girl. My friends and I prided ourselves on our foul mouths and our stunts, like sitting across from the jocks' table in the cafeteria and giving the guys crotch shots, then when they started elbowing each other and gawking, we shot them the finger and slammed our knees together. Or we collected gingerbread from lunch trays and molded them into shapes like turds and distributed them in water fountains.

The thing was, we were sick to death of boys having all the fun, so we started acting like them: We got drunk in the parking lot before school dances and rode real low in cars, elbows stuck out windows, tossing beer cans, flicking butts, and occasionally pulling down our pants and shaking our fannies at passing vehicles.

But even though we were very busy showing the world that girls could have fun if only they'd stop acting nice, eventually it troubled us all that the type of boys we liked—collegiate, popular, seniors—wouldn't touch us with a ten-foot pole.

One time I asked a guy in the Key Club why no guys liked me. "Am I ugly or stupid or something?"

"No." He scratched under his chin. "It's probably the things you say."

"What things?"

"I don't know."

"You think it's because I don't put out?"

"See? You shouldn't say things like that to a guy."

"Why?"

"It's not right."

"But why?"

"I don't know."

"Come on, is it because it's not polite or because it's about sex or because it embarrasses you? Tell me."

"You ask too many questions. You analyze too much, that's your problem."

To say that I analyzed too much is not to say I did well in school. Good grades, done homework—any effort abruptly ended in the tenth grade, when my mother laid the bad news on me that I would not be going to college. It was a Thursday night. I was doing the dishes, my father was sitting at the table doing a paint-by-numbers, and we were humming "Theme from Exodus" together. My mother was wiping the stove before she left for work at Bradlees, and for some reason she was stinked—maybe she had her period, or maybe it was because my father and I always hummed while I did the dishes and she was jealous. Neither of us acknowledged that we were basically harmonizing. It was more like it was just an accident that we were humming the same song. Our favorites were "'Bye 'Bye Blackbird," "Sentimental Journey," "Tonight," and "Exodus." After "Exodus," I said, "Hey, Ma. I was thinking I want to go to U Conn instead of Southern or Central. It's harder to get into, but it's a better school."

"And who's going to pay for it?"

It's odd that I never thought about the money, especially since my parents were borderline paupers and being poor was my mother's favorite topic. I just figured, naively, that anybody who was smart enough could go to college.

"I don't know. Aren't there loans or something?"

"Your father and I have enough bills. You better stop dreaming. Take typing. Get a *good* job when you graduate."

"I'm not going to be a secretary."

She lifted a burner and swiped under it. "We'll see," she said.

"I'm moving to New York."

"Keep dreaming." She dropped the burner back down.

So I gritted my teeth and figured I'd have to skip college and go straight to Broadway, but it pissed me off. Because I wasn't simply a great actress, I was smart too. I'd known this since the seventh grade, when I decided my family was made up of a bunch of morons with lousy taste in television. I exiled myself into the basement recreation room every night to get away from them. There were these hairy spiders down there, and I discovered if I dropped a Book of Knowledge on them they'd fist up into dots, dead as doornails. Then one night after a spider massacre, I opened a book up and discovered William Shakespeare—his quality-of-mercy soliloquy, to be exact. Soon I'd read everything in the books by him, and then by Whitman and Tennyson and Shelley. I memorized Hamlet's soliloquy and said it to the mirror behind the bar. To do this in the seventh grade made me think I was a genius. And now, to be told by my mother, who'd never read a book in her life, that I couldn't go to college was worse than infuriating, it was unjust. Somebody would have to pay.

That weekend my friends and I went around throwing eggs at passing cars. We drove through Choate, the ritzy prep school in the middle of town, and I had an inspiration. "Stop the car," I said. "Excuse me," I said to a little sports-jacketed Choatie crossing Christian Street. "Do you know where Christian Street is?"

"I'm not sure," he said, "but I think it's that street over there." He pointed to the next road over.

"You're standing on it, asshole!" I yelled, flinging an egg at the name tag on his jacket. I got a glimpse of his face as he watched the egg drool down his chest and I'll remember the look of disbelief as it changed to sadness till the day I die. We peeled out, my friends hooting and hollering and slapping me on the back.

I thought I saw a detective car round the bend and follow us down the street, but it was just my imagination. Now that my father'd been promoted from a regular cop to a detective, it was worse. Believe me, being a bad girl and having my father cruising around in an unmarked vehicle was no picnic. One time, I'd dressed up as a pregnant woman, sprayed gray in my hair, and bought a quart of gin, then went in a motorcade to the bonfire before the big Thanksgiving football game. We had the windows down even though it was freezing out and were singing "Eleanor Rigby" when we slammed into the car in front of us and the car in back slammed into us—a domino car crash. We all got out; there was no damage except a small dent in Ronald Kovacs's car in front. He waved us off, and we went to the bonfire.

Back home, I went directly to the bathroom to brush my teeth when the phone rang. In a minute my mother called, "Bev, your father's down the station. He wants to see you."

My heart stalled. "What about?"

"You know him. He never tells me anything."

I looked at myself in the mirror and said, "You are not drunk. You have not been drinking. You have done nothing wrong, and if that man accuses you, you have every reason in the world to be really mad." This was the Stanislavsky method of lying, and it worked wonders. I considered all my lying invaluable practice for the stage. There were countless times that I maintained not only a straight but a sincere face as my mother made me put one hand on the Bible, the other on my heart, and swear that I hadn't done something it was evident to the entire world only I could have done.

My father sat me in a small green room, where he took a seat behind a desk. "You were drinking," he said.

"No I wasn't," I said.

"You ever hear of Ronald Kovacs?"

"Yes. We were in a three-car collision. He slammed on his brakes in the middle of the motorcade, and we hit him."

"It's always the driver in the back's fault, no matter what the car in front does. That's the law. Maybe your friend wasn't paying too much attention. Maybe you were all loaded."

"You always think the worst. Somebody hit us from behind too, you know."

"Who was driving your car?"

"I'm not a rat like that jerk Kovacs."

"That's right. Be a smart ass. See where it gets you. I already know who was operating the vehicle. You better be straight with me or your friend, the driver, might end up pinched. It was Beatrice?"

"Yes."

"She wasn't drinking but you were?"

"*No!* Did you ever think that maybe Ronald Kovacs was drinking? Did you ever think that maybe he's trying to cover his own ass?"

"Watch your language."

I put on my best injured look and pretended to be choking back tears. It was easy because I was scared to death. Cops kept passing in the hall outside the door to the office. I was going out on a limb. If they found concrete evidence that I'd been drinking, my father would really be embarrassed. He might hit me when we got home, and I'd definitely be grounded, probably for the rest of my life.

"They're setting up the lie detector in the other room. We got it down from Hartford for a case we been working on," he said. "Will you swear on the lie detector that you're telling the truth?"

A bead of sweat dripped down my armpit. "Good. And bring in Ronald Kovacs and make him take it, too. Then you'll see who's a liar."

Turns out there was no lie detector; it was a bluff and I'd won the gamble.

When I got home, I played it for all it was worth with my mother. "He never trusts me. He always believes the worst. I can't stand it. How could you have married him?"

"You know your father. It's his nature to be suspicious."

"I wish he worked at the steel mill."

"You and me and the man in the moon. Then maybe I could pay the doctor bills. But that's not your father. He wanted to be a cop and make a difference. He didn't want to punch a time clock and have a boss looking over his shoulder."

When I was four, before my father became a cop, he pumped gas at the garage on the corner, and every day I brought him sandwiches in a paper bag. He'd smile like I'd just brightened his day when he saw me, then I sat on his lap while he ate. Sometimes I fell asleep, leaning my head against his chest, lulled by the warmth of his body and the rumble of trucks whooshing past. Sometimes I traced the red-and-green American Beauty rose on his forearm. I thought that flower was the most beautiful thing in the world back then. Now it was gray as newsprint, and whenever I caught a glimpse of it, I turned my eyes.

"You should've told him not to be a cop," I said. "It's ruining my life."

"It's not up to the wife to tell the husband what to do," my mother said.

"He tells you what to do all the time."

"The man wears the pants in the family."

"I'm never getting married."

"You'll change your tune."

"And end up like you? Never in a million years."

"You better not let your father catch you talking to me like that."

BEN FONG-TORRES
(1945–)

One of five children, Ben Fong-Torres was born in Alameda, California, to parents who had courted by mail and met only shortly before their marriage. His father, who emigrated in 1927, and his mother, who arrived in 1940, both used false identities to enter the United States because they needed to circumvent the Exclusion Act the Congress had enacted in 1882 to bar all Chinese—except for sons of United States citizens or Chinese merchants—from entering the country. Ben grew up in Oakland's Chinatown, where he spent much of his first ten years at the restaurant owned by his father. From 1962 to 1966, he attended San Francisco State College, majoring in radio-TV-film. From 1969 to 1981, he was the news editor of *Rolling Stone* magazine, interviewing entertainers such as Bob Dylan, Diane Keaton, Steve Martin, and Stevie Wonder. His interview with Ray Charles was awarded the Deems Taylor Award for Magazine Writing in 1974. From 1983 to 1992, he wrote feature articles and a radio column for the *San Francisco Chronicle,* complementing his career as a journalist with that of a part-time DJ, hosting and appearing on a range of radio and TV programs. In addition to the autobiography *The Rice Room: Growing Up Chinese-American—From Number Two Son to Rock 'N' Roll* (1994), Fong-Torres has published *Hickory Wind: The Life and Times of Gram Parsons* (1991), *The Hits Just Keep on Coming: The History of Top 40 Radio* (1998), and *Not Fade Away: A Backstage Pass to 20 Years of Rock and Roll* (1999). Presently, he is vice president of content at Collabrys, Inc.

---

from *The Rice Room*

The Mai Fong

The rice room—the *mai fong*—was the generic name for an area in the back of our father's restaurant.

From the time of my birth in 1945 until they sold the restaurant ten years later, the cafe at 710 Webster Street was my home away from home.

Sometimes, it was just plain home.

It is a bank now, but when I see the numbers over the doorway, it's my place. Outside is where I stood and played with firecrackers and came close to blowing off a thumb. Inside, straight past the row of tellers, I can still make my way through to the kitchen and beyond, past the door on the left that led out to the backyard. Straight ahead was the bank of iceboxes where we stored the soda pops and beer, and to their right were the cantankerous generators, the boxes on boxes of canned water chestnuts and bamboo shoots—and Old Dutch cleanser, whose label featured a scary, witchlike Dutch girl who always gave me the creeps. I'd get past the stacks of Dutch girls, the shiny, squared tin cans of soy sauce and peanut oil, and the crinkly paper packages of dried bean curd, turn left, and there I'd be again: the *mai fong*.

To the right was a tiny room with a bed, a chair, and a table, where we spent our infancies. To the far left was the rice room, a cold, concrete-floored, chicken-wired area. And setting them apart, but not very far, was our study room, where, under the light of a bare lightbulb strung from the low ceiling, we read and drew pictures and listened to a Mitchell table radio that shared a shelf with jars of fermented bean cakes and tins of salted fish.

Our babysitters were *The Lone Ranger* and *The Great Gildersleeve;* the machine-gunning *Gangbusters,* who were known as "G-men" as they went after criminals, and the *T-Man,* a rugged Federal Treasury agent who had his own bad guys to chase every week.

"Ah-*Ha-Nui!*—Sarah!"—we'd hear in the distance, and my sister would dash out of the room, headed to the kitchen.

"Ah-*Haw-Doy!*" and I'd be off, to the *chui fong*—the kitchen—to wash rice, or to a table at the rear of the dining room, where I'd sit and help shell prawns or strip the spines off sugar peas. Whatever we were old enough to learn to do, we did.

To us, the kitchen was a mysterious place. Our kitchen at home was so simple: an old Sparks stove, a refrigerator, sink, and table. At the New Eastern, it was a bustling *factory*. Almost an entire wall was taken up by a line of gigantic black woks. This was my father's stage. He strode the length of the four woks, each one fired up by gas flames underneath. Beneath him, planks of wood, raised off the ground an inch or two, served to give his legs and feet some spring, and to allow food particles to drip through, to be swept off the floor later.

The sink was the size of a bathtub; the refrigerator had glass doors and stretched three times as wide as the one at home. Every appliance was bigger, and there were things we never saw anywhere else, like the big cylindrical metal oven in which my father draped rods holding large marinated pieces of pork loin. We could hear the fire roaring from the bottom of this *loo-how*. My dad would go about his business, and then, always at exactly the right time, he'd wander over, lift off the top, and pluck out several rods of barbecued pork—glowing bright red, with black at the tips.

If I happened by at that magical moment, I'd stop. "*Yeet-gow!*" I'd say. One piece. And, taking a big Chinese cleaver, he'd deftly chop off a piece of the succulent, sweet meat. "One dollah!" he'd shout, then hand it over.

My father made the best food in town. Every now and then, he'd make a batch of *Jah-Don*—which meant "bombs," but which tasted infinitely better. They were Chinese cream puffs without the cream, but liberally dipped in sugar.

There was nothing he wouldn't try. If he tasted a candy he liked, he'd try to duplicate it himself. He was proud of a rock candy he whipped up once and determined to sell at the front counter of the New Eastern. We, of course, served as his guinea pigs, and we couldn't bring ourselves to tell him the sad truth: The candy was so hard that it was inedible. I rolled a piece around my mouth. "Tastes good, *Ba-Ba*," I said. Then, when he looked away, I spat it out.

Life in a Chinese restaurant gave us access to some strange snacks, most of which we grew to like. There were the *moy*, the salted or sugared preserved plums given so freely as gifts. The salted ones set off ticklish explosions inside our mouths, but once we adjusted, nothing rivaled the satisfaction of working the plum around, getting down to the plum seed.

There were the pickled scallions we'd pluck out of the jar, bulbous onion heads that we thought of as candy. Sometimes, Dad would get a sugar cane or two at the produce market and chop off inch-long pieces for us to suck on.

When we ventured beyond the rice room and kitchen, into the dining room, we'd run into the waiter, Gim Bok. He was a tall, spindly man with rimless glasses and thinning hair who liked to spin stories to us. Watching my little sister Shirley nibbling on an apple, he'd lean over.

"Don't eat the seed," he said, "or an apple tree will grow inside you."

"What?"

"Yes. Right inside your stomach, an apple tree!"

As kids we didn't stray from the restaurant, except to go across the street to the store where they sold comic books. As we grew, we did chores that took us up Webster Street, to the store where they cultivated bean sprouts and bean cake, or down Eighth Street, in the direction of home, where we'd pop into Hoy Chang and Company to pick up cigarettes and gum to sell at the front counter.

Beyond the immediate environs, there lay the unknown.

Everyone in Chinatown knew about Freddy, a shaggy-haired kid who lived just about a block below us, on Seventh Street on the lower skirt of Chinatown, Oakland. He was seven years old when he died. Our parents gave us some of the gruesome details a few days later. Freddy had been run over by a car and dragged for blocks. It was the first time I'd heard about death, and I couldn't get him out of my mind. It was the same for my older sister and brother. We couldn't blot out the visions of Freddy losing his life . . . right in our neighborhood, just around the corner from the New Eastern. I wondered what it had been like to be Freddy at that moment. I wondered about death.

■ ■ ■ ■ ■

Mother first tried to learn English around 1945, attending evening classes at Lincoln School, where she sat in a room of mostly Chinese immigrants, with a few from the Philippines and Mexico as well. She was inspired by a woman who'd been a shipmate on her trip from Hong Kong to America.

"My friend wanted to learn English so she would be able to talk with her children," Mother said. "But after a few classes, I decided it would be better to teach my children how to speak Chinese."

China regards itself the Middle Kingdom, a center of the universe superior to all around it. It calls itself *Joong Gok*—central state. In much the same way, my parents felt they didn't need English to survive. They'd lived their entire lives in a China away from China. Everyone they cared about spoke their tongue. So why struggle to learn a strange new one?

We saw no use for Cantonese, other than to appease our parents. We had enough on our hands, learning what to us was the most complicated language in the world, the one we'd be speaking and writing all our lives.

We picked up enough Cantonese by osmosis at home and in Chinatown to get across basic thoughts, and, I guess, our parents picked up some English through Jerry Lewis and Lucy. But without an effective common language, a wall arose between parents and children. Yes, we could talk and understand most of what the other was saying. But shadings, detail, nuances, turns of phrase . . . all of those, and much more, would be blocked by the omnipresent wall.

Over the years, the kids would encourage my mother to go back to evening school, but she resisted. English was far too complicated a language for her to learn. Besides, she had to take care of us and work in our restaurants, as well as do work at home for garment factories. Every night, it seemed, Mother stayed busy at her Singer, which she set up in the front foyer of the apartment. Soon, the area began to resemble an annex to the factory, its tables piled high with fabric, sewing patterns, and clothes in various stages of completion. To save money, she knitted sweaters for us, and we took turns holding the skeins of yarn out for her to roll into balls. These were the peaceful moments with Mother, when she'd talk about how hard Father was working, how many sacrifices they were making for the family.

"You must work hard, too," she said, and I knew to expect stories about China, and what the Communists were doing to our family in the village, and how important it was for us to do well, so that we could help provide for them.

This was the Chinese way. In American families, parents might dote on their children. In Chinese culture, filial piety was the highest ideal. The children had an obligation to support their parents. In China, a nuclear family included grandparents and in-laws, and the elders held equal rights to discipline the children.

Our grandmother, of course, was in China. Except for a worn black-and-white photograph of her, we knew nothing about *Po-Po* or our cousins, aunts, and uncles in Chek Hom or Gow Bay Hong.

But by our parents' constant references to them, we knew we didn't have the kind of family we saw on television. We had obligations: to work hard, so that we could send money back to the village, to work cooperatively, and, above all, to be respectful.

We were not to talk back. If we dared to say anything about friends at school being able to go more places or do more things than we did, our mother would admonish us about Americans.

"They don't care about family," she said, meaning that no race cared about family the way the Chinese did. In China, she said, grandparents were members of the household—and honored ones, too. "Chinese take care of one another," she said. "Americans take care of themselves."

Route 66

My father, restless working for others, had taken another offer. A Chinese Texan, whom I always knew as "Mr. Joe," was building a restaurant in Amarillo, along Route 66, the fabled highway that stretched like a twisted grin between Santa Monica and Chicago. Joe would run the restaurant while my father would be one of three partner-cooks. He assured my father that it was a no-lose deal. The partners would share in the profits of the restaurant, and if the business somehow lost money, Joe would absorb the loss.

My father accepted the deal, and he wanted me to go with him.

I didn't like the idea of being uprooted, leaving school and friends. But I had no choice. As bad a boy as my parents thought Barry was, he'd gone off to Reno and proven himself to my father. I felt like some of the clothes I wore: a hand-me-down, a boy who'd never be quite as big, as strong, as his older brother. This was my chance to prove myself worthy. I began to feel better about leaving.

One spring night, Sarah sat me down in the kitchen at our flat. She was sixteen, and she seemed envious that first Barry, and now I, had managed some kind of a getaway. "You're so lucky," she said. "No more Chinatown. You can do what you want." Sarah was a junior in high school, and all around her were Chinese boys being pressured to-ward college and white-collar careers.

We took a train to Texas in the summer of 1957. My father and I rarely talked, and I buried myself in the latest issue of *Mad* magazine. I'd recently discovered its inspired mix of goofiness and anarchy, and had a stack of issues with me.

As we crossed Nevada, on our way into Arizona, my father turned to me.

"Twelve years old," he said. "You're a big boy." I looked up, a little sheepishly, from my *Mad*.

"Barry was twelve when he went to Reno," my dad was saying. "In old times, I was twelve when I stopped school to work with my father." I put down my magazine. It occurred to me how rarely we ever talked. It wasn't just the language thing. At home, Mom had done most of the talking to the children. Now Dad was offering a bit of his history.

When he was twelve, he said, he was given the choice of continuing school, which he had attended for four years, or helping his father, a sundries salesman, make his rounds, carrying goods by shoulder to outlying villages and towns. Even if he contin-ued schooling, there was no way out for him. So he decided to help his father, walking as much as forty miles a day.

And now, I was twelve and headed for the Texas Panhandle.

It was spring when we arrived, but summer had beaten us there. We had to get used to temperatures surpassing one hundred by late morning. It was like Stockton, with no escape back to the saner climes of the Bay area. I couldn't wait for the building to go up—even a wall—just so there'd be a bit of shade. But despite the conditions, I got a daily kick watching a restaurant being built from the ground up, and to know it was being constructed from the sacks of cement, and the piles of cinderblocks and bricks, and the planks of lumber, and the buckets of tar and plaster scattered throughout the property.

The Ding How would be unlike any Chinese restaurant I'd ever seen. In Chinatown, buildings were old and flush against each other. Here, we were on open land, in what felt like the desert. Here, workers were putting up a sprawling ranch house of a restaurant, a contemporary white brick building topped and offset with Oriental touches—red awnings and a circular moon gate of polished, deep red bricks.

My father was a natural calligrapher who made strong, bold strokes with his brush pen, and he found his skill put to use right away. He wrote out the Chinese characters reading *Ding How*—"very good"—that would be transferred onto a marbled pattern on the entrance floor.

Watching the walls go up, I shared my father's optimism about the Ding How. But I also shared the reservations he had about the majority owner.

He was bigger and brasher than most Chinese men I'd ever met. He liked to wear large-brimmed hats, suits, and sunglasses. Once, before the Texas venture, he and his wife picnicked with our family by Lake Merritt in Oakland, and in every snapshot from that day, he stands aloof, looking off into some unknown distance.

While the Ding How was being built, we were put up at his house in Amarillo. It looked like the home of a man who'd done well for himself and his family, and it gave me hope that, someday, we'd live in a house just like this one.

But when the Ding How was set to open, we moved from the Joes' into a bungalow at the rear of the parking lot behind the restaurant. Besides my father and me, the two other cook-partners—Lee Sing and a man we would call "Little Joe"—would be living there.

It was little better than slave quarters, this low-slung, two-room shack with a bathroom entered only through my father's and my bedroom. We had no more furniture than in a jail cell; there was neither heating nor air conditioning, and the climate attracted an unending swarm of worms, which I swept off the front doorway several times a day.

Walking to and from the restaurant in the darkness of night, I had to be careful about not stepping on grasshoppers and crickets.

Ding How was designed for the tourists rolling through on Route 66. On the wide red awnings to the left and right of the front door were two neon signs: CHOP SUEY and CHOW MEIN. This was not a restaurant that was going to challenge diners. Chop suey wasn't even a Chinese dish when it was concocted in the mid-1800s in San Francisco for hungry gold miners. It was a dish a Chinese cook had slapped together from available vegetables and meat. *Chop suey* meant "bits and pieces," or a miscellany, and only its popularity among westerners forced it onto menus in Chinese restaurants. Chinese themselves never ate chop suey. (Chow mein is another matter. We love that stuff.)

To give Ding How's visitors a sense of the Orient, our waitresses, none of them Asian, wore red satin blouses with mandarin collars, and black slacks. Big Joe, dressed to look the wealthy Texan, played host. At the cashier's stand, a glassed-in counter displayed souvenirs for sale: ivory chopsticks, back-scratchers, plastic Chinese soup spoons, folding fans, and wisdom hats. By the counter there stood a rack of postcards, both naughty and nice. We sold a little book of risqué sayings attributed to Confucius, but written by a comedy writer, most likely not Chinese.

In a top-drawer restaurant like Ding How, there was no place for a kid like me. Big Joe had no interest in a low-overhead, family ambience. I was kept backstage, in the kitchen, doing occasional chores.

That was fine by me. It left me plenty of time in the bungalow, studying, reading my *Mad* magazines, drawing cartoons, watching Little Joe's TV set, and listening to the radio. I absorbed stars like Marvin Rainwater, Marty Robbins, and Gene Austin, as well as Top 40. But in my musical universe, there was still no one like Elvis.

In the heat and dust of summertime in the Panhandle, I began exploring my surroundings and got my first whiff of freedom.

Across the highway, I could indulge in one of my favorite American foods—chili and beans—and play an early electronic version of shuffleboard. On nights off from the restaurant, Lee Sing, he of the long peeing sessions, would sometimes take me to the local auditorium to take in some professional wrestling.

When summer turned to fall, I had to think about school. I had no idea where I'd be going. Amarillo in 1957 had segregated schools, and Mary, the head waitress at the restaurant, had to call the Amarillo school district office to tell them about this Chinese boy, and to ask whether I'd go to the regular school, Horace Mann Junior High, just up Route 66 on Buchanan Street, or across town to the Negroes' school, George Washington Carver.

Someone in the office determined that I would attend Horace Mann.

I was shocked by my sudden immersion into segregation, and by my lack of choice in the matter. I didn't care which school I'd go to. I'd mixed with all colors over the years. Besides, wherever I went, I'd be the only Chinese.

I enjoyed walking to school. I'd hike along Route 66, past hotels, truck-stop diners, bars and gas stations, a trailer park, and a bowling alley, to Buchanan Street. A left turn, a couple more blocks, and I'd be at Horace Mann.

It was a strange first few days, dealing with the wild shift in racial ratios. At Westlake, one in six kids had yellow skin. At Horace Mann, it was one in 433. Taken as a group, the students at Horace Mann were a portrait of youth before juvenile delinquency.

My classmates accepted me as just another new kid in town. They invited me to join them at the after-school hangout a block or so away from campus, where kids drank root beer floats and listened to rock and roll and rhythm and blues on the jukebox. Inside the jukebox, there were no racial borders, no segregation. The coolest sounds were being made by Elvis and Jerry Lee and Buddy Holly, but also by Little Richard and Chuck Berry. The kids would bop to Laverne Baker one minute and to cowboys like Johnny Cash or Marty Robbins the next. Rock and roll was an equalizer. And for me, it was more than a way to have fun or to feel like part of the crowd. It was a way to feel Americanized.

For my English elective, I chose speech and drama. Without having been told, I knew that I had what was known as a Chinese accent. Some sounds in English don't exist in Cantonese, and vice versa. Chinese words stand on their own as pictograph symbols; there is no alphabet. Cantonese, then, can sound sloppy. And so, too, would our English. I had trouble differentiating among various *ch* and *sh* sounds, and bridging words smoothly. In childhood, in Chinatown, it was neither good nor bad; it was just the way we were. In Texas, I decided to try and sound, as well as be, more "American."

I remember the shock I felt in physical education class when Coach Kile, a handsome young man, looked at me early in the semester, clapped his hands, and yelled, "Let's go, Chop Chop!"

For a kid who was longing to belong, it was a devastating blow. Trying only to fit in, I had been singled out; I was that round little yellow-skinned guy in the comic book. I was the Ching-Chong Chinaman. I had to be; after all, it was a teacher who was saying so.

And, of course, I was utterly powerless to fight back.

I ran with the rest of the boys in PE, taking solace in the fact that none of them took to calling me names. In speech class, I listened hard and learned to mimic Texas accents, to speak, as Shakespeare wrote, "trippingly on the tongue," to camouflage, in any way I could, the verbal vestiges of my Chinatown upbringing.

I tried to be cool. The passport to cooldom in 1957 was rock and roll. So, in the bungalow, in front of a mirror, I lip-synched to Elvis Presley songs.

One night, a banquet at the Ding How featured a band fronted by a cool-looking singer named Royce—slicked-back Elvis hair with a spit curl up front, flashy red jacket and black slacks. Royce sang rockabilly: Gene Vincent & His Blue Caps' "Lotta Lovin'," Buddy Knox's "Party Doll," and, of course, Elvis. For weeks, I couldn't get "You're Right, I'm Left, She's Gone" out of my mind. I'd run back to the bungalow for some more practice.

Once or twice, I got invited to parties, but I never went. It wasn't that I couldn't, although my father was opposed to my going out without a chaperone—like, for instance, Lee Sing. But I'd never attended a party with schoolmates before.

Life in Oakland had not prepared me for the wide open possibilities of the Panhandle of Texas. Now that I had a measure of freedom, I wasn't sure how to be free.

I had one schoolmate over. His name was Jackie Hines, and he came from a broken home. After school, he'd ride over on his bicycle and we'd hang out around the still-empty rear parking lot. He gave me my first bike lessons, even letting me use a spare bike he had at home.

One day, we were both riding around behind the Ding How, making circles in the concrete, when he jumped off, sat down against one of the five posts that held up the front roof of our bungalow, and waved me over.

I slowed my bike, using another of the posts to bring me to a dead stop, dismounted, and joined him on the ground.

"I found out something," he said.

"What?"

"It's about *sex*."

"So?" I was trying to be nonchalant, but he knew better.

"You already know how it's done?"

"Well . . . not *exactly*," I said, meaning I didn't know the first thing. He could have told me Santa brought babies, and I would have said, "So?"

Jackie then told me that a girl had told him how sex worked. "It usually happens in a bathroom," he said.

I became somewhat more alert. *This* was news.

"And then they take off their clothes, and he puts it in her."

"It" I didn't have to ask about. But where did *it* go?

Jackie shrugged. "Somewhere around the stomach, where the baby comes out."

I refrained from bringing up this wild rumor I'd heard—something about a stork— and I asked him a few more questions. What did kissing have to do with it? Was it fun? What's the deal with babies being part of it?

Jackie had no easy answers. The girl's information, after all, was based on sex being a phenomenon that took place in a restroom. Still, I knew more now than I ever had before.

At age twelve, I still had no interest in sex. At least not in knowing the morbid details. Back at Lincoln School, kids had burst out laughing after trapping victims in what was supposed to be a dirty joke.

You agreed to answer "Bendix"—the name of an appliance manufacturer—to every question posed.

"What kind of washing machine do you have?" they'd ask.

"Bendix."

"Where does your father work?"

"Bendix."

"What does your mother do?"

"Bendix."

The kids would roar. And I didn't have a clue.

It didn't occur to our parents to talk with us about sex. That wasn't the Chinese way. When Sarah had to confront her first period, she did it without our mother's involvement. She learned about sex through films shown in home economics. When Shirley expressed her first interest in going out on a date, she heard Mom's summary judgment: *"Hoy see how."* Translation: "A waste of time."

Having an older brother like Barry, I wasn't totally ignorant about sexual matters. Thanks to the magazines he acquired on our Sunday morning outings, I knew what naked women looked like. They had breasts, a muted gray zone where boys had penises, and they were usually playing volleyball.

But in Texas, my feelings about girls intensified. Given more time to myself than I had at home, I'd sit and watch TV. Besides Wally Cleaver going off on his first dates while an awed Beaver watched, there'd be these intensely romantic old movies late at night. Tender, unrequited love inevitably got requited. And I'd be like Beaver, watching and pining away for just one leftover shard of those magical feelings.

In real life, at Horace Mann, kids were going steady, exchanging ID bracelets and St. Christopher's medals to display their devotion to their one and only. It was love, eighth-grade-style, and I wanted some.

On nights when there were school dances or parties I couldn't attend, when I'd finished work and repaired across the rear parking lot to the bungalow, I'd turn on the radio and move around the concrete floor the way I saw kids doing on the local bandstand show. I didn't go as far as to dance with a broom, but I did think about Holly Clark.

She wasn't as cute as Milly Porter, who I imagined could step straight out of *Father Knows Best,* or as pretty as Marsha Giffin, who had the upturned nose and dimples of a model. Holly had naturally wavy brunette hair and a friendly face, and she wore neat blouses and crisply pleated skirts. But I liked her most because she laughed at my jokes and cartoons. And she didn't have a steady boyfriend.

And so, in the clumsy, adolescent, hiding-behind-jokes way I would adopt for much of my life, I attached myself to her, giving her a personalized ID bracelet—that's what all the other kids were doing—and deluding myself into thinking that we were, in some way, a couple.

Once or twice, I walked Holly home after school. At the front door of her family's house on Ridgemere Drive, I'd peek in through the front door, into her quiet, pin-neat, middle-class living room, and think: "This is the way it should be."

When the school year ended, she was off to a vacation with her family, and we never talked again.

For all the bold steps I took into uncharted territory in Texas, I still felt conspicuously small. Even for a person of average size, that's a common feeling in Texas. But when Coach Kile had called me "Chop Chop," I took it not only as a racial stab but also as a reminder that I was short.

And so, at the Ding How, I'd go into the men's room, where there was an overhead pipe. I'd get up on the toilet, reach up, and hang from the pipes, thinking I could stretch myself taller. I'd read the Charles Atlas ads in the back of comic books and think about sending away for muscles. I never did, and stayed puny.

Still, my sister Sarah had been right. I grew up in Texas, and my time there was pivotal. It was my first experience away from Chinatown, from Chinese peers, and from the family. Suddenly, on the eve of my teens, I had a respite from the matched set of expectations with which Chinese children are born. We were told early on that we had to study hard and become either a doctor, dentist, lawyer, or, if we weren't quite up to snuff, maybe an engineer.

We were going to do what our parents could not, they told us. While they had to struggle to earn a living and to raise their family, we would be the ones who would take full advantage of the opportunities offered by the Golden Mountains. We would make our fortunes by wearing white collars. Good children all, we would then repay our parents, helping to take care of them in their old age.

I had no such interests, and in Texas, away from such talk, I could fantasize about rock and roll stardom, about being on the radio, about drawing cartoons and writing jokes, or, failing such glamour jobs, commercial art. Since grade school, I'd known that I could draw—both Barry and I seemed to have inherited some of our father's artistic skills—and I got some cartoons into the *Oakland Tribune,* which published kids' stories and drawings in the Sunday paper.

Nosing around one day in the chief partner's office at the Ding How, I discovered the typewriter and, within a month or so of toying around, was hunting and pecking through most of my homework. In spring, using the typewriter and a rubber stamp kit, I even put together a personal magazine with stories and parodies I'd written. I let one or two friends see it, so that I could claim that the magazine had had some circulation beyond a couple of kindly Ding How waitresses.

The Ding How, from all appearances, was a solid success. Residents and travelers passing through Amarillo kept the restaurant full the first several months, and even when winter brought a lull, there seemed to be enough business to keep a crew of six waitresses constantly busy.

But my father never saw the profits. The main partner, the man whose brainchild the Ding How was, the one who put together the crew of partner-cooks, plowed the initial profits back into the restaurant. That was acceptable. But, after a while, my father was convinced that not all receipts were being properly registered, that at least one partner was pocketing a disproportionate share of the proceeds.

He confronted the others, and they, for various personal and business reasons, stood together.

"You got me here from Oakland, and now you cheat me!" my father shouted one day in Big Joe's office. Caught up in anger, he lost his voice and began to choke. I ran and fetched a glass of water so that he could continue his argument. But, three to one, it was hopeless.

I, his thirteen-year-old son, could do little. One night, knowing how frustrated my dad was while he was toiling through a dinner rush, I wandered out to the parking lot in front of the restaurant and stared at the elaborate sign of neon and lightbulbs that rose thirty feet high to beckon Route 66 travelers into the restaurant. After checking to be certain that no one was in the lot, I threw rocks at the sign until I knocked out one or two lightbulbs.

There, I thought, dashing toward the side alley to the back. That ought to teach them.

A few more arguments later, my father had had enough, and we were back on the railroad tracks, on our way home.

WARREN KLIEWER
(1931–98)

Warren Kliewer (pronounced *Klee-ver*) was born and raised in Mountain Lake, Minnesota, a predominately German-speaking, rural, Mennonite community that was to become the source of many of the themes of his stories, essays, poems, and plays. At age six, he was inspired by a *Peter and the Wolf* puppet show at the local lumber yard. He earned two degrees at the University of Minnesota, a B.A. magna cum laude in 1952 and an M.F.A. in theater arts in 1967, as well as an M.A. in English at the University of Kansas (1959). He combined his career as a writer, first, with that of a college professor and, later, with that of an actor, producer, and director. Kliewer taught at Bethany College in Lindsborg, Kansas, at Earlham College, and at Wichita University, where he established the playwriting program. From 1964 to 1971, he was coeditor of *Religious Theatre* magazine. In 1980, he founded the New Jersey–based East Lynne Company, a professional troupe devoted to researching, reviving, and educating the public about neglected plays of America's theatrical heritage; he directed most of the company's productions. He published two collections of poems, *Red Rose and Gray Cowl* (1960) and *Liturgies, Games, Farewells* (1974); a collection of poems and short plays titled *Moralities and Miracles* (1962); a collection of stories titled *The Violators* (1964); and the plays *The Berserkers* (1977) and *The Booth Brothers* (1978). His musical, *A Lean and Hungry Priest,* was included in *Playwrights for Tomorrow* (1975), an anthology edited by Arthur H. Ballet, and his plays, stories, poetry, and essays appeared in journals such as *Kansas Quarterly, Forum, Descant, Beloit Poetry Journal, Antioch Review,* and *Mennonite Life.*

Testing the Memory: An Introduction

Time passes, and you accumulate a storehouse of memories. More time passes, and you discover that looking up a long-lost old friend is as interesting as making a new one, that revisiting a dreary neighborhood where you once lived is as stimulating as exploring a new place. You find yourself choosing not to read a new book but to reread one that you had read many years earlier. I used to marvel at older people. "Why do they wallow in nostalgia?" I wondered. But time has passed. I no longer regard it as wallowing in the frivolous. Instead, it's a test. Every stage in life has its appropriate tests. In childhood we run and jump and flex our muscles. In early youth we fall in love and test our loyalty. We go into business and test our ingenuity. And there comes a stage in life when testing the memory is the new challenge.

"Ah, but memory plays tricks," people say, fretting about distortions and inaccuracies. I don't worry much about that anymore. Certainly I want to tell the truth. Most people do. But I also know that a correct recounting of the facts can sometimes create a plausible surface reality that deceives. I've read books, seen plays, and viewed a great many films and television shows in which the surface details were correct, but the truth had slipped between the facts. Besides, a bad memory can be fun. Memory plays tricks, does it? So does a magician. The illusion created by sleight of hand can be most entertaining. I have devoted my life to weaving fictions on stage and on the page, and I've grown to admire what a bad memory does to the past, making it simpler, clearer, more orderly, more symmetrical . . . more like a work of art.

These sketches are based on memory. If you are seeking facts, beware. For when I wrote them, I was in search of truths. And to serve that quest for truths, one must sometimes surrender to the rules dictated by bad memory or good art—two creative processes which may be more similar than one had thought.

Pigeon Hunting

Uncle John lived on a farm and had a disease. Not until I was almost an adult did I learn the name of the disease, but at the age of twelve I knew it wasn't something you could catch, and so I gave it no thought at all. Other things held my attention—his house, for example, a weathered white farmhouse with one story, one table, one bed, and two of everything else: rooms, windows, chairs, cups, forks. Over everything lay a film of old habits and accumulated dirt. The household was so rambunctiously dirty that a twelve-year-old boy could slog through the Minnesota April mud and over the threshold and into the house without breaking his stride. Adults, I thought, abhor filth. But we boys sought out dirty places to do dirty things, like scratching, licking the plate, belching when the need arose.

It's possible I misremember. Maybe Uncle John wasn't really dirty, just mercifully understanding of my need to escape good behavior. Who knows what he really thought. Maybe he sighed with relief after each of my occasional visits and leaped into a frenzy of tidying up the silt I had deposited. I do remember now what I hardly noticed then. Uncle John's house may or may not have been clean, but it certainly was orderly. He saved everything for all possible reasons: sentiment saved 1920s floral-design postcards, frugality saved bacon fat and old socks with holes and anything else that could be used in some other way someday. Every item in the house had been filed away in its own place. Because of that and because the table, stove, sink, and cabinet were arranged in a tight triangle in one corner, he could cook and eat an entire meal without taking more than two steps in any direction.

But after my courtesy call to the house, I always headed for the barn, even though it no longer held anything of value. It was a complete barn, originally built to embrace all the life of a farm. There were stanchions for milk cows, stalls for horses, pens for far-rowing pigs, and a hayloft you reached by clambering up on one-by-fours nailed un-evenly between joists. That was always my destination, the hayloft. The ground floor had low ceilings, and the vestiges of hay and straw and manure had moldered into gray-brown, earthlike mounds. Then if you'd climb straight up the sporadic ladder steps and squeeze through the two-foot-square hole, you'd emerge into cavernous space. It was a cathedral that did magical things. Your voice echoed. You could look down through the crack between your feet and squint your eyes and make things take new shapes.

Even though the farm animals were long gone, there was a new population up in the hayloft. Barn swallows built nests and brooded through the springs. Bats came and went throughout the year, gorging themselves fat on August mosquitoes. But the pi-geons got my whole attention one day. This flock had found a hole in the hayloft door and were roosting the winter away in the rafters. Having read a few issues of *Field and Stream* and having been given a .22 caliber rifle by my father and having shot a few tin cans off the tops of fence posts, I made plans for a pigeon hunt.

So on a bearable February Saturday—in Minnesota anything above zero degrees is considered bearable—I announced to my mother that we'd be eating pigeons for sup-per, and I put on my red-and-black checked hunting mackinaw with a special rubber-lined pocket at the back for stashing one's slaughtered game. I saddled my pony, tied my rifle onto the saddle, and set off on the five-mile trip northward to Uncle John's farm, expecting to return that afternoon with my game pocket stuffed with birds and stained with clotted, frozen blood.

City dwellers may cringe at the thought of eating pigeons. Rightly so, perhaps. City-dwelling pigeons often do degenerate when they pick up the eating habits of seagulls and the obsequiousness of panhandlers, and observing the rotted offal city pi-geons eat does not encourage one's appetite. But in the wild, pigeons, like all other species fending for themselves, are constantly culled by predators: hawks from above and skunks down below and the brutal Minnesota winter at any altitude. Wild pigeons survive for only that brief time when they are healthy and alert. Any wild pigeon still flying in February is sure to be in good health. Besides, my Uncle John's corncrib stood no more than thirty feet from the barn. What could be easier? An unlimited sup-ply of clean, nutritious corn. Each morning they'd fly down to the crib, gobble up as many kernels as their crops would hold, and waddle the thirty feet back to the barn where they'd spend the rest of the day digesting in the rafters and cooing on whatever topic it is that pigeons talk about.

A full belly breeds complacency. When I first crawled into the hayloft—an under-sized twelve-year-old encumbered by two pairs of pants, a flashy, stiff mackinaw, an earlapped cap, and mittens, and dragging behind me a skimpy .22 rifle—the pigeons showed their contempt by not moving an inch. I have no doubt they were saying snide things about town boys who venture into the country, and contemplating doing dis-gusting things on my head. Perched some twenty feet above me, they had no need to retreat. I moved slowly, eased myself down on one knee, removed my mittens, loaded my single-shot .22, drew a bead on a deliciously large cock pigeon, squeezed the trigger, and missed by at least a yard. And whoosh-whoosh-flap-flap! The whole flock vanished through the narrow hole in the hay door. These were, after all, wild pigeons.

You have never seen a space so empty as the hayloft at that moment. My life's purpose had gone out the hay door with them. Undeterred, I clambered down the makeshift ladder and found the pigeons outside shrewdly reorganized into battle formation. A few were roosting on the ridgepole of the barn, a few more atop the corncrib, and the rest circling around as reconnaissance squads, trying to figure out what the red nuisance down on the ground was up to.

With hindsight it's easy to see what I should have done: find a hiding place where I could be hidden from view and sheltered from the wind. For a .22 caliber bullet is easily deflected. Don't believe those legends of Davy Crockett which say that he could hit the eye of a squirrel at a hundred yards with a single ball from a double-action muzzle-loader. Davy Crockett never hunted in the cold prairie winds of Minnesota, where you have to predict gusts and calculate trajectories and compensate for the glare of sunlight on the ice. I did none of those things. Down on one knee I went, loaded with half-frozen fingers (you can't load a rifle while wearing mittens), and before the pigeons had a moment to sleuth out my maneuver, I aimed at that same cock pigeon defiantly parading along the peak of the roof and fired. I have no idea how wide I missed or how far the bullet traveled: I hope that it landed harmlessly in an empty field. I do know where the pigeons went: beyond the horizon. The entire flock rose in unison and flapped with purpose as if they had all decided to start a northward migration two months early.

Well, I thought, if they want to be shrewd, I'll be shrewd. Back up the ladder I went, hand over hand, mitten over mitten, and found a bit of debris and threw up a makeshift pigeon blind in a corner opposite to the hole in the hay door. And I squatted down to wait.

When the temperature is twenty degrees or so, sitting still for ten minutes seems like an hour. So I don't know how long I waited. Nothing came in but the wind. Time passed. I put the gun down on the floor. More time passed. I put my mittens back on. Nothing moved. I started thinking about the wood-burning stove in the house. I took my mittens off, unloaded, put my mittens back on, and started toward the ladder. Just at that moment the pigeon scout appeared in the hay door hole, cocked his head to look me over, and about-faced out into the cold sky again. The pigeons, it was obvious, had no intention of being breaded or gravied.

But cold though I was, a vestige of my racial memory of the hunter instinct still stirred somewhere below consciousness. I shivered my way down the ladder. I walked around inside the barn to peer out all the dirt-encrusted windows. Sure enough, about a third of the flock had stopped off at the corncrib and were preoccupied with stockpiling more corn. They'll never notice me, I thought. Greed gets them every time. I stole all the way around to the back of the barn, braced my gun against the corner, controlled my shivering with determined willpower, squeezed the trigger, and demolished an ear of corn about eighteen inches upwind of my target. Had I been wrong to compensate for the wind?

Now the pigeons were gone for good, I thought. In hunting you don't get a second chance. That may be why it appeals to grown-up men, but it's hard for a twelve-year-old to take. I couldn't make myself believe the pigeons would come back in less than two weeks, and I dreaded going back into the house. What would Uncle John say? He had a droll sense of humor which seemed funny while it hinted at other meanings. But what else could I do? I couldn't saddle up the pony and head home. I certainly couldn't go wandering aimlessly in the cold. So, bracing myself for humiliation, I headed for the house.

When he asked, "Get any?" I concentrated on stomping the snow off my boots and muttered, "No," without elaborating.

He nodded solemnly and changed the subject: "Cold out there?" His maneuver shouldn't be confused with tact. Farmers live by the unsentimental awareness that our survival is fed by the deaths of other creatures. So why should one spare the feelings of a kid who can't shoot straight? And yet, as I remember that day, his gesture seems almost delicate. A man who has learned to live with a disease does not make casual jokes about falling short.

"You hungry?" he asked. Now, I had a reputation in those days for devouring four or more meals a day, and many a relative smiled at my apparent compliment to her cooking. So I'm sure I said yes enthusiastically, even though Uncle John's cooking was known to be primitive and I considered his table manners slovenly. He drank his coffee, for example, by tipping the cup to spill the coffee and then sipping from the saucer. How embarrassing, I thought then, not knowing that he was merely preserving old folkways, an eighteenth-century way of cooling hot liquids.

The meal we ate that noon was a "brunch," though that word may not yet have been invented and certainly had not penetrated to a lonely farm five miles away from an isolated, German-speaking village. The bacon we ate was as black and the eggs as hard as Uncle John's old-fashioned cast-iron skillet. But being a cold twelve-year-old, I demolished every edible in sight and would have taken on the skillet as well if it had been handy.

Uncle John gave me no condolences on my failure. I didn't need sympathy, I needed three pigeons to feed three people. Well, pigeons are small, so six would have made a real meal, not just a nibble. Twelve would have been best of all. Twelve would have made me a real hunter with surplus game to share with the neighbors.

But I did get a bit of wildlife advice. Uncle John, as a result of the disease, spoke in a monotone and walked stooped over, so that he looked up at you from under his eyebrows. You had to listen carefully to catch his emphases. He muttered something about sitting still and not being so impatient and those pigeons didn't have anywhere else to go, so wait for them and they'll come to you.

It worked. It took the fortitude of an Eskimo to wait them out in the cold hayloft, but I brought down two pigeons. When the first one fell, the whole flock vanished out their escape hole. When the second pigeon fell, the whole flock with one mind fled to the next county or maybe even to California. Pigeons are not known for their intelligence, but two deaths in one day had been enough to persuade them that I had started a trend. I have no idea whether they ever came back. They certainly did not during the hour or two I waited.

The last time I saw Uncle John, he was living in a nursing home, leaning heavily on a walker, even more stooped over. His hair was neatly combed and he was wearing a clean, starched shirt. I wondered whether this was his idea or the women attendants who most certainly must have spent many hours wearing down his lifelong bachelor habits. He could still move around, but the multiple sclerosis had completely taken his voice away.

"You remember Warren?" my father asked.

Uncle John's face mimed great shock and surprise. He looked at me, shook his head, waved his arm laterally at what must have been my twelve-year-old height, pointed at me, shook his head again, and again waved his arm back and forth. Then he gave me the broadest grin I'd ever seen on his face. I nodded. He grinned again, as if he'd been saving his laughter for more than thirty years.

I'm not sure what happened to the rifle. I think it might have rusted away. It's just as well. If you can't shoot one supper's worth of overfed pigeons inside a hayloft, you might as well look for something else to do with your life, as Uncle John surmised long before I did.

The Best Christmas Present Ever

When I was a child, Christmas came but once a year, and that was too often. Girls always got the best Christmas presents: pretty things like dollhouses which you could spend months playing with, productive things you could make other things with, like miniature sewing machines. Well, I'll admit there were a couple of boys in rich families who made out just fine at Christmas. They got board games like Monopoly or complicated model airplane kits. I knew one boy who got a chemistry set, and he spent months mixing liquids to create foul odors. But what did I get for Christmas? Socks. A scarf. A flannel shirt. One year I got a book called *What Every Young Boy Should Know,* an introduction to sex, heavily weighted in the direction of exercise and cold water, and in the section dealing with physiology, there were no pictures. Some Christmas that was! Early in life I learned that there's no such thing as a guaranteed payoff.

But there was that exceptional year when Uncle Pete gave me a present. It was, in fact, in his farmhouse that this miraculous gifting occurred. The family lived about a mile and a half south of town, a short bicycle ride, but a torturous one because the road had been graveled with fist-sized rocks. It was in this farmhouse that my father's unmarried sister and four brothers gathered every year for the annual Christmas reunion, bringing along their wives and children, my aunts and cousins. On this particular morning everyone had, of course, attended church—everyone, that is, except a wife or two whose morning service was devoutly basting the ham in the oven. The festivities began just after noon with the feast—an enormous array of beans and corn and mashed potatoes and bread and rolls and relishes and pumpkin pie surrounding this shank of a pig that two or three months earlier had walked around in its pen some fifty yards from the kitchen.

Because the gathered clan was much too large for Uncle Pete and Aunt Anna's modest dining room table, the grown-ups ate at the first seating. We children waited. When the grown-ups were finished, the table was reset for us, and we were joined by Aunt Anna, who had been the presiding cook and now became the children's chaperon. Nowadays, it seems odd, maybe even cruel, to make children wait patiently for their meals. At this end of the twentieth century we've had many decades of psychologists and advertisers persuading us that children have sensibilities. But I lived my childhood in the last vestiges of a nineteenth-century European peasant tradition. Age had its privileges, and children went to the end of the line. We learned very quickly that people get rewards for growing up, and no one gets a prize for staying young and small. We kept our irritation to ourselves and entertained vague notions of growing up and sitting at the first table when the meat was still hot.

It was the waiting time after dinner that was hard to bear. The red-and-green wrapped packages were stacked and waiting under the Christmas tree, but the grown-ups were delaying. We children would drift like a small flock of lost sparrows into the kitchen where we'd watch the women putting food away, washing dishes, drying them, and laughing and talking as if this were a plain, old, ordinary day, not Christmas. We wanted to ask, "Aren't you almost done?" but no one dared. So we sparrows fluttered into the living room where the men had gone, as they said, "to digest." One had fallen asleep. Another was lost in thought. The rest were talking quietly, and it was only a matter of time before they too would drift off.

The silence made me nervous. I was sure that whatever was waiting for me hidden by red tissue paper was something that someone thought I needed, like a bathrobe. But being a part of the flock of cousins, I caught the fever of hope. There was always a tiny chance that someone had decided a Christmas present should be fun, not a duty. I looked hard at the package with my name on it. It didn't look like a bathrobe. Maybe . . . maybe . . .

But in that German-Russian Mennonite village, youth waited for age. This deference to age was, in fact, the reason we always gathered in Uncle Pete's house. The Christmas reunion had begun in my grandparents' house, and when they had both died, the locale passed to Uncle Pete's, not because it was the largest (which it wasn't) or because it was convenient (far from it), but because Uncle Pete was the oldest of the six living descendants. I understood all that, and I knew very well I couldn't hurry the grown-ups into anything they weren't ready for.

For that matter, no one, young or old, could hurry Uncle Pete along. He was his own pacesetter for whatever he was doing. He was determined to do all things once—thoroughly, making no mistakes, because he really hated to go back and do things over. So he had had to devote his life to being skillful. At what? At plowing or husking corn or whatever was needed, even little household chores. It was Uncle Pete who taught me how to fry eggs in such a way that you put a thin skin over a soft yolk. How many short-order cooks know how to do that?

I once saw his range of skills during what was probably the last hog-butchering on that farm. The relatives and neighbors gathered early on that chilly fall morning, and I was there watching everything, trotting along behind the men as they went out to the barn.

Uncle Pete, carrying the single-shot .22 rifle, squatted down behind a heavy-timbered gate and stuck the barrel through a gap. Another man herded the small white sow, balking and squealing, into an open space between two pens. When the sow had been maneuvered into the right spot, the herder moved back a few steps. The sow, surrounded on all sides by men and barriers, stood stock-still, as if to stop and think through this puzzling situation. All the watchers observed a hushed silence, and I stopped breathing. This was the moment Uncle Pete had been watching for. He squeezed the trigger. The .22 rifle's report echoed through the barn. A small, V-shaped incision appeared exactly between the eyes. The sow sighed and the legs collapsed beneath her. The living pig had become meat.

No howls or screams or fuss, no splashing blood accompanied that transformation. The victim probably felt no pain. And yet, Uncle Pete got up silently, discharged the shell case, wrapped the gun in a canvas cover, and without turning to look back, carried the weapon to its secure hiding place in the house. The killing itself, it seemed, was his most difficult moment in the process.

Two of the other men quickly hoisted the carcass and hung it by its own Achilles tendons on steel hooks, slit the throat to drain the blood into a waiting bucket, and dipped the carcass into a barrel of boiling hot water. Ten years old or so, I was amazed at the men's teamwork in efficiently attacking the flesh. The bristles were scraped off with four-inch round scrapers. Slits were drawn in the belly with long, delicate butcher knives. The guts spilled out into metal pans. The limbs were severed with cuts at the joints and deft twists of the cutters' wrists. The head came off, the hocks, the hams.

The limbless torso and all the smaller pieces were carried from the barn to the shiny metal table in the summer kitchen attached to the side of the house. There, as the torso was further divided, the small parts were sorted and sent on to this group of women or that group of men to be worked on. The scraps and trimmings were all collected into a vat where they were rendered down into lard and cracklings. Everything in that pig's body from snout to hoofs to organs was useful—everything, that is, but the tail and the sphincter. Even the intestines, I discovered late in the day, were thoroughly scrubbed and became the casings for sausages.

Uncle Pete coordinated all these small crews at work, and did so with the briefest of instructions. "Trim the fat." "Into that kettle." "Go help Anna." When I asked how sausages were made, his answer was, "Here. Watch." So I did. Intently. I observed every detail of every step as he stuffed the intestines over the spout at the bottom of the press and as he cranked the cast-iron handle to force the ground pork out into the casings, expanding them into full-sized sausages. But he explained nothing.

Uncle Pete was always laconic when he demonstrated or taught. Why use five words, he seemed to think, when you can say it in two? I have no memory of ever seeing him in a free and easy conversation with another person of his own age, let alone a child. That is why I am still haunted, a half century later, by his choice of the absolutely right gift for me on that miraculous Christmas of all Christmases. I doubt it was just dumb luck. Possibly someone else picked out the gift for him. Or is it possible that he was a careful and astute observer of his tiny nephew's habits? In either case someone was watching me, paying attention, taking note. How else could he, or someone, have known to buy the gift that I needed and desired more than anything else? A gift I wanted so deeply that even I didn't know what it was.

The preparation for gift-giving was a systematic lottery in those days. It began at the Thanksgiving family reunion. Someone who had a clear and elegant handwriting—one of the younger women, I supposed—wrote down each person's name on a tiny slip of paper. Someone else would go in search of a man's hat—often my father's since he always wore hats. The little slips were stirred and shuffled inside the upside-down crown of the hat, and we had a jolly little ceremony of drawing a name from the hat and then smiling and acting mysterious. No matter how dismayed we were by the gift-buying problem chance had given us, we smiled benignly. If someone caught you off guard, as my sister often did, and asked, "Did you get my name?" you were expected to say, "No." Christmas secrets were sacred. This was the only time of the year in our Mennonite community when we were encouraged to lie.

As that special Christmas day wore on, we children wore out, as usual. The grown-ups would not be hurried along. The dishes had to be dried, the men's digesting had to be accomplished, and so the little flock of children subsided into stupor. Even eager anticipation cannot be sustained. I sat in a corner and brooded about what my present was going to be. Probably mittens. And of course we didn't dare go outside and play. The grown-ups might forget we were there and start giving out the presents without us. We watched the grown-ups for any signs of activity. No one moved. We waited.

About three o'clock, maybe later, a couple of the women who had finished in the kitchen drifted into the living room and sat down next to their husbands, one of whom woke up. "Oh," he said. "Is it time?"

"Pretty soon," she replied. "Go back to sleep."

"No! No!" we children wanted to cry out, though of course we didn't. We sat up straighter and watched more intensely.

Another woman came from the kitchen and then another and another, and everyone was there except Aunt Anna, who was still in the kitchen putting the last few pots and kettles away in the cupboards. "Why doesn't she come?" we children wondered. "Doesn't she realize what she's doing to us?" Five minutes passed, or six or seven. Finally, Aunt Anna arrived. She found a chair. The grown-ups looked at each other. All we heard was the sound of breathing. That was a good sign. No one had anything to say. It meant no one would start an interesting conversation and delay us for another half hour. "Well," someone finally said, "who wants to be Santa Claus?" It had begun.

This democratic choosing of a "Santa Claus" never surprised me then but it does now in retrospect. One would think Uncle Pete as patriarch would have passed out the gifts. He was the oldest, after all, and we were gathering in his house. It wasn't that he was shy, but he seemed to defer to the pleasure children got from the ceremony. So when he sensed that a child was ready to take a step forward, Uncle Pete would step back.

That's how he happened to give me a lesson in frying eggs. "I'll show you how to do it right," he said one day when the subject had come up in conversation. He began by stirring up the fires in the wood cookstove, making one side of the stove moderately hot and the other side much hotter. Using a black, cast-iron skillet, he started the eggs on the moderate side and kept them there until the egg whites began to harden and the yolks were still soft and runny. Then he switched the skillet to the hot side, sprinkled a few drops of water into the hot skillet, and quickly clapped on a cover. The water instantly turned into hissing steam. After about thirty seconds he removed the cover. The steam escaped. The soft yolks were covered with a thin translucent skin. "Try those," he said. I did, and nodded my appreciation vigorously. Even that silent gesture of appreciation must have seemed excessive, for he turned my compliment aside by merely grunting. The success of the lesson, after all, spoke for itself.

So if Uncle Pete did not need compliments on his cooking, I suppose it's not surprising that he didn't need to play the patriarch. Better to let the children pass out the Christmas presents. And by this memorable Christmas it had become the custom for the youngest girl to get that job. Uncle Pete would sit back and smile at the pleasure my younger cousin was getting from this playful ceremony.

By the time she began her duties, it was about three-thirty, and I was permanently planted in a corner. My mind dwelt on things I didn't want but someone probably thought I needed—dark brown, useful woolen scarves and ugly red caps with earflaps. And as I watched the others, I saw no point in hoping. Young and old, uncles, aunts, boy cousins, girls, all were opening their wrapped gifts and smiling wanly at the giver and saying things like, "Oh, that's nice. Yes." Christmas was living up, or down, to its reputation.

My turn came. The package was brought to me. I laid it on my knees. Its weight told me it wasn't socks, or anything wearable. Too heavy. I'd run out of guesses. Like everyone else, I unwrapped slowly, delaying the moment when I'd have to say thank you for something I hadn't chosen and would never use. But the flimsy paper made the unwrapping go too fast.

For a moment I stared at the present, or rather, presents. There were two. Books. One was tan with light blue letters. *Five Little Peppers and How They Grew*. The second was red with black letters. *Robin Hood*. For a moment, unable to speak, I stared at the books, then dropped them to the floor, slid down off my chair, and with a fierce, open-mouthed scream raced across the room. Uncle Pete's eyes grew huge as he saw a tiny boy racing toward him, whooping all the way, then hurling himself into a bear hug and a slobbery kiss. When I slid to the floor again, Uncle Pete settled back with a self-satisfied grin. To this day I do not know who chose that Christmas present, but whoever it was, Uncle Pete believed for a moment he had done the shopping.

Before long I had slipped out of the family circle and witnessed no more of the gifting ceremony. The rest of the afternoon I spent devouring words. When it was time to go home and my mother came looking for me, I had finished the first half of

Robin Hood. By the end of the next day I had finished both fat books. I probably never reread the story of the Pepper family, and only remember that it was about good people who did nice things. But I delved into *Robin Hood* again and again, and made the book come to life by organizing the neighbor boys into a band of roving archers. We called each other Will Scarlet or Friar Tuck or "Thou varlet!" Battling in the backyard with long staffs, sneakily outwitting the Sheriff of Nottingham, journeying days and nights through imaginary dense woods, we learned that we could become whatever we were able to name. We hid out in my father's arbor, a small, shady shelter covered with grapevines, and through the power of words and images it became Sherwood Forest. We became older or stronger or fatter, we were able to transport ourselves back a thousand years, because we had learned that we could become whatever we could say.

Uncle Pete gave me the book. But who chose that moment for the book to be given? I continue to ponder that mystery, and have as yet no answer. I am sure, however, that until the flimsy tissue paper fell away and revealed the red cover and the title, I did not know how desperately ready I was to receive that book and all that followed. *Robin Hood* became for a time my metaphor. That book became my door into the world of imagination. And once that door opens, as those who distrust and fear the imagination well know, it can never again be shut.

JAMES McBRIDE
(1957–)

The eighth child of Rachel and Andrew McBride, a Baptist minister, James McBride was raised in the Red Hook housing projects in Brooklyn and in St. Albans, Queens. His mother (née Rachel Deborah Shilsky), the daughter of an abusive Orthodox Jewish rabbi, married an African-American man and became a devout Christian. Before McBride had reached his first birthday, his father had died and his mother married Hunter Jordan, a devoted husband with whom she had four more children. James dropped out of Benjamin Cardozo High School in Queens in the tenth grade after the death of his stepfather. Formerly a straight-A student, he became a truant, began to drink and use marijuana, and engaged in shoplifting and stealing. When the family moved to Wilmington, Delaware, he attended Pierre S. DuPont High School, an all-black public school, where he joined the marching band, concentrated on playing the trombone and tenor sax, and was selected to go to Europe with the American Youth Jazz Band. His love of music helped him to turn his life around when Oberlin College accepted him because of his music and writing talent. He earned a B.A. at Oberlin College and a master's degree in journalism at Columbia. His memoir, *The Color of Water: A Black Man's Tribute to His White Mother* (1996), emphasizes the high level of achievement he and his eleven siblings were enabled to attain through his mother's determination. In 2002, he published *Miracle at St. Anna,* which depicts the battles in Italy fought against the Germans by African-American soldiers in 1944.

---

from *The Color of Water*

Black Power

When I was a boy, I used to wonder where my mother came from, how she got on this earth. When I asked her where she was from, she would say, "God made me," and change the subject. When I asked her if she was white, she'd say, "No. I'm light-skinned," and change the subject again. Answering questions about her personal history did not jibe with Mommy's view of parenting twelve curious, wild, brown-skinned children. She issued orders and her rule was law. Since she refused to divulge details about herself or her past, and because my stepfather was largely unavailable to deal with questions about himself or Ma, what I learned of Mommy's past I learned from my siblings. We traded information on Mommy the way people trade baseball cards at trade shows, offering bits and pieces fraught with gossip, nonsense, wisdom, and sometimes just plain foolishness. "What does it matter to you?" my older brother Richie scoffed when I asked him if we had any grandparents. "You're adopted anyway."

My siblings and I spent hours playing tricks and teasing one another. It was our way of dealing with realities over which we had no control. I told Richie I didn't believe him.

"I don't care if you believe me or not," he sniffed. "Mommy's not your real mother. Your real mother's in jail."

"You're lying!"

"You'll see when Mommy takes you back to your real mother next week. Why do you think she's been so nice to you all week?"

Suddenly it occurred to me that Mommy *had* been nice to me all week. But wasn't she nice to me all the time? I couldn't remember, partly because within my confused eight-year-old reasoning was a growing fear that maybe Richie was right. Mommy, after all, did not really look like me. In fact, she didn't look like Richie, or David—or any of her children for that matter. We were all clearly black, of various shades of brown, some light brown, some medium brown, some very light-skinned, and all of us had curly hair. Mommy was, by her own definition, "light-skinned," a statement which I had initially accepted as fact but at some point later decided was not true. My best friend Billy Smith's mother was as light as Mommy was and had red hair to boot, but there was no question in my mind that Billy's mother was black and my mother was not. There was something inside me, an ache I had, like a constant itch that got bigger and bigger as I grew, that told me. It was in my blood, you might say, and however the notion got there, it bothered me greatly. Yet Mommy refused to acknowledge her whiteness. Why she did so was not clear, but even my teachers seemed to know she was white and I wasn't. On open school nights, the question most often asked by my schoolteachers was: "Is James adopted?" which always prompted an outraged response from Mommy.

I told Richie: "If I'm adopted, you're adopted too."

"Nope," Richie replied. "Just you, and you're going back to your real mother in jail."

"I'll run away first."

"You can't do that. Mommy will get in trouble if you do that. You don't want to see Ma get in trouble, do you? It's not her fault that you're adopted, is it?"

He had me then. Panic set in. "But I don't want to go to my real mother. I want to stay here with Ma . . ."

"You gotta go. I'm sorry, man."

This went on until I was in tears. I remember pacing about nervously all day while Richie, knowing he had ruined my life, cackled himself to sleep. That night I lay wide awake in bed waiting for Mommy to get home from work at two a.m., whereupon she laid the ruse out as I sat at the kitchen table in my tattered Fruit of the Loom underwear. "You're not adopted," she laughed.

"So you're my real mother?"

"Of course I am." Big kiss.

"Then who's my grandparents?"

"Your grandpa Nash died and so did your grandma Etta."

"Who were they?"

"They were your father's parents."

"Where were they from?"

"From down south. You remember them?"

I had a faint recollection of my grandmother Etta, an ancient black woman with a beautiful face who seemed very confused, walking around with a blue dress and a fishing pole, the bait, tackle, and line dragging down around her ankles. She didn't seem real to me.

"Did you know them, Ma?"

"I knew them very, very well."

"Did they love you?"

"Why do you ask so many questions?"

"I just want to know. Did they love you? Because your own parents didn't love you, did they?"

"My own parents loved me."

"Then where are they?"

A short silence. "My mother died many, many years ago," she said. "My father, he was a fox. No more questions tonight. You want some coffee cake?" Enough said. If getting Mommy's undivided attention for more than five minutes was a great feat in a family of twelve kids, then getting a midnight snack in my house was a greater thrill. I cut the questions and ate the cake, though it never stopped me from wondering, partly because of my own growing sense of self, and partly because of fear for her safety, because even as a child I had a clear sense that black and white folks did not get along, which put her, and us, in a pretty tight space.

In 1966, when I was nine, black power had permeated every element of my neighborhood in St. Albans, Queens. Malcolm X had been killed the year before and had grown larger in death than in life. Afros were in style. The Black Panthers were a force. Public buildings, statues, monuments, even trees, met the evening in their original bland colors and reemerged the next morning painted in the sparkling "liberation colors" of red, black, and green. Congas played at night on the streets while teenyboppers gathered to talk of revolution. My siblings marched around the house reciting poetry from the Last Poets, a sort of rap group who recited in-your-face poetry with conga and fascinating vocal lines serving as a musical backdrop, with songs titled "Niggers Are Scared of Revolution" and "On the Subway." Every Saturday morning my friends and I would pedal our bicycles to the corner of Dunkirk Street and Ilion Avenue to watch the local drag racers near the Sun Dew soft drink factory, trying to see who could drive the fastest over a dip in the road that sent even the slowest-moving car airborne. My stepfather hit that dip at fifteen miles an hour in his '64 Pontiac and I bounced high in my seat. These guys hit it at ninety and their cars flew like birds, barreling through the air and landing fifteen feet away, often skidding out of control, sometimes smacking against the wall of the Sun Dew factory before wobbling away in a pile of bent metal, grilles, and fenders. Their cars had names like "Smokin' Joe" and "Miko" and "Dream Machine" scrawled on the hoods, but our favorite was a gleaming black, souped-up GTO with the words "Black Power" written in smooth white script across the hood and top. It was the fastest and its driver was, of course, the coolest. He drove like a madman, and after leaving some poor Corvette in the dust, he'd power his mighty car in a circle, wheel it around, and do a victory lap for us, driving by at low speed, one muscled arm angling out the window, his car rumbling powerfully, while we whistled and cheered, raising our fists and yelling, "Black power!" He'd laugh and burn rubber for us, tires screeching, roaring away in a burst of gleaming metal and hot exhaust, his taillights flashing as he disappeared into the back alleyways before the cops had a chance to bust him. We thought he was God.

But there was a part of me that feared black power very deeply for the obvious reason. I thought black power would be the end of my mother. I had swallowed the white man's fear of the Negro, as we were called back then, whole. It began with a sober white newsman on our black-and-white television set introducing a news clip showing a Black Panther rally, led by Bobby Seale or Huey Newton or one of those young black militant leaders, screaming to hundreds and hundreds of angry African-American students, "Black power! Black power! Black power!" while the crowd roared. It frightened the shit out of me. I thought to myself, *These people will kill Mommy*. Mommy, on the other hand, seemed unconcerned. Her motto was, "If it doesn't involve your going to school or church, I could care less about it and my answer is no whatever it is."

She insisted on absolute privacy, excellent school grades, and trusted no outsiders of either race. We were instructed never to reveal details of our home life to any figures of authority: teachers, social workers, cops, storekeepers, or even friends. If anyone asked us about our home life, we were taught to respond with, "I don't know," and for years I did just that. Mommy's house was an entire world that she created. She appointed the eldest child at home to be "king" or "queen" to run the house in her absence and we took it from there, creating court jesters, slaves, musicians, poets, pets, and clowns. Playing in the street was discouraged and often forbidden and if you did manage to slip out, "Get your butt in this house before dark," she would warn, a rule she enforced to the bone. I often played that rule out to its very edge, stealing into the house at dusk, just as the last glimmer of sunlight was peeking over the western horizon, closing the door softly, hoping Mommy had gone to work, only to turn around and find her standing before me, hands on hips, whipping belt in hand, eyes flicking angrily back and forth to the window, then to me, lips pursed, trying to decide whether it was light or dark outside. "It's still light," I'd suggest, my voice wavering, as my siblings gathered behind her to watch the impending slaughter.

"That looks like light to you?" she'd snap, motioning to the window.

"Looks pretty dark," my siblings would chirp from behind her. "It's definitely dark, Ma!" they'd shout, stifling their giggles. If I was lucky a baby would wail in another room and she'd be off, hanging the belt on the doorknob as she went. "Don't do it again," she'd warn over her shoulder, and I was a free man.

But even if she had any interest in black power, she had no time to talk about it. She worked the swing shift at Chase Manhattan Bank as a typist, leaving home at three p.m. and returning around two a.m., so she had little time for games, and even less time for identity crises. She and my father brought a curious blend of Jewish-European and African-American distrust and paranoia into our house. On his end, my father, Andrew McBride, a Baptist minister, had his doubts about the world accepting his mixed family. He always made sure his kids never got into trouble, was concerned about money, and trusted the providence of the Holy Father to do the rest. After he died and Mommy remarried, my stepfather, Hunter Jordan, seemed to pick up where my father left off, insistent on education and church. On her end, Mommy had no model for raising us other than the experience of her own Orthodox Jewish family, which despite the seeming flaws—an unbending nature, a stridency, a focus on money, a deep distrust of all outsiders, not to mention her father's tyranny—represented the best and worst of the immigrant mentality: hard work, no nonsense, quest for excellence, distrust of authority figures, and a deep belief in God and education. My parents were nonmaterialistic. They believed that money without knowledge was worthless, that education tempered with religion was the way to climb out of poverty in America, and over the years they were proven right.

Yet conflict was a part of our lives, written into our very faces, hands, and arms, and to see how contradiction lived and survived in its essence, we had to look no farther than our own mother. Mommy's contradictions crashed and slammed against one another like bumper cars at Coney Island. White folks, she felt, were implicitly evil toward blacks, yet she forced us to go to white schools to get the best education. Blacks could be trusted more, but anything involving blacks was probably slightly substandard. She disliked people with money yet was in constant need of it. She couldn't stand racists of either color and had great distaste for bourgeois blacks who sought to emulate rich whites by putting on airs and "doing silly things like covering their couches with plastic and holding teacups with their pinkies out." "What fools!" she'd hiss. She wouldn't be bothered with parents who bragged about their children's accomplishments, yet she insisted we strive for the highest professional goals. She was against welfare and never applied for it despite our need, but championed those who availed themselves of it. She hated restaurants and would not enter one even if the meals served were free. She actually preferred to be among the poor, the working-class poor of the Red Hook housing projects in Brooklyn, the cement mixers, bakers, doughnut makers, grandmothers, and soul-food church partisans who were her lifelong friends. It was with them that she and my father started the New Brown Memorial Baptist Church, a small storefront church which still stands in Red Hook today. Mommy loves that church and to this day still loves Red Hook, one of the most dangerous and neglected housing projects in New York City. On any given day she'll get up in the morning, take the New Jersey Transit train from her home in Ewing, New Jersey, to Manhattan, then take the subway to Brooklyn, and wander around the projects like the Pope, the only white person in sight, waving to friends, stepping past the drug addicts, smiling at the young mothers pushing their children in baby carriages, slipping into the poorly lit hallway of 80 Dwight Street while the young dudes in hooded sweatshirts stare balefully at the strange, bowlegged old white lady in Nikes and red sweats who slowly hobbles up the three flights of dark, urine-smelling stairs on arthritic knees to visit her best friend, Mrs. Ingram, in apartment 3G.

As a boy, I often found Mommy's ease among black people surprising. Most white folks I knew seemed to have a great fear of blacks. Even as a young child, I was aware of that. I'd read it in the paper, between the lines of my favorite sport columnists in the *New York Post* and the old *Long Island Press,* in their refusal to call Cassius Clay Muhammad Ali, in their portrayal of Floyd Patterson as a "good Negro Catholic," and in their burning criticism of black athletes like Bob Gibson of the St. Louis Cardinals, whom I idolized. In fact I didn't even have to open the paper to see it. I could see it in the faces of the white people who stared at me and Mommy and my siblings when we rode the subway, sometimes laughing at us, pointing, muttering things like, "Look at her with those little niggers." I remember when a white man shoved her angrily as she led a group of us onto an escalator, but Mommy simply ignored him. I remember two black women pointing at us, saying, "Look at that white bitch," and a white man screaming at Mommy somewhere in Manhattan, calling her a "nigger lover." Mommy ignored them all, unless the insults threatened her children, at which time she would turn and fight back like an alley cat, hissing, angry, and fearless. She had a casual way of ignoring affronts, slipping past insults to her whiteness like a seasoned boxer slips punches. When Malcolm X, the supposed demon of the white man, was killed, I asked her who he was and she said, "He was a man ahead of his time." She actually liked Malcolm X. She put him in nearly the same category as her other civil rights heroes, Paul Robeson, Jackie Robinson, Eleanor Roosevelt, A. Philip Randolph, Martin Luther King, Jr., and the Kennedys—any Kennedy. When Malcolm X talked about "the white devil" Mommy simply felt those references didn't apply to her. She viewed the civil rights achievements of black Americans with pride, as if they were her own. And she herself occasionally talked about "the white man" in the third person, as if she had nothing to do with him, and in fact she didn't, since most of her friends and social circle were black women from church. "What's the matter with these white folks?" she'd muse after reading some craziness in the *New York Daily News*. "They're fighting over this man's money now that he's dead. None of them wanted him when he was alive, and now look at them. Forget it, honey"—this is Mommy talking to the newspaper—"your husband's dead, okay? He's dead—poop! You had your chance. Is money gonna bring him back? No!" Then she'd turn to us and deliver the invariable lecture: "You don't need money. What's money if your mind is empty! Educate your mind! Is this world crazy or am I the crazy one? It's probably me."

Indeed it probably was—at least, I thought so. I knew of no other white woman who would board the subway in Manhattan at one o'clock every morning and fall asleep till she got to her stop in Queens forty-five minutes later. Often I could not sleep until I heard her key hit the door. Her lack of fear for her safety—particularly among blacks, where she often stuck out like a sore thumb and seemed an easy target for muggers—had me stumped. As a grown man, I understand now, understand how her Christian principles and trust in God kept her going through all her life's battles, but as a boy, my faith was not that strong. Mommy once took me to Harlem to visit my stepsister, Jacqueline, whom we called Jack and who was my father's daughter by a previous marriage and more like an aunt than a sister. The two of them sat in Jack's parlor and talked into the night while Jack cooked big plates of soul food, macaroni and cheese, sweet potato pies, and biscuits for us. "Take this home to the kids, Ruth," Jack told Ma. We put the food in shopping bags and took it on the subway without incident, but when we got off the bus in St. Albans near our house, two black men came up behind us and one of them grabbed Mommy's purse. The shopping bag full of macaroni and cheese and sweet potato pies burst open and food flew everywhere as Mommy held on to her purse, spinning around in a crazy circle with the mugger, neither saying a word as they both desperately wrestled for the purse, whirling from the sidewalk into the dark empty street like two ballerinas locked in a death dance. I stood frozen in shock, watching. Finally the mugger got the purse and ran off as his buddy laughed at him, and Mommy fell to the ground.

She got up, calmly took my hand, and began to walk home without a word.

"You okay?" she asked me after a few moments.

I nodded. I was so frightened I couldn't speak. All the food that Jack had cooked for us lay on the ground behind us, ruined. "Why didn't you scream?" I asked, when I finally got my tongue back.

"It's just a purse," she said. "Don't worry about it. Let's just get home."

The incident confirmed my fears that Mommy was always in danger. Every summer we joined the poor inner-city kids the Fresh Air Fund organization sent to host families or to summer camps for free. The luckier ones among my siblings got to stay with host families, but I had to go to camps where they housed ten of us in a cabin for two weeks at a time. Sometimes they seemed closer to prison or job corps than camp. Kids fought all the time. The food was horrible. I was constantly fighting. Kids called me Cochise because of my light skin and curly hair. Despite all that, I loved it. The first time I went, Mommy took me to the roundup point, a community center in Far Rockaway, once the home of middle-class whites and Jews like playwright Neil Simon, but long since turned black, and it seemed that the only white person for miles was my own mother. The camp organizers set up a table inside where they removed our shoes and shirts and inspected our toes for athlete's foot, checked us for measles and chicken pox, then sent us outside to board a yellow school bus for the long journey to upstate New York. As I sat on the bus peering out the window at Mommy, the only white face in a sea of black faces, a black man walked up with his son. He had a mustache and a goatee and wore black leather pants, a black leather jacket, a ton of jewelry, and a black beret. He seemed outstandingly cool. His kid was very handsome, well dressed, and quite refined. He placed his kid's bags in the back of the bus and when the kid went to step on the bus, instead of hugging the child, the father offered his hand, and father and son did a magnificent, convoluted black-power soul handshake called the "dap," the kind of handshake that lasts five minutes, fingers looping, thumbs up, thumbs down, index fingers collapsing, wrists snapping, bracelets tingling. It seemed incredibly hip. The whole bus watched. Finally the kid staggered breathlessly onto the bus and sat behind me, tapping at the window and waving at his father, who was now standing next to Mommy, waving at his kid.

"Where'd you learn that handshake?" someone asked the kid.

"My father taught me," he said proudly. "He's a Black Panther."

The bus roared to life as I panicked. A Black Panther? Next to Mommy? It was my worst nightmare come true. I had no idea who the Panthers truly were. I had swallowed the media image of them completely.

The bus clanked into gear as I got up to open my window. I wanted to warn Mommy. Suppose the Black Panther wanted to kill her? The window was stuck. I tried to move to another window. A counselor grabbed me and sat me down. I said, "I have to tell my mother something."

"Write her a letter," he said.

I jumped into the seat of the Black Panther's son behind me—his window was open. The counselor placed me back in my seat.

"Mommy, Mommy!" I yelled at the closed window. Mommy was waving. The bus pulled away.

I shouted, "Watch out for him!" but we were too far away and my window was shut. She couldn't hear me.

I saw the Black Panther waving at his son. Mommy waved at me. Neither seemed to notice the other.

When they were out of sight, I turned to the Black Panther's son sitting behind me and punched him square in the face with my fist. The kid held his jaw and stared at me in shock as his face melted into a knot of disbelief and tears.

MARY McCARTHY
(1912–89)

Born in Seattle, Washington, and orphaned at the age of six when her parents died in the flu epidemic of 1918, McCarthy was raised mainly by two sets of wealthy but rigid grandparents, in strictly religious households, Catholic and Protestant. She was educated at Vassar College in Poughkeepsie, New York, where she studied literature and graduated with honors. During the '30s, McCarthy was active in the leftist movement and for many years was associated with the *Partisan Review,* as an editor and theater critic. Between 1945 and 1982, she taught and lectured at Bard, Sarah Lawrence, and Vassar colleges, and at University College, London. She was sued in the 1980s by the playwright Lillian Hellman after McCarthy stated, in an interview, that "every word she [Hellman] writes is a lie, including *and* and *the.*" McCarthy's first published work was *The Company She Keeps* (1941), a collection of loosely connected stories about New York intellectuals. *The Oasis* (1949) depicted artists in a utopian society. The novel for which she is best known, *The Group* (1962), examined the lives of eight Vassar graduates in the '30s. It was turned into a movie in which Candice Bergen made her screen debut. *The New York Times* described it as the "worst misfire of a movie in many years . . . an insult to a generation of human beings." Among her other works are *The Groves of Academe* (1952), *Venice Observed* (1956), *Memories of a Catholic Girlhood* (1957), *The Stones of Florence* (1959), *Cast a Cold Eye* (1963), *The Humanist in the Bathtub* (1964), *Vietnam* (1967), *Cannibals and Missionaries* (1979), *Ideas and the Novel* (1980), *How I Grew* (1987), *Never Too Old to Learn* (1988), and *Between Friends: The Correspondence of Hannah Arendt and Mary McCarthy 1949–1975* (1995).

---

from *Memories of a Catholic Girlhood*

A Tin Butterfly

The man we had to call Uncle Myers was no relation to us. This was a point on which we four orphan children were very firm. He had married our great-aunt Margaret shortly before the death of our parents and so became our guardian while still a benedict—not perhaps a very nice eventuality for a fat man of forty-two who has just married an old maid with a little income to find himself summoned overnight from his home in Indiana to be the hired parent of four children, all under seven years old.

When Myers and Margaret got us, my three brothers and me, we were a handful; on this there were no two opinions in the McCarthy branch of the family. The famous flu epidemic of 1918, which had stricken our little household en route from Seattle to

Minneapolis and carried off our parents within a day of each other, had, like all God's devices, a meritorious aspect, soon discovered by my grandmother McCarthy: a merciful end had been put to a regimen of spoiling and coddling, to Japanese houseboys, iced cakes, picnics, upset stomachs, diamond rings (imagine!), an ermine muff and neckpiece, furred hats and coats. My grandmother thanked her stars that Myers and her sister Margaret were available to step into the breach. Otherwise, we might have had to be separated, an idea that moistened her hooded grey eyes, or been taken over by "the Protestants"—thus she grimly designated my grandfather Preston, a respectable Seattle lawyer of New England antecedents who, she many times declared with awful emphasis, had refused to receive a Catholic priest in his house! But our Seattle grandparents, coming on to Minneapolis for the funeral, were too broken up, she perceived, by our young mother's death to protest the McCarthy arrangements. Weeping, my Jewish grandmother (Preston, born Morganstern), still a beauty, like her lost daughter, acquiesced in the wisdom of keeping us together in the religion my mother had espoused. In my sickbed, recovering from the flu in my grandmother McCarthy's Minneapolis house, I, the eldest and the only girl, sat up and watched the other grandmother cry, dampening her exquisite black veil. I did not know that our parents were dead or that my sobbing grandmother—whose green Seattle terraces I remembered as delightful to roll down on Sundays—had just now, downstairs in my grandmother McCarthy's well-heated sun parlor, met the middle-aged pair who had come on from Indiana to undo her daughter's mistakes. I was only six years old and had just started school in a Sacred Heart convent on a leafy boulevard in Seattle before the fatal November trek back east, but I was sharp enough to see that Grandmother Preston did not belong here, in this dour sickroom, and vain enough to pride myself on drawing the inference that something had gone awry.

We four children and our keepers were soon installed in the yellow house at 2427 Blaisdell Avenue that had been bought for us by my grandfather McCarthy. It was situated two blocks away from his own prosperous dwelling, with its grandfather clock, tapestries, and Italian paintings, in a block that some time before had begun to "run down." Flanked by two-family houses, it was simply a crude box in which to stow furniture, and lives, like a warehouse; the rooms were small and brownish and for some reason dark, though I cannot think why, since the house was graced by no ornamental planting; a straight cement driveway ran up one side; in the back, there was an alley. Downstairs, there were a living room, a "den," a dining room, a kitchen, and a lavatory; upstairs, there were four bedrooms and a bathroom. The dingy wallpaper of the rooms in which we children slept was promptly defaced by us; bored without our usual toys, we amused ourselves by making figures on the walls with our wet tongues. This was our first crime, and I remember it because the violence of the whipping we got surprised us; we had not known we were doing wrong. The splotches on the walls remained through the years to fix this first whipping and the idea of badness in our minds; they stared at us in the evenings when, still bored but mute and tamed, we learned to make shadow figures on the wall—the swan, the rabbit with its ears wiggling—to while away the time.

It was this first crime, perhaps, that set Myers in his punitive mold. He saw that it was no sinecure he had slipped into. Childless, middle-aged, he may have felt in his slow-turning mind that his inexperience had been taken advantage of by his wife's grandiloquent sister, that the vexations outweighed the perquisites; in short, that he had been sold. This, no doubt, was how it must have really looked from where he sat—in a brown leather armchair in the den, wearing a blue work shirt, stained with sweat, open at the neck to show an undershirt and lion-blond, glinting hair on his chest. Below this were workmen's trousers of a brownish-gray material, straining at the buttons and always gaping slightly, just below the belt, to show another glimpse of underwear, of a yellowish white. On his fat head, frequently, with its crest of bronze curly hair, were the earphones of a crystal radio set, which he sometimes, briefly, in a generous mood, fitted over the grateful ears of one of my little brothers.

A second excuse for Myers's behavior is manifest in this description. He had to contend with Irish social snobbery, which looked upon him dispassionately from four sets of green eyes and set him down as "not a gentleman." "My father was a gentleman and you're not"—what I meant by these categorical words I no longer know precisely, except that my father had had a romantic temperament and was a spendthrift; but I suppose there was also included some notion of courtesy. Our family, like many Irish Catholic new-rich families, was filled with aristocratic delusions; we children were always being told that we were descended from the kings of Ireland and that we were related to General "Phil" Sheridan, a dream of my great-aunt's. More precisely, my great-grandfather on this side had been a streetcar conductor in Chicago.

But at any rate Myers (or Meyers) Shriver (or Schreiber—the name had apparently been Americanized) was felt to be beneath us socially. Another count against him in our childish score was that he was a German, or, rather, of German descent, which made us glance at him fearfully in 1918, just after the armistice. In Minneapolis at that time, there was great prejudice among the Irish Catholics, not only against the Protestant Germans, but against all the northern bloods and their hateful Lutheran heresy. Lutheranism to us children was, first of all, a religion for servant girls and, secondly, a sort of yellow corruption associated with original sin and with Martin Luther's tongue rotting in his mouth as God's punishment. Bavarian Catholics, on the other hand, were singled out for a special regard; we saw them in an Early Christian light, brunette and ringleted, like the Apostles. This was due in part to the fame of Oberammergau and the Passion Play, and in part to the fact that many of the clergy in our diocese were Bavarians; all through this period I confided my sins of disobedience to a handsome, dark, young Father Elderbush. Uncle Myers, however, was a Protestant, although, being too indolent, he did not go to church; he was not one of us. And the discovery that we could take refuge from him at school, with the nuns, at church, in the sacraments, seemed to verify the ban that was on him; he was truly outside grace. Having been impressed with the idea that our religion was a sort of logical contagion, spread by holy books and good example, I could never understand why Uncle Myers, bad as he was, had not caught it; and his obduracy in remaining at home in his den on Sundays, like a somnolent brute in its lair, seemed to me to go against nature.

Indeed, in the whole situation there was something unnatural and inexplicable. His marriage to Margaret, in the first place: he was younger than his wife by three years, and much was made of this difference by my grandmother McCarthy, his wealthy sister-in-law, as though it explained everything in a slightly obscene way. Aunt Margaret, née Sheridan, was a well-aged quince of forty-five, with iron-gray hair shading into black, a stiff carriage, high-necked dresses, unfashionable hats, a copy of *Our Sunday Visitor* always under her arm—folded, like a flail—a tough dry skin with soft colorless hairs on it, like dust, and furrowed and corrugated, like the prunes we ate every day for breakfast. It could be said of her that she meant well, and she meant especially well by Myers, all two hundred and five pounds, dimpled double chin, and small, glinting, gross blue eyes of him. She called him "Honeybunch," pursued him with attentions, special foods, kisses, to which he responded with tolerance, as though his swollen passivity had the character of a male thrust or assertion. It was clear that he did not dislike her, and that poor Margaret, as her sister said, was head over heels in love with him. To us children, this honeymoon rankness was incomprehensible; we could not see it on either side for, quite apart from everything else, both parties seemed to us very old, as indeed they were, compared to our parents, who had been young and handsome. That he had married her for her money occurred to us inevitably, though it may not have been so; very likely it was his power over her that he loved, and the power he had to make her punish us was perhaps her strongest appeal to him. They slept in a bare, ugly bedroom with a tall, cheap pine chiffonier on which Myers's black wallet and his nickels and dimes lay spread out when he was at home—did he think to arouse our cupidity or did he suppose that this stronghold of his virility was impregnable to our weak desires? Yet, as it happened, we did steal from him, my brother Kevin and I—rightfully, as we felt, for we were allowed no pocket money (two pennies were given us on Sunday morning to put into the collection plate) and we guessed that the money paid by our grandfather for the household found its way into Myers's wallet.

And here was another strange thing about Myers. He not only did nothing for a living but he appeared to have no history. He came from Elkhart, Indiana, but beyond this fact nobody seemed to know anything about him—not even how he had met my aunt Margaret. Reconstructed from his conversation, a picture of Elkhart emerged for us that showed it as a flat place consisting chiefly of ball parks, poolrooms, and hardware stores. Aunt Margaret came from Chicago, which consisted of the Loop, Marshall Field's, assorted priests and monsignors, and the black-and-white problem. How had these two worlds impinged? Where our family spoke freely of its relations, real and imaginary, Myers spoke of no one, not even a parent. At the very beginning, when my father's old touring car, which had been shipped on, still remained in our garage, Myers had certain seedy cronies whom he took riding in it or who simply sat in it in our driveway, as if anchored in a houseboat; but when the car went, they went or were banished. Uncle Myers and Aunt Margaret had no friends, no couples with whom they exchanged visits—only a middle-aged, black-haired, small, emaciated woman with a German name and a yellowed skin whom we were taken to see one afternoon because she was dying of cancer. This protracted death had the aspect of a public execution, which was doubtless why Myers took us to it; that is, it was a spectacle and it was free, and it inspired restlessness and depression. Myers was the perfect type of rootless municipalized man who finds his pleasures in the handouts or overflow of an industrial civilization. He enjoyed standing on a curbstone, watching parades, the more nondescript the better, the Labor Day parade being his favorite, and next to that a military parade, followed by the commercial parades with floats and girls dressed in costumes; he would even go to Lake Calhoun or Lake Harriet for doll-carriage parades and competitions of children dressed as Indians. He liked bandstands, band concerts, public parks devoid of grass; skywriting attracted him; he was quick to hear of a department-store demonstration where colored bubbles were blown, advertising a soap, to the tune of "I'm Forever Blowing Bubbles," sung by a mellifluous soprano. He collected coupons and tinfoil, bundles of newspaper for the old rag-and-bone man (thus interfering seriously with our school paper drives), free samples of cheese at Donaldson's, free tickets given out by a neighborhood movie house to the first installment of a serial—in all the years we lived with him, we never saw a full-length movie but only those truncated beginnings. He was also fond of streetcar rides (could the system have been municipally owned?), soldiers' monuments, cemeteries, big, coarse flowers like cannas and cockscombs set in beds by city gardeners. Museums did not appeal to him, though we did go one night with a large crowd to see Marshal Foch on the steps of the Art Institute. He was always weighing himself on penny weighing machines. He seldom left the house except on one of these purposeless errands, or else to go to a ball game, by himself. In the winter, he spent the days at home in the den, or in the kitchen, making candy. He often had enormous tin trays of decorated fondants cooling in the cellar, which leads my brother Kevin to think today that at one time in Myers's life he must have been a pastry cook or a confectioner. He also liked to fashion those little figures made of pipe cleaners that were just then coming in as favors in the better candy shops, but Myers used *old* pipe cleaners, stained yellow and brown. The bonbons, with their pecan or almond topping, that he laid out in such perfect rows were for his own use; we were permitted to watch him set them out, but never—and my brother Kevin confirms this—did we taste a single one.

In the five years we spent with Myers, the only candy I ever had was bought with stolen money and then hidden in the bottom layer of my paper-doll set; the idea of stealing to buy candy and the hiding place were both lifted from Kevin. Opening my paper-doll box one day, I found it full of pink and white soft-sugar candies, which it seemed to me God or the fairies had sent me in response to my wishes and prayers, until I realized that Kevin was stealing, and using my paper-doll box for a cache; we had so few possessions that he had no place of his own to hide things in. Underneath the mattress was too chancy, as I myself found when I tried to secrete magazines of Catholic fiction there; my aunt, I learned, was always tearing up the bed and turning the mattress to find out whether you had wet it and attempted to hide your crime by turning it over. Reading was forbidden us, except for schoolbooks and, for some reason, the funny papers and magazine section of the Sunday Hearst papers, where one read about leprosy, the affairs of Count Boni de Castellane, and a strange disease that turned people to stone creepingly from the feet up.

This prohibition against reading was a source of scandal to the nuns who taught me in the parochial school, and I think it was due to their intervention with my grandmother that finally, toward the end, I was allowed to read openly the Camp Fire Girls series, *Fabiola,* and other books I have forgotten. Myers did not read; before the days of the crystal set, he passed his evenings listening to the phonograph in the living room: Caruso, Harry Lauder, "Keep the Home Fires Burning," "There's a Sweet Little Nest," and "Listen to the Mocking Bird." It was his pleasure to make the four of us stand up in a line and sing to him the same tunes he had just heard on the phonograph, while he laughed at my performance, for I tried to reproduce the staccato phrasing of the sopranos, very loudly and off key. Also, he hated long words, or, rather, words that he regarded as long. One summer day, in the kitchen, when I had been ordered to swat flies, I said, "They disappear so strangely," a remark that he mimicked for years whenever he wished to humiliate me, and the worst of this torture was that I could not understand what was peculiar about the sentence, which seemed to me plain ordinary English, and, not understanding, I knew that I was in perpetual danger of exposing myself to him again.

So far as we knew, he had never been in any army, but he liked to keep smart military discipline. We had frequently to stand in line, facing him, and shout answers to his questions in chorus. "Forward *march*!" he barked after every order he gave us. The Fourth of July was the only holiday he threw himself into with geniality. Anything that smacked to him of affectation or being "stuck-up" was subject to the harshest reprisals from him, and I, being the oldest, and the one who remembered my parents and the old life best, was the chief sinner, sometimes on purpose, sometimes unintentionally.

When I was eight, I began writing poetry in school: "Father Gaughan is our dear parish priest/ And he is loved from west to east." And "Alas, Pope Benedict is dead,/ The sorrowing people said." Pope Benedict at that time was living, and, as far as I know, in good health; I had written this opening couplet for the rhyme and the sad idea; but then, very conveniently for me, about a year later he died, which gave me a feeling of fearsome power, stronger than a priest's power of loosing and binding. I came forward with my poem and it was beautifully copied out by our teacher and served as the school's elegy at a memorial service for the Pontiff. I dared not tell that I had had it ready in my desk. Not long afterward, when I was ten, I wrote an essay for a children's contest on "The Irish in American History," which won first the city and then the state prize. Most of my facts I had cribbed from a series on Catholics in American history that was running in *Our Sunday Visitor*. I worked on the assumption that anybody who was Catholic must be Irish, and then, for good measure, I went over the signers of the Declaration of Independence and added any name that sounded Irish to my ears. All this was clothed in rhetoric invoking "the lilies of France"—God knows why, except that I was in love with France and somehow, through Marshal MacMahon, had made Lafayette out an Irishman. I believe that even Kosciusko figured as an Irishman *de coeur*. At any rate, there was a school ceremony, at which I was presented with the city prize (twenty-five dollars, I think, or perhaps that was the state prize); my aunt was in the audience in her best mallard-feathered hat, looking, for once, proud and happy. She spoke kindly to me as we walked home, but when we came to our ugly house, my uncle silently rose from his chair, led me into the dark downstairs lavatory, which always smelled of shaving cream, and furiously beat me with the razor strop—to teach me a lesson, he said, lest I become stuck-up. Aunt Margaret did not intervene. After her first look of discomfiture, her face settled into folds of approval; she had been too soft. This was the usual tribute she paid Myers's greater discernment—she was afraid of losing his love by weakness. The money was taken, "to keep for me," and that, of course, was the end of it. Such was the fate of anything considered "much too good for her," a category that was rivaled only by its pendant, "plenty good enough."

We were beaten all the time, as a matter of course, with the hairbrush across the bare legs for ordinary occasions, and with the razor strop across the bare bottom for special occasions, like the prize-winning. It was as though these ignorant people, at sea with four frightened children, had taken a Dickens novel—*Oliver Twist*, perhaps, or *Nicholas Nickleby*—for a navigation chart. Sometimes our punishments were earned, sometimes not; they were administered gratuitously, often, as preventive medicine. I was whipped more frequently than my brothers, simply by virtue of seniority; that is, every time one of them was whipped, I was whipped also, for not having set a better example, and this was true for all four of us in a descending line. Kevin was whipped for Preston's misdeeds and for Sheridan's, and Preston was whipped for Sheridan's, while Sheridan, the baby and the favorite, was whipped only for his own. This naturally made us fear and distrust each other, and only between Kevin and myself was there a kind of uneasy alliance. When Kevin ran away, as he did on one famous occasion, I had a feeling of joy and defiance, mixed with the fear of punishment for myself, mixed with something worse, a vengeful anticipation of the whipping *he* would surely get. I suppose that the two times I ran away, his feelings were much the same—envy, awe, fear, admiration, and a certain evil thrill, collusive with my uncle, at the thought of the strop ahead. Yet, strange to say, nobody was beaten on these historic days. The culprit, when found, took refuge at my grandmother's, and a fearful hush lay over the house on Blaisdell Avenue at the thought of the monstrous daring and deceitfulness of the runaway; Uncle Myers, doubtless, was shaking in his boots at the prospect of explanations to the McCarthy family council. The three who remained at home were sentenced to spend the day upstairs, in strict silence. But if my uncle's impartial application of punishment served to make us each other's enemies very often, it did nothing to establish discipline, since we had no incentive to behave well, not knowing when we might be punished for something we had not done or even for something that by ordinary standards would be considered good. We knew not when we would offend, and what I learned from this, in the main, was a policy of lying and concealment; for several years after we were finally liberated, I was a problem liar.

Despite Myers's quite justified hatred of the intellect, of reading and education (for he was right—it *was* an escape from him), my uncle, like all dictators, had one book that he enjoyed. It was *Uncle Remus,* in a red cover—a book I detested—which he read aloud to us in his den over and over again in the evenings. It seemed to me that this reduction of human life to the level of talking animals and this corruption of language to dialect gave my uncle some very personal relish. He knew I hated it and he rubbed it in, trotting my brother Sheridan on his knee as he dwelt on some exploit of Br'er Fox's with many chuckles and repetitions. In *Uncle Remus,* he had his hour, and to this day I cannot read anything in dialect or any fable without some degree of repugnance.

A distinction must be made between my uncle's capricious brutality and my aunt's punishments and repressions, which seem to have been dictated to her by her conscience. My aunt was not a bad woman; she was only a believer in method. Since it was the family theory that we had been spoiled, she undertook energetically to remedy this by quasi-scientific means. Everything we did proceeded according to schedule and in line with an overall plan. She was very strong, naturally, on toilet-training, and everything in our life was directed toward the after-breakfast session on "the throne." Our whole diet—not to speak of the morning orange juice with castor oil in it that was brought to us on the slightest pretext of "paleness"—was centered around this levee. We had prunes every day for breakfast, and cornmeal mush, Wheatena, or farina, which I had to eat plain, since by some medical whim it had been decided that milk was bad for me. The rest of our day's menu consisted of parsnips, turnips, rutabagas, carrots, boiled potatoes, boiled cabbage, onions, Swiss chard, kale, and so on; most green vegetables, apparently, were too dear to be appropriate for us, though I think that, beyond this, the family had a sort of moral affinity for the root vegetable, stemming, perhaps, from everything fibrous, tenacious, watery, and knobby in the Irish peasant stock. Our desserts were rice pudding, farina pudding, overcooked custard with little air holes in it, prunes, stewed red plums, rhubarb, stewed pears, stewed dried peaches. We must have had meat, but I have only the most indistinct recollection of pale lamb stews in which the carrots outnumbered the pieces of white, fatty meat and bone and gristle; certainly we did not have steak or roasts or turkey or fried chicken, but perhaps an occasional boiled fowl was served to us with its vegetables (for I do remember the neck, shrunken in its collar of puckered skin, coming to me as my portion, and the fact that if you sucked on it, you could draw out an edible white cord), and doubtless there was meat loaf and beef stew. There was no ice cream, cake, pie, or butter, but on rare mornings we had johnnycake or large woolly pancakes with Karo syrup.

We were not allowed to leave the table until every morsel was finished, and I used to sit through half a dark winter afternoon staring at the cold carrots on my plate, until, during one short snowy period, I found that I could throw them out the back window if I raised it very quietly. (Unfortunately, they landed on the tar roofing of a sort of shed next to the back porch, and when the snow finally melted, I met a terrible punishment.) From time to time, we had a maid, but the food was so wretched that we could not keep "girls," and my aunt took over the cooking, with sour enthusiasm, assisted by her sister, Aunt Mary, an arthritic, white-haired, wan, devout old lady who had silently joined our household and earned her keep by helping with the sewing and dusting and who tried to stay out of Myers's way. With her gentle help, Aunt Margaret managed to approximate, on a small scale, the conditions prevailing in the orphan asylums we four children were always dreaming of being let into.

Myers did not share our diet. He sat at the head of the table, with a napkin around his neck, eating the special dishes that Aunt Margaret prepared for him and sometimes putting a spoonful on the plate of my youngest brother, who sat next to him in a high chair. At breakfast, he had corn flakes or shredded wheat with bananas or fresh sliced peaches, thought by us to be a Lucullan treat. At dinner, he had pigs' feet and other delicacies I cannot remember. I only know that he shared them with Sheridan, who was called Herdie, as my middle brother was called Pomps, or Pompsie—childish affectionate nicknames inherited from our dead parents that sounded damp as gravemold in my aunt Margaret's flannelly voice, which reminded one of a chest rag dipped in asafetida to ward off winter throat ailments.

In addition to such poultices, and mustard plasters, and iron pills to fortify our already redoubtable diet, we were subject to other health fads of the period and of my great-aunt's youth. I have told elsewhere of how we were put to bed at night with our mouths sealed with adhesive tape to prevent mouth-breathing; ether, which made me sick, was used to help pull the tape off in the morning, but a grimy, gray, rubbery remainder was usually left on our upper lips and in the indentations of our pointed chins when we set off for school in our heavy outer clothes, long underwear, black stockings, and high shoes. Our pillows were taken away from us; we were given a sulphur-and-molasses spring tonic, and in the winter, on Saturdays and Sundays, we were made to stay out three hours in the morning and three in the afternoon, regardless of the temperature. We had come from a mild climate, in Seattle, and at fifteen, twenty, or twenty-four below zero we could not play, even if we had had something to play with, and used simply to stand in the snow, crying, and beating sometimes on the window with our frozen mittens, till my aunt's angry face would appear there and drive us away.

No attempt was made to teach us a sport, winter or summer; we were forbidden to slide in Fairoaks Park nearby, where in winter the poorer children made a track of ice down a hill, which they flashed down sitting or standing, but I loved this daring sport and did it anyway, on the way home from school, until one day I tore my shabby coat on the ice and was afraid to go home. A kind woman named Mrs. Corkerey, who kept a neighborhood candy store across from our school, mended it for me, very skillfully, so that my aunt never knew; nevertheless, sliding lost its lure for me, for I could not risk a second rip.

The neighbors were often kind, surreptitiously, and sometimes they "spoke" to the sisters at the parochial school, but everyone, I think, was afraid of offending my grandparents, who diffused an air of wealth and pomp when they entered their pew at St. Stephen's Church on Sunday. Mrs. Corkerey, in fact, got herself and me in trouble by feeding me in the mornings in her kitchen above the candy store when I stopped to pick up her daughter, Clarazita, who was in my class. I used to lie to Mrs. Corkerey and say that I had had no breakfast (when the truth was that I was merely hungry), and she went to the nuns finally in a state of indignation. The story was checked with my aunt, and I was obliged to admit that I had lied and that they did feed me, which must have disillusioned Mrs. Corkerey forever with the pathos of orphaned childhood. It was impossible for me to explain to her then that what I needed was her pity and her fierce choleric heart. Another neighbor, Mr. Harrison, a well-to-do old bachelor or widower who lived in the corner house, used sometimes to take us bathing, and it was thanks to his lessons that I learned to swim—a strange antiquated breast stroke—copied from an old man with a high-necked bathing suit and a beard. In general, we were not supposed to have anything to do with the neighbors or with other children. It was a rule that other children were not allowed to come into our yard or we to go into theirs, nor were we permitted to walk to school with another boy or girl. But since we were in school most of the day, five days a week, our guardians could not prevent us from making friends despite them; other children were, in fact, very much attracted to us, pitying us for our woebegone condition and respecting us because we were thought to be rich. Our grandmother's chauffeur, Frank, in her winter Pierce-Arrow and summer Locomobile, was well known in the neighborhood, waiting outside church on Sunday to take her home from Mass. Sometimes we were taken, too, and thus our miserable clothes and underfed bodies were associated with high financial status and became a sort of dubious privilege in the eyes of our classmates.

We both had enviable possessions and did not have them. In the closet in my bedroom, high on the top shelf, beyond my reach even standing on a chair, was a stack of cardboard doll boxes, containing wonderful French dolls, dressed by my Seattle grandmother in silks, laces, and satins, with crepe-de-Chine underwear and shoes with high heels. These and other things were sent us every year at Christmastime, but my aunt had decreed that they were all too good for us, so they remained in their boxes and wrappings, verboten, except on the rare afternoon, perhaps once in a twelve-month or so, when a relation or a friend of the family would come through from the West, and then down would come the dolls, out would come the baseball gloves and catchers' masks and the watches and the shiny cars and the doll houses, and we would be set to playing with these things on the floor of the living room while the visitor tenderly looked on. As soon as the visitor left, bearing a good report of our household, the dolls and watches and cars would be whisked away, to come out again for the next emergency. If we had been clever, we would have refused this bait and paraded our misery, but we were too simple to do anything but seize the moment and play out a whole year's playtime in this gala hour and a half. Such techniques, of course, are common in concentration camps and penal institutions, where the same sound calculation of human nature is made. The prisoners snatch at their holiday; they trust their guards and the motto "Carpe diem" more than they do the strangers who have come to make the inspection. Like all people who have been mistreated, we were wary of being taken in; we felt uneasy about these visitors—Protestants from Seattle—who might be much worse than our uncle and aunt. The latter's faults, at any rate, we knew. Moreover, we had been subjected to propaganda: we had been threatened with the Seattle faction, time and again, by our uncle, who used to jeer and say to us, "*They*'d make you toe the chalk line."

The basis, I think, of my aunt's program for us was in truth totalitarian: she was idealistically bent on destroying our privacy. She imagined herself as enlightened in comparison with our parents, and a super-ideal of health, cleanliness, and discipline softened in her own eyes the measures she applied to attain it. A nature not unkindly was warped by bureaucratic zeal and by her subservience to her husband, whose masterful autocratic hand cut through our nonsense like a cleaver. The fact that our way of life resembled that of an orphan asylum was not a mere coincidence; Aunt Margaret strove purposefully toward a corporate goal. Like most heads of institutions, she longed for the eyes of Argus. To the best of her ability, she saw to it that nothing was hidden from her. Even her health measures had this purpose. The aperients we were continually dosed with guaranteed that our daily processes were open to her inspection, and the monthly medical checkup assured her, by means of stethoscope and searchlight and tongue depressor, that nothing was happening inside us to which she was not privy. Our letters to Seattle were written under her eye, and she scrutinized our homework sharply, though her arithmetic, spelling, and grammar were all very imperfect. We prayed, under supervision, for a prescribed list of people. And if we were forbidden companions, candy, most toys, pocket money, sports, reading, entertainment, the aim was not to make us suffer but to achieve efficiency. It was simpler to interdict other children than to inspect all the children with whom we might want to play. From the standpoint of efficiency, our lives, in order to be open, had to be empty; the books we might perhaps read, the toys we might play with figured in my aunt's mind, no doubt, as what the housewife calls "dust catchers"—around these distractions, dirt might accumulate. The inmost folds of consciousness, like the belly button, were regarded by her as unsanitary. Thus, in her spiritual outlook, my aunt was an early functionalist.

Like all systems, my aunt's was, of course, imperfect. Forbidden to read, we told stories, and if we were kept apart, we told them to ourselves in bed. We made romances out of our schoolbooks, even out of the dictionary, and read digests of novels in the *Book of Knowledge* at school. My uncle's partiality for my youngest brother was a weakness in him, as was my aunt Mary's partiality for me. She was supposed to keep me in her room, sewing on squares of cheap cotton, making handkerchiefs with big, crude, ugly hems, and ripping them out and making them over again, but though she had no feeling for art or visual beauty (she would not even teach me to darn, which is an art, or to do embroidery, as the nuns did later on, in the convent), she liked to talk of the old days in Chicago and to read sensational religious fiction in a magazine called the *Extension*, which sometimes she let me take to my room, with a caution against being caught. And on the Sunday walks that my uncle headed, at the end of an interminable streetcar ride, during which my bigger brothers had to scrunch down to pass for under six, there were occasions on which he took us (in military order) along a wooded path, high above the Mississippi River, and we saw late-spring harebells and, once, a coral-pink snake. In Minnehaha Park, a favorite resort, we were allowed to play on the swings and to examine the other children riding on the ponies or on a little scenic railway. Uncle Myers always bought himself a box of Cracker Jack, which we watched him eat and delve into, to find the little favor at the bottom—a ritual we deeply envied, for, though we sometimes had popcorn at home (Myers enjoyed popping it) and even, once or twice, homemade popcorn balls with molasses, we had never had more than a taste of this commercial Cracker Jack, with peanuts in it, which seemed to us the more valuable because *he* valued it and would often come home eating a box he had bought at a ball game. But one Sunday, Uncle Myers, in full, midsummer mood, wearing his new pedometer, bought my brother Sheridan a whole box for himself.

Naturally, we envied Sheridan—the only blond among us, with fair red-gold curls, while the rest of us were all pronounced brunets, with thick black brows and lashes—as we watched him, the lucky one, munch the sticky stuff and fish out a painted tin butterfly with a little pin on it at the bottom. My brothers clamored around him, but I was too proud to show my feelings. Sheridan was then about six years old, and this butterfly immediately became his most cherished possession—indeed, one of the few he had. He carried it about the house with him all the next week, clutched in his hand or pinned to his shirt, and my two other brothers followed him, begging him to be allowed to play with it, which slightly disgusted me, at the age of ten, for I knew that I was too sophisticated to care for tin butterflies and I felt in this whole affair the instigation of my uncle. He was relishing my brothers' performance and saw to it, strictly, that Sheridan clung to his rights in the butterfly and did not permit anybody to touch it. The point about this painted tin butterfly was not its intrinsic value; it was the fact that it was virtually the only toy in the house that had not been, so to speak, socialized, but belonged privately to one individual. Our other playthings—a broken-down wooden swing, an old wagon, a dirty sandbox, and perhaps a fire engine or so and some defaced blocks and twisted secondhand train tracks in the attic—were held by us all in common, the velocipedes we had brought with us from Seattle having long ago foundered, and the skipping rope, the jacks, the few marbles, and the pair of rusty roller skates that were given us being decreed to be the property of all. Hence, for a full week this butterfly excited passionate emotions, from which I held myself stubbornly apart, refusing even to notice it, until one afternoon, at about four o'clock, while I was doing my weekly chore of dusting the woodwork, my white-haired aunt Mary hurried softly into my room and, closing the door behind her, asked whether I had seen Sheridan's butterfly.

The topic wearied me so much that I scarcely lifted my head, answering no, shortly, and going on with my dusting. But Aunt Mary was gently persistent: Did I know that he had lost it? Would I help her look for it? This project did not appeal to me, but in response to some faint agitation in her manner, something almost pleading, I put down my dustcloth and helped her. We went all over the house, raising carpets, looking behind curtains, in the kitchen cupboards, in the Victrola, everywhere but in the den, which was closed, and in my aunt's and uncle's bedroom. Somehow—I do not know why—I did not expect to find the butterfly, partly, I imagine, because I was indifferent to it and partly out of the fatalism that all children have toward lost objects, regarding them as irretrievable, vanished into the flux of things. At any rate I was right: we did not find it and I went back to my dusting, vindicated. Why should *I* have to look for Sheridan's stupid butterfly, which he ought to have taken better care of? "Myers is upset," said Aunt Mary, still hovering, uneasy and diffident, in the doorway. I made a slight face, and she went out, plaintive, remonstrant, and sighing, in her pale, high-necked, tight-buttoned dress.

It did not occur to me that I was suspected of stealing this toy, even when Aunt Margaret, five minutes later, burst into my room and ordered me to come and look for Sheridan's butterfly. I protested that I had already done so, but she paid my objections no heed and seized me roughly by the arm. "Then do it again, Miss, and mind that you find it." Her voice was rather hoarse and her whole furrowed iron-gray aspect somewhat tense and disarrayed, yet I had the impression that she was not angry with me but with something in outer reality—what one would now call fate or contingency. When I had searched again, lackadaisically, and again found nothing, she joined in with vigor, turning everything upside down. We even went into the den, where Myers was sitting, and searched all around him, while he watched us with an ironical expression, filling his pipe from a Bull Durham sack. We found nothing, and Aunt Margaret led me upstairs to my room, which I ransacked while she stood and watched me. All at once, when we had finished with my bureau drawers and my closet, she appeared to give up. She sighed and bit her lips. The door cautiously opened and Aunt Mary came in. The two sisters looked at each other and at me. Margaret shrugged her shoulders. "She hasn't got it, I do believe," she said.

She regarded me then with a certain relaxing of her thick wrinkles, and her heavy-skinned hand, with its wedding ring, came down on my shoulder. "Uncle Myers thinks you took it," she said in a rusty whisper, like a spy or a scout. The consciousness of my own innocence, combined with a sense of being let into the confederacy of the two sisters, filled me with excitement and self-importance. "But I didn't, Aunt Margaret," I began proclaiming, making the most of my moment. "What would I want with his silly old butterfly?" The two sisters exchanged a look. "That's what I said, Margaret!" exclaimed old Aunt Mary sententiously. Aunt Margaret frowned; she adjusted a bone hairpin in the coiled rings of her unbecoming coiffure. "Mary Therese," she said to me, solemnly, "if you know anything about the butterfly, if one of your brothers took it, tell me now. If we don't find it, I'm afraid Uncle Myers will have to punish you." "He *can't* punish me, Aunt Margaret," I insisted, full of righteousness. "Not if I didn't do it and *you* don't think I did it." I looked up at her, stagily trustful, resting gingerly on this solidarity that had suddenly appeared between us. Aunt Mary's pale old eyes watered. "You mustn't let Myers punish her, Margaret, if you don't think she's done wrong." They both glanced up at the Murillo Madonna that was hanging on my stained wall. Intelligence passed between them and I was sure that, thanks to our Holy Mother, Aunt Margaret would save me. "Go along, Mary Therese," she said hoarsely. "Get yourself ready for dinner. And don't you say a word of this to your uncle when you come downstairs."

When I went down to dinner, I was exultant, but I tried to hide it. Throughout the meal, everyone was restrained; Herdie was in the dumps about his butterfly, and Preston and Kevin were silent, casting covert looks at me. My brothers, apparently, were wondering how I had avoided punishment, as the eldest, if for no other reason. Aunt Margaret was rather flushed, which improved her appearance slightly. Uncle Myers had a cunning look, as though events would prove him right. He patted Sheridan's golden head from time to time and urged him to eat. After dinner, the boys filed into the den behind Uncle Myers, and I helped Aunt Margaret clear the table. We did not have to do the dishes, for at this time there was a "girl" in the kitchen. As we were lifting the white tablecloth and the silence pad, we found the butterfly—pinned to the silence pad, right by my place.

My hash was settled then, though I did not know it. I did not catch the significance of its being found at *my* place. To Margaret, however, this was grimly conclusive. She had been too "easy," said her expression; once again Myers had been right. Myers went through the formality of interrogating each of the boys in turn ("No, sir," "No, sir," "No, sir") and even, at my insistence, of calling in the Swedish girl from the kitchen. Nobody knew how the butterfly had got there. It had not been there before dinner, when the girl set the table. My judges therefore concluded that I had had it hidden on my person and had slipped it under the tablecloth at dinner, when nobody was looking. This unanimous verdict maddened me, at first simply as an indication of stupidity—how could they be so dense as to imagine that I would hide it by my own place, where it was sure to be discovered? I did not really believe that I was going to be punished on such ridiculous evidence, yet even I could form no theory of how the butterfly had come there. My first base impulse to accuse the maid was scoffed out of my head by reason. What would a grown-up want with a silly six-year-old's toy? And the very unfairness of the condemnation that rested on me made me reluctant so transfer it to one of my brothers. I kept supposing that the truth somehow would out, but the interrogation suddenly ended and every eye avoided mine.

Aunt Mary's dragging step went up the stairs, the boys were ordered to bed, and then, in the lavatory, the whipping began. Myers beat me with the strop, until his lazy arm tired; whipping is hard work for a fat man, out of condition, with a screaming, kicking, wriggling ten-year-old in his grasp. He went out and heaved himself, panting, into his favorite chair and I presumed that the whipping was over. But Aunt Margaret took his place, striking harder than he, with a hairbrush, in a businesslike, joyless way, repeating, "Say you did it, Mary Therese, say you did it." As the blows fell and I did not give in, this formula took on an intercessory note, like a prayer. It was clear to me that she was begging me to surrender and give Myers his satisfaction, for my own sake, so that the whipping could stop. When I finally cried out "All right!" she dropped the hairbrush with a sigh of relief; a new doubt of my guilt must have been visiting her, and my confession set everything square. She led me in to my uncle, and we both stood facing him, as Aunt Margaret, with a firm but not ungentle hand on my shoulder, whispered, "Just tell him, 'Uncle Myers, I did it,' and you can go to bed." But the sight of him, sprawling in his leather chair, complacently waiting for this, was too much for me. The words froze on my tongue. I could not utter them to *him*. Aunt Margaret urged me on, reproachfully, as though I were breaking our compact, but as I looked straight at him and assessed his ugly nature, I burst into yells. "I didn't! I didn't!" I gasped, between screams. Uncle Myers shot a vindictive look at his wife, as though he well understood that there had been collusion between us. He ordered me back to the dark lavatory and symbolically rolled up his sleeve. He laid on the strop decisively, but this time I was beside myself, and when Aunt Margaret hurried in and tried to reason with me, I could only answer with wild cries as Uncle Myers, gasping also, put the strop back on its hook. "You take her," he articulated, but Aunt Margaret's hairbrush this time was perfunctory, after the first few angry blows that punished me for having disobeyed her. Myers did not take up the strop again; the whipping ended, whether from fear of the neighbors or of Aunt Mary's frail presence upstairs or sudden guilty terror, I do not know; perhaps simply because it was past my bedtime.

I finally limped up to bed, with a crazy sense of inner victory, like a saint's, for I had not recanted, despite all they had done or could do to me. It did not occur to me that I had been unchristian in refusing to answer a plea from Aunt Margaret's heart and conscience. Indeed, I rejoiced in the knowledge that I had *made* her continue to beat me long after she must have known that I was innocent; this was her punishment for her condonation of Myers. The next morning, when I opened my eyes on the Murillo Madonna and the Baby Stuart, my feeling of triumph abated; I was afraid of what I had done. But throughout that day and the next, they did not touch me. I walked on air, incredulously and, no doubt, somewhat pompously, seeing myself as a figure from legend: my strength was *as* the strength of ten because my *heart* was pure! Afterward, I was beaten, in the normal routine way, but the question of the butterfly was closed forever in that house.

In my mind, there was, and still is, a connection between the butterfly and our rescue, by our Protestant grandfather, which took place the following year, in the fall or early winter. Already defeated, in their own view, or having ceased to care what became of us, our guardians, for the first time, permitted two of us, my brother Kevin and me, to be alone with this strict, kindly lawyer, as we walked the two blocks between our house and our grandfather McCarthy's. In the course of our walk, between the walls of an early snow, we told Grandpa Preston everything, overcoming our fears and fixing our minds on the dolls, the baseball gloves, and the watches. Yet, as it happened, curiously enough, albeit with a certain aptness, it was not the tale of the butterfly or the other atrocities that chiefly impressed him as he followed our narration with precise legal eyes but the fact that I was not wearing my glasses. I was being punished for breaking them in a fall on the school playground by having to go without; and I could not see why my account of this should make him flush up with anger—to me it was a great relief to be free of those disfiguring things. But he shifted his long, lantern jaw and, settling our hands in his, went straight as a writ up my grandfather McCarthy's front walk. Hence it was on a question of health that this good American's alarms finally alighted; the rest of what we poured out to him he either did not believe or feared to think of, lest he have to deal with the problem of evil.

On health grounds, then, we were separated from Uncle Myers, who disappeared back into Elkhart with his wife and Aunt Mary. My brothers were sent off to the sisters in a Catholic boarding school, with the exception of Sheridan, whom Myers was permitted to bear away with him, like a golden trophy. Sheridan's stay, however, was of short duration. Very soon, Aunt Mary died, followed by Aunt Margaret, followed by Uncle Myers; within five years, still in the prime of life, they were all gone, one, two, three, like ninepins. For me, a new life began, under a happier star. Within a few weeks after my Protestant grandfather's visit, I was sitting in a compartment with him on the train, watching the Missouri River go westward to its source, wearing my white-gold wristwatch and a garish new red hat, a highly nervous child, fanatical against Protestants, who, I explained to Grandpa Preston, all deserved to be burned at the stake. In the dining car, I ordered greedily, lamb chops, pancakes, sausages, and then sat, unable to eat them. "Her eyes," observed the waiter, "are bigger than her stomach."

Six or seven years later, on one of my trips east to college, I stopped in Minneapolis to see my brothers, who were all together now, under the roof of a new and more indulgent guardian, my uncle Louis, the handsomest and youngest of the McCarthy uncles. All the old people were dead; my grandmother McCarthy, but recently passed away, had left a fund to erect a chapel in her name in Texas, a state with which she had no known connection. Sitting in the twilight of my uncle Louis's screened porch, we sought a common ground for our reunion and found it in Uncle Myers. It was then that my brother Preston told me that on the famous night of the butterfly, he had seen Uncle Myers steal into the dining room from the den and lift the tablecloth, with the tin butterfly in his hand.

KATE SIMON
(1912–90)

One of the three children of Jacob and Lina Grobsmith, Kate Simon (originally named Kaila) was born in Warsaw, Poland. She emigrated to America at the age of four, settling first in Harlem and, when she was just under six years old, moving to 178th Street and Lafontaine Avenue in the Bronx. The family occupied a railroad flat on the top floor in a five-story tenement. Her selfish and tyrannical father treated Kate and her brother in vastly different ways because of his thoroughly sexist views. As an adult, she concluded: "he was a man who should never have married and never had children. In his time, that was not conceivable; now it is." After earning a B.A. at Hunter College of the City University of New York, Simon worked for the Book-of-the-Month Club, *Publishers Weekly,* and from 1952 to 1955 as a freelance writer for Alfred A. Knopf. She began to publish her widely acclaimed travel guides in 1959 with *New York: Places and Pleasures* (revised in 1971). Among her numerous guides are *Mexico: Places and Pleasures* (1965), *Paris: Places and Pleasures* (1967), *London: Places and Pleasures: An Uncommon Guidebook* (1968), *Italy: The Places in Between* (1970), *Rome: Places and Pleasures* (1972), and *England's Green and Pleasant Land* (1974). In 1988, she published a social, cultural, and political history of the Gonzaga family, wealthy aristocrats of northern Italy's Lombardy region: *A Renaissance Tapestry: The Gonzaga of Mantua.* She authored three autobiographical volumes: *Bronx Primitive: Portraits in a Childhood* (1982), which was chosen by the National Book Critics Circle as one of the most distinguished books published in that year; *A Wider World: Portraits in an Adolescence* (1986); and *Etchings in an Hourglass* (1990), concerning the death of her daughter.

---

from *Bronx Primitive*

The Movies and Other Schools

Life on Lafontaine offered several schools. School-school, P.S. 59, was sometimes nice, as when I was chosen to be Prosperity in the class play, blond, plump, dressed in a white pillowcase banded with yellow and green crepe paper, for the colors of grasses and grain, and waving something like a sheaf of wheat. The cringing days were usually Fridays, when arithmetic flash cards, too fast, too many, blinded me and I couldn't add or subtract the simplest numbers. (For many years, into adulthood, I carried around a sack of churning entrails on Friday mornings.) The library, which made me my own absolutely special and private person with a card that belonged to no one but me, offered hundreds of books, all mine and no tests on them, a brighter, more generous

267

school than P.S. 59. The brightest, most informative school was the movies. We learned how tennis was played and golf, what a swimming pool was and what to wear if you ever got to drive a car. We learned how tables were set, "How do you do? Pleased to meet you," how primped and starched little girls should be, how neat and straight boys should be, even when they were temporarily ragamuffins. We learned to look up soulfully and make our lips tremble to warn our mothers of a flood of tears, and though they didn't fall for it (they laughed), we kept practicing. We learned how regal mothers were and how stately fathers, and of course we learned about Love, a very foreign country like maybe China or Connecticut. It was smooth and slinky, it shone and rustled. It was petals with Lillian Gish, gay flags with Marion Davies, tiger stripes with Rudolph Valentino, dog's eyes with Charlie Ray. From what I could see, and I searched, there was no Love on the block, nor even its fairy-tale end, Marriage. We had only Being Married, and that included the kids, a big crowded barrel with a family name stamped on it. Of course, there was Being Married in the movies, but except for the terrible cruel people in rags and scowls, it was as silky as Love. Fathers kissed their wives and children when they came home from work and spoke to them quietly and nobly, like kings, and never shouted or hit if the kids came in late or dirty. Mothers in crisp dresses stroked their children's heads tenderly as they presented them with the big ringletted doll and the football Grandma had sent, adding, "Run off and play, darlings." "Darling," "dear" were movie words, and we had few grandmothers, most of them dead or in shadowy conversation pieces reported from At Home, the Old Country. And "Run off and play" was so superbly refined, silken gauze to the rough wool of our hard-working mothers whose rules were to feed their children, see that they were warmly dressed in the wintertime, and run to the druggist on Third Avenue for advice when they were sick. Beyond that it was mostly "Get out of my way." Not all the mothers were so impatient. Miltie's mother helped him with his arithmetic homework; my mother often found us amusing and laughed with and at us a lot. From other apartments, on rainy afternoons: Joey—"What'll I do, Maaa?" His Mother—"*Va te ne! Gherradi!*" (the Italian version of "Get out of here"); Lily—"What'll I do, Maaa?" Mrs. Stavicz—"Scratch your ass on a broken bottle." I sometimes wished my mother would say colorful, tough things like that but I wasn't sure I wouldn't break into tears if she did, which would make her call me a *"pianovi chasto"* (as I remember the Polish phrase), a delicate meringue cake that falls apart easily, which would make me cry more, which would make her more lightly contemptuous, and so on. Despite my occasional wish to see her as one of the big-mouth, storming women, I was willing to settle for her more modest distinction, a lady who won notebooks in her English class at the library and sang many tunes from "Polish operettas" that, with later enlightenment, I realized were *The Student Prince* and *The Merry Widow*.

Being Married had as an important ingredient a nervous father. There must have been other kitchens, not only ours, in which at about seven o'clock, the fathers' coming-home time, children were warned, "Now remember, Papa is coming home soon. He's nervous from working in the factory all day and riding in the crowded El.

Sit quiet at the table, don't laugh, don't talk." It was hard not to giggle at the table, when my brother and I, who played with keen concentration a game of mortal enemies at other times, became close conspirators at annoying Them by making faces at each other. The muffled giggles were stopped by a shout of "Respect!" and a long black look, fork poised like a sword in midair while no one breathed. After the silent meal came the part we disliked most, the after-dinner lecture. There were two. The first was The Hard Life of the Jewish worker, the Jewish father, the deepest funereal sounds unstopped for the cost of electricity (a new and lovely toy but not as pretty as throbbing little mazda lamps) for which he had to pay an immense sum each time we switched it on and off, like the wastrels we were. Did we think butter cost a penny a pound that we slathered it on bread as if it were Coney Island mud pies? Those good expensive shoes he bought us (he was an expert shoe worker, a maker of samples, and tortured us with embarrassment when he displayed his expertise to the salesman, so don't try to fool him), which were old and scuffed and dirty within a week, did we know how much bloody sweat was paid for them? The second lecture was the clever one whose proud, sententious repetitions I listened to with shame for him, wanting to put my head down not to see my handsome father turn into a vaudeville comic whose old monologues strained and fell. This lecture was usually inspired by my brother who, in spite of the "nervous" call, dashed at my father as soon as he heard the key in the lock with "Hello, Pa. Gimme a penny?" That led it off: "You say you want a penny, *only* a penny. I've got dimes and quarters and half-dollars in my pockets, you say, so what's a penny to me? Well, let's see. If you went to the El station and gave the man four cents, he wouldn't let you on the train, you'd need another penny. If Mama gave you two cents for a three-cent ice-cream cone, would Mrs. Katz in the candy store give it to you? If Mama had only forty-eight cents for a forty-nine-cent chicken, would the butcher give it to her?" And on and on, a carefully rehearsed long slow aria, with dramatic runs of words and significant questioning pauses. Once or twice I heard my mother mutter as she went out of the room, "That Victrola record again," but her usual policy was to say nothing. She was not afraid of my father, nor particularly in awe of him. (I heard him say frequently how fresh she was, but with a smile, not the way he said it to us.)

In none of my assiduous eavesdropping on the street did I ever hear any mention of unhappy marriage or happy marriage. Married was married. Although a Jewish divorce was a singularly easy matter except for the disgrace it carried, the Jewish women were as firmly imbedded in their marriages as the Catholic. A divorce was as unthinkable as adultery or lipstick. No matter what—beatings, infidelity, drunkenness, verbal abuse, outlandish demands—no woman could run the risk of making her children fatherless. Marriage and children were fate, like being skinny, like skeletal Mr. Roberts, or humpbacked, like the leering watchman at the hat factory. *"Es is mir beschert,"* "It is my fate," was a common sighing phrase, the Amen that closed hymns of woe.

My mother didn't accept her fate as a forever thing. She began to work during our school hours after her English classes had taught her as much as they could, and while

I was still young, certainly no more than ten, I began to get her lecture on being a woman. It ended with extraordinary statements, shocking in view of the street mores. "Study. Learn. Go to college. Be a schoolteacher," then a respected, privileged breed, "and don't get married until you have a profession. With a profession you can have men friends and even children, if you want. You're free. But don't get married, at least not until you can support yourself and make a careful choice. Or don't get married at all, better still." This never got into "My mother said" conversations with my friends. I sensed it to be too outrageous. My mother was already tagged "The Princess" because she never went into the street unless fully, carefully dressed: no grease-stained housedress, no bent, melted felt slippers. Rarely, except when she was pregnant with my little sister, did she stop for conversations on the street. She was one of the few in the building who had gone to classes, the only mother who went out alone at night to join her mandolin group. She was sufficiently marked, and though I was proud of her difference, I didn't want to report her as altogether eccentric. In the community fabric, as heavy as the soups we ate and the dark, coarse "soldier's bread" we chomped on, as thick as the cotton on which we practiced our cross-stitch embroidery, was the conviction that girls were to marry as early as possible, the earlier the more triumphant. (Long after we moved from the area, my mother, on a visit to Lafontaine to see appealing, inept little Fannie Herman who had for many years been her charge and mine, met Mrs. Roth, who asked about me. When my mother said I was going to Hunter College, Mrs. Roth, looking both pleased and sympathetic, said, "*My* Helen married a man who makes a nice living, a laundry man. Don't worry, your Katie will find a husband soon." She knew that some of the boys of the block wound up in City College, but a girl in college? From a pretty, polite child, I must have turned into an ugly, bad-tempered shrew whom no one would have. Why else would my marrying years be spent in college?)

I never saw my mother and father kiss or stroke each other as people did in the movies. In company she addressed him, as did most of the Jewish women, by our family name, a mark of respectful distance. They inhabited two separate worlds, he adventuring among anti-Semites to reach a shadowy dungeon called "Factory," where he labored ceaselessly. In the evening he returned to her world for food, bed, children, and fighting. We were accustomed to fighting: the boys and, once in a while, fiery little girls tearing at each other in the street; bigger Italian boys punching and being punched by the Irish gangs that wandered in from Arthur Avenue; females fighting over clotheslines—whose sheets were blocking whose right to the sun—bounced around the courtyard constantly. The Genoese in the houses near 178th Street never spoke to the Sicilians near 179th Street except to complain that somebody's barbaric little southern slob had peed against a northern tree. To my entranced ears and eyes, the Sicilians seemed always to win, hotter, louder, faster with *"Fangu"*—the southern version of *"Fa' in culo"* (up yours)—than the aristocrats who retired before the Sicilians could hit them with *"Mortacci"*—the utterly insupportable insult. My brother and I fought over who grabbed the biggest apple, who hid the skate key, and where he put my baby picture, I lying on a white rug with my bare ass showing, a picture he threatened to pass among his friends and humiliate me beyond recovery. I would have to kill him.

These sorts of fighting were almost literally the spice of daily life, deliciously, lightly menacing, grotesque and entertaining. The fighting between my mother and father was something else entirely, at times so threatening that I still, decades later, cringe in paralyzed stupidity, as if I were being pelted with stones, when I hear a man shouting. The fights often concerned our conduct and my mother's permissiveness. My father had a rich vocabulary which he shaped into theatrical phrases spoken in a voice as black and dangerous as an open sewer. The opening shot was against my brother, who was six or seven when the attacks began. He was becoming a wilderness boy, no sense, no controls, dirty, disobedient, he did badly in school (not true: with a minimum of attention he managed mediocrity). There was no doubt that he would become a bum, then a thief, wind up alone in a prison cell full of rats, given one piece of bread a day and one cup of dirty water. He would come out a gangster and wind up in the electric chair.

When it was my turn, I was disobedient and careless; I didn't do my homework when I should, I didn't practice enough, my head was always in a book, I was always in the street running wild with the Italian and Polish beasts. I didn't take proper care of my brother, I climbed with boys, I ran with boys, I skated with them on far streets. Mr. Kaplan had seen me and told him. And how would this life, this playing with boys, end? I would surely become a street girl, a prostitute, and wind up being shipped to a filthy, diseased brothel crawling with hairy tropical bugs, in Buenos Aires. My mother's response was sharp and short: we acted like other children and played like other children; it was he who was at fault, asking more of us than he should. And enough about prisons and electric chairs and brothels. He went on shouting, entranced by his gorgeous words and visions, until she left the room to wash the dishes or scrub the kitchen floor. We, of course, had heard everything from our bedroom; the oratory was as much for us as for our mother. When the big rats in the windowless cell came to our ears, my brother began to shake with terror beyond crying. I tried to comfort him, as accustomed a role as trying to maim him. I didn't know what a street girl was, and I certainly didn't know what a brothel was, but I wasn't afraid—I was too angry. If our father hated us so, why didn't he go away? I didn't examine consequences, who would feed us and pay the rent. I just wanted him out, out, dead.

Other fights were about money, and that, too, involved us. How dare she, without consulting him, change from a fifty-cent-a-lesson piano teacher to another—and who knows how good *he* was?—who charged a dollar? What about the embroidered tablecloth and the stone bowl with the pigeons that she bought from the Arab peddler, that crook. Did she realize how hard he had to work to pay for our school supplies each fall? And add to that the nickel for candy to eat at the movies every Saturday, and the ten cents each for the movie and the three cents for ice-cream cones on Friday nights. And God only knew how much money she slipped us for the sweet garbage we chewed on, which would certainly rot our teeth, and where would he get the money for dentists? Maybe she thought she was still in her shop in Warsaw, dancing and singing and spilling money like a fool. And on and on it went. These tirades, too, were answered very briefly. Our lives were meager enough. Did he ever think of buying us even the cheapest toy, like the other fathers did, instead of stashing every spare penny in the bank and taking it out only for his relatives? The ignorant Italians he so despised, they had celebrations for their children. Where were our birthday presents?

Long silences followed these fights and we became messengers. "Tell your mother to take my shoes to the shoemaker." "Aw, Pa, I'm doing my homework. Later." "Tell your mother I have no clean shirts." "Aw, Pa, I'm just sitting down to practice. I'll tell her later." We used the operative words "homework" and "practice" mercilessly while he seethed at our delays. My mother heard all these instructions but it was her role neither to notice nor to obey. Those were great days and we exploited our roles fattily, with enormous vengeful pleasure.

One constant set of squabbles that didn't circle around us concerned her relaxed, almost loose judgments of other people. She showed no sympathy when he complained about the nigger sweeper in the factory who talked back to him, when he complained about the Italian who reeked of garlic and almost suffocated him in the train. Most loudly he complained about her availability, spoiling his sleep, letting his supper get cold, neglecting her own children, to run to any Italian idiot who didn't know to take care of her own baby. Let them take care of their own convulsions or get some Wop neighbor to help. It was disgraceful that she sat on Mrs. Santini's porch in open daylight trying to teach her not to feed her infant from her own mouth. If the fat fool wanted to give it germs, let her. If it died, she'd, next year, have another; they bred like rabbits. Why didn't my mother mind her own business, what the hell did these people, these foreign ignoramuses, mean to her? The answer was short and always the same, *"Es is doch a mench,"* yet these are human beings, the only religious training we ever had, perhaps quite enough.

There were fights with no messengers, no messages, whispered fights when the door to our bedroom was shut tight and we heard nothing but hissing. The slow unfolding of time and sophistications indicated that these were fights about women, women my father saw some of those evenings when he said he was going to a Workmen's Circle meeting. There was no more "Tell your mother," "Tell your father," and except for the crying of our baby, no more evening sounds. No Caruso, no Rosa Ponselle, no mandolin practice, no lectures. My father busied himself with extra piecework, "skiving" it was called, cutting with breathtaking delicacy leaf and daisy designs into the surface of the sample shoes to be shown to buyers. She, during one such period, crocheted a beaded bag, tiny beads, tiny stitches. We watched, struck dumb by their skill, and because it was no time to open our mouths about anything, anything at all. The silence was dreadful, a creeping, dark thing, a night alley before the murderer appears. The furniture was waiting to be destroyed, the windows to be broken, by a terrible storm. We would all be swept away, my brother and I to a jungle where wild animals would eat us, my parents and the baby, separated, to starve and burn alone in a desert. School now offered the comforts of a church, the street its comforting familiarities, unchanging, predictable. We stayed out as long as we could, dashing up for a speedy supper, and down again. On rainy nights we read a lot, we went to bed early, anything to remove us from our private-faced parents, who made us feel unbearably shy.

One spring evening, invited to jump Double Dutch with a few experts, uncertain that I could leap between two ropes whipping in rapid alternation at precisely the exact moment, and continue to stay between them in small fast hops from side to side, I admitted a need, urgent for some time, to go to the toilet. I ran up the stairs to find our door locked, an extraordinary thing. Maybe they had run away. Maybe they had killed each other. Sick with panic, I kept trying the door, it wouldn't give. Then I heard the baby making squirmy, sucking baby noises. No matter what, my mother would never leave the baby, and anyway, maybe they were doing their whispering fighting again. Still uneasy, I knocked on the Hermans' door and asked to use their toilet. When I came out, I asked Fannie Herman if she knew whether my parents were at home. Yes, she said. Her door was wide open and she would have seen or heard them come out, but they hadn't. The Double Dutch on the street was finished when I got down so I joined the race, boys and girls, around the block, running hard, loving my pumping legs and my swinging arms and my open mouth swallowing the breeze. When most of the kids had gone home and it was time for us, too, I couldn't find my brother, who was hiding from me to destroy my power and maybe get me into trouble. I went up alone. The door had been unlocked, and as I walked uneasily through the long hallway of our railroad flat with wary steps, I heard sounds from the kitchen. My mother was sitting on a kitchen chair, her feet in a basin of water. My father was kneeling before her on spread newspaper. Her plump foot rested in his big hand while he cut her toenails, flashing his sharp work knife, dexterous, light, and swift. She was splashing him a little, playing the water with her free foot. They were making jokes, lilting, laughing. Something, another branch in the twisted tree that shaded our lives, was going to keep us safe for a while.

Coney and Gypsies

Our baby sister was in a perverse way a great boon. She was frail, easily caught cold, had pinworms that had to be purged, which sometimes made her sicker, and was a troubled teether. With each tooth she had a fever and cried a lot. The first doctor we ever saw in our house—the obstetrician came and went behind our closed bedroom door; Dr. James was a fast-moving black shadow—was called in for the baby several times. It must have been an affluent time to afford doctors' visits, a time when my father brought home fairy-princess shoes to decorate. The extra piecework money he made was also spent for two summer weeks in Coney Island when my sister was nine or ten months old, teething and sickish all the time. Sea air was what the baby needed, my mother kept saying. After all, hadn't she cured us of whooping cough by spending days with us on the Staten Island ferry? And Coney Island wasn't so expensive and my father could come out a couple of times a week maybe and have all day Sunday on the beach and the boardwalk.

It was arranged, and after royal farewells to our less fortunate friends, the rich consoling and soaring over their poor relatives, we dragged the baby's crib and our bundles to El Dorado, the house in Coney Island, a ramshackle wooden place with a big porch. The several vacationing families like us each had one room crammed with two or three beds and clothing hooks on the walls. There was one community toilet and one large kitchen in which all the women cooked, whether separately or together I never found out. (That sort of summer living, whether at the beach or in the legendary "mountains," was known as a *kuch alein,* cook for yourself, the cheapest way to give one's children fresh air and escape for a week or two some of the exigencies of marriage.) The baby must have been quite sick because my usually careful mother let us loose on Coney Island every day for two weeks. After a breakfast of cold cereal with a couple of other children at one of the kitchen tables and a visit to the toilet, with two or three lunch nickels tied in a handkerchief knotted to a shoulder strap of my bathing suit, and instructions not to go too far into the water, not to buy candy with our lunch money, and to be back for supper at six, we were off.

We fought little or not at all during those weeks, too happy to want anything but what was: walking long streets staring at old people nodding on porches, at two kids with braces on their legs (the sea air was recommended for children with polio), who hopped up and down the stairs of one house like crooked birds, at the brilliant beach balls and shovels like derricks in shops on the boardwalk, at the machine in one shop that folded and kept folding skeins of taffy, at the fat plopping people and skinny stick people, at the white-skinned with red masks of sunburn, at the negro grasshopper children leaping and flying on their faraway street. It was a dazzling new world, like those in the movie travelogues that closed with, "As the sun sinks slowly in the west . . . ," and it was all ours. When it grew hot, we walked over to the sea and dared each other to go farther and farther out into the water. Both of us were several times dragged out in the undertow and grabbed by adults who demanded, "Where's your mother? Why doesn't she watch you?" and thrust us back on shore. After daring and daring more, being thrown and twisted, blinded and deafened by the water, shouted at by frightened and annoyed strangers, we became more cautious by silent accord and spent more time making sand castles and burying each other "up to the neck, keep away from my mouth and ears." We were both eager to spend the lunch money as soon as we left our house, and did it the first day, but learned to be patient after hours of hunger pangs. Lunch was a five-cent hot dog at any of dozens of stands, loaded with sauerkraut and, if we had an extra nickel, an ear of corn out of a big steaming cauldron. Dividing it was difficult: it didn't always break into two just halves, a meticulously observed principle, so we tried other solutions; one of them meant counting the rows of kernels, and if they were even, he crunched two rows and I the next two, and so on. If that didn't work out justly, the loser sucked on the cob, or got to lick the paper of a melting Baby Ruth on those days we decided against corn. Popcorn should have been easier, but counting out kernels, one for you, one for me, was too time-consuming for something we didn't care that much about, so we let it go. The tacit goal was to live as peaceably as we could in this paradise, "with liberty and justice for all," the Snake of Contention tied in his tree.

We found the Gypsies. They came through our Bronx streets from time to time, two or three women in big swinging skirts like colored winds, dusty long black hair, flashing gold teeth, and bold hands that demanded money, unlike the quivering old bums who bashfully begged. We were told to avoid them; they were filthy, they were thieves, and they kidnapped children. Our Coney Island Gypsies sat in a store behind a draped entrance, just off the boardwalk. The front of the shop was decorated with a naked head marked off in sections, probably for "studying bumps," which I had heard about from Helen Roth's big sister. Next to the cut-up head were a hand with lines on it and a watery picture of a glassy ball. Over the entrance, FORTUNES TOLD. COME RIGHT IN. We spent a good deal of time examining the head, the hand, and the glassy ball, trying to figure out how they told fortunes. Did a bump on the front slice of the head mean rich or smart? Could the glass ball show you a picture of whom you would marry? The lines on the hand, maybe they showed who would work hard, like the men who carried coal to the cellar, and who would have a soft job, like a teacher or librarian. All the fortune-telling we knew was a pick board crammed with little papers that, for a penny, could be poked out and unfolded to tell us, "You will marry rich," "You will be a success," "You will travel"—dumb things, we said; not altogether incredible, we thought. But this was the real goods, arcane, high-class fortune-telling that required mysterious charts and globes and the strange wisdoms of women in long red and pink satin skirts.

As we stood one day, edging toward the side of the draped doorway, a young woman in a long skirt and earrings like chandeliers came out and said, in recognizable English, "Hello. You're here again. Want some cake?" We were afraid and as usual much more afraid to confess fear. After hesitating, feeling shy, poking each other in and out of the doorway, we entered, looking for the cake. It was there, big and covered with chocolate icing, on a folding table, near it an older glittering Gypsy lady holding a knife. She gave us large chunks and cups of black tea with a lot of sugar. Was this the way they poisoned children to take them away, inert and senseless? Between small bites of the cake I waited for a numbed tongue, dizziness, pains in my stomach, anything ominous. I felt fine and my brother was doing well, babbling about our family and the sick baby and we had to take her here to the healthy air and we lived in the Bronx and he couldn't shut up. The young woman told the older one who had cut the cake what my brother was saying in her language—Romany, she explained—and invited me to sit down on a long low cushion if I wanted to. I sank to the purple and green flowers of the cushion, feeling as if I were floating, and accepted another piece of cake. While my brother continued entertaining the ladies, who smiled at him and each other broadly, I looked around. It was the most beautiful place I had ever been in. On the walls were intricately woven mazes of deep colors, little flowers and leaves caught in boxes of dark blue and red. Near these hangings were long spills of sky-blue satin. Other than the small table and two chairs there was no furniture, only cushions, heaps of them in brilliant colors and patterns. Near the back of the store, more and more like an Arab tent in the movies, there was an open cabinet of dark wood, carved as delicately as the shoes my father carved, on one of its shelves the glassy ball pictured outside. One lamp of metal with hundreds of little holes in it spread soft spots of light like stars. Sounds and smells of cooking came from behind a far curtain, but I never saw that room.

We didn't know when to leave, what the polite way of being with Gypsies was, so we stayed talking and staring, until the older woman said it was probably time to go home, our mother must be expecting us. Nothing was ever said about the Gypsies at home, though we went there frequent afternoons, always hanging around outside, near the skull and hand, waiting to be noticed and invited in. Sometimes we were offered sandwiches instead of cake, not too disappointing because we assumed that the strange meat in the sandwiches was ham or pork, of rarer value than cake. Sometimes the purple door drapes were folded together for a long time. That meant a customer and we tiptoed away, aching to peek through the folds to see Gypsy magic. We didn't dare risk the anger of the black-haired, black-eyed queens with the gold chains and earrings. They might yet hit us or poison us and sell us to other Gypsies.

The afternoon we said our last good-bye in Coney Island, the older woman, who had shown a great interest in the baby's teething and fevers, gave us a bone ring attached to a twisted, hornlike piece of coral, saying it was a teething ring, the coral attached for good luck. If our baby bit on it, she would feel much better and make nice strong teeth, too. I thanked her and thanked her again, nodding to be emphatic and to show I understood as she put the ring into my hand. We said good-bye—no kissing, no hugging, no handshaking, a great relief. As we walked home my brother asked to see the ring and, turning it around and around, decided it was old, used, and maybe full of germs. (It was old, used, and probably an antique that I regret not having saved.) We couldn't take it home, couldn't tell where we had gotten it. Even if we said we had found it, my mother would have thrown it away. So we dropped it into a sewer opening and forgot it.

The two weeks of freedom and being Gypsy children were not as easily forgotten. There was still a month before school started and we ran wild. The block wasn't enough anymore, even the empty lot. We snooped in the Italian market, a hundred times bigger than the local greenstores and butchers, hung with walls of salamis and cheeses like big clubs tied with ropes, all the way up on 183rd Street and Arthur Avenue. We skated far along Tremont to stare down on the tracks below Park Avenue, peering far downtown as we waited for trains that never seemed to run. But there was good garbage on the tracks, the rare sight of dozens of whiskey bottles along with the more familiar rotten oranges, old shoes, and mice rustling in torn bags of bread crusts and chicken bones.

It didn't last; we knew it wouldn't. We burst in, disheveled and streaked with dirty sweat, late one evening after our father had arrived. He ordered us into the bathroom to wash and comb our hair, declaring that we had become animals in Coney Island, it was time we were better controlled. My mother said nothing, but after that she took us and the baby, who was somewhat easier, to the park every afternoon to play quietly within her vision. I didn't mind, I read. But it was hard for my brother to live in circumscribed space, although he tried after our mother shouted him back from a game of Indians and Cowboys, himself both Indian and Cowboy, tracking fast and far.

During the hottest days we took off for Orchard Beach after an hour of scurrying preparation: Where are your bathing suits, put them on; put the bananas into the big shopping bag; I wonder if the eggs are hard-boiled yet; put your shirts and pants on over your bathing suit; Katie, run down to the grocery and buy six rolls, there's money on the table; don't put on those shoes, wear your old sneakers; not that dress, wear the blue one; hold the baby while I take the eggs out; take her bottle of milk out of the icebox and wrap it in a diaper so it won't get too warm; wrap up the towels in the old blanket and tie some string around it; leave the grapes alone, we'll need them on the beach when we're thirsty; here, the eggs are ready, wrap them up with the farmer cheese. Are we ready? Everything in the shopping bag? Did you put in your shovel? Hold the baby while I close the fire-escape window and lock the door.

My mother carrying the baby, my brother with the rolled blanket, and I with the shopping bag went to Tremont Avenue to wait for the summer trolley, a chariot of the gods served by Mercury. It clanged, it swayed, it screeched, and when its delicate wand slipped the wires in the sky, it shot little lightnings. Mercury got down from his daring ledge that ran the length of the trolley and coaxed the capricious wand that bent and quivered back to its wire. When he wasn't mastering electricity (at times, I thought, like a young, graceful Ben Franklin, without the spectacles and the moral wisecracks), our hero swung from open row to row, collecting fares, tapping change from the coin-shaped tubes on his chest, ripping transfers off a pad, one foot on his narrow ledge, one swinging in the air behind him, like Mercury, like a bird taking off.

We transferred to another trolley and yet another, riding into a place that had lawns around the houses and trees to screen them from the trolley tracks. We got off where the tracks were gritty and pulled our feet through the hot sand toward the water. It was never as crowded as Coney Island nor as interesting. We couldn't go into the water over our heads, we didn't eat hot dogs, only wholesome everyday food, we couldn't throw sand at each other because it might get into the baby's face. The sailboats in the distance were pretty to watch, dipping and straightening like ice skaters, and we argued about cloud shapes, was it a giant or a rhinoceros (surprising to find the same discussion in *Hamlet*). We carefully sucked and picked the threads off peach pits, preparing them for endless rubbing on the sidewalk to wear them down until they could be worn as rings, theoretically. (It took so long to make a peach ring, demanding much more patience than any of us had, that although reports kept coming in about magnificent rings on Monterey and on Arthur, we on Lafontaine never accomplished even one.)

It was nice on Orchard Beach, with the trolley rides, the big bag of food to dip into, the sailboats, the clouds, the water and watching it flow into the canals we dug near the water's edge, but it wasn't Coney Island; nothing ever again was.

GARY SOTO
(1952–)

Born and raised in Fresno, California, Gary Soto recalls picking grapes and chopping cotton along with migrant farm workers to earn the money to buy new clothes for the opening of school. A Mexican-American, he writes fiction that often depicts poor Hispanic characters trying to solve their problems and succeed. He received a B.A. in English at California State University at Fresno and an M.F.A. at the University of California at Irvine. He has been awarded fellowships by the California Arts Council, the National Endowment for the Arts, and the Guggenheim Foundation. His memoir, *Living up the Street,* won the 1985 Before Columbus Foundation's American Book Award and his *New and Selected Poems* was a 1995 finalist for the National Book Award and the Los Angeles Times Award. Among his numerous collections of poetry are *The Elements of San Joaquin* (1977), *Where Sparrows Work Hard* (1981), *Black Hair* (1985), *A Natural Man* (1999), and *One of a Kind Faith* (2003). Among his prose works are *Baseball in April and Other Stories* (1990), *A Summer Life* (1990), *Taking Sides* (1991), *Pacific Crossing* (1992), *Jesse* (1994), *Buried Onions* (1997), *Petty Crimes* (1998), *Amnesia in a Republican County* (2003), and *The Afterlife* (2003). A resident of Berkeley, California, he serves as the young person's ambassador for both the United Farm Workers of America and the California Rural Legal Assistance.

---

from *Living up the Street*

Looking for Work

One July, while killing ants on the kitchen sink with a rolled newspaper, I had a nine-year-old's vision of wealth that would save us from ourselves. For weeks I had drunk Kool-Aid and watched morning reruns of *Father Knows Best,* whose family was so uncomplicated in its routine that I very much wanted to imitate it. The first step was to get my brother and sister to wear shoes at dinner.

"Come on, Rick—come on, Deb," I whined. But Rick mimicked me and the same day that I asked him to wear shoes he came to the dinner table in only his swim trunks. My mother didn't notice, nor did my sister, as we sat to eat our beans and tortillas in the stifling heat of our kitchen. We all gleamed like cellophane, wiping the sweat from our brows with the backs of our hands as we talked about the day: Frankie our neighbor was beat up by Faustino; the swimming pool at the playground would be closed for a day because the pump was broken.

Such was our life. So that morning, while doing in the train of ants which arrived each day, I decided to become wealthy, and right away! After downing a bowl of cereal, I took a rake from the garage and started up the block to look for work.

We lived on an ordinary block of mostly working-class people: warehousemen, egg candlers, welders, mechanics, and a union plumber. And there were many retired people who kept their lawns green and the gutters uncluttered of the chewing gum wrappers we dropped as we rode by on our bikes. They bent down to gather our litter, muttering at our evilness.

At the corner house I rapped the screen door and a very large woman in a muumuu answered. She sized me up and then asked what I could do.

"Rake leaves," I answered, smiling.

"It's summer, and there ain't no leaves," she countered. Her face was pinched with lines; fat jiggled under her chin. She pointed to the lawn, then the flower bed, and said: "You see any leaves there—or there?" I followed her pointing arm, stupidly. But she had a job for me and that was to get her a Coke at the liquor store. She gave me twenty cents, and after ditching my rake in a bush, off I ran. I returned with an unbagged Pepsi, for which she thanked me and gave me a nickel from her apron.

I skipped off her porch, fetched my rake, and crossed the street to the next block where Mrs. Moore, mother of Earl the retarded man, let me weed a flower bed. She handed me a trowel and for a good part of the morning my fingers dipped into the moist dirt, ripping up runners of Bermuda grass. Worms surfaced in my search for deep roots, and I cut them in halves, tossing them to Mrs. Moore's cat who pawed them playfully as they dried in the sun. I made out Earl whose face was pressed to the back window of the house, and although he was calling to me I couldn't understand what he was trying to say. Embarrassed, I worked without looking up, but I imagined his contorted mouth and the ring of keys attached to his belt—keys that jingled with each palsied step. He scared me and I worked quickly to finish the flower bed. When I did finish Mrs. Moore gave me a quarter and two peaches from her tree, which I washed there but ate in the alley behind my house.

I was sucking on the second one, a bit of juice staining the front of my T-shirt, when Little John, my best friend, came walking down the alley with a baseball bat over his shoulder, knocking over trash cans as he made his way toward me.

Little John and I went to St. John's Catholic School, where we sat among the "stupids." Miss Marino, our teacher, alternated the rows of good students with the bad, hoping that by sitting side-by-side with the bright students the stupids might become more intelligent, as though intelligence were contagious. But we didn't progress as she had hoped. She grew frustrated when one day, while she was dismissing class for recess, Little John couldn't get up because his arms were stuck in the slats of the chair's backrest. She scolded us with a shaking finger when we knocked over the globe, denting the already troubled Africa. She muttered curses when Leroy White, a real stupid but a great softball player with the gift to hit to all fields, openly chewed his host when he made his First Communion; his hands swung at his sides as he returned to the pew looking around with a big smile.

Little John asked what I was doing, and I told him that I was taking a break from work, as I sat comfortably among high weeds. He wanted to join me, but I reminded him that the last time he'd gone door-to-door asking for work his mother had whipped him. I was with him when his mother, a New Jersey Italian who could rise up in anger one moment and love the next, told me in a polite but matter-of-fact voice that I had to leave because she was going to beat her son. She gave me a homemade popsicle, ushered me to the door, and said that I could see Little John the next day. But it was sooner than that. I went around to his bedroom window to suck my popsicle and watch Little John dodge his mother's blows, a few hitting their mark but many whirring air.

It was midday when Little John and I converged in the alley, the sun blazing in the high nineties, and he suggested that we go to Roosevelt High School to swim. He needed five cents to make fifteen, the cost of admission, and I lent him a nickel. We ran home for my bike and when my sister found out that we were going swimming, she started to cry because she didn't have the fifteen cents but only an empty Coke bottle. I waved for her to come and three of us mounted the bike—Debra on the crossbar, Little John on the handlebars and holding the Coke bottle which we would cash for a nickel and make up the difference that would allow all of us to get in, and me pumping up the crooked streets, dodging cars and potholes. We spent the day swimming under the afternoon sun, so that when we got home our mom asked us what was darker, the floor or us? She feigned a stern posture, her hands on her hips and her mouth puckered. We played along. Looking down, Debbie and I said in unison, "Us."

That evening at dinner we all sat down in our bathing suits to eat our beans, laughing and chewing loudly. Our mom was in a good mood, so I took a risk and asked her if sometime we could have turtle soup. A few days before I had watched a television program in which a Polynesian tribe killed a large turtle, gutted it, and then stewed it over an open fire. The turtle, basted in a sugary sauce, looked delicious as I ate an afternoon bowl of cereal, but my sister, who was watching the program with a glass of Kool-Aid between her knees, said, "Caca."

My mother looked at me in bewilderment. "Boy, are you a crazy Mexican. Where did you get the idea that people eat turtles?"

"On television," I said, explaining the program. Then I took it a step further. "Mom, do you think we could get dressed up for dinner one of these days? David King does."

"*Ay, Dios,*" my mother laughed. She started collecting the dinner plates, but my brother wouldn't let go of his. He was still drawing a picture in the bean sauce. Giggling, he said it was me, but I didn't want to listen because I wanted an answer from Mom. This was the summer when I spent the mornings in front of the television that showed the comfortable lives of white kids. There were no beatings, no rifts in the family. They wore bright clothes; toys tumbled from their closets. They hopped into bed with kisses and woke to glasses of fresh orange juice, and to a father sitting before his morning coffee while the mother buttered his toast. They hurried through the day making friends and gobs of money, returning home to a warmly lit living room, and then dinner. *Leave It to Beaver* was the program I replayed in my mind:

"May I have the mashed potatoes?" asks Beaver with a smile.

"Sure, Beav," replies Wally as he taps the corners of his mouth with a starched napkin.

The father looks on in his suit. The mother, decked out in earrings and a pearl neck-lace, cuts into her steak and blushes. Their conversation is politely clipped.

"Swell," says Beaver, his cheeks puffed with food.

Our own talk at dinner was loud with belly laughs and marked by our pointing forks at one another. The subjects were commonplace.

"Gary, let's go to the ditch tomorrow," my brother suggests. He explains that he has made a life preserver out of four empty detergent bottles strung together with twine and that he will make me one if I can find more bottles. "No way are we going to drown."

"Yeah, then we could have a dirt clod fight," I reply, so happy to be alive.

Whereas the Beaver's family enjoyed dessert in dishes at the table, our mom sent us outside, and more often than not I went into the alley to peek over the neighbor's fences and spy out fruit, apricot or peaches.

I had asked my mom and again she laughed that I was a crazy *chavalo* as she stood in front of the sink, her arms rising and falling with suds, face glistening from the heat. She sent me outside where my brother and sister were sitting in the shade that the fence threw out like a blanket. They were talking about me when I plopped down next to them. They looked at one another and then Debbie, my eight-year-old sister, started in.

"What's this crap about getting dressed up?"

She had entered her profanity stage. A year later she would give up such words and slip into her Catholic uniform, and into squealing on my brother and me when we "cussed this" and "cussed that."

I tried to convince them that if we improved the way we looked we might get along better in life. White people would like us more. They might invite us to places, like their homes or front yards. They might not hate us so much.

My sister called me a "craphead," and got up to leave with a stalk of grass dangling from her mouth. "They'll never like us."

My brother's mood lightened as he talked about the ditch—the white water, the broken pieces of glass, and the rusted car fenders that awaited our knees. There would be toads, and rocks to smash them.

David King, the only person we knew who resembled the middle class, called from over the fence. David was Catholic, of Armenian and French descent, and his closet was filled with toys. A bear-shaped cookie jar, like the ones on television, sat on the kitchen counter. His mother was remarkably kind while she put up with the racket we made on the street. Evenings, she often watered the front yard and it must have upset her to see us—my brother and I and others—jump from trees laughing, the unkillable kids of the very poor, who got up unshaken, brushed off, and climbed into another one to try again.

David called again. Rick got up and slapped grass from his pants. When I asked if I could come along he said no. David said no. They were two years older so their affairs were different from mine. They greeted one another with foul names and took off down the alley to look for trouble.

I went inside the house, turned on the television, and was about to sit down with a glass of Kool-Aid when Mom shooed me outside.

"It's still light," she said. "Later you'll bug me to let you stay out longer. So go on."

I downed my Kool-Aid and went outside to the front yard. No one was around. The day had cooled and a breeze rustled the trees. Mr. Jackson, the plumber, was watering his lawn and when he saw me he turned away to wash off his front steps. There was more than an hour of light left, so I took advantage of it and decided to look for work. I felt suddenly alive as I skipped down the block in search of an overgrown flower bed and the dime that would end the day right.

Deceit

For four years I attended St. John's Catholic School where short nuns threw chalk at me, chased me with books cocked over their heads, squeezed me into cloak closets and, on slow days, asked me to pop erasers and to wipe the blackboard clean. Finally, in the fifth grade, my mother sent me to Jefferson Elementary. The principal, Mr. Buckalew, kindly ushered me to the fifth grade teachers, Mr. Stendhal and Mrs. Sloan. We stood in the hallway with the principal's hand on my shoulder. Mr. Stendhal asked what book I had read in the fourth grade, to which, after a dark and squinting deliberation, I answered: *The Story of the United States Marines*. Mr. Stendhal and Mrs. Sloan looked at one another with a "you take him" look. Mr. Buckalew lifted his hand from my shoulder and walked slowly away.

Mrs. Sloan took me into her classroom where, perhaps, the most memorable thing she said to us all year was that she loved to chew tar.

Our faces went sour. "What kind of tar?"

"Oh, street tar—it's like gum." Her hands were pressed into a chapel as she stared vacantly over our heads in some yearning for the past.

And it was an odd year for me because there were months on end when I was the sweet kid who wanted to become a priest. In turn, there were the months when I was your basic kid with a rock in his hand.

When the relatives came over to talk to me and pat me on the head, they often smiled and asked what I wanted to be when I grew up.

"A priest," I would say during those docile months, while if they caught me during the tough months I would answer, "A hobo, I think."

They would smile and chuckle, "Oh, Gary."

Although I was going to public school, my brother, sister, and I were still expected to go to church. We would dress in our best clothes, with Debra in a yellow bonnet that she would throw into a bush just around the corner. "Stupid thing," she muttered as she hid it under the leaves with the intention of getting it later.

After a month or so Rick and Debra didn't have to go to church; instead they lounged in their pajamas drinking hot chocolate and talking loudly of how they were going to spend the morning watching television. I was, as my mom described me, a "short-tail devil in need of God's blessings."

So each Sunday I put on a white shirt and stepped into a pair of pants that kicked around my ankles, my white socks glowing on my feet in the dark pews of St. John's Cathedral. I knelt, I rose, and I looked around. I muddled prayers and knocked my heart with a closed hand when the priest knelt and the altar boy followed with a jingle of the bell.

For the first few weeks I went to church, however reluctantly, but soon discovered the magazine rack at Mayfair Market, which was only two blocks from the church. I read comics and chewed gum, with only a sliver of guilt about missing Mass pricking my soul. When I returned home after the hour that it took to say a Mass, my mom was in the kitchen but didn't ask about the Mass—what the priest said or did I drop the quarter she had given me into the donation basket. Instead, she handed me a buttered tortilla as a reward for being a good boy, and I took it to eat in my bedroom. I chuckled under my breath, "God, this is great."

The next week at the magazine rack I read about Superman coming back to life, chewed gum, and took swigs of a Coke I had bought with money intended for the far-reaching wicker basket. But the following week I came up with another idea: I started happily up the street while my mom looked out the front window with hands on hips, but once around the corner I swung into the alley to see what I could do.

That Sunday I played with Little John, and the following week I looked through a box of old magazines before dismantling a discarded radio. I gutted it of its rusty tubes and threw them, one by one, at a fence until a neighbor came out and told me to get the hell away.

Another Sunday I went up the street into the alley and climbed the fence of our backyard. Our yard was sectioned into two by a fence: The front part was neatly mowed, colored with flowers and cemented with a patio, while the back part was green with a vegetable garden, brown with a rusty incinerator, and heaped with odd junk—ruined bicycles, boards, buckled wheelbarrows. I climbed into the back part of our long yard and pressed my face between the slats: Rick was hoeing a flower bed while Debra was waiting to clean up with a box in her hands. My mom was washing down the patio.

I laughed to myself and then made a cat sound. When no one looked up, I meowed again and Mom looked in my direction for a second, then lowered her eyes to the water bouncing off the patio. I again laughed to myself, but quieted when Rick opened the gate to dump a load of weeds into the compost. I was smiling my evilness behind an old dismantled gate, and when he left I meowed again, chuckled to myself, and climbed the fence into the alley to look around for something to do.

This would continue all through the summer of my twelfth year, and by fall Mom said I didn't have to go to church because she had seen an improvement in my ways.

"See, I told you, *m'ijo*," she said over dinner one night. "The nuns would be very proud of you."

I swallowed a mouthful of beans and cleared my throat. "Yes, Mom."

Still, when relatives showed up at the door to talk to my mom in Spanish, I hung around to comb my hair and wait for them to open their purses or fiddle deeply in their pockets for a nickel or dime. They would pat my head and ask me what I wanted to be when I grew up. "A priest," I would answer, to which they would smile warmly, "Oh, Gary," and give over the coin.

PIRI THOMAS
(1928–)

Piri Thomas was born Juan Pedro Tomas Montanez in Harlem Hospital in New York City to parents who had emigrated to the United States from Puerto Rico and Cuba. In a misguided attempt to help their child become assimilated, they changed his name to John Peter Thomas. He chose the name he cherishes, Piri, because his mother had referred to him as "*Mira* Piri," and only discovered many years later that "Piri" is a woman's name. He was raised in Spanish Harlem until his parents moved the family to Babylon, Long Island. There he experienced such intense racism and humiliation that at the age of fourteen he returned to his East Harlem neighborhood alone, often sleeping on rooftops, in backyards, or briefly in the houses of different friends. A gang member involved in armed robbery, he spent seven years in prison. There he earned a diploma by taking the high school equivalency test at Comstock State Prison in New York, and then he began to write. He has asserted that "for all its horror, prison for me turned out to be a painful blessing. I was in a place where I would either die or be refined." Thomas has published *Down These Mean Streets* (1967); *Savior, Savior, Hold My Hand* (1972); and *Seven Long Times* (1974), which depicts the brutal and dehumanizing conditions of New York's prisons; as well as *Stories from El Barrio* (1978). His play, *The Golden Streets,* was performed in Puerto Rico in 1972. The author of two television documentaries about drug rehabilitation, *Petey & Johnny* and *The World of Piri Thomas,* he now lives in Berkeley, California, where he is at work on a sequel to *Down These Mean Streets* titled *A Matter of Dignity.*

---

from *Down These Mean Streets*

Alien Turf

Sometimes you don't fit in. Like if you're a Puerto Rican on an Italian block. After my new baby brother, Ricardo, died of some kind of germs, Poppa moved us from 111th Street to Italian turf on 114th Street between Second and Third Avenue. I guess Poppa wanted to get Momma away from the hard memories of the old pad.

I sure missed 111th Street, where everybody acted, walked, and talked like me. But on 114th Street everything went all right for a while. There were a few dirty looks from the spaghetti-an'-sauce cats, but no big sweat. Till that one day I was on my way home from school and almost had reached my stoop when someone called: "Hey, you dirty fuckin' spic."

The words hit my ears and almost made me curse Poppa at the same time. I turned around real slow and found my face pushing in the finger of an Italian kid about my age. He had five or six of his friends with him.

"Hey, you," he said. "What nationality are ya?"

I looked at him and wondered which nationality to pick. And one of his friends said, "Ah, Rocky, he's black enuff to be a nigger. Ain't that what you is, kid?"

My voice was almost shy in its anger. "I'm Puerto Rican," I said. "I was born here." I wanted to shout it, but it came out like a whisper.

"Right here inna street?" Rocky sneered. "Ya mean right here inna middle of da street?"

They all laughed.

I hated them. I shook my head slowly from side to side. "Uh-uh," I said softly. "I was born inna hospital—inna bed."

"Ummm, *paisan*—born inna bed," Rocky said.

I didn't like Rocky Italiano's voice. "Inna hospital," I whispered, and all the time my eyes were trying to cut down the long distance from this trouble to my stoop. I couldn't help thinking about kids getting wasted for moving into a block belonging to other people.

"What hospital, *paisan*?" Bad Rocky pushed.

"Harlem Hosptial," I answered, wishing like all hell that it was 5 o'clock intead of just 3 o'clock, 'cause Poppa came home at 5. I looked around for some friendly faces belonging to grown-up people, but the elders were all busy yakking away in Italian. I couldn't help thinking how much like Spanish it sounded. Shit, that should make us something like relatives.

"Harlem Hospital?" said a voice. "I knew he was a nigger."

"Yeah," said another voice from an expert on color. "That's the hospital where all them black bastards get born at."

I dug three Italian elders looking at us from across the street, and I felt saved. But that went out the window when they just smiled and went on talking. I couldn't decide whether they had smiled because this new whatever-he-was was gonna get his ass kicked or because they were pleased that their kids were welcoming a new kid to their country. An older man nodded his head at Rocky, who smiled back. I wondered if that was a signal for my funeral to begin.

"Ain't that right, kid?" Rocky pressed. "Ain't that where all black people get born?"

I dug some of Rocky's boys grinding and pushing and punching closed fists against open hands. I figured they were looking to shake me up, so I straightened up my humble voice and made like proud. "There's all kinds of people born there. Colored people, Puerto Ricans like me, an'—even spaghetti-benders like you."

"That's a dirty fuckin' lie"—*bash*, I felt Rocky's fist smack into my mouth—"you dirty fuckin' spic."

I got dizzy and then more dizzy when fists started to fly from everywhere and only toward me. I swung back, *splat, bish*—my fist hit some face and I wished I hadn't, 'cause then I started getting kicked.

I heard people yelling in Italian and English and I wondered if maybe it was 'cause

I hadn't fought fair in having hit that one guy. But it wasn't. The voices were trying to help me.

"Whas'sa matta, you no-good kids, leeva da kid alone," a man said. I looked through a swelling eye and dug some Italians pushing their kids off me with slaps. One even kicked a kid in the ass. I could have loved them if I didn't hate them so fuckin' much.

"You all right, kiddo?" asked the man.

"Where you live, boy?" said another one.

"Is the *bambino* hurt?" asked a woman.

I didn't look at any of them. I felt dizzy. I didn't want to open my mouth to talk, 'cause I was fighting to keep from puking up. I just hoped my face was cool-looking. I walked away from that group of strangers. I reached my stoop and started to climb the steps.

"Hey, spic," came a shout from across the street. I started to turn to the voice and changed my mind. "Spic" wasn't my name. I knew that voice, though. It was Rocky's. "We'll see ya again, spic," he said.

I wanted to do something tough, like spitting in their direction. But you gotta have spit in your mouth in order to spit, and my mouth was hurt dry. I just stood there with my back to them.

"Hey, your old man just better be the janitor in that fuckin' building."

Another voice added, "Hey, you got any pretty sisters? We might let ya stay onna block."

Another voice mocked, "Aw, fer Chrissake, where ya ever hear of one of them black broads being pretty?"

I heard the laughter. I turned around and looked at them. Rocky made some kind of dirty sign by putting his left hand in the crook of his right arm while twisting his closed fist in the air.

Another voice said, "Fuck it, we'll just cover the bitch's face with the flag an' fuck 'er for old glory."

All I could think of was how I'd like to kill each of them two or three times. I found some spit in my mouth and splattered it in their direction and went inside.

Momma was cooking, and the smell of rice and beans was beating the smell of Parmesan cheese from the other apartments. I let myself into our new pad. I tried to walk fast past Momma so I could wash up, but she saw me.

"My God, Piri, what happened?" she cried.

"Just a little fight in school, Momma. You know how it is, Momma, I'm new in school an' . . ." I made myself laugh. Then I made myself say, "But Moms, I whipped the living—outta two guys, an' one was bigger'n me."

"*Bendito,* Piri, I raise this family in Christian way. Not to fight. Christ says to turn the other cheek."

"Sure, Momma." I smiled and went and showered, feeling sore at Poppa for bringing us into spaghetti country. I felt my face with easy fingers and thought about all the running back and forth from school that was in store for me.

I sat down to dinner and listened to Momma talk about Christian living without really hearing her. All I could think of was that I hada go out in that street again. I made up my mind to go out right after I finished eating. I had to, shook up or not, cats like me had to show heart.

"Be back, Moms," I said after dinner, "I'm going out on the stoop." I got halfway to the stoop and turned and went back to our apartment. I knocked.

"Who is it?" Momma asked.

"Me, Momma."

She opened the door. *"Qué pasa?"* she asked.

"Nothing, Momma, I just forgot something," I said. I went into the bedroom and fiddled around and finally copped a funny book and walked out the door again. But this time I made sure the switch on the lock was open, just in case I had to get back real quick. I walked out on that stoop as cool as could be, feeling braver with the lock open.

There was no sign of Rocky and his killers. After a while I saw Poppa coming down the street. He walked like beat tired. Poppa hated his pick-and-shovel job with the WPA. He couldn't even hear the name WPA without getting a fever. *Funny,* I thought, *Poppa's the same like me, a stone Puerto Rican, and nobody in this block even pays him a mind. Maybe older people get along better'n us kids.*

Poppa was climbing the stoop. "Hi, Poppa," I said.

"How's it going, son? Hey, you sure look a little lumped up. What happened?"

I looked at Poppa and started to talk it outta me all at once and stopped, 'cause I heard my voice start to sound scared, and that was no good.

"Slow down, son," Poppa said. "Take it easy." He sat down on the stoop and made a motion for me to do the same. He listened and I talked. I gained confidence. I went from a tone of being shook up by the Italians to a tone of being a better fighter than Joe Louis and Pedro Montanez lumped together, with Kid Chocolate thrown in for extra.

"So that's what happened," I concluded. "And it looks like only the beginning. Man, I ain't scared, Poppa, but like there's nothin' but Italianos on this block and there's no me's like me except me an' our family."

Poppa looked tight. He shook his head from side to side and mumbled something about another Puerto Rican family that lived a coupla doors down from us.

I thought, *What good would that do me, unless they prayed over my dead body in Span-ish?* But I said, "Man! That's great. Before ya know it, there'll be a whole bunch of us moving in, huh?"

Poppa grunted something and got up. "Staying out here, son?"

"Yeah, Poppa, for a little while longer."

From that day on I grew eyes all over my head. Anytime I hit that street for anything, I looked straight ahead, behind me and from side to side all at the same time. Sometimes I ran into Rocky and his boys—that cat was never without his boys—but they never made a move to snag me. They just grinned at me like a bunch of hungry alley cats that could get to their mouse anytime they wanted. That's what they made me feel like—a mouse. Not like a smart house mouse but like a white house pet that ain't got no business in the middle of cat country but don't know better 'cause he grew up thinking he was a cat—which wasn't far from wrong 'cause he'd end up as part of the inside of some cat.

Rocky and his fellas got to playing a way-out game with me called "One-finger-across-the-neck-inna-slicing-motion," followed by such gentle words as "It won't be long, spico." I just looked at them blank and made it to wherever I was going.

I kept wishing those cats went to the same school I went to, a school that was on the border between their country and mine, and I had amigos there—and there I could count on them. But I couldn't ask two or three amigos to break into Rocky's block and help me mess up his boys. I knew 'cause I had asked them already. They had turned me down fast, and I couldn't blame them. It would have been murder, and I guess they figured one murder would be better than four.

I got through the days trying to play it cool and walk on by Rocky and his boys like they weren't there. One day I passed them and nothing was said. I started to let out my breath. I felt great; I hadn't been seen. Then someone yelled in a high, girlish voice, "Yoo-hoo . . . Hey, *paisan* . . . we see yoo . . ." And right behind that voice came a can of evaporated milk—whoosh, clatter. I walked cool for ten steps then started running like mad.

This crap kept up for a month. They tried to shake me up. Every time they threw something at me, it was just to see me jump. I decided that the next fucking time they threw something at me I was gonna play bad-o and not run. That next time came about a week later. Momma sent me off the stoop to the Italian market on 115th Street and First Avenue, deep in Italian country. Man, that was stompin' territory. But I went, walking in the style which I had copped from the colored cats I had seen, a swinging and stepping down hard at every step. Those cats were so down and cool that just walking made a way-out sound.

Ten minutes later I was on my way back with Momma's stuff. I got to the corner of First Avenue and 114th Street and crushed myself right into Rocky and his fellas.

"Well-l, fellas," Rocky said. "Lookee who's here."

I didn't like the sounds coming out of Rocky's fat mouth. And I didn't like the sameness of the shitty grins spreading all over the boys' faces. But I thought, *No more! No more! I ain't gonna run no more.* Even so, I looked around, like for some kind of Jesus miracle to happen. I was always looking for miracles to happen.

"Say, *paisan*," one guy said, "you even buying from us *paisans*, eh? Man, you must wantta be Italian."

Before I could bite that dopey tongue of mine, I said, "I wouldn't be a guinea on a motherfucking bet."

"Wha-at?" said Rocky, really surprised. I didn't blame him; I was surprised myself. His finger began digging a hole in his ear, like he hadn't heard me right. "Wha-at? Say that again?"

I could feel a thin hot wetness cutting itself down my leg. I had been so ashamed of being so damned scared that I had peed on myself. And then I wasn't scared anymore; I felt a fuck-it-all attitude. I looked real bad at Rocky and said, "Ya heard me. I wouldn't be a guinea on a bet."

"Ya little sonavabitch, we'll kick the shit outta ya," said one guy, Tony, who had made a habit of asking me if I had any sen-your-ritas for sisters.

"Kick the shit outta me yourself if you got any heart, you motherfuckin' fucker,"

I screamed at him. I felt kind of happy, the kind of feeling that you get only when you got heart.

Big-mouth Tony just swung out, and I swung back and heard all of Momma's stuff plopping all over the street. My fist hit Tony smack dead in the mouth. He was so mad he threw a fist at me from about three feet away. I faked and jabbed and did fancy dance steps. Big-mouth put a stop to all that with a punch in my mouth. I heard the home cheers of "Yea, yea, bust that spic wide open!" Then I bloodied Tony's nose. He blinked and sniffed without putting his hands to his nose, and I remembered Poppa telling me, "Son, if you're ever fighting somebody an' you punch him in the nose, and he just blinks an' sniffs without holding his nose, you can do one of two things: fight like hell or run like hell—'cause that cat's a fighter."

Big-mouth came at me and we grabbed each other and pushed and pulled and shoved. *Poppa*, I thought, *I ain't gonna cop out. I'm a fighter too.* I pulled away from Tony and blew my fist into his belly. He puffed and butted my nose with his head. I sniffed back. *Poppa, I didn't put my hands to my nose.* I hit Tony again in the same weak spot. He bent over in the middle and went down to his knees.

Big-mouth got up as fast as he could, and I was thinking how much heart he had. But I ran toward him like my life depended on it; I wanted to cool him. Too late, I saw his hand grab a fistful of ground asphalt which had been piled nearby to fix a pothole in the street. I tried to duck; I should have closed my eyes instead. The shitty-gritty stuff hit my face, and I felt the scrappy pain make itself a part of my eyes. I screamed and grabbed for two eyes with one hand, while the other I beat some kind of helpless tune on air that just couldn't be hurt. I heard Rocky's voice shouting, "Ya scum bag, ya didn't have to fight the spic dirty; you could've fucked him up fair and square!" I couldn't see. I heard a fist hit a face, then Big-mouth's voice: "Whatta ya hittin' me for?" and then Rocky's voice: "*Putana!* I ought ta knock all your fuckin' teeth out."

I felt hands grabbing at me between my screams. I punched out. *I'm gonna get killed,* I thought. Then I heard many voices: "Hold it, kid." "We ain't gonna hurt ya." "*Je-sus,* don't rub your eyes." "Ooooohhhh, shit, his eyes is fulla that shit."

You're fuckin' right, I thought, *and it hurts like* coño.

I heard a woman's voice now: "Take him to a hospital." And an old man asked: "How did it happen?"

"Momma, Momma," I cried.

"Comon, kid," Rocky said, taking my hand. "Lemme take ya home." I fought for the right to rub my eyes. "Grab his other hand, Vincent," Rocky said. I tried to rub my eyes with my eyelids. I could feel hurt tears cutting down my cheeks. "Come on, kid, we ain't gonna hurt ya," Rocky tried to assure me. "Swear to our mudders. We just wanna take ya home."

I made myself believe him, and trying not to make pain noises, I let myself be led home. I wondered if I was gonna be blind like Mr. Silva, who went around from door to door selling dish towels and brooms, his son leading him around.

"You okay, kid?" Rocky asked.

"Yeah," what was left of me said.

"A-huh," mumbled Big-mouth.

"He got much heart for a nigger," somebody else said.

A *spic,* I thought.

"For anybody," Rocky said. "Here we are, kid," he added. "Watch your step."

I was like carried up the steps. "What's your apartment number?" Rocky asked.

"One-B—inna back—ground floor," I said, and I was led there. Somebody knocked on Momma's door. Then I heard running feet and Rocky's voice yelling back, "Don't rat, huh, kid?" And I was alone.

I heard the door open and Momma say, "*Bueno,* Piri, come in." I didn't move. I couldn't. There was a long pause; I could hear Momma's fright. "My God," she said finally. "What's happened?" Then she took a closer look. "Ai-eeee," she screamed. *"Dios mío!"*

"I was playing with some kids, Momma," I said, "an' I got some dirt in my eyes." I tried to make my voice come out without the pain, like a man.

"Dios eterno—your eyes!"

"What's the matter? What's the matter?" Poppa called from the bedroom.

"Está ciego!" Momma screamed. "He is blind!"

I heard Poppa knocking things over as he came running. Sis began to cry. Blind, hurting tears were jumping out of my eyes.

"Whattya mean, he's blind?" Poppa said as he stormed into the kitchen. "What happened?" Poppa's voice was both scared and mad.

"Playing, Poppa."

"Whatta ya mean, 'playing'?" Poppa's English sounded different when he got warm.

"Just playing, Poppa."

"Playing? Playing got all that dirt in your eyes? I bet my ass. Them damn Ee-ta-liano kids ganged up on you again." Poppa squeezed my head between the fingers of one hand. "That settles it—we're moving outta this damn section, outta this damn block, outta this damn shit."

Shit, I thought, *Poppa's sure cursin' up a storm.* I could hear him slapping the side of his leg, like he always did when he got real mad.

"Son," he said, "you're gonna point them out to me."

"Point who out, Poppa? I was playin' an'—"

"Stop talkin' to him and take him to the hospital," Momma screamed.

"Pobrecito, poor Piri," cooed my little sister.

"You sure, son?" Poppa asked. "You was only playing?"

"Shit, Poppa, I said I was."

Smack—Poppa was so scared and mad, he let it out in a slap to the side of my face.

"Bestia! Ani-*mul!*" Momma cried. "He's blind, and you hit him."

"I'm sorry, son, I'm sorry," Poppa said in a voice like almost-crying. I heard him running back into the bedroom, yelling, "Where's my pants?"

Momma grabbed away fingers that were trying to wipe away the hurt in my eyes. *"Caramba,* no rub, no rub," she said, kissing me. She told Sis to get a rag and wet it with cold water.

Poppa came running back into the kitchen. "Let's go, son, let's go. Jesus! I didn't mean to smack ya, I really didn't," he said, his big hand rubbing and grabbing my hair gently.

"Here's the rag, Momma," said Sis.

"What's that for?" asked Poppa.

"To put on his eyes," Momma said.

I heard the smack of a wet rag, *blapt,* against the kitchen wall. "We can't put nothing on his eyes. It might make them worse. Come on, son," Poppa said nervously, lifting me up in his big arms. I felt like a little baby, like I didn't hurt so bad. I wanted to stay there, but I said, "Let me down, Poppa, I ain't no kid."

"Shut up," Poppa said softly. "I know you ain't, but it's faster this way."

"Which hospeetal are you taking him to?" Momma asked.

"Nearest one," Poppa answered as we went out the door. He carried me through the hall and out into the street, where the bright sunlight made a red hurting color through the crap in my eyes. I hear voices on the stoop and on the sidewalk: "Is that the boy?"

"A-huh. He's probably blinded."

"We'll get a cab, son," Poppa said. His voice loved me. I hear Rocky yelling from across the street, "We're pulling for ya, kid. Remember what we . . ." The rest was lost to Poppa's long legs running down to the corner of Third Avenue. He hailed a taxi and we zoomed off toward Harlem Hospital. I felt the cab make all kinds of sudden stops and turns.

"How do you feel, *hijo?*" Poppa asked.

"It hurts like hell."

"You'll be okay," he said, and as an afterthought added, "Don't curse, son."

I heard cars honking and the Third Avenue el roaring above us. I knew we were in Puerto Rican turf, cause I could hear our language.

"Son."

"Yeah, Poppa."

"Don't rub your eyes, fer Christ sake." He held my skinny wrist in his one hand, and everything got quiet between us.

The cab got to Harlem Hospital. I heard change being handled and the door opening and Poppa thanking the cabbie for getting here fast. "Hope the kid'll be okay," the driver said.

I will be, I thought. *I ain't gonna be like Mr. Silva.*

Poppa took me in his arms again and started running. "Where's emergency, mister?" he asked someone.

"To your left and straight away," said a voice.

"Thanks a lot," Poppa said, and we were running again. "Emergency?" Poppa said when we stopped.

"Yes, sir," said a girl's voice. "What's the matter?"

"My boy's got his eyes full of ground-up tar an'—"

"What's the matter?" said a man's voice.

"Youngster with ground tar in his eyes, doctor."

"We'll take him, mister. You just put him down here and go with the nurse. She'll take down the information. Uh, you the father?"

"That's right, doctor."

"Okay, just put him down here."

"Poppa, don't leave me," I cried.

"Sh, son, I ain't leaving you. I'm just going to fill out some papers an' I'll be right back."

I nodded my head up and down and was wheeled away. When the rolling stretcher stopped, somebody stuck a needle in me and I got sleepy and started thinking about Rocky and his boys, and Poppa's slap, and how great Poppa was, and how my eyes didn't hurt no more . . .

I woke up in a room blind with darkness. The only lights were the ones inside my head. I put my fingers to my eyes and felt bandages. "Let them be, sonny," said a woman's voice.

I wanted to ask the voice if they had taken my eyes out, but I didn't. I was afraid the voice would say yes.

"Let them be, sonny," the nurse said, pulling my hand away from the bandages. "You're all right. The doctor put the bandages on to keep the light out. They'll be off real soon. Don't you worry none, sonny."

I wished she would stop calling me sonny. "Where's Poppa?" I asked cool-like.

"He's outside, sonny. Would you like me to send him in?"

I nodded. "Yeah." I heard walking-away shoes, a door opening, a whisper, and shoes walking back toward me. "How do you feel, *hijo*?" Poppa asked.

"It hurts like shit, Poppa."

"It's just for a while, son, and then off come the bandages. Everything's gonna be all right."

I thought, *Poppa didn't tell me to stop cursing*.

"And son, I thought I told you to stop cursing," he added.

I smiled. Poppa hadn't forgotten. Suddenly I realized that all I had on was a hospital gown. "Poppa, where's my clothes?" I asked.

"I got them. I'm taking them home an'—"

"Whatta ya mean, Poppa?" I said, like scared. "You ain't leavin' me here? I'll be damned if I stay." I was already sitting up and feeling my way outta bed. Poppa grabbed me and pushed me back. His voice wasn't mad or scared anymore. It was happy and soft, like Momma's.

"Hey," he said, "get your ass back in bed or they'll have to put a bandage there too."

"Poppa," I pleaded. "I don't care, wallop me as much as you want, just take me home."

"Hey, I thought you said you wasn't no kid. Hell, you ain't scared of being alone?"

Inside my head there was a running of *Yeah, yeah, yeah,* but I answered, "Naw, Poppa, it's just that Momma's gonna worry and she'll get sick an' everything and—"

"Won't work, son," Poppa broke in with a laugh.

I kept quiet.

"It's only for a couple days. We'll come and see you an' everybody'll bring you things."

I got interested but played it smooth. "What kinda things, Poppa?"

Poppa shrugged his shoulders and spread his big arms apart and answered me like he was surprised that I should ask. "Uh . . . fruits and . . . candy and ice cream. And Momma will probably bring you chicken soup."

I shook my head sadly. "Poppa, you know I don't like chicken soup."

"So we won't bring chicken soup. We'll bring what you like. Goddammit, whatta ya like?"

"I'd like the first things you talked about, Poppa," I said softly. "But instead of soup I'd like"—I held my breath back, then shot it out—"some roller skates!"

Poppa let out a whistle. Roller skates were about $1.50, and that was rice and beans for more than a few days. Then he said, "All right, son, soon as you get home, you got 'em."

But he had agreed too quickly. I shook my head from side to side. Shit, I was gonna push all the way for the roller skates. It wasn't every day you'd get hurt bad enough to ask for something so little like a pair of roller skates. I wanted them right away.

"Fer Christ sakes," Poppa protested, "you can't use 'em in here. Why, some kid will probably steal 'em on you." But Poppa's voice died out slowly in a "you win" tone as I just kept shaking my head from side to side. "Bring 'em tomorrow," he finally mumbled, "but that's it."

"Thanks, Poppa."

"Don't ask for no more."

My eyes were starting to hurt like mad again. The fun was starting to go outta the game between Poppa and me. I made a face.

"Does it hurt, son?"

"Naw, Poppa. I can take it." I thought how I was like a cat in a movie about Indians, taking it like a champ, tied to a stake and getting like burned toast.

Poppa sounded relieved. "Yeah, it's only at first it hurts." His hand touched my foot. "Well, I'll be going now . . ." Poppa rubbed my foot gently and then slapped me the same gentle way on the side of my leg. "Be good, son," he said and walked away. I heard the door open and the nurse telling him about how they were gonna move me to the ward 'cause I was out of danger. "Son," Poppa called back, "you're *un hombre*."

I felt proud as hell.

"Poppa."

"Yeah, son?"

"You won't forget to bring the roller skates, huh?"

Poppa laughed. "Yeah, son."

I heard the door close.

REBECCA WALKER

(1969–)

The daughter of Alice Walker, the Pulitzer Prize–winning author, and
Mel Leventhal, a white civil rights lawyer, Rebecca Walker was
born in a newly desegregated hospital in Jackson, Mississippi. Her maternal great-great-great-great-great-great-great-grandmother, May Poole,
was a slave who walked from Virginia to Florida with a baby on each
hip, and her paternal great-grandmother, Jennie, was a landlord of
Harlem apartments. When Rebecca was eight years old, her parents
separated, and when their divorce was finalized, her mother moved to
San Francisco while her father lived first in Washington, DC, and later
in New York. Her parents decided that their form of shared custody
would require that the child spend alternate periods of two years with
each of them. In negotiating the very different environments of each
parent, Walker asserts, she had to become "well trained in not breaking
the code, not saying something too white around black people or too
black around whites." She attended a private San Francisco high school
(the Urban School) and graduated cum laude from Yale University in
1992. While still a college student, she began contributing articles to
Ms. Magazine, and later published works in *Harper's, The Utne Reader,
Spin,* and *Vibe.* In 2001, she published *Black, White and Jewish: Autobiography of a Shifting Self.* She has also edited two collections, *Telling
the Truth and the Changing Face of Feminism* (1995) and *Putting
Down the Gun: New Masculinity* (2003). A cofounder of the Third Wave
Foundation—a national, philanthropic, activist organization for women
between the ages of fifteen and thirty—Walker has been named one of
the fifty future leaders of America by *Time* magazine.

---

from *Black, White and Jewish*

I stop making sense in third grade. Right after my parents sit me down and tell me
they are not getting along, that me and Mama are going to move to another neighborhood and Daddy will come to pick me up on weekends. They might as well have told
me we were moving to live with penguins on the North Pole, but I nod my head and
help Mama pack books and generally move as if nothing is wrong, as if there isn't this
big crack in the middle of the painting that is supposed to be my life.

Because we have to live on the tiny amount of money my mother makes writing,
Mama and I move into a floor-through on the other side of Prospect Park one-fourth
the size of our house on Midwood. My room is the size of the bathroom in the old
house, with just a bed and a tall, skinny chest of drawers which I climb on a lot, sometimes sitting on top and staring out the window for hours at the trees blowing and the
people walking by. When Mama comes home from work, she cooks dinner for us,

scrambled eggs and bacon, or a magic soup she learned how to make from her father out of whatever vegetables we have in the fridge tossed into chicken broth.

While she cooks I do homework, or I stretch out on the blue velvet couch in our living room, listening to music Mama asks me to put on the phonograph to drown out the sounds that come muffled through our ceiling: another half-black half-white child screaming, wrestling with his white mother who always looks exhausted when I see her in the hallway. Mama and I listen to Phoebe Snow singing "Teach Me Tonight," or the Beatles singing "Come Together," or our favorite, the soundtrack from *Jesus Christ Superstar*.

Late at night we talk quietly in the bathroom, me handing her the Vitabath and washing her back, the bright orange washcloth huge in my eight-year-old hand. In the mornings I climb into her bed and press my face against the soft blue flannel of her nightgown, inhaling her clean, spicy scent. One cold night we sit upright in the bed with the tall wooden headboard, and she dictates to me how she wants her funeral. You have to make sure it is this way, she says, and I nod. There should be a party, she says, smoothing lotion down one arm. Lots of people dancing. She pauses as I write that down on the legal pad. And don't let them put me in a big ugly coffin. N-o u-g-l-y c-of-f-i-n, I write. I should be buried in a simple pine box and S-t-e-v-i-e W-o-n-d-e-r should be playing over the PA.

I don't know. Mama put me in this new school over here near where we live now, she and me in three rooms the size of one of the floors of our old house, mine and Mama and Daddy's house. We went to the little office on the first floor with Mama's new boyfriend and she filled out the papers and the people looked me up and down and shuffled some other papers, and then Mama said I needed to be in the gifted class and the woman behind the desk looked at me again, harder, like she was trying to see through to my brain. And then I was in a classroom with Mrs. Leone helping her staple orange leaves made out of construction paper to the wall around the blackboard. And then I was walking down the hallway with my new class, following the green line painted on the waxy concrete floor, and then we were in the auditorium for assembly and then I was in Mr. Ward's music class, just like that.

It is dark in Mr. Ward's music room. There is wood on the walls, which is weird because our school, PS 321, is made of cement and other hard materials, like metal, which is in skinny bars on the windows. Mama's new boyfriend says this is because our school was built in the fifties, when they thought you could prepare for an A-bomb. Mr. Ward is handing out instruments from a big cardboard box next to his piano bench. He tries to distribute them evenly throughout the room, so it's not just the kids in front who get the good instruments, but there are way more of us than there are cymbals and drums and guitars so most of us get plastic yellow recorders with one part missing.

I feel out of my element here in Mr. Ward's class, like everyone knows how to make music but me, even though I can tell by the way the other kids are banging and blowing that this is not true. It is true that I am much more comfortable in reading class, where I whiz through the SRA colors like a bat out of hell. I'm in the third grade, but according to the purple and red folders I am up to in SRA, I read at the seventh-grade level. I get one hundreds on all of my spelling tests, and Mrs. Leone puts them up on the closet doors next to the SRA folders at the back of the room.

Sometimes when I am in her class I feel like it's just me and her in the room and none of the other kids is there at all. It's sort of like that in Mr. Ward's class, too, except I don't feel like I'm here with Mr. Ward. Here I'm just alone with all of these other kids with names and faces but not much else. When Mr. Ward tells me to, I put my fingertips on a couple of the holes and blow through the mouthpiece of my recorder. I try to focus on what Mr. Ward is saying, but he's not teaching us notes or chords or anything else about music. He seems bored and aggravated, especially by the boys in the back who won't be quiet and do what he says. When everyone starts playing their instruments and making an awful, loud, horrible noise that hurts my ears, Mr. Ward just spaces out and looks at us like he doesn't know how we all got to be here together in the basement of some public school in Brooklyn.

Bryan Katon is sitting with his legs crossed on my left, closer to the music stands by the door, beating on a drum. If I close my eyes I can almost smell him. Bryan has milky white skin and red freckles. He has sandy brown hair that always falls in front of his eyes, like Linus on *Charlie Brown*. Bryan lives way out in Bay Ridge somewhere but his parents own the dry-cleaning store across the street from school, the one next to the pizza parlor where we all go for lunch. If I walk to school early enough I sometimes see Bryan getting out of a black car with his parents. He crosses the street and goes into school while his father rolls up the gate in front of the cleaners.

Bryan Katon is the boy I like. I don't know why I like him, I just do. I like the way he is kind of tough and has a lot of friends and talks in a choppy, offhand way, like he doesn't care if anyone is listening. I like the way his parents give him money when he asks for it. I like it that his mother and father are right across the street. The one time I go into Katon Cleaners with Bryan at lunchtime, it is all warm inside and his mother smiles when we come in and asks him why he is late, like she was worried. For a split second I imagine myself back behind the counter with her, getting lost in all the hanging skirts and blouses and suits, breathing in all those fumes and pressing my cheeks against the silky plastic bags. I imagine that she tells me to stop, that I could hurt myself, in that same worried voice.

I tell Sarah that Bryan Katon is the boy I like. Sarah is my friend but I don't trust her all the way. This year I'm paranoid. I don't trust any of my friends all the way. Not Donna, not Siobhan, and not Jamie, who I sometimes meet on the corner in the mornings so we can walk to school together. I trust Karen but she lives by my old house and now she goes to a private school six blocks away and I never see her. I'm never sure what the new friends are going to do, if they are going to stop being my friends one day for no good reason, or what.

To protect myself, I start to buy my friends things with money I take from my mother's purse. I like the way it feels to pay for something at the register, to be able to give my friends something they want. I feel safer, older, bigger, knowing that they look to me as some kind of provider, even if it is only because I have the money: nickels and dimes and quarters paid out in bubble gum and sets of jacks and plastic-topped containers filled with goopy, green Slime.

And because I know things they don't, things I learn from reading books like *Forever*, by Judy Blume, which I bought for myself at the bookstore for $2.95. I know, for instance, that a penis can have a name and feel really soft and good inside of a girl. But this is something I am not supposed to know, only I don't know that I'm not supposed to know it until one day I am reading paragraphs from *Forever* to my friend Sasha. We are sitting in the front window of her mother's clothing store on Seventh Avenue, a couple of blocks up from the cleaners and the pizza parlor. There is sun coming in through the windows, and the floor underneath is covered in this cushy beige carpet that makes me want to lie down and take a nap. I see Sasha's mother's feet walk over to where we are sitting and then I hear her ask to see what we are reading.

When I look up at Sasha's mother I see her looking at the book like the woman in the office at school looked at me, trying to see through to my brain. Then she tells me that Sasha isn't allowed to read books like *Forever* and I should go home because Sasha isn't allowed to play with me anymore. That's how I find out that I'm not supposed to know about boys putting their penises inside of girls' vaginas.

So Sarah tells Bryan and then Bryan tells me, in front of his friends, after school one day when it is cold and there is dirty gray snow on the ground and we all are leaving to go home, that he doesn't like black girls. Bryan Katon tells me that he doesn't like black girls. Bryan Katon, the boy that I like, tells me that he doesn't like black girls, and I think, with this big whoosh that turns my stomach upside down and almost knocks me over, is that what I am, a black girl? And that's when all the trouble starts, because suddenly I don't know what I am and I don't know how to be not what he thinks I am. I don't know how to be a not black girl.

My stepmother is a not black girl. When she picks me up on Fridays after school in her tall, brown suede boots for the weekend, I wait inside school a little longer, until I am sure Bryan is outside and will see me go over to her and be hugged by her. I want him to see her take my backpack from me and take my hand, and I want him to see me get into her car. And when my grandma Miriam comes to pick me up on other days I do the same thing, I make a big fuss in front of school so that he will see that I am related to not black girls.

I start to brush my hair straight, a hundred times every night before I go to sleep, like I see Jan Brady do on *The Brady Bunch*. Jan Brady is a not black girl. I roll my hair in pink rollers when I am at my grandma's house so that I will have bangs, so that my hair will look more like the not black girls in my class. And I tell my stepmother that I want the doll she says I should want, because all girls want dolls, and even though I have not ever had a baby doll and I am not all that interested in a plastic baby that eats colored mush and then poops it out, I think, this must be part of being a not black girl.

At school Mrs. Leone tells us that we, our class, are going to put on a play for the whole school. She tells us this from the front of the classroom, where she walks back and forth looking out at our faces. Some of you will make the sets for the show, some will make costumes, and some of you, she says, will act. The play is *The Wizard of Oz,* she says, and hands short rectangular stacks to the first person in each row to pass backward until we all have our own wad of mimeographed sheets to hold.

I rush through my pages, inhaling the sweet, tart, mediciny odor of the purplish blue ink. Who do I want to be? We read the whole play out loud, and everyone who wants to act tries different parts on, to see which one fits. Mrs. Leone has me try the Lion, Auntie Em, the Wizard himself. I do not notice that she has only not black girls read the words underneath Dorothy's name, I am too excited by the idea of acting, reading out loud, and making my voice change to match what I think each character should sound like. By the end of classtime it all is decided. I will play the Wicked Witch of the West.

I don't tell my mother too much about the play, and she doesn't ask. It isn't a big deal, I say, hoping she won't see through my mask of nonchalance; I don't want to hurt her. I don't want to lie, either, but how else am I going to convince her not to come to see me on Play Night? How else can I explain that Bryan Katon doesn't like black girls and if she comes he will definitely know that I am, in fact, a black girl, and all of my other efforts to be a not black girl will be washed away? How else can I stay with her and still leave?

On the night of the play, as I am trying on my black witch's cape and pointy hat for the umpteenth time, I beg her not to come. I will be too nervous, I say, I won't be able to remember my lines if you are there, I say. Please, Mama, don't come. She looks at me strangely, like the woman in the office did, trying to see through to my brain. I hold my breath but she doesn't push. She takes me at my word and I go, free, alone, out into the night. When I look out from the stage I can make out my grandmother's white face in the dark crowd. I think, Mama is not here, Mama is at home. I think, surely Bryan will see my grandmother. I think, surely Bryan will like me now.

At the end, when all the parents and teachers stand up and clap for us, I feel an unexpected sadness come into my body, a heat inching up from someplace underneath the skin on my face. I picture Mama lying in her big bed by the window, alone, the lamp giving off a pool of yellow light as she reads, silently wondering about Play Night. Even though everyone says I was good, my mama, the one with the most important voice, can never say this to me.

Shame sticks to me like sweat.

TOBIAS WOLFF
(1945–)

Born in Birmingham, Alabama, Tobias Wolff was raised in Chinook, Washington, and educated at Oxford and Stanford universities. A veteran of Vietnam, he became a reporter for *The Washington Post* and subsequently taught creative writing and literature at Goddard College, Arizona State University, Syracuse University, and Stanford University. Wolff has commented that "so many of the things in our world tend to lead us to despair. It seems to me that the final symptom of despair is silence, and that storytelling is one of the sustaining arts. . . . The very act of being a writer seems to me to be an optimistic act." He is a recipient of a Wallace Stegner Fellowship in creative writing at Stanford University, two National Endowment for the Arts Fellowships, a Guggenheim Fellowship, the St. Lawrence Award for Fiction, the Rea Award for Excellence in the Short Story, and three O. Henry Awards. He has published a novella about his experience in the army, "The Barracks Thief" (1984), which won a PEN/Faulkner Award for Fiction, and the full-length novel *Old School* (2003). Among his collections of stories are: *In the Garden of the North American Martyrs* (1981), *Back in the World* (1985), and *The Night in Question* (1997). Wolff has published two memoirs: *This Boy's Life* (1989), which was the basis of a 1993 film starring Leonardo DiCaprio and Robert DeNiro; and *In Pharaoh's Army: Memories of the Lost War* (1994). Presently, he lives in northern California and teaches at Stanford University.

---

from *This Boy's Life*

We lived in a boardinghouse in West Seattle. At night, if my mother wasn't too tired, we took walks around the neighborhood, stopping in front of different houses to consider them as candidates for future purchase. We went for the biggest and most pretentious, sneering at ranches and duplexes—anything that smelled of economy. We chose half-timbered houses, houses with columns, houses with sculpted bushes in front. Then we went back to our room, where I read novels about heroic collies while my mother practiced typing and shorthand so she wouldn't fall behind in her new job.

Our room was in a converted attic. It had two camp beds and between them, under the window, a desk and chair. It smelled of mildew. The yellow wallpaper was new but badly hung and already curling at the edges. It was the kind of room that B-movie detectives wake up in, bound and gagged, after they've been slipped a Mickey.

The boardinghouse was full of old men and men who probably only seemed old. Besides my mother only two women lived there. One was a secretary named Kathy. Kathy was young and plain and shy. She stayed in her room most of the time. When people addressed her she would look at them with a drowning expression, then softly ask them to repeat what they had said. As time went on, her pregnancy began to show through the loose clothes she wore. There didn't seem to be a man in the picture.

The other woman was Marian, the housekeeper. Marian was big and loud. Her arms were as thick as a man's, and when she pounded out hamburger patties the whole kitchen shook. Marian went with a marine sergeant from Bremerton who was even bigger than she was but more gentle and soft-spoken. He had been in the Pacific during the war. When I kept after him to tell me about it he finally showed me an album of photographs he'd taken. Most of the pictures were of his buddies. Doc, a man with glasses. Curly, a man with no hair. Jesus, a man with a beard. But there were also pictures of corpses. He meant to scare me off the subject with these pictures but instead they made me more interested. Finally Marian told me to stop bothering him.

Marian and I disliked each other. Later we both found reasons for it, but our dislike was instinctive and mysterious. I tried to cover mine with a treacly stream of yes ma'ams and no ma'ams and offers of help. Marian wasn't fooled. She knew I didn't like her, and that I was not the young gentleman I pretended to be. She went out a lot, running errands, and she sometimes saw me on the street with my friends—bad company, from the looks of them. She knew I combed my hair differently after I left the house and rearranged my clothes. Once, driving past us, she yelled at me to pull up my pants.

■ ■ ■ ■ ■

My friends were Terry Taylor and Terry Silver. All three of us lived with our mothers. Terry Taylor's father was stationed in Korea. The war had been over for two years but he still hadn't come home. Mrs. Taylor had filled the house with pictures of him, graduation portraits, snapshots in and out of uniform—always alone, leaning against trees, standing in front of houses. The living room was like a shrine; if you didn't know better you would have thought that he had not survived Korea but had died some kind of hero's death there, as Mrs. Taylor had perhaps anticipated.

This sepulchral atmosphere owed a lot to the presence of Mrs. Taylor herself. She was a tall, stooped woman with deep-set eyes. She sat in her living room all day long and chain-smoked cigarettes and stared out the picture window with an air of unutterable sadness, as if she knew things beyond mortal bearing. Sometimes she would call Taylor over and wrap her long arms around him, then close her eyes and hoarsely whisper, "Terence! Terence!" Eyes still closed, she would turn her head and resolutely push him away.

Silver and I immediately saw the potential of this scene and we replayed it often, so often that we could bring tears to Taylor's eyes just by saying "Terence! Terence!" Taylor was a dreamy thin-skinned boy who cried easily, a weakness from which he tried to distract us by committing acts of ferocious vandalism. He'd once been to juvenile court for breaking windows.

Mrs. Taylor also had two daughters, both older than Terry and full of scorn for us and all our works. "Oh, *God*," they'd say when they saw us. "Look what the cat dragged in." Silver and I suffered their insults meekly, but Taylor always had an answer. "Does your face hurt?" he would say. "I just wondered, it's killing me." "Is that sweater made of camel's hair? I just wondered, I thought I saw two humps."

But they always had the last word. As girls went they were nothing special, but they were girls, and empowered by that fact to render judgment on us. They could make us cringe just by rolling their eyes. Silver and I were afraid of them, and confused by Mrs. Taylor and the funereal atmosphere of the house. The only reason we went there was to steal Mrs. Taylor's cigarettes.

We couldn't go to my place. Phil, the man who owned the boardinghouse, had no use for kids. He rented the room to my mother only after she promised that I would be quiet and never bring other kids home with me. Phil was always there, reeking of chewing tobacco, drooling strings of it into the chipped enamel mug he carried with him everywhere. Phil had been badly burned in a warehouse fire that left his skin blister-smooth and invested with an angry glow, as if the fire still burned somewhere inside him. The fingers of one hand were welded together.

He was right not to want me around. When we passed one another in the hallway or on the stairs, I couldn't keep my eyes from him and he saw in them no sympathy or friendliness, only disgust. He responded by touching me constantly. He knew better but could not help himself. He touched me on the shoulders, on the head, on the neck, using all the gestures of fatherly affection while measuring my horror with a cold bitter gaze, giving new pain to himself as if he had no choice.

My place was off-limits and Terry Taylor's was full of trolls, so we usually ended up at Silver's apartment. Silver was an only child, clever, skinny, malicious, a shameless coward when his big mouth brought trouble down on us. His father was a cantor who lived in Tacoma with his new wife. Silver's mother worked all day at Boeing. That meant we had the apartment to ourselves for hours at a stretch.

But first we made our rounds. As we left school we followed girls at a safe distance and offered up smart remarks. We drifted in and out of stores, palming anything that wasn't under glass. We coasted stolen tricycles down the hills around Alkai Point, standing on the seats and jumping off at the last moment to send them crashing into parked cars. Sometimes, if we had the money, we took a bus downtown and weaved through the winos around Pioneer Square to stare at guns in the windows of pawnshops. For all three of us the Luger was the weapon of choice; our passion for this pistol was profound and about the only passion we admitted to. In the presence of a Luger we stopped our continual jostling of each other and stood wide-eyed.

Television was very big on the Nazis then. Every week they screened new horrors, always with a somber narrator to remind us that this wasn't make-believe but actual history, that what we were seeing had really happened and could happen again if we did not maintain ourselves in a state of vigilance. These shows always ended the same way. Overviews of ruined Berlin. Grinning GIs rousting the defeated Aryan soldiery from their hiding places in barn and cave and sewer. Himmler dead in his cell, hollow-eyed Hess in Spandau. The now lathered-up narrator crowing, "Thus was the high-flying Prussian eagle brought to ground!" and "Thus did the little Führer and his bullyboys turn tail and run, giving up forever their dream of *The Thousand Year Reich!*"

But these glimpses of humiliation and loss lasted only a few minutes. They were tacked on as a pretense that the point of the show was to celebrate the victory of goodness over evil. We saw through this fraud, of course. We saw that the real point was to celebrate snappy uniforms and racy Mercedes staff cars and great marching, thousands of boots slamming down together on cobbled streets while banners streamed overhead and strong voices sang songs that stirred our blood though we couldn't understand a word. The point was to watch Stukas peel off and dive toward burning cities, tanks blowing holes in buildings, men with Lugers and dogs ordering people around. These shows instructed us further in the faith we were already beginning to hold: that victims are contemptible, no matter how much people pretend otherwise; that it is more fun to be inside than outside, to be arrogant than to be kind, to be with a crowd than to be alone.

Terry Silver had a Nazi armband that he swore was genuine, though anyone could see he'd made it himself. As soon as we reached his apartment Silver would get this armband from its hiding place and slip it on. Then he would strut around and treat Taylor and me like lackeys. We let him do it because of the candy Mrs. Silver left out in crystal bowls, because of the television set, and because without Silver to tell us what to do we were reduced to wandering the sidewalks, listlessly throwing rocks at signs.

First we made a few calls. Taylor and I listened in on the extension in Mrs. Silver's bedroom while Silver did the talking. He looked up people with Jewish-sounding names and screamed at them in pig German. He ordered entire banquets of Chinese food for his father and stepmother. Sometimes he called the parents of kids we didn't like and assumed the voice and manner of a Concerned Adult—teacher, coach, counselor—just touching base to ask whether there was some problem at home that might account for Paul's unusual behavior at school the other day. Silver never laughed, never gave himself away. When he was being particularly plausible and suave, Taylor and I had to stuff Mrs. Silver's coverlet in our mouths and flail the mattress with our fists.

Then, bumping each other with our hips to make room, the three of us would press together in front of Mrs. Silver's full-length mirror to comb our hair and practice looking cool. We wore our hair long at the sides, swept back into a ducktail. The hair on top we combed toward the center and then forward, with spit curls breaking over our foreheads. My mother detested this hairdo and forbade me to wear it, which meant that I wore it everywhere but at home, sustaining the distinctness of two different styles with gobs of Butch Wax that left my hair glossy and hard and my forehead ringed with little pimples.

Unlit cigarettes dangling from the corners of our months, eyelids at half-mast, we studied ourselves in the mirror. Spit curls. Pants pulled down low on our hips, thin white belts buckled on the side. Shirts with three-quarter-length sleeves. Collars raised behind our necks. We should have looked cool, but we didn't. Silver was emaciated. His eyes bulged, his Adam's apple protruded, his arms poked out of his sleeves like pencils with gloves stuck on the ends. Taylor had the liquid eyes and long lashes and broad blank face of a cow. I didn't look that great myself. But it wasn't really our looks that made us uncool. Coolness did not demand anything as obvious as that. Like chess or music, coolness claimed its own out of some mysterious impulse of recognition. Uncoolness did likewise. We had been claimed by uncoolness.

At five o'clock we turned on the television and watched *The Mickey Mouse Club*. It was understood that we were all holding a giant bone for Annette. This was our excuse for watching the show, and for me it was partly true. I had certain ideas of the greater world that Annette belonged to, and I wanted a place in this world. I wanted it with all the feverish, disabling hunger of first love.

At the end of every show the local station gave an address for Mousketeer Mail. I had begun writing Annette. At first I described myself in pretty much the same terms as I had in my letters to Alice, who was now very much past tense, with the difference that instead of owning a ranch my father, Cap'n Wolff, now owned a fleet of fishing boats. I was first mate, myself, and a pretty fair hand at reeling in the big ones. I gave Annette some very detailed descriptions of my contests with the friskier fellows I ran up against. I also invited her to consider the fun to be had in visiting Seattle. I told her we had lots of room. I did not tell her that I was eleven years old.

I got back some chipper official responses encouraging me to start an Annette fan club. In other words, to organize my competition. Fat chance. But when I upped the ante in my letters to her, they stopped sending me anything at all. The Disney Studio must have had a kind of secret service that monitored Mousketeer Mail for inappropriate sentiments and declarations. When my name went off the mailing list, it probably went onto some other list. But Alice had taught me about coyness. I kept writing Annette and began to imagine a terrible accident in front of her house that would almost but not quite kill me, leaving me dependent on her care and sympathy, which in time would turn to admiration, love . . .

As soon as she appeared on the show—Hi, I'm Annette!—Taylor would start moaning and Silver would lick the screen with his tongue. "Come here, baby," he'd say, "I've got six inches of piping hot flesh just for you."

We all said things like that—it was a formality—then we shut up and watched the show. Our absorption was complete. We softened. We surrendered. We joined the club. Taylor forgot himself and sucked his thumb, and Silver and I let him get away with it. We watched the Mousketeers get all excited about wholesome projects and have wimpy adventures and talk about their feelings, and we didn't laugh at them. We didn't laugh at them when they said nice things about their parents, or when they were polite to each other, or when they said, "Hey, gang . . ." We watched every minute of it, our eyes glistening in the blue light, and we went on staring at the television after they had sung the anthem and faded away into commercials for toothpaste and candy. Then, blinking and awkward, we would rouse ourselves and talk dirty about Annette.

Sometimes, when *The Mickey Mouse Club* was over, we went up to the roof. Silver's apartment building overlooked California Avenue. Though the street was busy we chose our targets carefully. Most days we didn't throw anything at all. But now and then someone would appear who had no chance of getting past us, like the man in the Thunderbird.

Thunderbirds had been out for only a year now, since '55, and because they were new and there weren't that many of them they were considered somewhat cooler than Corvettes. It was early evening. The Thunderbird was idling before a red light at the intersection, and from our perch behind the parapet we could hear the song on the radio—"Over the Mountain, Across the Sea"—and hear too, just below the music, the full-throated purr of the engine. The black body glistened like obsidian. Blue smoke chugged from the twin exhausts. The top was rolled back. We could see the red leather upholstery and the blond man in the dinner jacket sitting in the driver's seat. He was young and handsome and fresh. You could almost smell the Listerine on his breath, the Mennen on his cheeks. We were looking right down at him. With the palm of his left hand he kept the beat of the song against the steering wheel. His right arm rested on the back of the empty seat beside him, which would not remain empty for long. He was on his way to pick someone up.

We held no conference. One look was enough to see that he was everything we were not, his life a progress of satisfactions we had no hope of attaining in any future we could seriously propose for ourselves.

The first egg hit the street beside him. The second egg hit the front fender. The third egg hit the trunk and splattered his shoulders and neck and hair. We looked down just long enough to tally the damage before pulling our heads back. A moment passed. Then a howl rose skyward. No words—just one solitary soul cry of disbelief. We could still hear the music coming from his radio. The light must have changed, because a horn honked, and honked again, and someone yelled something, and another voice answered harshly, and the song was suddenly lost in the noise of engines.

We rolled back and forth on the roof for a while. Just as we were getting ready to go back down to Silver's apartment, the Thunderbird screeched around the corner up the block. We could hear the driver cursing. The car moved slowly toward the light, combusting loudly. As it passed below we peered over the parapet again. The driver was scanning the sidewalks with stiff angry jerks of his head. He seemed to have no idea where the eggs had come from. We let fly again. One hit the hood with a loud boom, another landed in the seat beside him, the last exploded on the dashboard. Covered with egg and eggshell, he rose in his seat and bellowed.

There was more honking at the light. Again he tore away and again he came back, still bellowing. Six eggs were left in the carton. Each of us took two. Silver knelt by the edge, risking a few hurried glances into the street while holding his arm out behind him to keep us in check until the moment was right. Then he beckoned furiously and we reared up beside him and got rid of our eggs and dropped back out of sight before they hit. The driver was looking up at the building across the street; he never laid eyes on us. We heard the eggs smack the pavement, boom against the car. This time there was no cry of protest. The silence made me uncomfortable and in my discomfort I grinned at Silver, but Silver did not grin back. His face was purple and twitching with anger as if he had been the one set upon and outraged. He was beside himself. Breathing loudly, clenching and unclenching his jaw, he leaned over the edge and cupped his hands in front of his mouth and screamed a word I had heard only once, years before, when my father shouted it at a man who had cut him off in traffic.

"Yid!" Silver screamed, and again, "Yid!"